# Passions and Constraint

STEPHEN HOLMES

# PASSIONS and CONSTRAINT

## *On the Theory of Liberal Democracy*

THE UNIVERSITY OF CHICAGO PRESS

*Chicago and London*

The University of Chicago Press, Chicago 60637
The University of Chicago Press, Ltd., London

Printed in the United States of America
04 03 02 01 00 99 98 97 5 4 3 2
ISBN 0-226-34968-3 (cloth)
ISBN 0-226-34969-1 (paperback)

Permission to reprint earlier versions or portions of articles that have appeared elsewhere is gratefully acknowledged: Chapter 1 appeared in *The American Prospect* 7 (Fall 1991): 81–96; chapter 2, in Jane Mansbridge, ed., *Beyond Self-Interest* (Chicago: University of Chicago Press, © 1990 by The University of Chicago; all rights reserved); chapter 3, in Mary G. Dietz, ed., *Thomas Hobbes and Political Theory* (Lawrence: University of Kansas Press, 1990); chapter 4, in J. Roland Pennock and John Chapman, eds., *Religion, Morality, and the Law, NOMOS* 30 (Copyright © 1987 by New York University); chapter 5, in Jon Elster and Rune Slagstad, eds., *Constitutionalism and Democracy* (New York: Cambridge University Press, 1988); chapter 6, in Marcelo Dascal and Ora Gruengard, eds., *Knowledge and Politics* (Boulder, CO: Westview Press, 1989); chapter 7, in Jon Elster and Rune Slagstad, eds., *Constitutionalism and Democracy* (New York: Cambridge University Press, 1988); chapter 8, in Donald Moon, ed., *Responsibility, Rights, and Welfare* (Boulder, CO: Westview Press, 1988).

Library of Congress Cataloging-in-Publication Data

Holmes, Stephen, 1948–
Passions and constraint : on the theory of liberal democracy / Stephen Holmes.
p. cm.
Includes bibliographical references and index.
1. Liberalism. 2. Democracy. I. Title.
JC574.H65 1995 94-33748
320.5′1—dc20 CIP

♾ The paper used in this publication meets the minimum requirements of the American National Standard for Information Sciences—Permanence of Paper for Printed Library Materials, ANSI Z39.48—1984.

FOR JAMIE

# CONTENTS

# ACKNOWLEDGMENTS

Thanks go first to Cass Sunstein who, in literally hundreds of early-morning sidewalk conversations, has endlessly urged me to quit lampooning antiliberals and to say something constructive about liberalism itself. I am also indebted to Jon Elster, whose writings on the passions and on strategies of self-binding have opened up theoretical perspectives on liberal politics that are still far from being fully explored. The thematically connected essays gathered in this book have been criticized with wonderful acuteness by both Sunstein and Elster, and by other maliciously witty friends: Samuel Beer, Kiren Chaudhry, Ann Davies, David Franklin, Albert Hirschman, Helge Høibraaaten, David Laitin, Larry Lessig, Nancy Maull, John McCormick, Richard Posner, John Rawls, Ian Shapiro, Paul Starr, and Bernie Yack. I am grateful to them all. Protests and encouragements from my editor, John Tryneski, have also moved me reluctantly to improve this book.

A week before her unexpected death, Judith Shklar devoted a high-spirited evening in Chicago to searching criticisms of an earlier draft; it is bitter to be unable to thank her as she deserves. Finally, for financial support, I am pleased to thank the Russell Baker Fund of the University of Chicago Law School.

# PREFACE

Limited government is, or can be, more powerful than unlimited government. The paradoxical insight that constraints can be enabling, which is far from being a contradiction, lies at the heart of liberal constitutionalism. Frustrated at times by the failure of democratic governments to address serious problems, domestic and international, critics may be tempted to see liberal institutions, such as the separation of powers, as outmoded hindrances to problem-solving action. But blaming liberalism for political weakness suggests a lack of historical perspective. By restricting the arbitrary powers of government officials, a liberal constitution can, under the right conditions, *increase* the state's capacity to focus on specific problems and mobilize collective resources for common purposes. The recent collapse of so many communist regimes, apparently debilitated by a *lack* of constitutional restraints, has driven this surprising lesson home.

Admittedly, liberalism is not about to triumph across the globe. Authoritarianisms and fundamentalisms still abound, and ethnocracy is on the rise. But, for the time being, the superiority of constitutional democracies over their nearest rivals, from both an economic and a military perspective, seems unchallenged. Contemporary circumstances are especially favorable, therefore, for rethinking the liberal tradition. It now seems obvious that liberalism can occasionally eclipse authoritarianism as a technique for accumulating political power. However temporary, the current world supremacy of liberal-democratic polities would be incomprehensible if liberalism really were, as friendly and unfriendly commentators alike sometimes assume, a quasi-anarchical war against the state. Liberalism is not allergic to political power. It should now be clear that, for good or ill, liberalism is one of the most effective philosophies of state building ever contrived.

Neither progressives nor conservatives devote much attention to the positive or enabling side of liberal constitutionalism, however. Despite their ideological disputes, both agree that liberalism conspires to weaken the state. And they add, in differing tones of voice, that liberalism is especially adept at enfeebling the democratic and redistributionist state. Left-wingers scorn liberalism for placing limits on electoral majorities and for discouraging forms of state intervention meant to compensate for inequalities in the nonpolitical sphere. Right-wingers praise liberalism on exactly the same grounds. Liberalism, to be sure, is a pliant term that can be kneaded easily into uncommon shapes. If we define it narrowly, as identical to libertarianism, and thereby bleed it of all concern for democracy and welfare, then "liberalism" will indeed be antidemocratic and antiwelfarist. But liberalism should be kept distinct from libertarianism. Redefinition games, in any case, obscure the fundamental issues at stake. It is more useful to ask: What are the elements of liberalism, however we color this difficult concept, that make liberals, by necessity, inimical to democracy and the welfare state? Three facets of liberal theory dominate the discussion: constitutional constraints on majority rule, the identification of individual freedom with an absence of government involvement in civil society, and a celebratory attitude toward the principle of self-interest. All three ideas are routinely adduced to prove the incompatibility of traditional liberal principles with both popular self-rule and state provision for the poor. The purported demonstration fails, however. When examined more closely, the basic principles of liberal theory provide a plausible foundation for democratic government and (within limits) for regulatory and redistributionist policies in large nation-states.

All this may seem anomalous, but the arguments that lead to such counterintuitive conclusions are commonsensical and can be stated quite succinctly. Constitutional restraints on temporary majorities are designed to facilitate rather than to paralyze democracy; liberal principles are compatible with any form of state provision that fosters individual autonomy; and the idea of self-interest has two undeniably humanistic implications. First, far from entailing a repudiation of all moral norms, a positive attitude toward self-interest reflects a civilized desire to control irrational and aggressive human passions, often referred to by eighteenth-century writers as mankind's "inflammable humors." Second, self-interest is an intrinsically egalitarian and universalist principle. All human beings have interests and, from a political perspective, their interests are of equal worth. The idea of universal self-interest, therefore, supports a policy of political and economic inclusion. These considerations imply that support for democracy and the welfare state are perfectly compatible with uncontroversially liberal commitments. Those who advocate a strengthening of democracy and an improvement in welfare policy, as a result, do not have to be anti-liberal in the way that many of them still apparently believe they must. Furthermore, popular self-government and public provision for the poor become unrealistic (and perhaps undesirable) ideals if separated from the premises and trappings of liberal constitutionalism. And the liberal tradition, while far from homogeneous, lends unexpectedly strong support to the development of democratic, regulatory, and redistributionist politics in a modern context. Such contentions, stated here with telegraphic brevity, are not what most contemporary political theory teaches us to expect. To explain and defend them is the central purpose of this book.

# INTRODUCTION

*Why has government been instituted at all? Because the passions of men will not conform to the dictates of reason and justice without constraint.*

—ALEXANDER HAMILTON

Passions and constraint, irrational motivations and institutional limitations, are two paramount themes of classical liberal theory. How can destructive and self-destructive emotions be transformed into, or replaced by, socially constructive and self-beneficial ones? And how can social interactions be submitted to binding rules without sacrificing or impairing human freedom? The essays collected in this volume, focusing on such questions, do not provide a comprehensive account of liberal political thought. They nevertheless advance an interconnected sequence of theoretical claims meant to change the way we think about liberalism. They aim not to survey the field, one might say, so much as to plow it up, providing a fresh view of the undersoil. My principal arguments have been broached in the Preface. But more needs to be said about the contribution of the individual chapters, composed on different occasions over a number of years, to the underlying argument of the book. I especially need to explain why I proceed so unconventionally, devoting two central chapters to the preliberal theorists, Hobbes and Bodin.

## Rudiments of Liberal Thought

The liberal tradition is difficult to summarize in brief compass. Lasting several centuries and reformulated in many different countries in response to dramatically changing problems, liberalism contains many different strands and tensions. Some liberals are optimists, for example, believing that technological progress is inevitably accompanied by moral progress, while others are pessimists, worried about the irrepressible human tendency to abuse power and hoping to stave off catastrophe, if only for a time. Similarly, some liberals celebrate material well-being, while others cling unflinchingly to human dignity. Some stress utility, while others stress rights. Some emphasize valuable consequences such as peace, education, and prosperity, while others emphasize moral values such as fairness or autonomy. More concretely, some contemporary liberals are free-speech absolutists, while others favor substantial restrictions on pornography, advertising, hate speech, and so forth. Some endorse affirmative action, others oppose it. Some antipaternalists advocate a decriminalization of narcotics, while others think that the free sale of addictive substances cannot be justified by invoking voluntary consent. These pros and cons are a vital part of liberal political culture—for liberalism continues to be a field of contest, not an unambiguous creed that demands total allegiance and stigmatizes dissent. To acknowledge this lack of perfect unanimity, some historians choose to speak of liberalisms rather than liberalism. But the plural form is probably more evasive than helpful, for it too assumes an underlying affinity among the doctrines in question. Intraliberal disputes, in any case, however important, should not blind us to the broad consensus on fundamentals that makes all such disagreements compatible with political coexistence and cooperation. To grasp the rudiments of liberalism, without sacrificing the pluralism and diversity of the movement, it will prove useful to mine the works of a handful of classical liberals including Locke, Montesquieu, Adam Smith, Kant, Madison, and John Stuart Mill. In chapter 1, I offer a synoptic account of their kindred forms of liberalism, based on the various themes to be developed in the remainder of the book. Their thinking turns out to be much less hostile to democracy and welfare than critics have often assumed.

## Self-Interest

Misinterpretations of liberalism routinely begin by putting a false construction on the concept of self-interest. The primacy of *self-interest* in liberal thought has been persistently misdescribed as a celebration of unbridled egoism, an embrace of crass materialism, and a repudiation of the common good. The liberal affirmation of the rational and calculating pursuit of economic advantage should be viewed less censoriously, however, and in its original historical context (chapter 2). All classical liberals were perfectly aware that most human behavior is noncalculating, habitual, and emotional and that most human goals are nonmaterial. Their psychological premises were messy, eclectic, and rich—not austere, parsimonious, and reductionistic. Yet detractors repeatedly, not to say repetitiously, associate liberalism with an unrealistic and simplistic conception of mankind as instrumentally rational and naturally self-regarding. When making this unflattering case they invariably invoke Hobbes, who is purported to be the originator of what later became the "characteristically liberal" (that is, reductionistic) approach to human motivation.

## Hobbes's Passions

Hobbes was no liberal. If I were concerned solely with the separation of powers, judicial independence, religious toleration, freedom of public discussion, and legal controls on the police, I would never include Hobbes in a book on liberalism. But any commentator who wants to explore the psychological presuppositions of liberal theory must also discuss Hobbes (chapter 3). In my view, liberalism's sleepless detractors are correct to discern many important parallels and overlaps between Hobbesian and liberal psychology. (Some liberals drew their psychology directly from Hobbes, while others were simply influenced by the same traditions of thought on which he drew.) So liberalism's critics are right to this extent. They walk into a mistake only when they ascribe to Hobbes the empirically implausible view that human beings are, for the most part, instrumentally rational and naturally self-regarding.

Hobbes held no such unrealistically reductionistic view and, as a consequence, could not have bequeathed it to his liberal successors. To state such a revisionary claim in a few lines may attract attention. But my aim here is to demonstrate it unanswerably, by a careful and exhaustive exegesis of an important Hobbesian text. If successful, this exercise may encourage students of the origins of liberalism to scrap one of their fondest assumptions. For Hobbes, and for the liberal writers who admittedly accepted his psychological premises, individuals are compulsive and impulsive, creatures of habit and victims of emotional frenzy. Moreover, most people, as classical liberals followed Hobbes in describing them, turn out to be obsessively concerned with relative social status and hypersensitive to social slights and humiliations. Dispassionate assessment of their current situation is seldom within their reach. Their ability to forgo inherited emotional reactions and adapt rationally to new circumstances is slight. Such personal foibles have immense political implications, for brutal and uncompromising enmities dominate human history, and only a few of them can be traced to cool-headed competition for scarce material resources. *Cruelty arises more often from noncalculating passions than from calculating interests.* This insight, already clearly formulated in antiquity, was to become one of the central premises of classical liberalism. As John Stuart Mill remarked, "it is not from the separate interests, real or imaginary, of the majority, that minorities are in danger; but from its antipathies of religion, political party, or race."[1] The rational pursuit of individual or group advantage sometimes plays an important role in life, but it has never been, and will never be, the dominant or most worrisome human style.

Modern economics has accustomed us to the parsimonious image of man as a "rational maximizer." To read works written two or three hundred years ago with the eyes of a modern economist, therefore, is to be profoundly misled. Those who project present-day assumptions into the past will logically conclude that Hobbes (and the liberals who followed him) conceived of human beings as economic animals. They will infer, anachronistically, that classical liberal theory presupposed a reductionistic conception of psychological processes. In fact, the favorable attitude toward self-interest displayed by classical liberals resulted from an underlying belief, inherited in part from ancient Stoicism and wholly alien to mainstream economic theory today, that individuals rationally pursue their true advantage only in rare circumstances. The classical liberal theory of self-interest must be reinterpreted as a normative doctrine, therefore, and not a descriptive one. The principal aim of liberals who wrote favorably of self-interest was to bridle destructive and self-destructive passions, to reduce the social prestige of mindless male violence, to induce people, so far as possible, to act rationally, instead of hot-bloodedly or deferentially, and to focus on material goals such as economic wealth, instead of spiritual goals such as avenging a perceived slight or compelling neighbors to attend church. The importance of *this* Hobbesian legacy—subsequently enriched by liberals to include an appreciation of human dignity, individual and cultural diversity, and political democracy—remains beyond dispute.

## The Morality of Self-Interest

There is nothing immoral or amoral about trying to build a social order on the basis of universal self-interest, so understood. The fallacy of associating self-interest with moral skepticism or nihilism becomes especially clear when we reflect on the *universality* attributed by liberals to the rational pursuit of personal advantage. To focus on self-interest is to emphasize a motivation that all human beings equally share. The same cannot be said of civic virtue or insight into the common good. Preliberal political theorists usually assumed that social elites were "higher types," driven by worthier motives or attached to nobler causes than the rest of mankind. Liberals exploded this flattering fiction with the revelation that rulers, too, are self-interested creatures, despite their picture-window virtues and purportedly privileged insight into the worthiest goals of the community. Liberals also assumed that, for political purposes, no individual's interest should be seen as intrinsically more valuable than another's. (That is the egalitarian principle upon which Jeremy Bentham's thinking coincides with Immanuel Kant's.) In this way, liberalism laid the anthropological foundations for democratic theory. Since *all* human beings are partial to themselves, it is imperative to construct political institutions based on a realistic assessment of potential rulers and their motives. Like the Grand Inquisitor, brilliantly modeled upon them, old-European political elites traditionally claimed that the masses of mankind are basically weak and stupid and need to be ruled. Liberals agreed, but went on to universalize the point. As ordinary men, *rulers too need to be ruled.* Institutions such as a free press, checks and balances, and periodic accountability before a national electorate can help discipline the stubborn partiality of officeholders. Liberal democracy strives to billet mighty decision makers in conspicuous sites where they can be carefully monitored and where their personal interests will not drift impossibly aloft from the interests of the community at large.

The concept and practice of democracy, according to this line of argument, is anchored not in a nonliberal theory of civic virtue and selfless devotion to the common good, but in a liberal theory of universal self-interest. Traditional autocratic and aristocratic regimes gained public legitimacy by advertising the special virtues of rulers, not to mention these rulers' unrivaled insight into the common advantage. Liberalism helped lay the foundations for democracy by doubting, even heckling, such conceits. The theoretical compatibility of universal self-interest (no exceptions allowed for "the few") and collective self-rule (all voices counted equally) implies the inadequacy of the routine contrast between liberalism and republicanism. Much of this book, in fact, is devoted to questioning this unhappy dichotomy.

## The Constitutional Idea

Liberalism and republicanism are not opposites. They were perfectly compatible in the seventeenth and eighteenth centuries. Classical works of the period, such as James Harrington's *Oceana* and Trenchard and Gordon's *Cato's Letters,* can be categorized only as liberal-republican; they effortlessly combine a commitment to popular sovereignty with an acceptance of both constitutional limitations and, within the bounds of justice, the private pursuit of personal interests. The polities that are organized most democratically today also limit the power of officeholders and accept the legitimacy of the individual's attempt to improve his own condition, so long as such strivings respect the rights of others. The *theoretical* grounds for construing liberalism and republicanism as alternative models of political life are also weak. Limited government is not, in principle, a hindrance to self-government. Religious toleration and restrictions on the discretionary powers of lethally armed policemen do not present insurmountable obstacles to democratic self-rule.

The key concept for understanding the interdependence of liberalism and democracy is *constitutionalism*. Indeed, the widespread notion that constitutional constraints are somehow inherently antidemocratic reflects a common but one-sided understanding of what a constitution does. Constitutions restrict the discretion of power-wielders because rulers, too, need to be ruled. But constitutions not only limit power and prevent tyranny, they also construct power, guide it toward socially desirable ends, and prevent social chaos and private oppression. The American Constitution, for example, was designed "to rescue us from impending anarchy."[2] More comprehensively, liberal constitutions are crafted to help solve a whole range of political problems: tyranny, corruption, anarchy, immobilism, unaccountability, instability, and the ignorance and stupidity of politicians.[3] Constitutions are multifunctional. It is, therefore, a radical oversimplification to identify the constitutional function exclusively with the prevention of tyranny.

It is also excessively negative. The positive or facilitative dimensions of constitutionalism must be taken into account. A constitution is an instrument of government. It establishes rules that help put democracy into effect. It creates an institutional framework that, if it functions properly, makes decision making more thoughtful and mistakes easier to learn from and correct. It prevents power-wielders from invoking secrecy and shutting themselves off, as they are naturally inclined to do, from criticisms, counterarguments, and fresh ideas. At the same time, it mobilizes collective resources for solving collective problems. No surprise, then, that advocates of strong government have also recognized the advantages to be gained from constitutional limitations on sovereign power. That is the conclusion to be drawn from the works of the most renowned theorist of European absolutism, Jean Bodin, whose strategic acceptance of constitutional restraints has been regrettably ignored.

## Bodin and the Case against Negative Constitutionalism

Why include a chapter on Bodin in a book on liberalism? A chapter on Hobbes can be tolerated, at a stretch, for other commentators and political theorists have discussed him voluminously in many histories of liberal thought. But Bodin? Was he not an "absolutist"? Did he not invent the ideas of unlimited sovereignty and the all-powerful state? Did he not claim that the king must be *legibus solutus,* or unconstrained by higher law? And was not constitutional thought born in protest *against* the striving for unbridled power typical of the centralizing monarchies Bodin defended and admired? So why Bodin?

I have chosen to focus on Jean Bodin for a very specific reason (chapter 4). A reconsideration of his thought is simply the most economical and eye-catching way to overturn a normally unquestioned premise of constitutional theory: that *constitutions are designed primarily to limit the power of the sovereign* (whether royal, as it used to be, or popular, as it is today). This misleading but almost universally accepted premise has enormous consequences and is by no means harmless. In my view, it presents the most formidable obstacle to a fruitful theoretical exploration of the relation between constitutionalism and democracy. Bodin is a pivotal writer, for my purposes, because he draws our attention to the mutually reinforcing relationship between sovereignty and constitutional restraints. Many students of Bodin assume, almost without thinking about it, that this relation is necessarily hostile. For sovereignty to assert itself, they reason, constitutional restraints have to be thrown off. For constitutional restraints to be effective, on the other hand, sovereignty has to be weakened, paralyzed, tied down. This is common sense, but it is not right, and it is not Bodin.

Whenever political theorists interpret constitutionalism as a reaction *against* sovereign power, centralization, and state building, they are committing themselves to the same approach embraced by most misinterpreters of Bodin. Without reflecting deeply on the question, they are choosing *negative constitutionalism,* the doctrine that constitutions are primarily preventive or inhibitory devices, meant to check or repress tyranny and other abuses of power. Negative constitutionalism is more than a theory; it is a way of seeing and evaluating political institutions. Originating with platitudes about the opposition of "liberalism" to "absolutism," it has now become an unargued premise of much theorizing about the relation between constitutionalism and democracy. Replace the royal sovereign with the popular sovereign, and what you get is the seemingly obvious idea that constitutionalism's main function today is to prevent the "excesses of democracy." Only constitutional restraints can prevent the "tyranny of the majority," defend individual rights against abusive rulers, and so forth.

This idea is true up to a point, but not beyond. One of the main purposes in this book, therefore, is to demonstrate the limits of negative constitutionalism as an unargued premise of democratic theory. Constitutions are enabling devices, not merely disabling ones. They can be instruments of state-building, for instance, or Union-building, if we consider the Constitution drafted in Philadelphia in 1787. To understand the inadequacy of negative constitutionalism, it is vital that we return first to the origin of the idea, and question the seemingly obvious assumption that constitutions were originally formulated *against* the sovereignty of kings. A close reading of Bodin exposes the inadequacy of this premise, and therefore should help us place the theory of constitutionalism itself on new foundations. For Bodin may be considered the father of *positive constitutionalism.* Royal sovereignty, he argued, can be reinforced, rather than subverted, by constitutional limitations. This is a remarkable claim, which later liberals (such as James Madison) picked up and applied boldly to the sovereignty of the people.

A constitution is a facilitative document, Bodin argues, not merely a constraining one. It is not merely a chain meant to fetter the will of the sovereign. Once we recognize how this paradoxical line of argument, developed brilliantly in *Les six livres de la république* [*The Six Bookes of a Commonweal*] (1576), was eventually extended to liberal regimes, we begin to see constitutionalism in a fresh light. A democratic constitution, for instance, can ensure that the will of the sovereign people is formed through open public debate where criticism of past mistakes is more or less uninhibited and where individuals inside or outside the government can propose and advocate new ways to attack common problems. Only a constitution that limits the capacity of political decision makers to silence their sharpest critics, for example, can enhance the intelligence and legitimacy of decisions made.

## Why Liberalism Is Not Anti-Democratic

But if democracy means majority rule, then how can constitutional limitations, which a majority may not easily modify or circumvent, be compatible with democratic principles? That majoritarianism itself presupposes certain restrictions on the will of the majority is the *paradox of democracy* (chapter 5). This paradox reveals why liberalism, far from being inherently antirepublican or antidemocratic, is actually constitutive of democracy in any large modern society. To see why, we need only ask: Under what conditions will the numerical majority of citizens in a modern state maintain some modest influence over processes of political decision making? How can the people act, *as* a people, to enforce its will, at least occasionally, upon its rulers? Can citizens exercise their sovereign power outside all procedural mechanisms for aggregating their separate wills into one? Urban mobs may take to the streets and seize city hall, of course. But demagogues with paramilitary support who christen themselves "the representatives of the people" do not thereby become so. In large states, at least, ochlocracy is never majoritarian. The power of the street (in the capital city) is never the power of the numerical majority. So how can the majority make its voice heard?

Through competitive elections and public discussions. Neither of these historically rare mechanisms are available in a state of nature or condition of sovereignless anarchy, obviously enough. Both are highly artificial constructs, requiring patient acceptance of elaborate procedures, institutions, rules. Without regular elections and open debates in civic forums such as the press, and without the political culture that makes both seem legitimate in the eyes of the public, majoritarianism is purely fictitious. The idea that the people as a whole wield the *pouvoir constituant,* prior to all procedural restraints, and outside the discipline of electoral law, may be a useful legal fiction. (It serves to deny that any single subgroup may rightfully seize extraconstitutional power.) But to say that "the people" of a modern nation-state, while truly *legibus solutus,* or unbound by law, can spontaneously choose a new political order, is unrealistic. It is unrealistic even if we put aside the democratically unanswerable question of who is a member of the community. For a society with millions of citizens, even where the membership question is uncontestedly resolved, there is no such thing as a collective choice outside of all prechosen procedures and institutions. (Although a coup d'état may certainly be embellished with whatever populist imagery the seizers of power can purchase or invent.) Both elections in which contending political parties lose and gain power, and public discussions conducted largely through a free and pluralistic press, depend upon the entrenchment of liberal constitutionalism. This suggests that *liberalism is a necessary, though not sufficient, condition for some measure of democracy in any modern state.*

That modern democracy cannot exist outside of a liberal constitutionalist framework should be a truism, in fact, but, to some political theorists, it still sounds like an eccentricity, if not a heresy. By elaborating on this idea, I aim to refute both those radical republicans who denigrate liberal constitutionalism as a sinister plot and those dogmatic libertarians who extol it as a clever ploy. Both romantic democrats and conservative antidemocrats are on the wrong track. Unless the majority agrees to restrict itself along liberal-constitutional lines, it will have no chance to act as a majority. Although self-binding is enabling in the long run, it is psychologically difficult in the short run, which is precisely when it has to occur. Collectivities are no more fond of restricting their own freedom of choice than are individuals. As a result, democratic majorities have learned to enlist a kind of collective *stare decisis* to help them limit the range of options they have readily available. They may describe their decision to limit themselves (not to oppress minorities, for example) as acquiescence in the will of an earlier majority that ratified the constitution. But democratic commitment to rules of the game that are difficult to change has nothing to do with ancestor worship. The present generation accepts some of the decisions of the past because, on balance, they are good decisions, improving the quality of present deliberations and making present problems easier, not harder, to solve. Liberal constitutions remain morally binding, therefore, only because of sustained popular consent. Such collective self-limitation works tolerably well in practice, at least in a handful of countries, even though it remains poorly understood in theory.

## Gag Rules

Another and no less fundamental form of collective self-restriction is the decision to exclude certain emotionally charged and rationally irresolvable issues from the public agenda. Even John Stuart Mill, who was probably the greatest liberal advocate of freewheeling debate, recognized the disadvantages of uninhibited discussion in some settings (chapter 6). Rules that preclude cooperation-shattering debate of emotionally charged issues I call *gag rules* (chapter 7). Despite the democratic commitment to freedom of speech, all functioning democracies curb or channel political debate. Liberal-democratic polities invariably remove certain overheated topics from political discussion. The most obvious example is religion. Democratic majorities in multidenominational societies are more likely to resolve their other problems rationally if religious disputes are confined to the private sphere. Indeed, negative liberty (freedom from politics) is vital to positive liberty (participation in politics) in precisely this sense. The decision to protect individual conscience from interference by public officials is simultaneously a decision to secularize political life, to remove from the public agenda issues that are impossible to resolve by either argument or compromise. In other words, private freedom serves public freedom. The privatization of religion has been a fairly successful method for fostering political cooperation in multidenominational societies. (Not all troublesome issues can be dealt with in this sequestering manner, however. Most notably, attempts to handle problems of racial diversity, using methods of avoidance that have functioned fairly well in the case of religion, have not been, and probably never will be, particularly successful.) Rules that protect the private sphere, at any rate, are not always aimed *against* politics. Sometimes they are designed to *improve* politics, to make public debate more rational. When this is the case, liberalism can again be said to reinforce democracy.

Moreover, the liberal democratic societies that exist today do not sacralize the private sphere. They are not based on a wholly favorable or unqualifiedly protective attitude toward private action. The greatest threat to freedom, all liberals agree, is the concentration of power. *This is true whether power is concentrated in the public or in the private realm.* Even libertarians, as a result, support some accumulation of power in the hands of the state. Without public power, they recognize, private power-wielders would terrorize ordinary people and engross collective resources. (The total incapacity of the state to "interfere" in civil society, for example, does not make contemporary Somalia into a libertarian ideal.) As a consequence, laws designed to protect consumers or the environment from injurious private action, while condemned by some libertarians, cannot be labeled, in principle, as illiberal. What makes liberalism unique as a political doctrine, arguably, is its simultaneous concern with both public and private abuses of concentrated power. This is just as true today as it was in the seventeenth and eighteenth centuries. Even though liberals, in principle, favor strong protections for private property, they also distrust forms of ownership, for instance, that translate easily into political influence or authority. Ownership of the media is an obvious example. Attempts to regulate the news media, in ways compatible with a constitution devoted to freedom of the press, reflect a perfectly liberal concern with the political misuse of accumulated private power.

## Why Liberalism Is Not Antiwelfarist

Free-market systems not only engender potentially abusable private power, they also produce various forms of relative disadvantage. Those who assert that liberalism is essentially antidemocratic often add that liberalism is essentially antiwelfarist as well, meaning disinclined to use the taxing power to alleviate economic distress. But this second accusation is just as questionable as the first. For one thing, every major liberal theorist, from Locke to Mill, emphatically endorsed state provision in case of dire necessity (chapter 8). Why did they do this? Did they advocate poor relief because of a vestigial Christian heritage that was being steadily rinsed away at the time? Or does secular liberalism itself contain moral principles that enjoin the provision of some basic resources to all citizens?

Misled by a deceptively clear dichotomy between latitudes and entitlements, many detractors of liberalism assume that the classical liberal state was designed to protect freedoms without providing resources. The plausibility of this charge, too, disintegrates upon inspection. The liberal state provides publicly financed schooling to all, for instance, and the institutional means for private litigation. The jury system is costly, but federal and state governments in the United States *must* provide it in certain cases. Equal access to the law, while sometimes more an ideal than a reality, expresses a liberal commitment not merely to the provision but even to the *just distribution* of collective resources. Such examples suggest that liberal hostility to "entitlements" has been exaggerated by enemies on both the left and the right.

Liberalism, in all its variants, affirms the value of individual achievement. But the achievement ethic does not rule out some form of state help. Publicly financed education, for instance, is a redistributive investment in otherwise underdeveloped human capacities. It is a form of state help designed to prepare *all* citizens for *individual* achievement. Especially targeted are those individuals whose families give them little support in this regard. Similarly, the meritocratic ethic demands that some sort of compensatory action be taken to counteract the anti-individualist implications of modern inheritance law, which permits a *de facto* bequeathing of parental social status. Why should children be hopelessly snared in a web of underprivilege into which they were born through no fault of their own? The public provision of universal elementary education, jury trials in specified cases, and so forth, are especially important to those whose inherited resources are meager or nonexistent. On what principled grounds, given these precedents, can a liberal government refuse to tax the moderately affluent to provide, say, some minimum of health care to the children of the poor? This demonstration of compatibility between classical liberalism and modern welfare politics is "merely" historical, it should be said. It explodes the libertarian claim to be the true heir of classical liberalism; but it does not, in itself, refute the more important libertarian claim to be, morally and economically, the most attractive political philosophy. Like the other essays collected here, therefore, the concluding chapter on the liberal foundations of the welfare state should be read as a first step or opening bid, by no means as a final word.

# 1

# The Liberal Idea

*L'état n'est pas par lui-même un antagoniste de l'individu. L'individualisme n'est possible que par lui.*
—DURKHEIM

Liberalism is neither a vague Zeitgeist nor the outlook of modern man, but a clearly identifiable set of principles and institutional choices endorsed by specific politicians, publicists, and popular movements. The early history of liberalism, in fact, cannot be detached from the political history, in the seventeenth and eighteenth centuries, of England and Scotland, the Netherlands, the United States, and France. The political theorists who have most cogently articulated and defended liberal aspirations—Milton, Spinoza, Locke, Montesquieu, Hume, Voltaire, Beccaria, Blackstone, Smith, Kant, Bentham, Madison, Hamilton, Constant, Tocqueville, and J. S. Mill—were deeply immersed in contemporary controversies. Each spent his life responding to local challenges, defending specific reforms, struggling with circumscribed problems. They jousted with different enemies and allied themselves with different social forces. Some were temperamentally audacious; others were more cautious, predisposed to hedging and compromise. Their epistemologies and metaphysical beliefs were sometimes diametrically opposed to each other's. They also deviated from one another on a wide range of policy questions. Some mixed liberal commitments with illiberal ones. None can be fully understood if plucked ahistorically from his political and intellectual context and forced to march in a canonical parade of liberal greats.

Examined from a distance, nevertheless, the positions they endorsed tend to converge. Their common liberalism—for we might as well call it that—has nothing whatsoever to do, as some of their critics contend, with "atomistic" individualism or a hostility to the common good.[1] So what did it involve? Liberals are sometimes said to advocate "the priority of liberty" or "the most extensive liberty consistent with the same liberty for all." While not totally false, these catchphrases are needlessly telegraphic. An open society, as classical liberals conceived it, would have to institutionalize, at a bare minimum, religious toleration, freedom of discussion, personal security, free elections, constitutional government, and the freedom to buy and sell in a market of goods and services. But much more was and is involved.

For expository purposes, it will be useful to construct an ideal type of the classical liberal theorist, to sketch, so to speak, a composite portrait of the writers listed above. There is no such individual as the Typical Liberal, needless to say. Given the colorful diversity of the leading liberals of the past, no stock description can be applied without qualification to any concrete case. Counterexamples can be discovered, therefore, to all the generalizations I am about to make. But the result will nonetheless be useful, providing a benchmark to orient our discussion of an immensely complex field of study.

The ideal-typical liberal, we can begin by saying, was simultaneously anticlerical and antimilitaristic. Church authorities, he argued, should not be allowed to use the coercive powers of the state to punish heterodoxy and enforce religious conformity. While warfare may sometimes be unavoidable, he also believed, it should be viewed as a human tragedy, not as a male sport. He was also opposed, in varying degrees, to hereditary monopolies, especially to the privileges of a few "great" families who owned large tracts of land. He scorned ties of vassalage and peonage. Protesting against the indignity suffered by those adults who, in traditional European societies, were treated as wards of social superiors, he aimed to universalize the condition of personal independence. He believed in the value of literacy and secular education for all, a fairer system of taxation, and the legitimacy of social mobility within and across generations. He welcomed immigration and freedom of movement in general. He supported the right to form private associations as well as the right to divorce. He opposed legal disabilities on religious minorities (so long as national security was not at stake). He endorsed the freedom to establish churches and to preach.

Legitimate authority, he argued, is based on popular consent, not on divine right or dynastic succession. He probably defended not merely electoral politics, but also the right of rebellion in some form. He advocated political pluralism and government by public discussion among provisionally elected and publicly accountable representatives. He hoped that bloody confrontation between armed factions could be, to some extent, replaced by rational bargaining and debate. Even in the absence of social homogeneity, he believed, coexistence and cooperation could be made possible by mutual tolerance for diverse customs, styles, and beliefs. He proposed a widening of the franchise, more or less in tandem with the expansion of literacy, the relaxation of religious orthodoxy, and the abatement of religious passions. He also favored impartial hearings, uniform procedures, and an independent judiciary, as well as laws that are clearly framed, publicly proclaimed, and fairly enforced. He prescribed the abolition of torture and savage punishments, legal checks on the police, guarantees against both retroactive legislation and arbitrary imprisonment, and jury trials in criminal cases. He tended to conceive punishment as a means of deterrence rather than as a form of revenge. He advocated civilian control of the military. And he admired science as a mental activity, or deepening of human understanding, not merely as an instrument for mastering nature.

Our ideal-typical liberal was devoted not only to legal equality, but also to equality of economic opportunity. He was more distressed by poverty and personal dependency, however, than by inequality of income or wealth. He therefore urged a wide and rapid diffusion of private property. He believed that contracts should be enforced. He favored the abolition of domestic customs barriers, free entry into trades and occupations, and the freedom to exchange goods and services. He welcomed the antipaternalism of the marketplace *(caveat emptor!)*, even while he strove to remove certain goods—such as public office, military exemptions, and favorable judicial verdicts—from the channels of economic exchange. In other words, he had a selective but still warmly welcoming attitude toward commercial society. In general, he looked favorably on commercialism because he believed that economic competition could foster innovation and the efficient use of scarce resources and thereby create, among other things, enough general prosperity to improve the lives of even the poorest members of the community. Underlying liberal political economy, in other words, was a liberal theory of justice. Adam Smith advocated free trade, for example, because he assumed it would maximize the welfare of "the lowest ranks of the people" and work "for the benefit of the poor and the indigent."[2] As inevitable side effects of a market system, economic inequalities are justified because they improve the absolute (not relative) living standard of the least advantaged.

This medley of moral tenets and favored practices provides the best starting point for an understanding of the liberal tradition. From this disorderly list, it is possible to extrapolate a loose set of norms or moral ideals that appear essential both to the thinking of liberal writers and the practice of liberal communities. The best place to begin, if we wish to cut to the core of liberalism, is with Locke: "Freedom of Men under Government, is, to have a standing Rule to live by, common to every one of that Society, and made by the Legislative Power erected in it."[3] Elaborating on this classic formula, we can say that the highest political values, from a liberal perspective, are psychological security and personal independence for all, legal impartiality within a single system of laws applied equally to all, the human diversity fostered by liberty, and collective self-rule through elected government and uncensored discussion. These are the aims or moral bases of liberalism. They explain what liberal institutions are for. They help distinguish liberalism from conservatism on the one hand and socialism on the other. Finally, they show that liberalism has a robust normative basis, and is not founded, as some have claimed, on radical moral skepticism.

## What Liberalism Is Against

The sheer miscellaneousness of the proposals canvassed so far suggests that liberals were just as interested in solving concrete problems as in elaborating a systematic philosophy of political life. But can we conjure more theoretical order out of so many assorted recommendations, commitments, and concerns? I think so. By inversion and simplification, for example, we can convert our unwieldy catalogue into a shorter list of liberalism's most-disliked institutions and regimes. Four classically illiberal arrangements leap to the eye: autocracy, aristocracy, theocracy, and collective ownership. (Today we might add identity politics and ethnocracy.) By reviewing very briefly what liberals were against, we can see in clearer terms what they were for, and why.

In an *autocratic* regime, a single and unaccountable faction, party, or clique monopolizes power, the press is censored or superintended by the government; individuals can be imprisoned for extensive periods without legal recourse; surveillance and informing are all-pervasive; the secret police seizes or is given enormous discretion to liquidate unreliable individuals and enforce political subservience; the ordinary police is poorly monitored and controlled; in some cases, finance and industry are nationalized and the economy is centrally managed; criticism of political rulers is forbidden and, therefore, government is likely to be capricious, oppressive, corrupt, and grossly misinformed. In an *aristocracy,* access to privilege is determined almost wholly by pedigree; land ownership is the key to life; a closed oligarchy monopolizes political power; and social mobility within and across generations is minimal. In a *fundamentalist theocracy* or clerical authoritarian regime, a small clerisy dictates the moral destiny of the vast majority, bigotry is rewarded, innovation is sacrificed to indoctrination, intellectual exchange is quashed, education relentlessly controlled, deviations punished, orthodoxy enforced.

All three of these regimes are patently illiberal. None stirs any sympathy among liberal intellectuals. Outrage is expressed whenever their vestiges are discovered in liberal societies today. Remedies are proposed (and sometimes applied). To the extent that autocracy, aristocracy, and theocracy are decried, liberal rhetoric, at least, has triumphed.

It is different with *communism* and the principle of economic leveling on which it is purportedly built. During the greater part of this century, the socialist tradition, despite its trumpeted embrace of "progress," has assiduously cultivated and kept alive an archaic inequality taboo, inherited, it seems, from subsistence economies of the distant past. (The archaic roots of communism may partly explain the extraordinary contagiousness of authoritarian socialism in nonindustrial countries where traces of an old communalist ethos remain strong.) What characterizes liberalism, by contrast, is its unembarrassed repudiation of ancient and Christian prohibitions on inequality of resources. While adamantly opposed to any sort of caste system, liberalism is notoriously tolerant of newly emergent disparities in income and wealth. Our ideal-typical liberal, as mentioned, is intensely concerned with poverty and economic dependency, that is, with absolute levels of well-being (including a "bottom floor" of decent subsistence) as well as economically entrenched relations of mastery and control. And he is scandalized when rich men manage to buy politicians and judges. Inequality of wealth itself, however, *when detached from problems of dependency, poverty, and corruption,* is not viewed by most liberals as an unacceptable social evil. Critics often assert that liberal acquiescence in economic inequality stems from a profound belief that superior talents "deserve" superior rewards. But this is a dubious claim. Our ideal-typical liberal accepts inequality of resources, in fact, because he sees it as the inevitable side effect of a productive economy. He rejects the inequality taboo not because it is the expression of irrational envy (although it may have been this as well), but rather because it is an infallible formula for reproducing scarcity and exacerbating dependency. Collective ownership, aimed at equalizing conditions, is not only economically inefficient, it also destroys the independent and decentralized resources on which political opposition is based.

Nowhere in this book do I offer a concise definition of liberalism. In what follows, I will simply analyze a series of basic political concepts—state power, interests, rights, democracy, and welfare. By examining each of these concepts in turn, I will be able to explain how liberalism's basic moral commitments are embodied in concrete political proposals and institutional arrangements. This will also allow me to explore the role played in liberal thought and practice by the unfamiliar principles discussed separately in subsequent chapters.

## State Power

Liberalism is classically defined as an attempt to limit the power of the state for the sake of individual freedom. The ideal-typical liberal, it is true, was justifiably afraid of political tyranny. His driving concern, historians have repeatedly argued, was to prevent hypertrophic or whimsical government from oppressing individuals and groups. The essence of liberalism, from this perspective, lay in techniques for taming absolute power.[4] There are good reasons for emphasizing the antipower ethos within the liberal tradition. For while liberals have a better grasp of economic realities than socialists and communists, the most obvious superiority of liberal over Marxist thought stems from liberalism's persistent concern for—and Marxism's infamous blindness to—abuses of accumulated political power.

In fact, the antityrannical strand has always been, and remains today, a vital element within liberal thought. But it is not the whole story. To identify liberalism with a crusade to restrict state power is inadequate. For one thing, liberal states have, since the very beginning, proved breathtakingly powerful.[5] The twentieth century provides some outstanding examples of the superiority of liberalism over autocracy from purely military and administrative perspectives. It is enlightening to reread, after the events of 1989, the speeches that Alexander Solzhenitsyn delivered in the United States during the 1970s. There we learn that the West—infected by the spirit of liberalism—is becoming weaker and weaker, while the Soviet Union is roaring with doomlike inevitability toward world domination.[6] This prognosis has been spectacularly refuted by events.

The dramatic story of nineteenth-century Britain is another case in point. The age of free trade and the industrial revolution, of course, was simultaneously the age of the British Empire. Shockingly enough, a small island off the northwest coast of Europe gained mastery over a third of the globe. The classic country of political liberalism did not display state weakness in any obvious sense. Britain even proved strong enough, eventually, to *shed* its empire without suffering an internal political collapse. When estimating the relative strength of alternative institutional arrangements, in fact, we should ask, What political regimes can stably survive invasion, military defeat, loss of empire, civil war, and so forth? Liberal polities have done *relatively* well in such trying circumstances. Their relative success, like Britain's path to world empire, is understandable only because liberal institutions help increase the capacity of the state to mobilize internal resources for collective purposes.

That liberal institutions could be militarily strengthening was already clear in the seventeenth century. As Locke wrote, "That Prince who shall be so wise and godlike as by established laws of liberty to secure protection and incouragement to the honest industry of Mankind against the oppression of power and narrownesse of Party, will quickly be too hard for his neighbors."[7] In the same spirit, Voltaire and Montesquieu praised England not only for its liberties, but also for its power—for the ships crowding its harbors. Oppression, they both argued, weakens the state. Intolerance deepens sectarian conflict and drives useful citizens abroad. Censorship blocks the flow of information vital for the governance of a large nation. Cruel and excessive punishments crush the spirit of ordinary citizens, depriving the government of their active collaboration. Heavy-handed regulations on trade decrease the private wealth that might eventually be tapped for the public treasury. A liberal polity is much better situated than a tyrannical one for enlisting citizen cooperation in the pursuit of common objectives. Voltaire, and even Montesquieu, identified liberalism with a welcome magnification (along some dimensions) of state power.

This line of reasoning makes perfect sense. It is implausible, after all, to view liberal rights as naturally incompatible with political power, as if such rights could flourish when the state withers away. State power and liberty are interdependent, not simply opposed. As Immanuel Kant, among others, made clear, rights (including property rights) are defined and enforced by the government. Referring to "natural rights," Émile Durkheim, too, convincingly wrote that "the State creates these rights, gives them an institutional form, and makes them into realities."[8] To violate liberal rights is to disobey the liberal state. In a sovereignless condition, rights can be imagined but not experienced. In a society with a weak state, such as Lebanon for the past decade, or with virtually no state, such as Somalia today, rights themselves are nonexistent or underenforced. Statelessness means rightlessness, as stories of migrating Kurds, Vietnamese and Caribbean boatpeople, and many others, have also made abundantly clear.

The positive correlation between individual rights and state capacities is an important theme in the history of liberal thought. An emblematic figure in this regard is Pierre Bayle, one of the originators of the liberal defense of religious toleration. Bayle was a theorist of toleration, but he was simultaneously an "absolutist," that is, an advocate of increased powers for the crown or centralized state. The logic of his position may be unfamiliar to those who understand liberalism as vehemently antistatist. But the Baylean linkage of liberal rights to sovereignty is actually quite straightforward. In his day, political opponents of the Church naturally enlisted the support of the secular power. Only a powerful centralized state could protect individual rights against local strongmen and religious majorities. Only an energetic and resourceful state could defend the weak against the strong. In France, more specifically, only a powerful state could defang the church, resisting the pressure of ecclesiastics to persecute the Protestant minority. (Bayle was a Protestant.) Most historians of liberalism claim that liberalism was born in protest against state power.[9] This is an accurate, but still one-sided, picture. Bayle's liberal defense of toleration was born in protest against a *lack* of state power. His liberalism was most lucidly displayed in his plea to extend the state's protection to vulnerable Huguenots.[10]

Libertarian rhetoric about "getting the government off our backs" makes the positive correlation between individual rights and state power difficult to comprehend. The history of liberal political theory offers a better guide. I have just mentioned Bayle. Dozens of other texts reinforce the same idea—that personal liberty and governmental capacities can be mutually reinforcing. Consider, to pick a British example, David Hume's famous essay, "Of Commerce." What does Hume argue in this classic defense of liberal political economy? He contends, essentially, that Britain should deregulate commercial and industrial life and welcome the accumulation of private wealth, because such a system will increase the resources available to the state. Banning the luxury trade would be self-defeating for a modern nation. As it turns out, "manufactures encrease the power of the state" by creating resources "to which the public may lay claim."[11] An autocratic government, intent upon controlling all economic life, will decrease the stock of private wealth and thereby indirectly undermine its own power. Kant reformulated the same point, articulating a lesson in 1784 that the leaders of the Communist bloc absorbed only late in the day: "Civil freedom can no longer be so easily infringed without disadvantage to all trades and industry, and especially to commerce, in the event of which the state's power in its external relations will also decline."[12]

Not private property and freedom of contract alone, but almost all typically liberal institutions can be justified on the grounds that they strengthen the state's capacity to govern and solve collective problems. Consider, by way of further illustration, one of the most fundamental institutions of liberal constitutionalism: liberty of discussion. Libertarians might defend freedom of speech by arguing that the sphere of individual liberty must be maximally expanded while the sphere of state power must be contracted to a proportional degree. But the ideal-typical liberal conceived free discussion in another way. Kant was wholly representative when he argued that a government should never stifle freedom of the press because, in so doing, it would lose access to vital information and undermine its own capacity to govern. Legally protected outlets for public complaint both discourage conspiratorial intrigue and enhance the legitimacy (and hence the effective power) of the government. As we shall see, theorists of absolutism, such as Bodin, had already drawn attention to the advantages of uncensored free-spokenness for the power of the state. His book *Les six livres de la république* provided a series of extremely influential *raison d'état* arguments for constitutional limits on governmental power. That limited government can be more powerful than unlimited government, as I try to demonstrate in chapter 4, is Bodin's principal legacy to the liberal tradition. More specifically, if a king wants to learn promptly about the misdeeds of his own agents, he ought to create an outspoken Estates General where representatives from the entire kingdom can come together and complain openly under a prior grant of immunity.[13] In this way, *assembléisme* can contribute directly to the assertion and maintenance of effective sovereign power. Freedom of speech in a national assembly is an indispensable tool of the modern "art of governance."

What can we learn by looking at such preliberal arguments for typically liberal political institutions? We can learn, at the very least, to question the conventional interpretation of liberal theory as ardently antistatist. The name of Bodin is almost synonymous with the idea of sovereignty or state power. If *he* could argue in favor of constitutional restrictions on power as clever techniques for increasing the government's capacity to govern, then we cannot be justified in assuming, without further argument or evidence, that liberals who embraced similar institutions were necessarily enemies of sovereign power.

Admittedly, an anarchical impulse can be discerned in some liberal theorists, such as Tom Paine, and even in Locke (and perhaps in all natural-rights theorists). But our ideal-typical liberal was certainly no anarchist. He was opposed to capricious and oppressive authority, not to authority in general. He embraced "the firmness and efficiency of government" as a means both to prevent anarchy and to enforce impartial laws against the grain of human partiality or self-love.[14] (More recently, even libertarians have come to accept state power as an indispensable instrument for enforcing competition.) Because they assumed that political rulers will ordinarily be human, and therefore partial to themselves and potentially unjust, classical liberals devised institutional machinery to contain authority within legal channels. Such a constitutionalizing of authority is antiauthoritarian. But opponents of whimsical and brutal rule did not therefore yearn for a crippled or helpless state.

As the countries of the former East bloc struggle to establish constitutional democracies in difficult circumstances today, we should ask ourselves again how the United States managed to launch a stable liberal-republican regime at the end of the eighteenth century. The endurance of the Constitution written at Philadelphia in 1787 was not foreordained. Members of the Constituent Assembly in Paris in 1791, whose ideals were not radically discrepant from those of the American Founders, produced a respectable, if not perfect, liberal constitution which guttered to a swift and miserable end. Why did the Americans succeed and the French fail? There are many reasons, of course, stemming from the vastly different political, religious, economic, demographic, and military situations of the two countries. (While the French were saddled with Louis XVI, the United States was favored with George Washington, and so forth.) But one additional reason deserves to be pointed out. Unlike their French contemporaries, the American framers devised their Constitution *after a period of frustration with the weakness of the central government.* The Articles of Confederation presented "a striking spectacle of a government destitute even of the shadow of constitutional power to enforce the execution of its own Laws." Under that document, "the government of the Union had gradually dwindled into a state of decay, approaching nearly to annihilation."[15] The framers aimed, therefore, not only to prevent tyranny, but also to create an energetic government with the capacity to govern, to rule effectively, and to "promote the general Welfare." This devotion to governmental energy and effectiveness, this passion for state building, was virtually absent at the Paris Constituent Assembly. Framed in response to the unpredictable arbitrariness of monarchical rule, the French Constitution of 1791 proved so constricting that, when the first crisis struck, authorities were driven to slough it off and govern extraconstitutionally. By contrast, the desire simultaneously to limit and reinforce the state resulted, in the American case, in a stable constitutional regime that was neither tyrannical nor weak.

When granting powers to the government, the American framers looked for guidance to the great European liberals. What capacities should government be assigned, from a liberal point of view? These powers are not trivial. The ability to defend the country from foreign invasion and to regulate political and economic intercourse with other nations are usually mentioned first. But what domestic powers should a liberal state possess? What public goods must a liberal government provide? The ideal-typical liberal expected the government to keep the peace internally, providing security from private as well as public violence. (That is, government had to create both a capable police force and reliable mechanisms for monitoring and controlling this police force.) The liberal state was also expected to provide a stable currency and to define property rights, and enforce property law, contract law, trespass law, and patent law in court. No rules for the inheritance or conveyance of property exist in the state of nature, wrote Blackstone; they have to be created conventionally, by political means.[16] Civil society, therefore, was society "civilized" by the state. The government imposed civilization on a territorially bounded population not only by concentrating the legitimate use of violence in its own hands, but also by establishing and enforcing the private law framework of civil society.

The legitimate functions of the liberal state, in fact, were significant and diverse. Constitutional government had a significant allocative role, for instance. It had to make available judicial institutions for private litigation. It had to deliver fair procedures in criminal cases, allowing a reasonable defense for the accused. It had to provide poor relief. (The principles behind traditional poor relief were attacked by Malthus, it is true, but not by our ideal-typical liberal.) And the liberal state had to provide a whole series of other public goods, including, in many cases, canals, highways, safe water, street lights, sewers.

Such state help was conceived as providing the preconditions for self-help. This idea was nowhere more apparent than in liberal advocacy of subsidized education. Adam Smith, for one, favored a publicly financed (though not necessarily publicly operated) system of compulsory elementary education aimed to improve the condition of the indigent. Mill, too, held it to be "the duty of the government" to supply "pecuniary support to elementary schools, such as to render them accessible to all the children of the poor." Far from being a road to serfdom, government intervention was meant to enhance individual autonomy. Publicly financed schooling, as Mill wrote, is "help toward doing without help."[17]

## Interests

From a Marxist perspective, the primary liberal right is the right to economic liberty: the right to own property, to make contracts, to enter into business, to choose one's career or occupation, to buy and sell, to exchange goods and services. But is it true that our ideal-typical liberal would have viewed economic rights as somehow primary or exemplary? According to Max Weber, freedom of conscience was the first and basic liberal right.[18] More generally, liberals embraced religious toleration, freedom of discussion, the right to criticize government officials, the right to a reasonable defense in criminal trials, and prohibitions against bodily torture, all for independent reasons—not merely because such practices were good for trade. However important, economic liberty was merely one among the core practices valued by liberals.

This is not to deny the sympathetic emphasis that many liberals placed on market freedoms and economic self-interest. Even liberals committed to redistribution, such as John Rawls, endorse core market institutions.[19] The role of self-interest in liberal theory, however, has been poorly understood. All too often, commentators assume that liberals who adopt a friendly attitude toward self-interest are advocating some sort of hyperegoistical, beggar-thy-neighbor attitude in which nothing matters but the pursuit of personal and material gain. This is an overly theatrical view of the liberal tradition.

Liberals are often accused of psychological reductionism.[20] They purportedly believed that human beings are propelled by rational self-interest alone, as if benevolence, love of others, and devotion to the common good were wholly unreal motivations. This accusation is reckless. Before the nineteenth century, as my next two chapters are designed to show, motivational reductionism was virtually unknown. Traditional psychology was dominated by a mélange of Stoic, Epicurean, Aristotelian, and Augustinian theory. Most human behavior was understood to spring from unthinking habit or irrational passions. Rational choice of action was exceptional. Self-destructive and wasteful conduct was rampant. Most individuals were compulsive or impulsive, hidebound by custom or racked by passing frenzies. Ideological creeds, psychological identification with cultural groups or charismatic leaders, and chivalric or devotional behavioral codes—all these forces drove individuals to sacrifice their personal well-being and even their lives. For neo-Stoics with eyes to see, therefore, calculating and self-interested behavior was obviously a rare moral ideal. It could be achieved only by a few philosophers after a strenuous process of moral discipline, wherein irrational passions were systematically weakened and purged. It could certainly not be expected from everyone.

Given this cultural background, it is implausible to assume that our ideal-typical liberal would have been a motivational reductionist.

His focus on calculating self-interest must be understood in a subtler way. It was not a descriptive claim, first of all, but rather a normative recommendation. We can see this pattern most clearly, as I argue in chapter 3, in the writings of Thomas Hobbes, the preliberal theorist who probably exerted the greatest and most lasting influence on classical liberals. In a few scattered passages, Hobbes asserts that the coolly rational pursuit of self-interest on the part of affectless individuals can frustrate collective undertakings. But his basic argument is quite different. If most human beings most of the time were rational pursuers of their own self-interest, Hobbes explained, history would *not* be an endless chronicle of wasteful butchery and self-destruction. Civil wars are so frequent, instead, because at least some individuals are prepared to risk death for the sake of "higher" ideals such as glory and salvation, or perhaps to avenge a public humiliation inflicted on their cultural group. To eliminate the destructive violence of civil war, it is crucial to discredit all ideals that tempt individuals to defy death. This is the principal goal of Hobbes's reeducation campaign. In a morally reformed society, people will, for the most part, rationally pursue self-preservation, oblivious to the siren songs of aristocratic glory and religious redemption. Hobbes favored such an extirpation of irrational motivations, but he did not believe that most people could ever be wholly rescued from preposterous habits of mind. He cannot be accused of thinking that human beings are self-disciplined enough to become rational and self-interested in an emphatic sense.

The liberals who built upon Hobbesian foundations had a slightly more optimistic view. They too saw self-interest and strategic rationality as social ideals to be approximated, although still not perfectly achieved. They were less pessimistic than Hobbes because they thought that commercial society and predictable state authority had powerful psychological effects and could conceivably knock some modicum of sense into mankind. Montesquieu, for instance, believed that economic growth and legal constraints on public officials would discourage panicky, instrumentally irrational, and self-destructive behavior. Commercialism alone would weaken the vise-grip of xenophobia and bigotry, incite forethought, and sharpen people's awareness of the remote consequences of their actions. The spirit of commerce would not create noble souls, but it might solve certain social problems by subtly transforming dominant styles of interaction. Bentham aside, none of the classical liberals thought that human beings were programmed *at birth* to be calculating maximizers of individual well-being. (For some overpowering evidence, see Montesquieu's *Persian Letters.*)

Rational self-interest might emerge as a common, if not preponderant, human style, but only after a massive and long-term reform of social manners.

There is another, even more important, flaw in conventional accounts of the liberal attitude toward self-interest. It is often assumed that liberal devotion to self-interest implies a purely prudential account of practical reason. If self-interest is a legitimate motive, then practical reasoning must be exclusively instrumental, a matter of discovering the most effective means to achieve given goals. This formulation is misleading, however. There is an implicit moral component hidden in the liberal emphasis on *universal* self-interest, as mentioned in the Introduction and argued at greater length in chapter 2. To say that *all* individuals are motivated by self-interest is to assert that, from a political perspective, all human beings are fundamentally the same. For political purposes, no individual can lay claim to motives that are morally superior to his neighbor's. There are no higher types. Everyone has interests, and one individual's interests are, in principle, as worthy of satisfaction as another's. The right to rule cannot be grounded in natural superiority, therefore, as Kantians and utilitarians agree. All people, including rulers, are driven by self-interest. As a result, constitution makers must craft institutions, such as periodic and competitive elections, that shape and channel the interests of rulers so that they artificially coincide with the interests of the ruled. The concept of universal self-interest can thus be said to lay the anthropological foundations for democracy. (This explains why seventeenth- and eighteenth-century "republicans," such as Harrington, expressed exactly the same cautious enthusiasm about self-interest as did Locke.)

The liberal concept of self-interest, to repeat, contains an implicit reference to some sort of universalistic and egalitarian norm. This norm was explicitly affirmed, moreover, not merely implied. "The sum of all we drive at," wrote Locke, "is that every man may enjoy the same rights that are granted to others."[21] Not satisfied with indirect references to moral equality, classical liberals uniformly endorsed a norm of fairness meant to override self-interest in case of conflict. Later advocates of *universal* state-financed education were expressing the very same liberal commitment to an egalitarian norm. (The ideal-typical liberal's refusal to take the next step and advocate economic equality was due not to the tepidness of his egalitarian commitments, but to his double conviction that, first, such an arrangement would impoverish the entire society including its worst-off members and, second, no government armed with such massive redistributionist and regulatory powers could be trusted to act in the interests of society.)

There is nothing shameful, in any case, about the pursuit of personal advantage. This concession is a distinctive innovation of the modern humanism to which all liberals subscribed. Self-interest is not a sign of moral depravity or cowardice, though it may express a novel insouciance toward would-be social "superiors." Advantage seeking nevertheless presents an important social problem. Government is necessary, as Locke and the others argued, precisely because individuals are partial to themselves. The passions of men will not conform to the dictates of justice without constraint. Our ideal-typical liberal endorsed self-interest, then, but also worried about it, because he was acutely conscious of the damaging effects of human partiality. A self-interested individual will prefer that everyone else obey the law, while he or she continues to disobey it. Such an arrangement would be in the individual's private interest, but it would also be wrong from a liberal point of view. To benefit from the self-restraint of others, while continuing to benefit from one's own lack of self-restraint, is flagrantly unjust or unfair. Individuals who exempt themselves from otherwise universal constraints implicitly assert, contrary to liberal principles, that they are special, superior, higher types.

Liberalism is a norm-based, not an interest-based, theory. The *prohibition on self-exemption* has always been, and still is, one of its core norms. This norm—the injunction to play by rules which apply equally to all—was most systematically expounded by Kant, but it is unambiguously advanced in the works of all liberal theorists. It would be in an individual's interest to make an exception of himself; he would prefer to free-ride on the taxes paid by his neighbors or to break the laws against industrial pollution whenever convenient while benefiting from the well-monitored behavior of others. But he cannot be permitted to do this because self-exemption from generally valid laws would be unfair. For our ideal-typical liberal, in short, a norm of fairness overrides the motive of self-interest.

## Rights

The ideal-typical liberal also believed that rights were specified and maintained by state power. And he saw economic liberty as only one kind of right, of no greater importance than, say, freedom of speech, the right to a fair trial, freedom from bodily fear, freedom of conscience, the right to education, or the right to vote. In "On the Jewish Question," the young Marx accused bourgeois rights of destroying community. Why controls on the whimsy of policemen equipped with deadly weapons should be seen as meanly anticommunal has never been clear. In fact, liberal rights do not protect the atomized individual from society. They protect fragile channels of social communication (such as the press) from being infiltrated, subdued, destroyed by political authorities. It is not surprising that authoritarian regimes, based on fear, are much more "atomistic" than liberal societies organized around rights.

One of the greatest obstacles to a fresh understanding of such rights is the tyranny of false polarities. Political theory lives in thrall to a sequence of binary schemes: individualism vs. community, self-interest vs. virtue, negative liberty vs. positive liberty, limited government vs. self-government. Indeed, the history of modern political theory has recently been reconstructed as a running battle between two supposedly rival traditions: liberalism vs. republicanism. Republicanism, it appears, was everything that liberalism was not. Republicans believed in virtue, community, citizen involvement in politics, while liberals were devoted to base self-interest, personal security, and private independence. This stylized contrast between liberalism and republicanism, as already mentioned, does not provide an accurate picture of the real alternatives confronting seventeenth- and eighteenth-century political thought.

One source of the misleading antithesis between liberalism and republicanism is Isaiah Berlin's famous essay on negative and positive liberty.[22] The faults of this stimulating essay are well-known. For one thing, Berlin employs the term "positive liberty" in an ambivalent sense. He uses it to mean both the romantic realization of the real self and the democratic organization of government. This is an unfortunate conflation, however, since collective self-rule and individual self-fulfillment have no necessary connection with one another. Indeed, if Wilhelm von Humboldt was right, self-fulfillment is possible only in a condition where a large degree of freedom from politics is secured.[23]

Similarly, democratic procedures are presumably valuable because they improve the quality of political decisions, not primarily because they enhance the spiritual beauty of the decision makers.

Another major problem with Berlin's position is his claim that negative and positive liberty are themselves logically, institutionally, and historically unrelated. It is easy, he says, to have one without the other. This is a perplexing claim, for political participation has obviously proved to be an indispensable tool for protecting individuals against capricious, corrupt, and tyrannical government.[24] Such, after all, was the essential meaning of "no taxation without representation." Conversely, the protection of private rights provides a crucial precondition for "positive liberty" in both senses. If the police can smash down doors at midnight and drag away families to unknown dungeons or graves, a citizen's chances for "personal fulfillment" will be drastically curtailed, as will his desire to participate actively in political life. There is no good reason, again, why controls on police misconduct should be considered either undemocratic or hostile to the flowering of the romantic self.

While Humboldt argued that limited government makes self-realization possible, his contemporary, James Madison, argued that limited government makes collective self-rule possible. These two claims are complementary and, taken together, provide good grounds for doubting the adequacy of Berlin's scheme. Madison's argument runs as follows. All attempts to organize stable popular government in the past have failed miserably. Republican regimes seem doomed to collapse into factionalism and anarchy. To escape from the intolerable chaos, some sort of democratically unaccountable Caesar or Cromwell will inevitably be handed unregulated power.[25] The constitutional problem is how to thwart this powerful historical pattern. How could the Americans design a democratically elected and popularly accountable government that, unlike all other republics throughout history, would have a decent chance to survive?

The practical answer to this question hinged upon a premise that seemed self-evident to the framers, the premise that liberal rights can be democracy reinforcing. For self-government to endure, Madison reasoned, it must be limited government in a special sense. For the will of the majority to prevail, outvoted minorities must be willing to comply with electoral results. They must not be inclined to resort to violence whenever they lose an election. To purchase minority compliance, the electoral majority must assure the electoral minority that its most precious values and rights will not be violated. A baseline of universal security, provided to all citizens, and public confidence that certain vital interests will not be subject to political control, should create a willingness among the outvoted to acquiesce peacefully in the decisions of the majority.

Madison's often maligned sensitivity toward property rights should also be seen in this light. While expecting and encouraging a greater diffusion of property ownership, Madison foresaw the maintenance in the United States of an important distinction between the rich and the poor. For a popular government to persist, moreover, the mass of poorer citizens must keep the confidence of the wealthy. Without the willing cooperation of the rich, no system as inherently unstable as collective self-rule could possibly last. If property-holders believe that democratic procedures will lead to confiscatory policies, they will refuse to go along. They will sabotage the workings of popular government, and they will use their private wealth to resist collective decisions. The poor will counterattack. The likely outcome is class warfare, social turmoil, and the general call for a dictator on horseback.

This line of reasoning may seem excessively cynical. Are property rights merely concessions that the many make to the few in order to purchase their cooperation in the workings of popular government? The impression of cynicism is mitigated, however, once we recall that Madison also assumed an economic rationale for property rights. (They are productive, not merely protective; they contribute to overall prosperity, enhancing the well-being of the poorest members of the community; with economic growth, the proportion of property owners in the population will increase.) What matters for present purposes, in any case, is the abstract pattern of Madison's thought. He does not conceive of limits on governmental power as covertly antidemocratic. On the contrary. Only such limits will permit democracy—or its closest realizable approximation—to endure.

Not only is positive liberty a necessary precondition for negative liberty but, so Madison's argument suggests, negative liberty is a necessary precondition for positive liberty. A market economy alone cannot guarantee the creation or persistance of a democratic government and liberal legal institutions. (Germany, for instance, has had more or less the same "market system" under the Kaiser, the Weimar Republic, Hitler, and the Federal Republic.) Without decentralized economic power, however, liberal democracy is very unlikely, if not wholly unable, to survive. Economic liberty is a necessary but not sufficient condition for the creation and endurance of a liberal-democratic or liberal-republican regime.

Of course, "negative liberty" does not refer solely to economic freedom. It refers, even more essentially, to *psychological security*.[26] In a liberal state, individuals generally assume that, if they obey the law, they will not be harassed, tortured, or killed by the police. They also assume a high degree of judicial predictability—that they will be governed "by established standing laws, promulgated and known to the People, and not by Extemporary Decrees."[27] The logical, psychological, and historical connection between negative and positive liberty becomes even more persuasive when we take the problem of security into account.

Individuals want their private rights protected because, among other reasons, personal security allows them to exercise their distinctive virtues and realize their different potentials, and also to participate—without inhibition or fear of reprisal—in public debate and processes of collective self-governance. Liberalism's critics seldom take the virtue-fostering, diversity-encouraging, and democracy-enabling functions of private rights into account. The last point is especially worth repeating. Citizens will not throng voluntarily to the public square if their homes can be ravaged at will by the police.

Finally, as I argue in chapter 7, negative liberty makes another crucial contribution to democratic government. Individual rights of religious conscience and group freedom of worship do not merely protect a nonpolitical (but still social) sphere. They also help keep divisive issues off the political agenda. By privatizing religion in a multidenominational society, liberal freedom helps make public discussion and majoritarian decision making more effective. By securing a "private space" for religious activity, constitutional government encourages citizens to engage in mutual learning and cooperation on a whole range of nonsacred issues. Separation of church and state unclutters the democratic agenda and creates an opportunity for collaboration across sectarian lines. Because rights are protective, in short, they can also be productive.

## Democracy

The claim that liberalism is inherently hostile to democracy is implausible from an historical point of view. Why should a commitment to private rights necessarily imply disdain for electoral politics and civic activism? Liberals generally believed that "a dependency on the people is, no doubt, the primary control on the government." Rather than rejecting democratic freedoms for the sake of private independence, they were "equally the friends . . . of public and personal liberty."[28] This should not be surprising, since the only countries in which the majority of citizens has any chance to exert a modicum of influence on political decisions are those with liberal-constitutionalist regimes. Moreover, the democratization of the franchise in the West did not abolish or even seriously threaten the primary predemocratic liberal gains: religious toleration, freedom of the press, constraints on police misbehavior, freedom of entry into occupations and trades, and so forth.[29] So whence, besides Berlin's misleading antithesis, derives the assumption that liberalism and democracy are mutually exclusive?

An unrealistic dream of "direct democracy" has played a role. True, liberals have always viewed political participation as voluntary rather than obligatory, and as part-time rather than full-time. In a large nation densely populated with busy citizens, collective decision making can occur only in a representative assembly. ("Infirmities of Health, and Avocations of Business," as Locke quaintly explained, "will necessarily keep many away from the publick Assembly.")[30] This assembly, liberals came to believe, must be informed and stimulated by national discussion conducted by means of a free press.

Those who identify democracy with direct full-time obligatory participation in public life, it is true, have traditionally pigeonholed liberals as antidemocrats. Aspiring to an unrealizable ideal, they have condemned liberals for the sin of being practical-minded. True, the ideal-typical liberal did not gaze back with nostalgia at the ancient Greek polis. But was his skepticism, in this regard, essentially antidemocratic? On the contrary. He admired the extraordinary freedom of discussion in the Greek assemblies. But he did not want to imitate most of the other characteristics of those impoverished, slave-holding, militaristic oligarchies which managed to consume themselves in class warfare.

The two-century-long struggle of the disenfranchised, including women, to gain the right to vote in liberal systems was a democratic struggle against antidemocratic forces. With whom, in this struggle, were "liberals" allied? Was liberalism basically a conservative ideology, supporting the exclusion of most people from active citizenship? Or was it a more progressive force, encouraging the gradual integration of all citizens into electoral politics as literacy spread and religious passions subsided?

Resistance to the universality of the vote, even by those who otherwise defended "universal" human rights, was based, to some extent, on fear of potentially confiscatory electoral majorities. Both Montesquieu and Blackstone, however, defended the British decision to limit the franchise to the propertied classes because the poor would predictably sell their vote for a meal.[31] Similarly, Mill and Tocqueville were distressed at the election of Louis Napoléon to the presidency of the Second French Republic by universal manhood suffrage. The fundamental source of resistance to a liberalization of the franchise, nevertheless, was *the reluctance of those who already had the vote to see their power diluted by newcomers.* That insiders have a tendency to defend their privileges against outsiders probably has more to do with human nature, however, than with the supposed niggardliness of liberalism as a political creed.

Indeed, despite practical reservations, liberals provided a strong theoretical basis for democratic politics, including the universal franchise, as it eventually developed. Even Montesquieu, who passes as a conservative breed of liberal, could write that "the legislative power should reside in the whole body of the people."[32] Lincoln's idea of government of the people, by the people, and for the people, in other words, was an extension, not a denial or reversal, of liberal ideas. *To be free,* for liberals, included the right *to obey laws made by oneself or one's representatives.* "Freedom to choose" was partly the freedom to choose collectively the laws under which all citizens must jointly live. Two vital political institutions in every liberal regime, therefore, are the franchise and a representative legislature. Citizens are bound to obey only those laws that are made by individuals expressly authorized to do so, laws framed by legislators whom the electorate can oust from office if it so decides. Locke already set forth these ideas with exemplary clarity. He insisted that the legislative power is "but a delegated Power from the People" and that "the Legislative being only a Fiduciary Power to act for certain ends, there remains still *in the People a Supream Power* to remove or *alter the Legislative,* when they find the *Legislative* act contrary to the trust reposed in them."[33] This is the classic liberal formulation of a right of rebellion. Democratic politics, as we now know it, is but a routinization of this original liberal right. Our legislators are our trustees whom we may remove from office when they violate our trust.[34] Madison was simply following his liberal predecessors when he asserted that "a dependence on the people" is "the primary control on government," more important even than the separation of powers.[35] The same can be said of Mill, who argued that "the ideally best form of government is that in which the sovereignty, or supreme controlling power in the last resort, is vested in the entire aggregate of the community."[36]

A subsidiary principle also reveals the interconnection between liberalism and democracy. This is the radically untraditional idea that *public disagreement is a creative force.* Among preliberal political theorists, the prevailing view was that uniformity of belief is a salutary social cement, indispensable for public order. John Milton was one of the first to reject this traditional idea, scorning what he called "obedient unanimity" and suggesting that a society could stably flourish without "a grosse and conforming stupidity."[37] The utility of public disagreement was the principal theme of his great work, *Areopagitica* (1644), written before Milton himself became a censor. This improbable idea had an earlier incarnation, among other places, in a few city-states of ancient Greece. But it was only encoded in the political systems of large nations during the liberal period. It is so radical that not even Rousseau, the father of modern radicalism, accepted it.

Liberal rights are not only protective, but productive as well. The principal purpose of freedom of speech, from this perspective, is less the protection of individual autonomy than the production of intelligent (the term is relative) political decisions. Participation in "the free market of ideas" does not guarantee personal fulfillment or independence, any more than it fosters an emotional-moral identification among citizens. Instead, as I argue in chapter 6, liberty of public discussion is a technique designed to enlist the decentralized imagination and knowledge of citizens, to expose errors, and to encourage new proposals. Moreover, the free market of ideas is an implicitly egalitarian idea. It assumes that every citizen can, in principle, make a useful contribution to public debate. (Milton wrote of "the voice of reason from what quarter soever it be heard speaking.")[38] Finally, a regime built around free-wheeling debate, in Milton's sense, is also based on human nature, at least in a loose sense. Human beings are animals capable of self-correction. Government by discussion is a political embodiment of the elemental human capacity to learn from experience and repair mistakes.

Suppose that a well-meaning constitutional engineer is struggling to organize a political system for a large nation in which the majority would have a modest chance to influence public policy. What would he do? He would certainly avoid conferring excessive power on urban mobs, who never represent more than a slim minority of the population. The only technique available would be electoral politics of some sort. When detached from periodic elections, in fact, "majoritarianism" degenerates into nothing better than an ideological cover for autocracy. Vote-tallying majoritarianism, in fact, is much less threatening to liberal values than most political theorists who fret about the "tyranny of the majority" assume. Realistically speaking, the tyranny of a numerical majority does not pose a significant threat in large commercial societies today. It certainly cannot compete in seriousness with the threat of ordinary tyranny, and that means, of course, the tyranny of a minority.

Liberal universalism, it should also be noted, implies that every individual's vote should count the same. The *only* morally justified decision-making rule in liberal politics is majoritarian. The logical derivation of majoritarianism from egalitarian individualism has been obscured by the fact that all liberal polities, while establishing free, competitive, and periodic elections, have also instituted a variety of countermajoritarian restraints. These constraints are routinely misinterpreted as evidence that the ideal-typical liberal nurses doubts about the justice of majority rule. This impression has been reinforced by the correct observation that almost all liberal thinkers prior to the twentieth century accepted some sort of restricted suffrage. But the reasoning here is faulty. To understand the underlying error we need to see how certain limitations on majority rule can be reconciled with a commitment to majoritarianism. The failure to resolve this puzzle has also helped spread the fallacy that liberal constitutionalism is somehow inherently antidemocratic. That is an unsatisfying conclusion, however, for all of the reasons already mentioned and, above all, because ongoing dependency of governing officials on the electorate remains the most important principle of constitutional government itself, superior even to the separation of powers.

Liberal limits on the power of electoral majorities have at least five justifications. Three follow directly from the majority principle itself, whereas the fourth and fifth have nonmajoritarian, but still "democratic," sources. First, the present majority must not be allowed to deprive future majorities of the right to correct earlier mistakes. Second, the present majority, to implement its decisions, needs the willing cooperation of outvoted minorities, whose personal rights must therefore be protected. Third, without freedom of debate, shielded from majority censorship and intimidation, elites will capture power and ensconce themselves beyond criticism, eventually confiscating the majority's own power.

Finally, there are two powerful nonmajoritarian, but still "democratic" principles at work behind liberal limitations on majority rule. One is the norm of fairness or impartiality. Majorities are not supposed to apply laws selectively or unequally, however advantageous this may seem. The second is the ideal of shrewd and sensible decision making. Political decisions will be more intelligent, it is assumed, if produced by a process of wide-open debate and subjected, even after they are made, to an ongoing process of criticism. The majority cannot silence its critics, even if it would love to do so. This prohibition insures that its decisions are more thoughtful and better informed than they otherwise would be. These last two restrictions are indeed antimajoritarian. They may be thought of as the "liberal" component in liberal democracy, I suppose. But they are not antidemocratic, unless "democracy" excludes (and how could it?) both impartiality and deliberation, both equality before the law and government by discussion.

A final point about majority rule. Conservatives and radicals alike enjoy citing the famous passage in the *Federalist Papers* where Madison writes that "the people in their collective capacity" should have no role in political life. This phrase has always seemed oddly dissonant with other passages where Madison insists that the constitution being framed will create a "popular government" in which "all power" is "derived from the people."[39]

The solution to this apparent inconsistency lies partly in federalism and partly in electoral politics, for reasons already discussed. To allow the people to *act collectively,* like the Roman mobs, is to create tumult and, as a consequence, to disenfranchise the majority. Only when the people act in smaller jurisdictions and *individually as voters* (rather than collectively as a mob), can some influence of the majority be secured over the long haul.

The problem with this arrangement, of course, is that the influence wielded by voters on election day is both slight and intermittent. To make popular participation compatible with rule by the (electoral) majority, liberalism makes it dangerously weak. What can be done to increase the marginal leverage that a majority exerts through popular elections? To this problem, some liberals suggested a new use for the old maxim: divide and rule. Traditionally, the *divide et impera* strategy had been employed by tyrants against their restive subjects. Liberals boldly turned this technique into a tool that the people could use against their rulers. By introducing internal divisions within ruling circles (including the split between government and opposition), liberals did not simply aim to prevent tyranny. They were trying to create a regime that was relatively easy to influence from below. A "balance" is not necessarily stable. On the contrary, some sorts of balance can be upset by a grain of sand. Indeed, the multibranch and multilevel government of the United States was originally conceived as a sensitive barometer for registering changes in public opinion, electorally expressed. This analysis (brilliantly advanced by Hamilton in *Federalist* no. 28), suggests again that liberalism and democracy, far from being enemies or rivals, can be mutually reinforcing.

## Welfare

Political theorists who view liberalism as inherently hostile to democracy often add that it is inherently hostile to the redistributionist welfare state as well. This second claim is as dubious as the first. For one thing, transfer programs presuppose the continued existence of private property. Only a vigorous market economy, relying on individual incentives, can produce a surplus worth distributing by political means. In fact, welfare measures were originally supported by politicians friendly to the market as a technique for improving liberal econo-mies and enhancing their chances of survival. Such policies were not designed to create equality of resources, or even to maximize the minimal holdings of social resources (as in the maximin principle), but only to establish in practice a "bottom floor" beneath which the indigent would not fall. This is why communists, who favored collective ownership, were consistently opposed to welfare, which they considered a subtle ploy to dampen the fighting spirit of the working classes. The socialist enemies of redistributionist politics, in other words, would not have understood Hayek's fears that the welfare state was a stepping stone on the road to a communist utopia. Quite the contrary. They despised the incipient welfare state because they saw it as a cul de sac, as blocking the path to collectivism, as irredeemably liberal.

The historical relation between eighteenth-century rights and modern welfare entitlements is, and will always remain, somewhat obscure. As I argue in chapter 8, however, the case for some sort of continuity between the two is stronger than most libertarians, at least, have led us to believe. Contrary to what they claim, we have no particular reason to think that classical liberals would have been hostile to a social safety net. Modest redistributions that support, say, health care for the indigent are not "tyrannical." They are not even remotely reminiscent of the cruel and oppressive acts in response to which the ideal of limited government first arose. How can constitutional principles originally designed to outlaw judicial torture and religious persecution plausibly be invoked to forbid the provision of prenatal care to the impoverished? In any case, classical liberals never attacked the principles underlying traditional poor relief. Spinoza's assertion that "the care of the poor is incumbent on the whole of society" was echoed by every major liberal theorist.[40] This near unanimity is difficult to explain, but it is probably due to the deep liberal commitment to psychological security. True, this value originally referred to protection from physical violence. But as the resources of liberal societies expanded enormously, it was only natural for the concept of security to be gradually stretched to include unemployment insurance and various other programs of "social security" compatible with a decentralized market economy.[41]

The government should protect citizens from force and fraud, libertarians argue, but it should take no "positive" action. Individuals are responsible for their own welfare. They should shift for themselves rather than expect to be pampered by a caretaker state. This is a common way of presenting the case against modern redistributionist politics, including the version currently installed in the United States. How much weight can such partisan reasoning bear? Not much. As an attempt to conceptualize the American constitutional system, at least, libertarianism seems remarkably deficient. In the United States, all liberal rights, including those enshrined in the first ten Amendments, are exercised on the basis of resources furnished by political agencies. Governing bodies alone, state or federal, are in a position to define and enforce property rights, for example. And what other institutions can provide citizens with a sense of physical security? The social contract, according to Locke, *required* individuals to surrender the right of violent self-defense to the state. This was and is an obligatory, not an optional, exchange. In a liberal society, therefore, self-help always depends upon state help. There is nothing at all illiberal, as a result, about the idea of an entitlement. Liberal citizens are *entitled* to a fair trial and to a high-school education, for example. To the extent that libertarians doubt this, they fall so far outside the liberal consensus as to become politically irrelevant. The widely endorsed plan to give tuition vouchers to every school-age child is illuminating in this regard. In the public discussion about vouchers, at least, all parties on the ideological spectrum, including the libertarian right, plainly accept the liberal state's duty to provide a minimum level of resources to *all* citizens. Entitlements to affirmative state action, then, are a staple of the liberal tradition. The controversy begins only when we ask, What sort of help, and how much, should the government provide? This is a proper topic for partisan debate among rival liberal schools, a debate which cannot be peremptorily closed by the assertion that "our" liberal Constitution forbids the government to provide individuals with resources of any kind.

Liberalism is individualistic, and the ideal-typical liberal believes that individuals should be rewarded for personal achievement and merit. In no actually existing liberal society, however, are benefits and burdens allocated wholly on the basis of individual desert. Many of society's delights are purchased by means of inherited resources, while its headaches fall disproportionately on those who are born without. The current rate of black infant mortality is only the most shocking example of a nonindividualistic pattern in the allocation of social goods. The saliency of inherited resources in all liberal societies, in fact, presents a huge dilemma for liberals. We cannot justify the vastly unequal distribution of inherited resources (including parental attention) on individualistic grounds. No infant *deserves* either to be reared in luxury or to shiver undernourished and poorly clothed in a dangerous and drug-ridden tenement. The ideal-typical liberal will acknowledge that inheritable property is indispensable for maintaining the prestige and cohesion of the family (the best environment we know for the socialization of individuals). He will also allow that the right to bequeath is itself a form of liberty, that it provides an incentive for industriousness and savings, and so forth. But liberal inheritance law remains a radical concession to a nonindividualistic institution, which suggests that the basic unit of society is the family, not the individual.

On the basis of ascriptive ties, not personal achievement or capacity, social status is handed down from one generation to the next in a quasi-monopolistic fashion. In historical perspective, intergenerational and intragenerational social mobility is an impressive feature of modern liberal societies. But inheritance of poverty—*chômeur fils de chômeur*—remains a stubborn reality. As a result, liberals who recognize the practical advantages of exceptional legal protections for the family unit have nevertheless logically sought to *redeem individualism* by providing vital support to children who are born (through no imaginable fault of their own) without inherited resources. Publicly subsidized and universal schooling is designed to diminish the role of (unequal) family wealth as a key to life. Child nutrition programs, too, are redistributive and yet wholly "individualistic"—aimed at helping *individuals* who are disadvantaged by their *involuntary* membership in a social group. They are attempts not to create a society of equals, of course, but simply to compensate, in a modest way, for a maldistribution of inherited resources, difficult to justify on liberal grounds.

Liberalism is nevertheless egalitarian in some sense. Political and legal equality extends, or should extend, across class, ethnic, racial, and religious lines.[42] For similar reasons, liberalism is universalistic. In principle, basic liberal rights should be extended charitably across all national borders. Why should someone starve, for example, because he or she happens to live on the wrong side of a political frontier? Can this be "justified" within a liberal framework? No. As a universalistic or cosmopolitan doctrine, liberalism is wholly unable to draw territorial boundaries or separate insiders from outsiders in a principled way. Liberal principles, such as inequality before the law and majority rule, are obviously useless for deciding who belongs to what community in the first place. This deficiency of liberalism is quite serious, since politically supportable frontiers between states are an indispensable precondition for the realization of the core liberal goals. Liberals have succeeded in realizing some of their ideals, in fact, only because they have compromised with the realities of national sovereignty erected on a preliberal basis. Liberal rights are meaningful only within the confines of pre-existing, territorially-bounded states, and only where there exists a rights-enforcing power. To the extent that no enforcing power operates between states or across borders, liberal rights are futile. So, our ideal-typical liberal will reason in the following manner. While it is morally obligatory to secure a "bottom floor" of subsistence to all humanity, it is (unfortunately) unrealistic to attempt domestic-scale redistributions across territorial borders, not only because of scarce resources, but also because of the location of sovereign power. Although this restriction flies in the face of liberal universalism, welfare rights will in fact be limited to conationals.

Contrast this argument to communitarian thinking about welfare. Communitarians argue that we owe special attention to conationals, and perhaps to coreligionists. This homogeneity principle does not depend on practical considerations. (Pragmatic reasons for limiting ourselves to supporting conationals might include the following: we can be more effective if we focus our resources in this way, or: transnational redistributions tend to encourage migration from the countryside into the cities, making poorer nations even more dependent on richer ones, and so forth.) Communitarians tend to justify the exclusive provision of welfare rights to conationals in a stronger way. They invoke solidarity or cultural identity. We are morally obliged to love our countrymen and prefer them to foreigners. Morality stops, or is severely diluted, when heterogeneity begins.

A liberal would demur. Being practical, of course, liberals are willing to compromise with irrational human passions. They recognize that, for psychological reasons, "a man is more attached to his family than to his neighborhood, to his neighborhood than to the community at large."[43] If a sense of common national citizenship makes inhabitants of Scarsdale accept income transfers that benefit inhabitants of Harlem by *overcoming* parochial affections and feelings of racial heterogeneity, there is nothing objectionable in that. A sense of shared nationality does seem to mobilize support for economic redistributions, *especially when citizenship appears to be coextensive with ethnicity*. European countries with higher degrees of ethnic homogeneity have been more successful in winning electoral support for transfer programs than welfare advocates in the ethnic crazy quilt of the United States. (In other words, the capacity for purely *civic* affections to heal racial and ethnic divisions seems disappointingly limited.) So communitarian considerations may be strategically useful, even for liberals. But homogeneity does not provide a *moral reason* for redistribution from a liberal point of view.

## Liberal Discontent

Classical liberals were reformers and social critics. They were not hand-holders and flag-wavers for established regimes. Today, no liberal in the United States would advocate a wholesale remaking of our constitutional, legal, and economic system. But neither can a liberal heir of Locke and Mill ignore the painfully illiberal features of our society. In many places, urban violence makes a mockery of the promise to protect every citizen from physical fear. Decaying schools represent a national betrayal of liberalism's pledge to the next generation. The steady increase of children living in poverty (raised by young, unemployed, and poorly educated unwed mothers), conflicts rudely with a liberal commitment to equal opportunity. The rising costs of litigation have thrown into doubt the principle of equal access to the law. Rising campaign expenditures suggest that economic inequality continues to be converted directly into political inequality, against all liberal norms. And how can liberals accept the continuing marginalization of women from positions where political and economic influence is wielded? Finally, black Americans still live to an appalling extent as a stigmatized caste. Infant mortality, poverty, unemployment, school and housing segregation, and reduced access to health care all indicate that social resources are being allocated according to skin color, not along individualistic lines.

A reconstruction of the liberal tradition cannot provide recipes for solving stubborn problems such as these. Indeed, no book of intellectual history and abstract theory can prescribe specific policies or institutional solutions without regard to costs, concrete alternatives, and predictable side effects. But reconceiving liberalism can help us understand why problems such as the ones just listed are problems from a liberal point of view. And it can embolden us to reaffirm today the aims that liberals have traditionally pursued. Liberalism will always remain an aspiration. It can never be fully realized or institutionalized. But it can provide a guide and stimulus to action. A liberal nation is a nation that keeps the worthier aims of liberalism steadily in view.

# 2

# The Secret History of Self-Interest

*What is to be gained by overturning the table, by hurling cups upon the floor, by dashing oneself against pillars, tearing the hair, and smiting the thigh and the breast?*

—SENECA

The concept of *self-interest* is one of the most remarkable coinages of modern European thought. Surviving in phrases such as "special interests" and "interest groups," it continues to play an important role in the self-description of contemporary liberal democracies. To study its origins and development, therefore, is to learn something essential about the prism through which we have come to interpret our lives. Unfortunately, for a variety of reasons, the evolution of the concept of self-interest has remained shrouded in obscurity. To dispel a few of the clouds and to disclose some surprising aspects of the idea's history, we must focus first on the often forgotten contrast between calculating interest and noncalculating passion.

### Liberalism and Self-Interest

The assumption that human beings are, by nature, rational maximizers of their own interest is sometimes presented as a key premise of classical liberal thought. Many unforgiving commentators, moreover, roundly condemn liberalism for this purported belief, which, they suggest, has demeaned mankind and all but destroyed patriotism and friendship. By rehabilitating self-interest, they claim, liberalism has provided cultural legitimacy to cool calculation, niggling selfishness, and indifference toward spiritual values and the common good. The easiest way to show that such broadsides are as misdirected as they are common is to demonstrate that their target is largely imaginary. Bentham aside, no classical liberal ever wrote that human beings are invariably engaged in the calculating pursuit of personal advantage. Neither Locke nor Mill, neither Smith nor Madison, thought this way. In perfect agreement with a long line of preliberal and nonliberal theorists, they were all perfectly aware that emotional and habitual behavior is extraordinarily widespread and refractory to rational control. They all assumed, quite realistically, that passions can crowd out interests. Human beings, they thought, are ceaselessly engaged in a wide range of noncalculating and nonselfish forms of behavior: punishing nonconformists, falling hopelessly in love, avenging group humiliations, looking wistfully out the window, pitying the unfortunate, spoiling for a fight, ruining other people's happiness, feeling petrified before an audience, gossiping pointlessly, blushing at a neighbor's embarrassment, hating themselves, trying to understand the past, and so forth.

These typical forms of behavior, it must be stressed, are *noncalculating* as well as nonselfish. Vast swatches of human life remain largely undisciplined by the arithmetic of cost-effectiveness since, as Spinoza wrote, "men seldom live under the guidance of reason."[1] This irrationality hypothesis, rather than any stress on nonselfish and nonmaterialistic aims, is a defining feature of classical liberal theory. An acute awareness of human irrationality, in fact, is what distinguishes seventeenth- and eighteenth-century liberalism most sharply from the neoclassical economics that is, in so many other ways, its most illustrious intellectual descendant. Twentieth-century economic thinking does not have an easy time dealing with self-hate and other forms of unhinged behavior that, however commonplace, veer close to clinical dementia. Indeed, contemporary economics has virtually no clue about how to treat surges of affect, bouts of apathy, panic, pique, rage, cold feet, unprovoked aggression, mental rigidity, tantrums and doldrums, petulance and waggishness, meekness and audacity, euphoria and despondency, thoughtlessness, alertness, cantankerousness, infatuation, resentment, excitability, embarrassment, paranoia, squeamishness, inertia, impetuousness, serenity, fidgetiness, paralysis, compulsiveness, or indeed any human behavior that remains fairly unschooled by calculation, foresight, and a prudential weighing of costs and benefits.[2] The liberal forefathers of neoclassical economics were much better equipped in this regard.

How did classical liberals, who did not share the methodological premises of late twentieth-century economists, view rationality and irrationality, selfish and selfless aims? The answer provided in this chapter falls under three headings. First, I want to document the exceptional finesse with which Adam Smith, David Hume, and some of their contemporaries analyzed the human psyche. A brief historical survey is meant to suggest the pitiful impoverishment that befell us, sometime in the nineteenth century, when Marxism and liberal economics conspired to assert the supremacy of rational self-interest and thus to extinguish an older and subtler tradition of moral psychology. Second, I hope to explain how the increasingly positive attitude toward rational self-interest, typical of a broad range of liberal theorists in the seventeenth and eighteenth centuries, was motivated not only by discontent with the aristocratic ideal of glory, but also by disenchantment with the Christian dogma of original sin. And third, I will contend that the postulate of *universal* self-interest, although logically incompatible with insight into the rich variety of human motives, first rose to cultural prominence because of its unmistakably egalitarian and democratic implications.

## Beyond Self-Interest

In his analysis of Adam Smith, the eminent economist George Stigler exhorts us to admire "the granite of self-interest" upon which the palace of economics is built. Throughout most of the *Wealth of Nations,* he writes, Smith took a hard line, explaining the endurance of colonialism, primogeniture, and slavery by invoking the self-interest of the principal actors involved. Unfortunately, Stigler continues, Smith failed to turn "the jaundiced eye of a master economist" upon political life. In thinking about politics, he was not hard but soft. He ascribed excessive influence to emotion and prejudice, and, shockingly, spied "failures of self-interest in guiding people's behaviour." If Smith had only been as tough-minded as Stigler and his colleagues, he would have recognized that every "alleged failure" of self-interest is "nonexistent or of negligible magnitude."[3]

Today this attitude toward self-interest is widespread among economists and the social scientists most influenced by them. But it was rare or unheard-of in the eighteenth century. For instance, according to Stigler's paraphrase of Smith, slavery panders to the pride of slaveholders, and therefore serves their self-interest.[5] Interpreted in this manner, pride is simply another form or emanation of self-interest. Throughout Smith's great economic treatise, however, interest was consistently *contrasted* with pride.[5] Although Britain would benefit from relinquishing its dominion over the American colonies, it was unlikely to do so: "Such sacrifices, though they might frequently be agreeable to the *interest,* are always mortifying to the *pride* of every nation." Because it is an unnatural means of enriching one child while beggaring his siblings, primogeniture is against "the real *interest* of a numerous family" even though it supports "the *pride* of family distinction." Landowners retain their slaves because they are driven by a natural inclination to bully and preside—even when such gratuitous domineering entails economic deprivation.[6]

Smith repeatedly states that self-interest, however robust, is merely one motive among others. He also assumes that people are sometimes rational, sometimes not. The majority of every class is usually governed by common prudence, yet Europe's landed nobility destroyed itself by a most imprudent vanity.[7] In other words, Smith concedes, indeed he stresses, the massive historical importance of self-destructive and noncalculating behavior. Under certain conditions, we must appeal to motives other than interest to understand not this or that scattered event, but even the drift of social and political change. His ideas about motivation, therefore, are distinct from, and perhaps more interesting than, those of his self-appointed successors. In explaining human action, he routinely invokes the distinction (common at the time) between "interests, born of calculation, and passions, based on impulse."[8] This opposition is fundamental—and not merely for those seeking to master the vocabulary of the *Wealth of Nations*.

## Against Simplicity

The hypothesis of universal self-interest, as everyone knows, has provoked its share of protest and disgruntlement. Antiliberal moralists bridle at what they consider an implied slur on human nature—a denial of the sincerity of self-sacrifice, for example. But the most persuasive complaint about the idea has a more liberal source as well as a more liberal purpose. According to a variety of prominent eighteenth-century theorists, the decision to lump together sharply dissimilar motives under the single category of "calculating self-interest" involved an undesirable *loss of information* about rudimentary psychological and behavioral processes. This is also the essence of Macaulay's subsequent jibe that to discover self-interest behind an action is to say, with tautological banality, that "a man had rather do what he had rather do."[9]

As economists will hasten to explain, of course, the hypothesis of rational self-interest is theory, not description. A deliberate simplification enables us to construct mathematically tractable models of human behavior that, in turn, yield testable predictions. This is an important consideration. But social scientists who, under the sway of economics, choose to see maximizing behavior everywhere they look should also admit that they are discarding an important dimension of, at least, Adam Smith's thought—for *he* obviously shared with many other eighteenth-century thinkers a concern about the uninformative character of the self-interest postulate.

A look at Smith's close friend, David Hume, whose psychological writings exerted a decisive influence on the *Wealth of Nations,* should help clarify what is at stake here. Hume emphatically denounced the false "love of simplicity" that underlies motivational reductionism. (In so doing, he, in turn, was echoing Shaftesbury, Hutcheson, and others.)[10] To say that patriots and misers, cowards and heroes all aim exclusively at "their own happiness and welfare" illustrates only how little we learn about behavior by adducing self-interest.[11] We can always *say* that the altruist includes the welfare of others in his own utility function. We can always *stipulate* that everything a person does, by definition, is meant to maximize his or her psychic income. But when the motivational reductionist traces all action to self-love or the rational pursuit of personal advantage, he "makes use of a different language from the rest of his countrymen, and calls things not by their proper names."[12] Theorists are free to indulge in such linguistic idiosyncrasy, of course. If they make no distinctions, then, naturally enough, everything will be the same. But why jettison well-entrenched and useful contrasts between, say, interested and disinterested or calculating and noncalculating behavior? A generic concept such as the maximization of personal utility (referring to "the" aim of all human choice) swallows up such distinctions. Is there anything wrong with that? Hume thinks so. The very idea of interest-driven behavior is meaningless, he argues, unless we can identify some behavior that is *not* interest-driven. The idea of calculating action loses all content if it can no longer be opposed to action that is *not* calculating. An accurate account of social action presupposes a fine-grained mapping of rival motivations and behavioral styles.[13] Ultimately, descriptions and explanations will be more straightforward if we adhere to common usage and frankly acknowledge the reality of disinterested impulses and noncalculating styles of conduct.[14]

Hume also denies that moral judgment is a pliant tool of our self-interest, narrowly understood. Conclusive evidence for this claim he finds in the praise we commonly bestow upon actions from which we cannot conceivably profit. A miser admires the niggardliness of a fellow miser in a purely disinterested fashion, perhaps from an aesthetic appreciation of penny-pinching, certainly not from any expectation of personal gain.[15] Sometimes we even praise the moral quality of actions that harm us. Although moral assessments and commitments affect behavior in important ways, they cannot always be boiled down to underlying interests. Furthermore, benevolence exists. A disinterested preference for the happiness of others has significant behavioral effects.[16]

Normally, a person will not step briskly upon "another's gouty toes," even if he finds it somewhat inconvenient to go around them.[17]

## Against Dichotomy

But fellow feeling and humanity are by no means the only disinterested emotions discussed by Hume. Mankind is also moved by "disinterested resentment," for example.[18] Indeed, Hume's rich account of the motivations vying with rational self-interest reveals the second most important aspect of his theory. He denies the completeness of binary schemes, such as egoism/altruism or selfishness/benevolence, just as vigorously as he denies the hypothesis of universal self-interest. Such simplifying dichotomies, too, obscure the range and diversity of human motives.

Hume identifies a wide array of violent and subrational emotions, all of them distinct, he believes, from both self-interest and social benevolence. In general, such emotions prove destructive to the community as well as to the individual.[19] They include principally "the disagreeable passions, fear, anger, dejection, grief, melancholy, anxiety, &c." Unlike self-interest, these sentiments are accompanied by immediate kinetic reactions, psychophysical outbursts or paralysis, without any intervening computation of costs and benefits. Interest induces strategic or instrumental action. Passion hurls us willy-nilly into consummatory or expressive acts. The "darker passions of enmity and resentment" are disinterested in an emphatic sense: they motivate self-destructive behavior. Violent passions can seize an individual's soul, provoke emotional upheaval, cloud his vision, envenom his existence, and ruin his simplest pleasures.[20] Such self-destructive impulses are no less common or powerful than benevolence and self-interest.

In the *Theory of Moral Sentiments,* Smith, too, replaces the egoism/altruism dichotomy with a trichotomy of social/selfish/unsocial passions.[21] Self-interest, on this scheme, is located somewhere between disinterested benevolence and disinterested malevolence, between virtue and vice.[22] Unsocial passions—such as envy and anger—blur the mind, tear at the breast, interfere with purposive conduct, and make rational comparison of alternatives next to impossible. Hume also stresses the sheer immediacy of malevolent impulses: "There are mental passions by which we are impelled immediately to seek particular objects, such as . . . vengeance *without any regard to interest.*" From Hume's perspective, therefore, revenge is disinterested: "Who sees not that vengeance, from the force alone of passion, may be so eagerly pursued, as to make us knowingly neglect every consideration of ease, interest, or safety; and, like some vindictive animals, infuse our very souls into the wounds we give an enemy." Because the hot-blooded pursuit of revenge can plunge people to their deaths, the contrast between the selfish and the vengeful—the selfish and the "unsocial"—is just as sharp as the more conventional contrast between the selfish and the social.[23]

## Selfless Cruelty

A platitudinously moralized dichotomy between (good) altruism and (bad) egoism makes it difficult to conceptualize something so elementary, not to say elemental, as *selfless cruelty.* It is easier to be cruel, on a large scale, when you act in the name of others, or in the name of an ideal, or even for the benefit of your victim, than when you act for your own sake. Blood revenge for a humiliation suffered by one's ascriptive group, even at the risk of one's own life, is a glaring example. Think, also, of those Catholic zealots in medieval France, described by Montesquieu, who rushed onto the scaffold where a Jew was about to be executed for having blasphemed the Virgin Mary: they subdued the public executioner and used their own knives to peel away slowly the sinner's skin.[24] They were not acting from egoistic or mercenary motives, but for the common good—as they saw it. Again, the egoism/altruism dichotomy is of no help here; neither bargain hunting nor gentle benevolence was involved. Nonselfish, but nonetheless sickeningly murderous behavior abounds in history. It is not marginal, but massively important. That is surely the way it appeared to those living in the wake of Europe's religious civil wars.

If our concepts commit us to the idea that whenever people overcome selfishness they necessarily act in a morally admirable manner, then our vision of political behavior is bound to be both selective and unfocused. A moralized selfish/selfless scheme blinds us in precisely this manner. Thus, any vocabulary lacking the category "selfless cruelty" is historically impoverished. It also provides an inadequate guide to the thought of the keenest observers of political life in early modern Europe.

## Interest in Hume

"Factions," as Locke remarked, "have been fatal to States and Kingdoms."[25] No surprise, therefore, that many seventeenth- and eighteenth-century political writers were obsessed with mankind's irrational psychological compulsion toward group enmity or *factionalism.* Faction is a third alternative between the private individual and the community as a whole. Not accidentally, Hume's "Of Parties in General," devoted entirely to this subject, is one of the best eighteenth-century sources for understanding how the concept of rational self-interest was molded and put to use during this phase in its long career.[26] (Madison's famous analysis of factionalism in *Federalist* no. 10 relies heavily on this essay.) Hume explains what self-interest is by explaining what self-interest is not. Factions are not mere interest groups. They can galvanize behavior that is simultaneously selfless and unspeakably vicious toward others. People may suppress their personal interests and even cease to weigh the consequences of their actions because of a natural "propensity" to fall into factions.[27] This joining or flocking instinct, the flip side of xenophobia, is a universal characteristic of mankind and one that can easily vanquish the natural propensity to truck and barter. Not even intense selfishness can prevent a person, in the right circumstances, from kindling in "the common blaze."[28]

Factions are deplorable, Hume believes, because they make communitywide cooperation impossible. Narrow group loyalties often prevent citizens from coming humanely to each other's assistance.[29] The mutual hostility of subgroups is a perverse but direct result of *selective* identification with other human beings. "Popular sedition, party zeal, a devoted obedience to factious leaders; these are some of the most visible, though less laudable effects of this social sympathy in human nature."[30] In short, Hume draws a sharp contrast between the inborn tendency to identify emotionally with an exclusive subgroup (factionalism) and strategic rationality in general, particularly the coolly calculating pursuit of personal advantage.

As Swift's famous tale of Big-Endians and Little-Endians was designed to show, violent factional conflicts often have astonishingly trivial origins. Hume adduces the example of a "difference between the colour of one livery and another in horse races."[31] Onlookers at the hippodrome in ancient Constantinople witnessed races between rival charioteers who were outfitted arbitrarily in blue and green. Identifying psychologically with one side or the other, rival factions fell into lethal conflict with one another. But why? Self-interest was not a decisive factor. Spur-of-the-moment rioting and mayhem, fueled by sudden enmity, are not calculating at all. They reflect instead something like "an original propensity" or primordial need: when you observe a conflict, you tend to identify yourself with one party or the other.[32] (Every sports fan experiences something of this kind.) The universal proclivity to fall into factions presumably results, at least in part, from this deep-rooted psychological impulse.

Hume does not stop here, however. He is not content with explaining the formation of factions by invoking a universal human tendency to form factions. Instead, he sets forth a bold typology for the various motives which lead individuals to cluster and divide into hostile groupings. At first, he does not even mention the compulsion to identify with a group in a situation of conflict, and instead presents a tripartite scheme, distinguishing among *interest-driven, affection-driven,* and *principle-driven* behavior.[33] On this basis, he then distinguishes among factions based on economic interest, factions based on attachment to a person, and factions based on abstract principles such as a theological dogma or the divine character of royalty. If we wanted to generalize, we could say that Hume here identifies three independent and mutually irreducible factors that exert causal force upon human action: interests, passions, and norms.

Several things should be said about this three-part scheme. First, although there is no insinuation whatsoever that interested behavior is always harmless, Hume obviously considers interests far less dangerous than a number of more violent and combustible passions.[34] Second, he assumes that a person's motives are always mixed, that interests, passions, and norms conspire together to shape every human action. Nevertheless, sometimes one motive predominates and sometimes others. We can therefore speak meaningfully of largely principle-driven, largely interest-driven, and largely affection-driven behavior. Third, within a single group, such as a religious sect or movement, Hume tends to correlate different motives with different roles—so that leaders and elites are ordinarily motivated by calculating interest while followers are usually motivated by noncalculating principle or affect.[35] Fourth, by distinguishing motives in this way, Hume makes it possible to analyze the causal interconnections between them. To use his example, a man may be a royalist from principle, but when he receives a sinecure from the king his ardor for his principles may suddenly redouble.[36]

Fifth, and still more strikingly, Hume explains how animosity among hostile factions is able to sustain itself even when it runs counter to every party's present interest.[37] Originally, he says, two groups may be divided by competition over a scarce resource or over some principle. With the passage of time, however, the original bone of contention vanishes but the animosity does not. Why? The answer Hume offers is simple. Certain emotional reactions become etched or ossified in the human mind, and they do not readily adapt to altered circumstances. Once human beings get used to responding in a certain way, inertia takes over and their actions become largely robotic or independent of external circumstances. People in motion cannot stop on a dime, even if that is what rational maximization and intelligent responsiveness to the immediate environment would require. Psychological rigidity makes maximization especially difficult, therefore, in turbulent conditions or when rapid social change is under way. What was initially an interest-based or principle-based enmity can easily become an inveterate or inherited one, out of joint with the times. Resentments, grudges, and hatreds are sometimes bequeathed from generation to generation, without requiring further stimulus from new conflicts of interest. Hence Hume supplements his original list. Alongside interest and principles, he places subrational affections. And he particularly stresses *inherited animosity,* a perverse form of affection which is disinterested, unprincipled, and wholly noncalculating.

Another politically important form of affection is infatuation with a leader. This is what Hume calls an "imaginary interest," whereby individuals attach themselves psychologically to a kingpin or guru whom they may never meet personally and from whom they can expect no material benefits whatsoever.[38] Starry-eyed fixation on prominent individuals, such as military chieftains, may sometimes inspire acts of personal foolhardiness or courage. But such adoration also has purely inward effects. For instance, hero worship allows devotees to live national events vicariously, to feel jazzed by imaginary involvement in large affairs. Psychological doting on the great, Hume adds, can sometimes arise from spite and the proclivity to factionalism: if we hate our neighbor sufficiently, we may express our loathing by identifying with *his* hero's most conspicuous enemy or rival.

Another complicating factor must also be mentioned here. Admittedly, "men are much governed by interest." Nevertheless, "even interest itself, and all human affairs, are governed by *opinion.*"[39] In other words, Hume never doubts the causal efficacy of disinterested ideas. He professes mock bafflement, nevertheless, at factions based on differences of religious dogma. Can the opinions that rule the world really be as doltish as those promoted by Christian sects? Hume mentions Morocco where racial wars are based on a "pleasant difference" of skin color which Europeans scorn.[40] But how much more absurd were Europe's religious civil wars, terrifying struggles provoked not by a clash of sentiment but based on a disagreement about a few abstruse phrases that one party accepts without understanding and the other rejects in the same manner. Despite the philosopher's perplexity, people are fiercely attached to their creeds—even to unintelligible or preposterous ones. Their emotional life often crystallizes around unfathomable doctrines and dogmas. The bloody conflicts about the meaning of the Eucharist, which originally split the reform churches, cannot be traced to conflicts of interest in a narrow sense. Why one sect is driven to persecute another so ferociously seems impossible to explain on a rational-actor model. Why *did* Europe drown itself in blood? Once again, Hume's answer is succinct. Human beings are emotionally flustered and roiled. They do not think about what they are doing. They are not instrumentally rational. Their minds are gnawed at by childish myths and unspeakable fears. They crave certainty. As a result, they often fail to grasp their private advantage or to act upon it strategically when they do.

So individuals are not always clear-eyed about their interests. But they are always impatient of being contradicted. We long mightily and involuntarily to find our own beliefs mirrored in those around us. Anyone who crosses our path we grab by the lapels; and we hammer the unlucky party into agreement because our minds are shocked by contrariness and fortified by consensus. This compulsive intolerance is not a symptom of arrogance but of insecurity. We do not coolly compare alternatives in such situations, but clutch desperately at any confirmation we can find that we are right. And what we seek is not a strategic ally in the pursuit of power or plenty but symbolic comfort from a fellow believer. This primitive psychological need for agreement explains why we are so "keen" in controversy, something neither self-interest nor even vanity could explain.[41]

After parties have been formed in any of these ways—from material interest, inheritance, emotional identification with a leader, or conformist attachment to an idea—new adherents can be won by the independent and powerful motive of imitativeness.[42] Here we have Hume's theory of *l'homme copie*. (A contemporary of Hume and Rousseau provided the following alternative to the opening to the *Social Contract:* man is born original, but everywhere he is a mere copy.)[43] Behavior is contagious and people copy others—in gait or cadence of speech, for instance—not because it is in their interest to do so, but because imitation comes naturally. "This is not only conspicuous in children, who implicitly embrace every opinion propos'd to them; but also in men of the greatest judgment and understanding, who find it very difficult to follow their own reason or inclination, in opposition to that of their friends and daily companions."[44] (An economist might argue that it is easier for an individual to discover what is fashionable or what other people are doing than to identify unambiguously his own interests. But this way of speaking makes imitation sound too much like a strategic reaction to scarcity of information. Hume has something much more instinctual in mind here, such as the spontaneous internalization of observed patterns by impressionable onlookers—presumably, say, the way Texans learn to lope.)

Finally, some people have nothing to do when they get up in the morning. They fall into factions from propinquity and from the lack of any better idea.[45] In a civil war when two factions have an exactly equal chance of winning, moreover, individuals who habitually act according to rational self-interest are at a loss for what to do. They cannot choose the side likely to benefit them most in the long run, since the eventual winner is perfectly incalculable. As a consequence, in rationally undecidable situations such as these, self-interest falls silent and individuals must be moved to action by some other motive such as affection, principle, habit, or imitation.[46]

As this brief exposition has probably made clear, Hume elaborates an unprudish, unhysterical, and humorous view of men and morals. His essay on factionalism testifies beautifully to the subtlety of eighteenth-century moral psychology characteristic, I claim, of virtually every classical liberal political theorist. Hume does not view self-interest as the hard rock on which all social life is reliably built. He clarifies the nature of self-interested and rational behavior by contrasting it with disinterested and irrational behavior. Compulsive and impulsive reactions as well as spontaneous sympathies and absurd antipathies provide a foil for "calculating self-interest," giving sharp contours to that idea. For Hume, and his mainstream liberal followers such as Smith and Madison, "interest" would be a useless category if it were not reserved for one motive contending with others. Each of them therefore rejects imperialistic attempts to explain *all* behavior by invoking the rational pursuit of personal advantage. Motivational reductionism was unattractive to classical liberals, among other reasons, because it robs "calculating self-interest" of the specificity it acquires when viewed against a backdrop of selfless urges and thoughtless acts.

## Passions and Interests

In *The Passions and the Interests,* Albert Hirschman explores the Humean contrast between calm and violent passions in a broad intellectual context.[47] Briefly, the main thesis of this highly original book is that the idea of self-interest was popularized, and self-interestedness itself morally endorsed, by a variety of seventeenth- and eighteenth-century thinkers. They looked favorably upon interest because they saw it as a relatively peaceful and harmless alternative to the violent passion for glory which had long inspired the military, aristocratic, and landed ruling classes of Europe. (Hobbes is an important figure in this story, as Hirschman sees, and as I shall explain more fully in the next chapter.) To understand what the advocates of self-interest were for, one must understand what they were against, and what they were up against. Some of the most intractable difficulties they faced resulted from the upper-class obsession with glory, an ideal that often had bloody and destructive consequences, including painful or even fatal externalities for the unlucky bystanders of glorious escapades.

The notion that self-interest was a *relatively* harmless and even beneficial passion was, according to Hirschman, a new and untraditional idea, contradicting the old association of avarice with sin.[48] Even though it eased the transition to commercial society, even though it eventually became—if we want to speak this way—the cornerstone of bourgeois or liberal ideology, its earliest advocates and defenders were not necessarily members of the "rising" middle class. Rather they were randomly distributed participants in the old order, weary of the destruction caused by glory, bent on reform, and hopeful that the mild passion for moneymaking, although admittedly ignoble and uncouth, could defeat and bury the violent passions that so ruinously stoked the endless cycles of civil butchery. Commerce is "low," but it is not the cruelest fate individuals and groups can inflict on each other. Interests are base, but they also raise the comfort level of social interaction. The self-interested agent is "cool and deliberate."[49] He is reliable, predictable, calculable, and susceptible to influence by others.[50] An individual who is flushed with a hot passion or in the grip of some abstract principle is more obstinate, less amenable to compromise, and less prone to cooperation than any rational seeker of private advantage. It is much easier to defend oneself against enemies fretting about their interests than against opponents reeling from selfless emotions and bursting with inspiring ideals. The most difficult adversaries to outwit or buy off are probably those seized by envy.[51]

Interest was originally viewed as an alternative to various dangerous and unpredictable motivations. Here lies the heart of Hirschman's argument. If we fail to discern the implicit contrast with violent passion, and continue, therefore, to conceive of interest as fundamentally inhumane, we will be at a loss to explain the relatively positive attitude toward economic interests displayed by obviously humane writers during the seventeenth and eighteenth centuries. If we ignore the irrational and destructive antonyms of self-interest, we may even stumble into the kind of error popularized by R. H. Tawney, who interpreted every liberal affirmation of calculating self-interest as a mean-spirited repudiation of brotherly love.[52]

For all its suggestiveness—which I have only touched on in this hopelessly brief synopsis—Hirschman's account of the history of "self-interest" has three shortcomings: (1) it focuses too single-mindedly on the pursuit of glory, slighting other irrational motivations with which interest was contrasted during this period; (2) it neglects the extent to which religion, particularly the idea of original sin, helped provoke new and more favorable attitudes toward self-interest; and (3) it mentions, but leaves undeveloped, the egalitarian implications of the postulate of *universal* self-interest. I return to the second and third points below. But first it will be useful to round out Hirschman's analysis of the antonyms of interest-driven behavior.[53] Following Hume's lead, we can construct a fuller list of the subrational motivations to which seventeenth- and eighteenth-century thinkers contrasted the calculating pursuit of private advantage. Here is Hume's catalog again: the intolerant adherence to abstract principle, inherited animosity, love of imitation, psychological infatuation with a leader, and psychological identification with a group. To these motives, he also adds the craving for approval, anger, envy, fear, grief, shame, depression, melancholy, and anxiety.[54]

A thoughtful reader of Hume, Adam Smith provides a similar survey of "disinterested" passions.[55] Among those he mentions are envy,[56] malice, the longing for revenge, parochial loyalty, eagerness to conform, the inclination to act as befits one's station, irrational avarice, zealotry, caprice, aversion to change, sheer habit, the instinct to imitate others, and the desire to be told what to do. This last impulse is worth stressing. Irrational "obsequiousness" toward the rich and the powerful is the flip side of *libido dominandi*. It, too, is a lamentable but natural "disposition" of the human soul.[57] We fawn and bend the knee unthinkingly, without knowing why. Superstitious submissiveness toward the great has enormous social consequences. Yet it is not necessarily a product of wily calculation. The unsocial passions in general make reasoning difficult. As motivational forces, nevertheless, they are just as "hard" as self-interest. Individuals in the thrall of such unsocial passions do not act from rational self-interest—not, at least, as the celebrated founder of modern economics understood that basic idea.

The urge to better one's condition is a forceful and persistent motive—a steady drip that gradually sculpts a hollow into the stone. But it remains one motive among others. Even those early modern theorists who emphasized man's natural proclivity for self-preservation admitted that this impulse was less than all-powerful. The survival instinct vies with a whole range of self-destructive passions. Francis Bacon listed the following emotions, all of which, in his view, could trump the desire for self-preservation: revenge, love, honor, shame, grief, fear, pity, and boredom.[58] This list overlaps remarkably with those advanced later by Hume and Smith. Intoxicated or stunned by such mental states, individuals will ignore the foreseeable consequences of their acts. Emotionally excited or overwrought, they will sacrifice not only their interests but even their lives. When storm waves of affect besiege the mind, strategies of self-preservation are quickly washed aside.

Passions and norms drive people to neglect their own advantage, rationally understood. Impulses, compulsions, and emotionally charged social taboos often propel behavior directly, without benefit of calculation or opportunistic reasoning. The question is, Where did Hume and Smith learn to appreciate this short-circuiting of strategic rationality? Direct observation and the study of political history gave them ample occasion to ponder the foibles and follies of mankind. But they were also well acquainted with a rich body of literature, including, for instance, Bacon's *Essays,* devoted to the analysis of noncalculating motives and self-destructive behavior. The study of emotional tumult and irrationality, in fact, stretches back to antiquity.[59] Scholars now seem to be agreed that "Stoic philosophy" was "the primary influence on Smith's ethical thought."[60] That is a very useful piece of information, for the Stoics were centrally concerned with perturbations and disorders of the soul. A passionate man, they believed, was mentally deranged and unable to pursue his own best interests (or, for that matter, any goal) in a clever and coherent fashion.[61] In the most complete ancient catalog of such disruptive motivations, Cicero included envy, compassion, anxiety, grief, depression, vexation, despondency, sluggishness, shame, fright, consternation, bewilderment, malice, rapture, ostentation, anger, hatred, and greed.[62] However personal advantage is defined, its methodical pursuit can be derailed by such turbulent passions, which the Stoics associated with the irrational prizing of worldly things over which we have no control.[63]

In Stoic philosophy, the most impressive example of an irrational passion was *malice,* the "pleasure derived from a neighbor's evil which brings no advantage to oneself."[64] Today we might say that the malicious individual includes the illfare of others as a positive argument in his own utility function. But to the Stoics, and to those influenced by them, this would have seemed a perverse way to talk. They were too impressed by the stark diversity of human motivations to sympathize with a reductionist psychology, however justified methodologically.

Thoughtfulness and thoughtlessness are obviously different. Self-preserving and self-destructive behavior are equally so. Commonsensical distinctions such as these dominated Stoic and neo-Stoic psychology. The Stoics described "anger," for example, as "giving no thought to itself if it can hurt another."[65] Cruelty can be heroically selfless, they also observed. An individual sometimes cuts off his nose to spite his face, which demonstrates beautifully how thoroughly demented passion-aroused conduct can be.[66] Only a diseased soul would pine for patently useless things or dread obviously harmless ones. Passion-motored behavior is sick and ungoverned by reason. Thus, rational choice is impossible until the individual has achieved a state of "apathy" or emotional serenity.[67] Equanimity or tranquility of mind, in turn, presupposes a strenuous process of self-discipline, a mental therapy in which the unruly passions are not moderated but extirpated.[68] The rational pursuit of utility, far from being universal, is a rare moral achievement, possible only for those who undergo an arduous dispositional training.

## The Principal Antonyms of Self-Interest

Stoic emphasis on both the variety of human motives and the rarity of rational goal seeking continued to exert a powerful influence on psychological theories up through the eighteenth century. Rational and truly self-interested behavior, conceived as rare and exceptional, was repeatedly contrasted with commonplace forms of irrational and self-destructive behavior. To exploit Hirschman's thesis fully, indeed, we need only provide a more systematic survey of the passions typically contrasted with the calculating pursuit of private advantage. After consulting many seventeenth- and eighteenth-century works from both England and France, I have managed to compile a list of the twenty-four most frequently discussed antonyms of self-interest. Disinterested benevolence and malevolence are opposed to the rational pursuit of personal advantage and, of course, to each other as well. With this in mind, I have attempted to organize the following catalog of antonyms in pairs. They are all set against the rational pursuit of private advantage; but each one is contrasted to a rival irrational motive as well.

According to numerous liberal and nonliberal writers of the seventeenth and eighteenth centuries, including Smith and Hume, deviations from calculating self-interest can be explained by the following passions:

1. Animosity, enmity, and hatred
2. Affection, attachment, and love

3. The relish of telling people what to do
4. The relish of being told what to do

5. Excessive pride, megalomania, and the desire to eclipse others
6. Self-deprecation, dejection, spiritlessness, and a failure to take an interest in oneself

7. The love of spewing vilification on others
8. Extreme indignation at social slights

9. Primordial inertness or the desire not to work
10. Primordial restlessness or the desire to do something, anything—to be where the action is

11. The need for consensus
12. Delight in conflict—it clarifies life—and the spirit of contradiction

13. The hatred of change
14. The love of change

15. The hatred of uncertainty
16. The love of uncertainty[69]

17. Instinctual imitativeness—monkey see, monkey do
18. The desire to be different

19. The obsessive desire to follow rules
20. The obsessive desire to break rules

21. Identification with the victors
22. Identification with the victims

23. Envy for merited or unmerited success
24. Pity for undeserved misfortune

This list, which could easily be lengthened or rearranged, is meant to be suggestive, not canonical. In the seventeenth- and eighteenth-century works I have consulted, all such impulsive or compulsive motives are described as noncalculating and disinterested. They are said to dictate responses "immediately," antecedent to all reflection, without the intervention of common prudence. They accompany behavior that is expressive or consummatory, not instrumental or strategic. To be sure, even the most irrational emotional outbursts can be *used* to gain a strategic advantage. An expert on bluffing, such as Thomas Schelling, could easily explain to Seneca *what is to be gained* by overturning the table, hurling cups onto the floor, dashing oneself against pillars, and so forth.[70] But would he be right? The possibility of using an emotion rationally does not imply that emotions are intrinsically rational. As Jon Elster has remarked, we can sometimes treat emotions strategically, as instruments to achieve our ends, only because passions are usually spontaneous and involuntary.[71] A reputation for vengefulness "without regard to interest" may well serve as a credible deterrent. But it exceeds credulity to assert that a rational actor can deliberately cultivate a vengeful disposition—an inclination, say, to infuse his soul into the wounds of his enemies—for such a clear-headed purpose. Moreover, if passions never drove us uncontrollably into committing imprudent and thoughtless acts, neighbors could not be so easily intimidated by shrewdly timed displays of frenzy or rage. Moreover, we would not be able to manipulate the emotional reflexes of others strategically if these emotional reactions did not occur naturally and nonstrategically.

My roster of the principal antonyms of self-interest, in any case, remains awkward in several respects. It gives insufficient prominence to habit or inherited folkways and patterns of response. It slights anger or rage (which classical authors, such as Seneca, considered the premier example of an irrational passion whereby violence immediately provokes counterviolence, in a knee-jerk fashion, without intervening calculations of advantage). Vengefulness and malice, too, are poorly represented. I have also excluded identification with a group, partly because of uncertainty about the "contrary" motivation with which it should be paired. (Is the passion for membership opposed to the xenophobic hatred of rival groups or to antisocial withdrawal into hermetic isolation?) And so on.

Moreover, I have accentuated negative and morally neutral motivations. I have done this, in part, because the list is already long enough, and my aim is to be exemplary, not exhaustive. Emphasizing the negative also helps corroborate Hirschman's thesis that self-interest was embraced because of the disagreeable alternatives. In any case, philanthropy, benevolence, romantic love,[72] patriotism, noble moral principles, and devotion to justice[73] are mentioned frequently by others. There is no need to go on flattering human nature. People sink below self-interest just as often as they soar above it—perhaps more often. In evaluating classical liberal attitudes toward interest-driven behavior and its opposite, we should never forget that "Disinterestedness is often created by Laziness, Pride, or Fear; and then it is no virtue."[74] The person who overcomes selfishness, as I said at the outset, can be, but is not necessarily, a moral hero.

Even in its present and truncated form, however, my checklist retains considerable interest. Unfortunately, it is not yet a *catalogue raisonné*. And I will not now undertake a point-by-point commentary on each irrational urge inventoried, but will let the twenty-four antonyms stand as if chiseled on a tablet. Even in their unglossed state, they provide striking evidence for the complexity of seventeenth- and eighteenth-century views of motivation. If I have convincingly suggested this complexity, which most classical liberal theorists took for granted, I have achieved one of the main objectives of this chapter.

I now turn to my other two themes. I focus first on religion and then on the norm of equality. In both cases, we need to examine some powerful but neglected forces that have also profoundly affected the way the concept of self-interest has evolved.

## Religion and Self-Interest

The interest/glory polarity loomed large in seventeenth-century political theory.[75] Students of the conflict between the commercial ethic and the chivalric ethic, however, should also keep the *biblical ethic* in mind. For one thing, Christian hostility toward pridefulness and glory-seeking helped pave the way for secular and "bourgeois" attacks on aristocratic sentiments and ideals.[76]

Hirschman emphasizes the labeling of avarice as a sin. But Christianity's role in the shaping of modern attitudes toward self-interest was not exhausted by its doomed attempt to shore up the faltering usury taboo. Hume, for example, saw Christianity as an almost intolerable moral provocation. He certainly conceived of commercial self-interest as a peaceful alternative to hot-gospeling and sectarian zealotry. Enthusiasm was just as socially undesirable, and just as incompatible with a calculating temperament, as the nobility's addiction to glory.[77]

Within Christian culture, moreover, the flesh was often described as the root of moral depravity.[78] The prison house of concupiscence was a principal sign of our fallen condition. Self-love itself was sometimes considered a sin.[79] Attentiveness to oneself can mean forgetfulness of God. Augustine even identified self-love with the hatred of God. Conversely, he coupled love of God with contempt for oneself.[80] This way of thinking is what Hume was referring to when he complained that Christianity often "represents . . . man to himself in such despicable colours, that he appears unworthy in his own eyes."[81] According to Voltaire, too, the Augustinian tradition had taught men to hate themselves and hold worldly pursuits in disdain.[82] For both Hume and Voltaire, the "rehabilitation" of self-love was inseparable from an attack on Christian severity and asceticism. By removing the pejorative connotations of personal advantage seeking, they hoped to make man appear worthy in his own eyes. At the very least, their hostility to religious self-abnegation helped reinforce their relatively welcoming attitude toward the principle of rational self-interest.[83]

Marx writes of "the spiritual egoism of Christianity," assuming that an obsession with one's personal salvation is fundamentally selfish and antisocial.[84] But this diagnosis may well underestimate the sincerity of Christian "self-denial."[85] Self-mortification means striving to be "dead to self."[86] One must love God for *His* sake, not in order to go to heaven, but from astonishment at His glory and selfless revulsion at the thought of His being blasphemed. Marx is partly right, nonetheless. Devotion to the glory of God sometimes required neglect of others as well as neglect of self. In the mystical tradition, the pious Christian was encouraged not only to feel "loathing" and "horror" for himself but also to turn away from "all earthly creatures."[87] This is precisely what Hume has in mind when he writes that "self-denial" and other "monkish virtues" are contrary to *both* private advantage *and* the public good.[88] Even Tocqueville, a liberal whose sympathy for religion far exceeded Hume's, could write pejoratively of Christianity's antihumanistic bias against worldly involvement.[89]

John Stuart Mill elaborates on this point, claiming that the distinction between active and passive characters is much more fundamental than the homiletic contrast between egoistic and altruistic motives. Religion, he believes, generally favors "the inactive character, as being more in harmony with the submission due to the divine will."[90] If you can get a person interested in himself, by contrast, you need apply little more than a gentle nudge to get him interested in others as well.[91] The large step is not from egoism to altruism, but from religiously induced "absence of desire" to a willingness to bestir oneself in the world at all.[92] Voltaire, for the same reason, insists that self-love assists human beings in loving others.[93] This coupling of selfishness and benevolence may seem counterintuitive today. But it made perfect sense in a cultural context where hatred of the world was a widely acclaimed moral ideal.

Significantly, the entry under "self-interest" in Diderot's *Encyclopédie* is an attack, in the spirit of Voltaire, on Augustinian misanthropy.[94] Nicole and Pascal are justly famous for having anticipated Smith's theory of the invisible hand. A society based on cupidity and self-love can be orderly and productive even if it is sinful.[95] But this "modern" aspect of their thinking is entirely neglected in the article on *Intérêt*. Here, the Jansenists are attacked for striving to make people ashamed of their natural and healthy self-love. Despite what such severe theologians suggest, it is a good thing to want to preserve yourself, for, as Spinoza had argued, "the effort for self-preservation is the first and only foundation of virtue."[96] Self-love is nothing more shameful than a steady desire for well-being and a wholesome attachment to sweet life. A natural result of our physical makeup, the self-love with which human beings come into the world turns out, when examined more closely, to be *morally neutral*—neither good nor bad.[97] A baby who suddenly stops crying to look at himself in a mirror deserves neither praise nor blame. Depending on how it is reshaped through education, primitive self-love will become just or unjust, a virtue or a vice. In its primal state, however, it cannot be classified in either way.[98] This argument, too, sheds important light on the modern "rehabilitation" of self-interest. Those who defended the idea of an inborn but morally neutral self-love were not celebrating avarice. They were attacking the idea of original sin—a form of guilt no one can possibly understand.

## Interest and Morality

The story I have told so far, while accurate enough, is clearly one-sided. Smith often contrasted self-interest with a variety of social and unsocial passions. But he also suggested, at least occasionally, that self-interest was *the* fundamental motivation spurring all human endeavor.[99] Thus, present-day economists who lay claim to Smith's legacy have not simply, without textual support, projected contemporary views back onto the *Wealth of Nations*. By selective citation, they can adduce Smith's own words in their defense. The confusing oscillation between an exclusive and an inclusive conception of self-interest was characteristic of Smith, in fact, and of other eighteenth-century liberal theorists as well.

Hirschman has already drawn attention to a seeming contradiction in the evolution of the concept of self-interest, in what he calls its semantic drift.[100] On the one hand, the concept became, in the course of the seventeenth and eighteenth centuries, progressively more narrow and specialized: having first meant any rational style of behavior, it came to refer exclusively to moneymaking. On the other hand, during the same period, the concept broadened to the point of becoming a tautology. Everything that anyone did became explainable as a consequence of interest. (This is the development that provoked Macaulay's sarcastic comment on James Mill.) But which is it? Did the concept become broader or narrower?

Both. The idea of self-interest simultaneously expanded and contracted. To explain this paradoxical development, we must penetrate even deeper into the secret history of the concept. Sometimes two seemingly contrary tactics were pursued for the same reason. By claiming that *all* actions were motivated by self-interest, theorists friendly to commercial society made it impossible to discredit moneymaking by smearing it as self-interested. But they also made the rational pursuit of economic gain seem relatively harmless by an opposite tack—by distinguishing interest from a variety of malevolent passions. So interest was identified both as one motive among others *and* as the basic motor of all human action. Smith, like many of his contemporaries, alternated dizzyingly between these two claims.

I have already explored at length the "narrowing strategy," the decision to contrast rational self-interest with various irrational motivations. I now look at the *political rationale* behind the "broadening strategy," the decision to identify rational self-interest with human motivation in general. Republican theorists in particular were prone to assert that it is "impossible for any Man to act upon any other Motive than his own Interest . . . in the larger Sense of the Word."[101] It is not difficult to see why. Self-interest is a profoundly egalitarian and democratic idea. Only a few have hereditary privileges, but everyone has interests. To acknowledge the legitimacy of interests is to say that all citizens, no matter what their socially ascribed status, have concerns that are worthy of attention. Far from being mean-spirited and selfish, this "rehabilitation" of interest made it morally obligatory, for the first time, to attend to "the interests of the excluded."[102] (For more textual evidence of the interest-equality connection in seventeenth- and eighteenth-century works, see the next section.)

At the end of the sixteenth century, Richard Hooker summarized traditional thinking with his claim that the common people are motivated by self-love, while religious and political elites are motivated by virtue and devotion to the common good.[103] Viewed in this context, the postulate of universal self-interest appears as a subversive doctrine, designed to remove all flattering obscurity about the motives of kings, aristocrats, and priests. It allowed republican theorists to declare, disrespectfully, that "the interest of the few is not the profit of mankind."[104] In other words, the exaggerated tendency to trace *all* action to self-interest was, to some extent, a by-product of modern egalitarianism. It implied, above all, that "Princes are but men, made as others."[105] To say that *all* individuals were motivated by self-interest was to universalize the status of the common man.

## Interest and Democracy

Not virtue alone, therefore, but self-interest, too, was an essential ingredient in modern republican ideology.[106] For one thing, collective self-rule remains practically infeasible until violent and unpredictable passions are replaced by calm and predictable ones. People who cannot "leave to the laws the avenging of their real or supposed wrongs" cannot possibly organize their political life democratically.[107] But republican theorists also viewed interest favorably because of its undeniably egalitarian connotations. As Tocqueville later wrote, "the moral authority of the majority is also founded on the principle that the *interest* of the greatest number should be preferred to that of those who are fewer."[108] The king and the nobility, of course, had benefited most from the self-oblivion of cannon fodder: "Tyranny being nothing else but the Government of one Man, or of a few Men, over many, against their Inclination and Interest."[109] The notion that it is always noble to close one's eyes to self-interest had also proved distressingly useful to the tax collector. Republican writers simply asked rulers to explain what advantages the average citizen might reap from paying taxes and dying in dynastic wars.

As it gradually seeped into common usage, the concept of self-interest accustomed people to discovering *conflicts of interest* in every sector of social life. Particular attention was paid to a discrepancy between the interests of citizens and the interests of wielders of power—a gap formerly papered over by uplifting rhetoric about the public good (understood well only by the virtuous few). The yawning gulf, in the *Wealth of Nations,* between the interests of the few and the interests of the many suggests what is wrong with an overemphasis on the invisible hand as the key to Smith's theory of social order. Rather than associating the notion of private interest with some sort of preestablished concord, indeed, he uses it to stress the semipermanent character of conflicts of interest—most notably the conflict of interest between merchants and the rest of the community.[110] He was fundamentally opposed to those medieval *Harmonielehren* that pictured society as a large organic body, differentiated and unified by a divinely ordained division of labor. Sharp material rivalries were much more formidable than such mythology allowed. Thus, despite the apparent inconsistency it entailed, Smith was drawn to broaden and universalize the idea of self-interest. The postulate of *universal* self-interest helped him demolish the old illusion that harmony was a natural by-product of hierarchy and subordination. (Smith admittedly boasted about the harmony of free-trade regimes in some passages, but only to outbid those mercantilist writers who claimed that harmonization could be orchestrated by a well-designed system of tariffs, bounties, and regulations.)

Every man wants to use others to advance *his* interests at the expense of *their* interests. Publicly to announce this permanent human partiality, of course, is to warn against it. The universality of the self-interest postulate, therefore, was not meant to "atomize" society, but simply to advise the weak not to be duped and exploited by the strong. As Trenchard and Gordon remarked: "All these Discoveries and Complaints of the Crookedness and Corruption of human Nature are made with no malignant Intention to break the Bonds of Society; but they are made to shew, that as Selfishness is the strongest Bias of Men, every Man ought to be upon his Guard against another, that he become not the Prey of another."[111] Liberals asked not the predators but the preyed-upon to open their eyes and notice the stubborn universality of self-interest.

Unless we see interests, we cannot see the "contrariety of Interests, which unavoidably happen in all Collections of Men."[112] The fact is, "different interests necessarily exist in different classes of citizens." By focusing on the "interfering interests" and "clashing interests" and "contending interests" that afflict every known society, on "the different interests and views of the various classes of the community," the principal modern theorists of self-interest can be said to have laid the anthropological foundations for democracy.[113] Assuming, for the sake of argument, that all men were driven by the rational pursuit of private advantage, self-interest theorists clearly posed—for the first time—the problem that modern democratic institutions were eventually designed to resolve: how to make the interests of rulers coincide with the interests of the ruled. For Trenchard and Gordon, "the only Secret . . . in forming a Free Government, is to make the Interests of the Governors and the Governed the same, as far as human Policy can contrive."[114] Princes, according to Locke, ordinarily "have distinct and separate interests from their People."[115] How is this immemorial gap to be overcome? By *electoral accountability.* "Frequent elections" turned out to be the only effective mechanism for guaranteeing "that the government in general should have a common interest with the people."[116] Republican theorists instructed citizens "to choose Representatives, whose Interests are at present the same with your own, and likely to continue the same."[117] Democratic institutions were said to provide "the means by which identity of interest may be insured between the representatives and the community at large."[118] Indeed, the very perfection of government was defined as the "identity of interest between the trustees and the community for whom they hold their power in trust."[119] Elections are necessary because a "governing class not accountable to the people are sure, in the main, to sacrifice the people to the pursuit of separate interests and inclinations of their own."[120] These and similar statements imply that the question answered by modern democratic procedures cannot even be formulated until the universality of self-interest is assumed.

One may speak, as Hirschman does, about a "rehabilitation" of self-interest in modern culture. But there was never any blanket endorsement of the idea. Liberals never acclaimed venality. The concept of "sinister interest" never disappeared from their works.[121] They did not cease worrying about "the corrupt combinations of selfish private interests."[122] Reformers remained acutely aware that vested interests routinely block useful reforms. According to Smith, moreover, every man should be free to follow his own interests in his own way, but only "as long as he does not violate the laws of justice."[123] Since every individual has *many* given interests, some good, some bad, the norm of justice must be invoked to discriminate between interests that should and those that should not be satisfied.[124] In Smith's view, the interests of monopolists are invariably unjust or morally illegitimate, and should be thwarted legislatively if possible. The classical formulation of this absolutely crucial distinction between just and unjust interests is found in the *Second Treatise*. There, Locke argues that law enlarges freedom, and not merely by restricting the behavior of criminals for the sake of honest men. Rather, "Law, in its true Notion, is not so much the Limitation as the direction of a free and intelligent agent to his *proper Interest,* and prescribes no further than is for the general Good of those under that Law."[125] *Proper interest* turns out to be a pivotal, but largely neglected, liberal idea. Hume calls such motives "real and permanent interests," while Madison refers to them as "the permanent and aggregate interests of the community." They are interests disciplined by the restraints of social coexistence and justice.[126] Proper interests are not merely the long-term interests of the individual, but rather those motivations compatible with "the general Good" of all.[127]

A further relevant consideration is this: writers in the Enlightenment tradition were ardent debunkers and unmaskers. In examining social arrangements, they never lost sight of the ultimate question, *cui bono*? Without wishing to imply that self-interest was the motive behind all human actions, they were naturally fond of exposing self-interested motives wrapped in rhetoric about heroic sacrifice and the common good.[128] Locke stated intriguingly that most human legislation was difficult to understand at first: the "positive Laws of Common-wealths" are so often obscure because they are the "intricate Contrivances of Men, following contrary and hidden interests put into Words."[129] Exposés of this sort, interminably repeated, eventually convey the impression that mercenary motives lurk behind every human act, however decked out in the robes of decency and benevolence. But this is a false impression. We must not misinterpret polemical skirmishes as psychological generalizations. The idea of *universal* self-interest, customary at the time of Adam Smith, had a political rationale. It suggested that citizens should distrust every public expression of disinterestedness on the part of the authorities. Such distrust was not merely cynical. It was also, at least potentially, democratic.

## Conclusion

It is plainly contradictory to say that rational self-interest is a universal motivation underlying all human action and to contrast, at the same time, private interest to a whole series of rival motivations (envy, anger, vengefulness, and so forth). Here lies a profound paradox—and a key for unlocking the "secret history" of self-interest. Self-interest was initially defined in opposition to noncalculating and self-destructive motivations. But a commitment to equality and a relish of exposé encouraged some influential modern theorists (some of the time) to overemphasize its exclusiveness and universality. As a result, this singularly cool and deliberate passion was conceived simultaneously in two contrary ways: as one impulse vying with others and as the fundamental motor propelling all human effort. This contradiction cannot be dissolved, but it can, as I have tried to show, be more or less adequately explained.

The second conception, the notion that interest is the principal driving force behind all behavior, has had an astonishingly triumphant career. In some quarters, "the granite of self-interest" has now been blessed as the rock of ages. The consistency, rigor, and explanatory success of this reductionist approach may be genuinely admirable. But, as Hume would have said, a methodological commitment to the maximization hypothesis has some empirical disadvantages. It obscures the *actual* motives of individual revenge seekers, for example. It classifies delirious self-hatred, acute emotional distress, and frantic self-torture as subvarieties of methodical self-interest—an odd use of language, to say the least. It also encourages a simplistic approach to the enduring problems posed by ethnic and religious factions. Selfless cruelty exists and has large-scale social effects. Fortunately, we may still consult the account of human motivation advanced by Smith and Hume themselves. They provide a clearer perspective on the irrational and mutually destructive behavior we read about every day. Their analysis of the human psyche is rich, not parsimonious. Ultimately, their attentiveness to the microfoundations of human irrationality makes social behavior—and self-interest itself—easier, not harder, to understand. The same can be said about the psychological thought of their great preliberal predecessor, Thomas Hobbes, to whom I now turn.

# 3

# Hobbes's Irrational Man

*Nous perdons encore la vie avec joie pourvu qu'on en parle.*

—PASCAL

Thomas Hobbes apotheosized unquestionable authority as the only practicable alternative to anarchy and disparaged political liberty in almost all its forms. Nevertheless he has been repeatedly enlisted as one of the major progenitors of liberal political theory.[1] The seemingly incongruous references to Hobbes in standard accounts of liberalism, in fact, are what justify a detailed examination of his writings here. What do those who, paradoxically enough, discern the roots of liberalism in Hobbesian thought have in mind? Some may be thinking of Hobbes's secular definition of the goal of the state as individual security and social peace, rather than salvation or godliness. But most of them want to emphasize Hobbes's philosophical anthropology. Hobbes was purportedly the first important political theorist to conceptualize man as a machine devoted solely or primarily to biological self-preservation. Liberals ostensibly acceded to this immoral picture of human nature, which is said to explain most of their intellectual and practical failings.

Widely accepted as a kind of orthodoxy, this incriminating genealogy is somewhat less than scholarly. Liberals *did* take over the main psychological premises of Hobbes's theory, but his most influential assumptions about human motivation are not the ones to which commentators have directed our attention. For Hobbes never defended the reductionist psychological theory which the detractors of liberalism commonly foist upon him. He emphatically *denied* that man is a rational animal who, by nature, is driven to preserve himself. This is a crucial insight for the student of liberalism. To demonstrate conclusively (by a close reading) that even Hobbes rejected the rational-actor model of human behavior will prove worthwhile if it helps force liberal historiography to rethink its fondest assumptions. It turns out that Hobbes's picture of the human psyche is closely akin to the other seventeenth-century views canvassed in chapter 2, views that were eventually taken up by impeccably liberal theorists such as Locke,

Smith, and Mill. In other words Hobbes shared, but did not invent, the psychological premises of liberalism. Like his contemporaries—Descartes, Spinoza, La Rochefoucauld, and La Bruyère—he merely built upon and refined two millennia of Western thinking about the complexities of human motivation. While largely extraneous to the institutional aspects of liberalism, therefore, his theoretical perspective, to which I now turn, will help us grasp more clearly the subtle psychological premises inherited by his liberal successors. Especially useful in this regard is Hobbes's often-neglected book, his commentary on the English civil wars.

## Hobbes's History of the Great Rebellion

*Behemoth* was completed in manuscript around 1668, when Hobbes was almost eighty years old. Some pirated editions were published in the late 1670s, but an authorized version of the book was not printed until 1682. In a letter of 19 June 1679, written a few months before his death, Hobbes explained the frustrating delay: "I would fain have published my *Dialogue of the Civil Wars of England,* long ago; and to that end I presented it to his Majesty: and some days after, when I thought he had read it, I humbly besought him to let me print it; but his Majesty, though he heard me graciously, yet he flatly refused to have it published."[2] Charles II may have hesitated to license the work, despite its outspoken championing of the royalist cause, because of its equally outspoken, but politically awkward, anticlericalism.[3]

Hobbes had developed an analytical framework for discussing sedition, rebellion, and the breakdown of authority in earlier works, particularly in *De Cive* (1642) and *Leviathan* (1651). His decision, late in life, to provide an account of the political convulsions that struck England between 1640 and 1660 gave him the opportunity to apply this framework historically. The book he dictated is cast as a discussion between a master, A, and his pupil, B. Unlike a straightforward narrative, the dialogue format allowed Hobbes to dispel the naivete of an inexperienced listener, while drawing useful lessons from events. It was a role he manifestly enjoyed.

Hobbes had lived in exile in France throughout the 1640s. His knowledge of the central episodes recounted in *Behemoth,* therefore, was almost wholly secondhand. Personal remoteness from the scene was of little importance, however. For Hobbes was concerned with "the history, not so much of those actions that passed in the time of the late troubles, as of their causes, and of the councils and artifice by which they were brought to pass" (45).[4] Indeed, he used this historical narrative largely as "a thread" on which to hang the "injustice, impudence, and hypocrisy," not to mention the "knavery, and folly," of the main participants in the civil war (119–20). The causes of the upheaval were not economic and legal, as James Harrington had argued in *Oceana* (1656), but rather psychological and ideological.[5] Civil war broke out because, under complex conditions of shifting political power, key actors were bewitched by irrational passions and tragically misled by doctrinal errors.[6]

The book is divided into four parts, or dialogues. Roughly speaking, the first dialogue contains Hobbes's analysis of the seed of rebellion, the civil war's long-term ideological origins, with emphasis on political and theological opinions. In the second dialogue, A and B concentrate on the growth of this seed, especially on the strategies of those who undermine and destroy political authority. The stress here falls on the art of words by which the people are indoctrinated and seduced. And the last two dialogues are devoted to a schematic chronicle of events between 1640 and 1660, interlarded, of course, with numerous philosophical commentaries and detours.

The biblical creature Behemoth (apparently a giant ox, hippopotamus, or elephant) appears in Job 40, immediately before the famous and mysterious passage about that frightening sea beast Leviathan, "king over all the children of pride" (Job 41:34), whom Yahweh alone, and no man, can control. Whatever the two creatures signify in the Old Testament, Hobbes employed Leviathan as a symbol for the peacekeeping state and Behemoth as a symbol for rebellion and civil war.[7] It takes one monster to subdue another.[8] More than ten years before completing *Behemoth,* Hobbes wrote sarcastically that his ecclesiastical critics should not "misspend" their time criticizing and attacking his works, "but if they will needs do it, I can give them a fit title for their book, *Behemoth against Leviathan.*"[9] In the end, *Behemoth* did not become the name of a book aimed at refuting *Leviathan,* but rather of a book aimed at excoriating *Leviathan*'s enemies.

As Hobbes's mocking suggestion for a title indicates, he associated the monster of rebellion and civil war with religion, with "the Kingdome of Darknesse,"[10] with the clergy first of all, but also with laymen in the grip of enthusiasm. Hobbes lavished blame upon bishops, Presbyterian ministers, and sectarian zealots. But he also attacked lawyers, merchants, soldiers, city dwellers, university men, Commons, Lords, and even the King's trusted advisers. Together, they constituted Behemoth, the multiheaded monster of rebellion.[11] Hobbes's approach to social causality was accusatory. To identify a "cause" of rebellion was to arraign a culprit. Religious troublemakers were favored, but every party to the civil war was incriminated at one point or another.

*Behemoth* is a brilliantly written book—a fierce, witty, biting royalist polemic. But what is its theoretical importance? Why does it remain essential reading for all students of Hobbes? And why should historians of liberalism pay it special heed? There are two reasons, I think.

First, it explodes one of the most common and persistent errors of Hobbes scholarship, an error that also spills over, as I have argued, into numerous works on the origins of post-Hobbesian liberalism. Even today, commentators continue to assert that Hobbes conceived of man as an animal propelled exclusively by the desire for self-preservation. This assertion cannot survive an attentive scrutiny of the relevant texts. Consider, for example, Hobbes's striking claim that "most men would rather lose their lives . . . than suffer slander."[12] This sort of remark certainly suggests that self-preservation is not invariably the strongest human longing. In *Leviathan,* similarly, Hobbes indicates that people fear invisible spirits more than death.[13] Airy phantoms have greater sway over distempered imaginations than do real and certain dangers. While fear is wired into human nature, moreover, the *object* of fear is variable, depending on an individual's constitution and education.[14] According to this line of reasoning, the primacy of the fear of death cannot possibly be an unchangeable attribute of the human mind.

Why have civil wars raged throughout history? Mankind is insanely self-destructive because, among other reasons, human beings dread dishonor and damnation more acutely than they fear death. The main argument of *Behemoth* reinforces this insight. Indeed, the book contains one of Hobbes's most explicit rejections of motivational reductionism. The passage about Ethiopian kings who commit suicide on the command of unarmed priests, to be discussed below, is a stunning rebuttal of the claim that the fear of death is *the* fundamental and overpowering human motive. But the entire work testifies to Hobbes's extraordinarily rich understanding of the human psyche. It places him unmistakably in the old and psychologically subtle tradition reconnoitered in chapter 2. Human motivations are much too disorderly and perverse, he assumes, to be reduced to self-preservation or the rational pursuit of private advantage.

*Behemoth* is an indispensable work for a second reason as well. It provides a marvelously clear illustration of Hobbes's theory of the origins and basis of political power. The most striking statement in the entire book is probably this: "The power of the mighty hath no foundation but in the opinion and belief of the people" (16). The ultimate source of political authority is not coercion of the body, but captivation of the mind. The subjective or psychological basis of authority provides the core of Hobbes's political science. His obsession with religion can be understood only when we recognize the all-importance of "opinion" in his analysis of human behavior, especially in his explanation of obedience and rebellion. *Behemoth,* focusing on seditious opinions, drives the point unrelentingly home.

I shall focus in this chapter on these two themes. I will first discuss Hobbes's antireductionist theory of human motivation. And I will then go on to explain his claim that opinion is the source and basis of power, with special emphasis on the way solid worldly authority can be constructed upon rationally unjustifiable religious beliefs.

## Motivational Reductionism

In some passages, admittedly, Hobbes strikes a cynical pose. When writing in this vein, he depicts rational and affectless advantage seeking as the principal or sole motor of human behavior. Even in matters of religion, the cool scramble for money and power is uppermost. The reason people call themselves "godly," for example, is to acquire more land (161). Beneath the surface, the devout are "just as other men are, pursuers of their own interests and preferments" (29). Despite appearances, religious controversies boil down to "questions of authority and power over the Church, or of profit, or of honour to Churchmen" (63). The sole rationale behind theological doctrines is to redirect "towards the clergy" obedience due to the Crown (71).[15] Even the King's Anglican allies opposed sedition only with an "eye to reward" (63).

Presbyterian ministers in particular are "impious hypocrites" (26) who seek power in order "to fill their purses" (89). They claim to interpret the Bible better than others only "for their advancement to benefices" (90). They focus on blasphemy and adultery, neglecting "the lucrative vices of men of trade or handicraft" in order to win merchant support and for sake of their own "profit" (25). They are shameless frauds and playactors: "No tragedian in the world could have acted the part of a right godly man better than these did" (24). But the charge of hypocritical advantage seeking is not aimed exclusively at Protestants. Under the reign of Charles I, courtiers converted to Catholicism for "hope of favour from the Queen" (60). Regardless of denomination, in fact, the "ambitious clergy" (13) are mountebanks who don "the cloak of godliness" (26) to sell the snake oil of superstition at a profit.[16]

One consequence of the reductionist approach to human motivation that Hobbes *sometimes* employs is a tendency to exaggerate the calculative powers and foresight of the rebels. From the very beginning, apparently, the Presbyterians and their allies in Parliament "were resolved to take from [the King] his royal power, and consequently his life" (102).[17] These prescient revolutionaries did not stumble backward into civil war, their pleas for a redress of grievances only slowly escalating into radically antiroyalist demands. Their appetites were not gradually whetted by successive concessions. At the very outset, instead, the clear-eyed "design of the Presbyterian ministers" was "to change the monarchical government into an oligarchy" (75).

If this sort of conspiracy thinking were dominant, *Behemoth*'s psychological portraits would corroborate the ordinary view of Hobbes while also being wholly unrealistic. Fortunately, Hobbes's account of motivation is much more complicated than his occasional stress on rational mastery and affectless opportunism would lead us to expect.[18]

## Self-Fulfilling Prophecies

To gain an initial sense of the psychological intricacy of Hobbes's theory, consider the fascinating passage, in the fourth dialogue, where he asserts that "prophecy" is "many times the principal cause of the event foretold" (188). Despite his physicalism, Hobbes is committed to the idea that, in some circumstances, the unreal controls the real. Equipped with imagination and language, human beings respond to the possible as well as to the actual, to the dreaded or anticipated future as well as to the experienced present. If the yet unreal future had no causal power, human beings could never be moved by threats of punishment or fear of violent death.

Hobbes introduces his analysis of self-fulfilling prophecies with a discussion of the "dreams and prognostications of madmen." These rantings can seriously injure the commonwealth because human beings always suffer anxiety from "the uncertainty of future time." Ideas in the head control behavior. More specifically, "foresight of the sequels of their actions" shapes what individuals subsequently do (188). But how does this curious process work?

If a prophet could convincingly "predict" that Oliver Cromwell was doomed to be defeated, then most people (supposed, for the sake of argument, to be rational and affectless opportunists) would desert his party, weakening it and insuring its defeat. Contrariwise, if a fortune-teller persuaded the majority that Cromwell's party was certain to win, then people would rush to join his coalition, making its victory inevitable. The struggle for sovereignty is fought on a battlefield of wholly unreal imaginings or rationally unjustifiable assumptions about the future. Whoever controls the future (or the idea people have of it) has unstoppable power.

This passage has interesting implications for Hobbes's theory of authority. It presupposes, of course, that individuals are basically advantage seekers, that they will always join the winner and desert the loser, "to deserve well" (188) of the victorious party. But it also attributes an important causal role in the chain of social events to ideas, fantasies, and baseless mental attitudes. The outcome of a civil war may depend on something as intangible as the capacity to dishearten foes and embolden allies. You cannot *explain* (much less foresee) social outcomes by reference to the postulate of universal self-interest. Human behavior, no matter how self-interested, remains unpredictable because it is guided partly by assessments of the future, assessments which in turn result from irrational traits of the mind (naive trust in prognostications, a gloomy disposition, etc.), not from the calculations of rational maximizers. On inspection, moreover, human aspiration often turns out to be "sottish ambition" (145)—not clear-eyed or self-serving, but drunken, uncontrollable, foolish, whimsical, stupid, and self-defeating.

## Irrationality

The behavior of passionless and calculating opportunists is ultimately controlled by less than rational, or even preposterous, assumptions about the future. But this modest qualification of rational-actor theory is not Hobbes's last word on the subject. Indeed, the very notion that human beings are, by nature, relentless pursuers of their own advantage conflicts wildly with *Behemoth*'s fabulous chronicle of human folly. As he had already laid down in *Leviathan,* "the most part of men, though they have the use of Reasoning a little way . . . yet it serves them to little use in common life." Since "Reason" is not given by nature but rather "attayned by Industry," it is no wonder that most people, being chronically indolent, are irrational most of the time.[19] Impulsiveness and compulsions, hysterical frenzy and aimless drifting, are more characteristic of man's history than eye-on-the-ball purposiveness, thoughtful self-preservation, or the sober cultivation of material interests. Students of "the prisoner's dilemma" assert that behavior which is individually rational can be socially irrational. A cool aversion to being suckered wreaks havoc on social cooperation. Although Hobbes argues this way in a few scattered passages, he emphatically does not conclude that society's greatest problems result from too much rationality on the part of individuals. Sometimes he focuses on slipshod reasoning and other cognitive defects, such as the inability of most people to follow "a long chain of consequences . . . to the end."[20] But he also stresses the sheer absurdity of the elemental human passions themselves, many of which propel men to self-destruction rather than self-preservation. In most cases, in fact, he traces the irrationality of behavior to the irrationality of an individual's motives—most notably, to an unreasonable skittishness about insult and public humiliation. If individuals were rational, they would seek reputation only to the extent that it would foster physical safety and material gain. Instead, they cultivate their name even when it obviously conflicts with their interests to do so. Haunted by envy, feelings of inferiority, and status deprivation, they are also mortified at the thought of losing face. These hauntings boggle the mind, interfering with a sober assessment of alternative courses of action. If individuals were rational, they would (for they easily could) develop thick skins against gratuitous signs of undervaluing. But they do not do this. They do not do it because they are *ir*rational fools.

Even when stressing the opportunism of fanaticism (25), Hobbes does not ascribe to humankind vast capacities for clearheadedness. Cromwell's fetishism about his lucky day, the third of September (183), and the King's appointment of Arundel to lead an army into Scotland, merely because his "ancestor had formerly given a great overthrow to the Scots" (30–31), reveal the elementary incapacity of human minds to learn from experience or absorb the most obvious truths about natural causality.[21] No rational actor would be as narcotized as most men patently are by such "foolish superstition" (31).

It is another extraordinary "infirmity of the people" that they "admire nothing but what they understand not" (96). Human beings can be easily conned with gibberish, "with words not intelligible" (164). Widespread gullibility has massive historical effects. For centuries, hare-brained parishioners admired the arguments of Catholic theology "because they understood them not" (17). They applauded these arguments not despite but because of their unintelligibility.

Conformism, deference, and group-think are further irrational reflexes of the human mind. Men are sheep. Out of a natural obsequiousness and need to be told what to do, "inferior neighbours" follow "men of age and quality" (54). Soldiers are "addicted to their great officers" (189), while subjects in general heed their "immediate captains" (39), be they preachers, gentlemen, or officers. Personal loyalty, a moral-emotional identification with local notables, has a tremendous grip on most subjects. The English people do not hate Catholicism because that religion is false; they are too ignorant and dim-witted to tell the difference between a true and false religion. No, they hate Catholicism because their preachers *tell* them it is detestable (60), and they docilely parrot whatever their superiors authoritatively declaim. Ordinary subjects, moreover, think that "boldness of affirmation" (69) is a proof of the thing affirmed. The more self-assured someone's tone of voice, the more persuasive he becomes. It is only because most people are credulous dupes that ecclesiastical imposture succeeds so well. Indeed, a pathetic incapacity for individual advantage seeking has always characterized the greater part of humanity: "What silly things are the common sort of people, to be cozened as they were so grossly" (158).

Even without schoolmasters, people will acquire their opinions by osmosis rather than by critical reflection—by being dunked in "the stream" (112) of public opinion. Within a group, a person can be "passionately carried away by the rest," which explains the paradox that "it is easier to gull the multitude, than any one man amongst them" (38). As he had written in *Leviathan,* "the Passions of men, which asunder are moderate, as the heat of one brand; in Assembly are like many brands, that enflame one another."[22] Whether in groups or alone, however, almost all individuals are "negligent" (17). *L'homme copie* irrationally imitates the beliefs and behavior patterns of those around him, failing to notice what he is doing. He acts without thinking, not in order to save time as hard-headed economists might imagine, but from mindlessness, impulsiveness, distraction, inveterate slovenliness, poor moral character, and an inborn penchant for imitating the preferences of close companions.

Dreamily indulging their wildest fantasies about the distant future, most people lack the gumption to think causally two steps ahead. Hobbes emphasizes this nearly universal myopia: "All men are fools which pull down anything which does them good, before they have set up something better in its place" (155).[23] Rebels are willing to overthrow an unsatisfactory regime only because they give no thought to the tyranny or anarchy that is bound to follow. Such everyday thoughtlessness (or failure to weigh costs and benefits) is not limited to commoners. In the early stages of the civil war, the Lords themselves proved stupendously obtuse. They did not understand that weakening the King would expose their own order to an attack by the Commons. The reason for this "folly in the Lords" (155) is most instructive. Great peers closed their eyes to the middle-range future, acquiescing in the Commons' assault on the Crown, "for fear of violence" (88) at the hands of London crowds. Panic at the thought of violent death clouds the mind and promotes irrational, shortsighted, and self-defeating behavior.

Failure to think causally about the probable consequences of one's actions usually has woeful consequences. Usually, but not always. Parliament's army was more successful than it should have been because its soldiers were heedless half-wits. They would have quaked spinelessly at danger "approaching visibly in glistering swords." But "for want of judgment," they "scarce thought of such death as comes invisibly in a bullet, and therefore were very hardly to be driven out of the field" (114). If soldiers have not mentally adjusted to the latest advance in weaponry, if they are irrationally prone to overestimate their good luck, or if, in the heat of action, they simply fail to think ahead, the threat of violent death ceases to operate as a sobering deterrent. In this exceptional case, a cognitive defect yields a behavioral advantage.

Hobbes's preoccupation with the sources of human irrationality, in sum, clashes rudely with the "rational-actor" approach that many commentators project onto his works. Despite a few memorable and citable passages, he does not conceive of man as an economic animal, engaging in preemptive strikes, rendering harmless those who might conceivably harm *him.* The pitiful and snarled mess which is the human mind cannot be painted with such a monochrome palette. To help us disentangle the complexities of Hobbes's position, we could do worse than to return to Hume's tripartite scheme, as outlined in the last chapter. Human behavior is motored not by self-interest alone, but simultaneously by passions, interests, and norms.[24]

## Norms

Throughout *Behemoth,* Hobbes invokes norms rhetorically. He speaks in favor of honesty, oath keeping, debt repayment, fair play (11),[25] gallantry (38), civility (125), decency, and loyalty.[26] With palpable sincerity, he denounces not only "wicked Parliaments" (154) but, more generally, "impudence and villainy" (86), flattery (110), "drunkenness, wantonness, gaming," and even "lewd women" (147). More seriously, he lashes out repeatedly against cruelty[27] and tyranny.[28] His stomach is particularly churned by the Judas-like sale of the King first to Parliament by the Scots (134) and subsequently to the Independents by the Presbyterians (155).

This is all quite touching. For our purposes, however, Hobbes's moral sentiments are beside the point. As he says, "what one calls vice, another calls virtue" (45). And a value-subjectivist can scarcely propose his own values as commitments readers are rationally compelled to accept.[29] Of course, if he employs morally charged language, he may be assuming that it will strike a chord. Hobbes invokes, for example, Christian and martial values to vilify merchants.[30] From this rhetorical maneuver, we can conclude nothing about his own values. We can say, with some certainty, however, that he thinks readers will respond sympathetically to traditional moral codes.

More important is Hobbes's empirical, rather than normative, approach to norms. Norms are *effective*. They are not simply rationalizations that can be peeled away to disclose an individual's single-minded obsession with personal advantage. People not only should, they actually do honor their plighted word, even when the personal costs of doing so are quite steep. So norms can sometimes override interests. Even when they do not do so, however, they can be uncommonly effective whenever countervailing interests cancel each other out or whenever interests prove inscrutable. Motives irreducible to self-interest are additionally powerful, in short, in complex choice situations where considerations of advantage do not clearly privilege one alternative over another.

Despite his torrent of jibes about religious hypocrisy, Hobbes straightforwardly asserts that the Queen's Catholicism was genuine and disinterested (61). Indeed, he assumes that people sincerely believe what they are taught to believe as children.[31] The passivity of primary socialization alone belies an exclusively instrumental interpretation of religion. Crafty prelates can use religion to serve their interests only because most subjects, indoctrinated from infancy, have a habitual or uncritical, that is, noninstrumental, attitude toward their faith.

The omnipresence of nonopportunistic behavior, it seems, can be inferred even from Hobbes's most cynical-sounding claims. The assertion that "there were very few of the common people that cared much for either of the causes, but would have taken any side for pay or plunder" (2) implies that the loyal few, at least, devoted to either King or Parliament, would have been somewhat less susceptible than most people to monetary rewards. Conversely, Hobbes's remark about "men that never look upon anything but their present profit" (142) refers not to the majority, but solely to those who have grown rich through trade and craft.

Hobbes's most arresting example of norm-driven behavior is this: members of the Commons passionately hated Wentworth *because he had once been a Parliamentary leader* (68). Such seething hatred cannot be reduced to the self-interest of the enraged party. Their animosity was not fueled by anticipated advantage. It was engendered instead by an implicit norm: deserters are intrinsically worse than people who have always been enemies, even if their behavior is the same.[32] Much more loathsome than any damage he did to Parliamentary interests while in the King's service was Strafford's heinous defection, his apostasy, his breach of a taboo. Equally rankling, perhaps, was his all too rapid rise from knight to earl, which did not injure Parliamentary interests, but rather violated a prevailing sense about how the status system was supposed to work. In other passages, Hobbes explicitly invokes status anxiety to explain why the Scottish nobility cooperated in the abolition of episcopacy: "Men of ancient wealth and nobility are not apt to brook, that poor scholars should (as they must, when they are made bishops) be their fellows" (29–30).[33] A compulsive attachment to inherited place, fused with trepidation about change, explains patterns of hostility unintelligible from the standpoint of rational self-interest alone.

Consistency is another causally effective norm. Having first protested against irregular royal taxes, Parliament eventually imposed irregular taxes of its own. It should thus have been hoist by its own petard (85). Such apt punishment is not always a mere hope; it can also be a fact. Priestly licentiousness, before Henry VIII's break with Rome, actually undermined clerical power. "The force of their arguments was taken away by the scandal of their lives" (18). The normative trespassing of priests, monks, and friars helped disgrace the Church and prepared the way psychologically for the English Reformation.

Norms exhibit exceptional causal force, once again, in the swaying of fence sitters. The moral principle that "the aggressor is in the wrong" seems to be a case in point. To win the cooperation, or at least compliance, of uncommitted moderates, the rebels worked hard "to make it believed that the King made war first upon the Parliament" (36). Similarly, the Dutch "wisely" (176) made it seem that English ships attacked *them.* (In his more cynical moods, admittedly, Hobbes makes it seem that the justice of the struggle, as opposed to naked national interest, seldom determines which side a hesitating third party will join).

## Names

Throughout *Behemoth,* Hobbes also stresses the politics of name calling and, especially, of name avoidance. Even when not backed up by the sword, "words" and "breath" possess enormous political force.[34] This is a little-explored dimension of Hobbes's nominalism: people react more emotionally to names than to facts.[35] Terms of obloquy are especially powerful in this regard. Cromwell did not dare assume the name of *king* (109) for fear of awakening the latent envy of subordinates. Aware that treason laws were draconian, supporters of Parliament anxiously explained that they should not be called *rebels.* It was "Parliament's artifice" (67), on the other hand, to affix the epithet *traitor* to anyone it aimed to kill. The label of treason has a particularly profound effect on waverers and temporizers. Thus, the capture and publication of the King's correspondence with France (about the possibility of introducing French troops into England) swelled Parliamentary ranks. And, of course, you can destroy an enemy by making him "odious to the people" (161). To this end, the Presbyterians drew execration upon the King's party by smearing it with the label of *Episcopalian* (89). They cast odium upon the Anglicans, in turn, by calumniating them with the name of *papists* (83). Recrimination with the tongue cannot be waived aside as a mere "externall thing."[36]

Public opinion is politically decisive. Hobbes calls the Commons' claim to be *King-in-Parliament* a "university quibble" (124). But he never doubts its subversive effect. To curry popular favor, Parliament cleverly denominated itself the *guardian of English liberties.* The Rump, in turn, confiscated the name of *Parliament* because, "being venerable amongst the people" (157), this nomenclature served their cause. Veneration attaches to names, and veneration is an important source of power. Vilification, too, requires a shrewd application of labels. By rhetorical skill, "the Parliament had made the people believe that the exacting of ship-money was unlawful" (60). They assailed ship-money, which was financially a very light tax, as a form of *illegal oppression* (37). Given the gracious receptivity of the human mind, such flung mud tends to stick. Hobbes's account of the Hampden affair assumes that most people are relatively indifferent to the monetary cost of taxation. The raucous to-do about ship-money arose less from damage to material interests than from ideologically induced hysteria, from symbolic politics, from the labeling of extraparliamentary taxation as a form of *tyranny.* The Commons was able "to put the people into tumult upon any occasion they desired" (69); that is, could drive them into actions contrary to the people's real interests. Few names were more useful in this regard than the name of *tyrant.* In reality, "no tyrant was ever so cruel as a popular assembly" (23). But the readers of Greek and Roman history propagated the fiction that "popular government" was *free,* while monarchical rule was *tyrannical.*[37]

Right and might are far from identical. In *Behemoth,* at least, the practical exchange of obedience for protection is overshadowed by old-style Stuart legitimacy. The dynastic right to rule is apparently valid independently of any real power to keep the peace. The possibility that Charles I might have forfeited his right to rule when he became unable to protect his subjects is mentioned, but not taken seriously (146). This curious twist in the argument might be dismissed as Hobbes's servile attempt to ingratiate himself with the restored Stuarts. But notice his causal claim. Mere names, such as King or Stuart, sway the popular mind. The right to rule cannot be inherited; but words, as tokens of public opinion, govern the world. Dynastic right thus has a potential for political power independent of any actual military strength. Residual "reverence" for the Crown was an important factor in the King's capacity to raise an army without Parliamentary support (35–36). True, *Behemoth* is not completely consistent on this point. Parliament's seizure of the power of self-perpetuation accomplished "a total extinction of the King's right" (74). Yet, somewhat later: "The right [to rule] was certainly in the King, but the exercise was yet in nobody" (135). Similarly, the King had "the right of defending himself against those that had taken from him the sovereign power" (108). Legitimate authority, in any case, is not automatically transferred to the wielder of superior military force. After the King's execution, the noncoincidence of right and might remained apparent: "If by power you mean the right to govern, nobody [here] had it. If you mean the supreme strength, it was clearly in Cromwell" (180).

Hobbes's deceptively positive attitude toward the Stuart "right to rule" implies nothing about his own theory of just authority. It shows only that he believed most people were outfitted with conventional minds. Custom, inertia, habit, and the enduring grip of ideas imbibed in infancy insure that "a rightful king living, an usurping power can never be sufficiently secured" (131). The very *name* of Stuart has a power to attract resources and allies far out of proportion to its bearer's current capacity to impose his will by force. The intangible power attached to family pedigree explains why, inevitably, "usurpers are jealous" (184) and also why the Stuarts returned with a mysterious inevitability to the throne.

Norms and names can be tools for some because they are not tools for all. Hypocrisy would be wholly pointless if everyone were fraudulent and no one was sincere. At one point, Hobbes claims that sects and fanatics were "Cromwell's best cards" (136) in the card game for sovereignty. The distinction, implicit here, between the calculating and the noncalculating, between the players and the played-with, is consistently drawn. Broadly speaking, there are two types of human being:

the cynic and the dupe.[38] Dupes vastly outnumber cynics. As a result, norms and names will always exert a decisive influence over the course of historical events.

## Teachings

Free speech and freedom of the press concerned Hobbes not as promises but as threats. The rebellion was driven by ideas that vexed the mind and distorted people's perception of their own advantage. Foremost among these "dangerous doctrines" (71) were the following: sovereignty may be divided; civil and spiritual power are distinct; the sovereign is subject to the law; private men can judge whether laws are just or unjust; private conscience justifies resistance, not to mention tyrannicide; England has a mixed constitution; and republics are free, while monarchies are tyrannical.[39] Seditious opinions such as these crept into English heads by way of books and public speech.

To a large extent, in fact, "this late rebellion of the presbyterians and other democratical men" (20) was a *reader's revolt,* an uprising led by unsupervised students of the Bible, on the one hand, and of Greek and Roman history, on the other.[40] As disruptive as the printed word were sermons from pulpits, "harangues" in Parliament, and "discourses and communication with people in the country" (23). England's problems were wrought by a joint looseness of pen and tongue. Lawyers "had infected most of the gentry of England with their maxims" (119), opposing the King's efforts to tax and conscript without consent and promulgating the notion of fundamental law, which was nothing but an invitation to regicide. Even the King's advisers had caught the doctrinal plague, falling "in love with *mixarchy*" and thus being irrationally "averse to absolute monarchy" (116).[41] This intellectual contagion had significant effects on the King's closest allies. Specifically, it "weakened their endeavor to procure him an absolute victory in the war" (114–15).

Hobbes reserves some of his bitterest criticisms for the two great centers of learning. He even claims that "the core of rebellion" lay in "the Universities" (58). From the universities, Presbyterians carted their theology into the churches. From the universities, gentlemen transported their politics into Parliament (23). It was Laud's great mistake "to bring . . . into the State his former controversies, I mean his squabblings in the University about free-will, and his standing upon punctilios concerning the service-book" (73). In a healthy society, these "unnecessary disputes" (62) would have remained quarantined within the ivory tower.

The universities were originally established as a Trojan horse for papal power in England, as an outpost for inculcating "absolute obedience to the Pope's canons and commands." University indoctrinators supported papal supremacy by employing "verbal forks," "distinctions that signify nothing" (41), and "unintelligible distinctions to blind men's eyes" (40). If you overlooked their dastardly political purpose (to erode secular authority), then Duns Scotus and Peter Lombard would seem to be "two of the most egregious blockheads in the world, so obscure and senseless are their writings" (41).

Apparently, those who first pitched theological dust into the eyes of readers were not themselves unseeing. By Hobbes's own day, however, university theologians had come to compose treatises "which no man else, nor they themselves, are able to understand" (17). The worst feature of the doctrines imported from the universities into the polity is that they are so opaque as to be endlessly "disputable" (55). Reasonable men will always disagree about what they imply. Thus, "the babbling philosophy of Aristotle . . . serves only to breed disaffection, dissension, and finally sedition and civil war" (95). Doctrines are politically dangerous because disagreements are politically dangerous. Intellectual discord engenders civic discord because parties coalesce around ideas. To introduce theological conflict into the public domain through the universities was "an excellent means to divide a kingdom into factions" (148). Faced with Anglican-Puritan or Arminian-predestinationist squabbles, Laud was disastrously wrong to think "that the state should engage in their parties, and not rather put them both to silence" (62).

Norms, names, and doctrines are politically decisive. This is especially true because "the power of the mighty hath no foundation but in the opinion and belief of the people" (16). Frequently neglected, as already mentioned, this remarkable pronouncement lies at the heart of the Hobbesian theory of power. To explain human behavior, appeals to self-interest are insufficient because, quite simply, "the Actions of men proceed from their Opinions."[42] Man may be a pleasure/pain machine, but whether he is vexed by a flung insult or gladdened by the burning down of a rival church depends on his beliefs, not on his nerve endings. The opinions that guide and misguide people's lives are not themselves the products of a rational pursuit of private advantage. Few opinions are picked up and dropped as strategic rationality decrees.[43] An individual does not ordinarily adopt opinions because they promote his self-preservation or material advantage. Beliefs are seldom so rational. Pascal, a younger contemporary, argued as follows: "Toute Opinion peut être préférable à la vie, dont l'amour paraît si fort et si naturel."[44] The love of life seems strong; but, in fact, men are willing to die for almost any belief, however crazy or illogical. This was Hobbes's dismayed conclusion as well.[45]

## Passions

The rebellious Presbyterians and Parliamentarians were driven to rebellion not only by contumacy, ambition, and love of gain, but also by *malice* and *envy* (23). Such bilious passions, too, complicate attempts to offer a rational explanation of human behavior. They cannot be smoothly inserted into the utility bundle of a rational maximizer because, at the extremes, they flummox the mind, making the weighing of costs and benefits next to impossible. At one point, Hobbes throws up his hands: "What account can be given of actions that proceed not from reason, but spite and such-like passions?" (169). Pascal's claim that the love of life, apparently so strong, can be overcome by almost any opinion, is nicely complemented by a remark of Francis Bacon's concerning emotion rather than belief: "There is no passion in the minds of man, so weake, but it Mates, and Masters, the Feare of Death."[46] Man is not a rational actor because his intellect is not a "dry light." On the contrary, "affections colour and infect the understanding."[47] As mentioned in chapter 2, the bewitching passions that, according to Bacon, regularly override the desire for self-preservation include revenge, love, honor, shame, grief, fear, pity, and boredom.[48] Having acted as Bacon's amanuensis during the composition of the *Essays,* Hobbes was thoroughly persuaded of the motivational power of mind-clouding emotions. He considered it a truism, for instance, that some men would rather lose their lives than endure slander.

And consider boredom. Many "seditious blockheads" are "more fond of change than either of their peace or profit" (113). They seek a "change of government" (38) for its own sake. Restlessness, fidgetiness, cabin fever, or love of novelty are the contraries of inertness, homesickness, and dread of change. None of these motives is particularly rational, none is selected for its instrumental value, and none can be reduced to self-interest.[49] For some people, change is simply tastier than material advantage, while boredom is more frustrating than material deprivation. A few lunatics even consider tedium to be worse than anarchy. Not a lack of foresight alone, but also a taste for innovation, an irrational sense that the grass is greener on the other side, explains why rebels will foolishly tear down a government before giving the least thought to what they can erect in its place (155).

Many of the passions to which Hobbes attributes causal force are rooted in vanity or the irrational desire for applause.[50] We yearn to be thought superior; and we resent it bitterly when people forget our names. Consider the Marian exiles. Before the dispersal, they were apparently satisfied with the status of the clergy in England. But when they observed the Presbyterians in Geneva, they experienced the psychological trauma of relative deprivation. Not hard interests but anxieties about comparative prestige led them, on returning home, to escalate their demands. They wanted "the same honour and reverence given to the ministry in their own countries" (22) as they had observed in Geneva. As a result, they "have endeavoured, to the great trouble of the Church and nation, to set up that government here, wherein they might domineer and applaud their own wit and learning" (136).

Emotions divert the mind unhealthily from material concerns. For example: "*Envy* is grief for the prosperity of such as ourselves, arising not from any hurt that we but from the good that they receive."[51] This other-regarding passion is socially rampant. Ministers envy bishops, whom they think less learned than themselves, while gentlemen envy privy councilors, whom they consider less wise (23).[52] Subordinate commanders envy victorious generals, which was one of the reasons why Cromwell did not feel he could safely assume the name of king (109). Envy at the level of states, "the emulation of glory between the nations" (30), has incalculable consequences. English dominion of the seas was "envied by all the nations" (176), while English merchants, in turn, envied Dutch prosperity (4). For the outcome of the civil war, no emotion was more decisive than the envy felt by the Scots toward the English.[53] Among neighboring nations, even when their interests coincide, "the less potent bears the greater malice" (32). An irrational obsession with comparative status explains the explosive energy of the less powerful.

While it sickens the envier, envy may gratify the envied. Indeed, the consumption of envy, a subtle variation on the consumption of praise, is one of mankind's most fatuous and common amusements. Even the charm of political participation stems from a foolish desire to consume the envy of nonparticipators, or so Hobbes assumes in his strikingly narcissistic concept of participation. Under Presbyterianism, "every minister shall have the delight of sharing in the government" (89), that is, shall enjoy a positional good the whole value of which depends upon most others being frustratingly excluded from it.

All men, of course, "think highly of their own wits" (23), a form of intellectual vanity that is inevitably and dangerously exacerbated by a university education. This vanity, it turns out, proved terribly damaging to the King's cause.[54] The Parliamentary party rapidly gained the support of gentlemen who had been passed over for office, that is, who felt their talents had gone unrecognized by the King (27, 155–56). Because man is the only animal obsessed with the adjectives attached by others to his name, stable government requires gag rules to stifle mutual insult, as well as an artful distribution of immaterial resources, especially status and prestige.[55]

In his abridged "translation" of the *Rhetoric,* Hobbes departed from Aristotle's original by adding intriguingly that individuals have a tendency "to hate" anyone "whom they have hurt," simply *because* they have hurt him.[56] Hatred, anger, contempt, and malice are even more irrational than moral psychologists have traditionally assumed. The Hirschmanian distinction between interests and passions, discussed in chapter 2, is beautifully illustrated by Hobbes's contrast between covetousness and malice. The Presbyterians sought political power in order to "satisfy not only their covetous humour with riches, but also their malice with power to undo all men that admired not their wisdom" (159). Such references to "malice" (25) abound. For example, the King's soldiers were stout; but "their valour was not sharpened so with malice as theirs were on the other side" (114).[57] This was no negligible defect, because "spite" is "more conducing to victory than valour and experience both together" (110). If individuals pursue power "farther than their security requires,"[58] they also pursue malice to irrational excess, being "more spiteful . . . than revenge required" (165). Splenetic behavior outruns advantage seeking and even surpasses the needs of retaliation. Discussing Parliament's "spiteful" veto against royal pardons, Hobbes again contrasts opportunism and malice: "All the rest proceeded from ambition, which many times well-natured men are subject to; but this proceeded from an inhuman and devilish cruelty" (107).

The need to have one's vanity massaged is closely akin to the need to avoid humiliation and "affront" (97). The pointless Dutch decision to insult some English ambassadors resulted in a military debacle (174). Names, it is worth repeating, are especially potent politically when they resonate with contempt. Thus, "the Irish nation did hate the name of subjection to England" (79), just as Parliament could not "endure to hear of the King's absolute power" (33). Essex agreed to lead the Parliamentary army because his wife's too-public dalliance had humiliated him at Court, calling his manliness into question, and exposing him to the disagreeable reputation of a cuckold.[59]

Power may be valued as an instrument for acquiring wealth or extorting praise. But it may also be desired for its own sake, as a consummatory, not an instrumental, good. *Libido dominandi* or the desire to "domineer" (136) is no more logical than the desire to be told what to do. It is just another subrational human passion with potentially anarchical consequences.[60] The Parliamentarians wanted to be "the people's masters" (164). Similarly, "Presbyterians are everywhere the same: they would fain be absolute governors of all they converse with" (167). Perversely enough, they find enjoyment in "a severe imposing of odd opinions upon the people" (169). In these passages, intriguingly, an advocate of uncritical obedience fans resentment against mastery and subordination.

## Irrationality and Religion

Despite his concern for earthly self-preservation, Hobbes is well informed about mankind's relish for martyrdom and otherworldly rewards. He introduces his history of the Long Parliament with an extensive excursus on transubstantiation, auricular confession, celibacy, and the medieval struggles between emperor and pope. He does so because he sees religion as a potent amalgam of opinion and passion, with an almost irresistible power to shape and misshape human behavior.

Christianity is especially dangerous. That, at least, is the message Hobbes had conveyed in the frontispiece to *Leviathan,* where the weapons of the Church were displayed as distressingly equal to the weapons of the state. Religious civil war, moreover, is singled out as Christianity's chief contribution to political development. Nothing similar ever occurred in the ancient world (63–64).[61] In fact, "the cause of all our late mischief" (55) was the spillover of abstruse theological disputes into the public realm. Belief cannot be directly commanded, but it can be indirectly induced. Christian authorities never forgot that "the tongue is the instrument of domination."[62] They cunningly poured enormous resources into the diffusion of sermons. As for the causes of rebellion: "The mischief proceeded wholly from the Presbyterian preachers, who, by a long practised histrionic faculty, preached up the rebellion powerfully" (159).[63] Here lies the uniqueness of Christianity: "Only in Christendom" is "liberty . . . given to any private man to call the people together, and make orations to them frequently, or at all, without first making the state acquainted." The "heathen Kings" committed no such mistake, because they "foresaw, that a few such orators would be able to make a great sedition" (16).[64] Practice is continuation of theory by similar means: "The doctrine of the Presbyterians" was "the very foundation of the then Parliament's treacherous pretensions" (82); and, of course, the King "was murdered, having been first persecuted by war, at the incitement of Presbyterian ministers"(95).[65]

As a book-centered religion, Christianity suggests anarchically that it is "lawful . . . for subjects to resist the King, when he commands anything that is against the Scripture" (50), that is, against any single individual's interpretation of Scripture.[66] The "doctrine" that moral obligations disclosed by private reading may override the duty to secular authority is calamitous. It "divides a kingdom within itself." Moreover, the preachers "who in the pulpit did animate the people to take arms in the defence of the then Parliament, alleged Scripture, that is, the word of God, for it" (50). A book-based and freely sermonizing religion will necessarily propagate anarchy. Various passages in the Bible dangerously imply that kings should lay down their sovereignty and submit themselves to ecclesiastical authority (6). But no realm can be stable so long as subjects may disobey the King's instructions whenever such commands seem "contrary to the command of God" (50). Unruliness becomes endemic once "private interpretation" (22) of the Bible becomes common; that is, once subjects themselves become "judge of the meaning of the Scripture" (50).[67] The promulgation of "evil principles" (204) by "seditious ministers" (50), "pretending to have a right from God" (2), provokes Hobbes to remark, daringly: "How we can have peace while this is our religion, I cannot tell" (57).

## The Power of the Pope

Bishop of Milan toward the end of the fourth century, Ambrose wrote saucily to Emperor Theodosius: "I prefer God to my sovereign."[68] The anarchical strain in Christianity thus long predated the Reformation. Scanning the past for dangerous precedents of this sort, Hobbes interpreted the execution of Charles I as a Protestant adaptation and implementation of the Jesuit doctrine of regicide. Atabalipa of Peru discovered that Catholic ecclesiastics would murder kings "when they have power" (11). Charles I learned the same lesson about their reformed counterparts.

In the Middle Ages, the papacy "encroached upon the rights of kings" (40), overturning the power of lay investiture.[69] Aware of the mind-entrancing power of propaganda, the Pope multiplied sermons and dispatched "preaching friars" (15) throughout Europe to spread his authority. With these unarmed battalions alone, the Church "found means to make the people believe, there was a power in the Pope and clergy, which they ought to submit unto, rather than to the commands of their own Kings, whensoever it should come into controversy" (13).

They taught "that we ought to be governed by the Pope, whom they pretended to be the vicar of Christ" (3), a clever formula, for everyone knew that "Christ was King of all the world" (12). Most important of all, the Pope claimed "a power of absolving subjects of their duties, and of their oaths of fidelity to their lawful sovereigns" (7). The natural result was an unstably divided sovereignty, the centuries-long conflict between *sacerdotium* and *imperium,* a conflict that Hobbes saw revived or reenacted in the battle between the King and a religiously inspired Parliament.

There "was never such another cheat in the world" (21) as the Pope. From early times, the occupant of the Holy See was uncannily shrewd, parlaying the "pretence of his power spiritual" (11) into real political power by a series of deft tactical maneuvers. By making marriage a sacrament, he gained a "monopoly of women" (7), that is, control over a question crucial for every King, legitimate succession. Even more cunning was the papal decision to impose celibacy on the clergy itself. By this seemingly self-abnegating move, the Pope insured that secular rulers, needing heirs, could never be priests and thus could never personally benefit from the indelible aura of sacerdotal authority. Priestly celibacy made every King *politically* impotent, depriving him of "the reverence due to him from the most religious part of his subjects" (13).

The Anglican bishops remained loyal to the Crown during the civil war. But their loyalty provided no evidence for the usefulness of Anglicanism to kings. Indeed, they refrained from personally decapitating His Majesty only because he and they were both hostile to the rebels and very unpopular with the common people (95). The bishops shared the delusion, common to all Christian clergy and inherited ultimately from the Pope, that they were not meant to be creatures of the King (89). They, too, claimed to exercise jurisdiction autonomously, "in the right of God" (19). They heartily approved when Henry VIII abolished the Pope's power in England, but only because, by sheerest coincidence, they simultaneously detected divine right in themselves. The culmination of Hobbes's attack on Anglicanism is that "the doctrine taught by those divines which adhered to the King . . . may justify the Presbyterians" (49). Anglicanism itself vindicates regicide by disgruntled subjects.[70]

To B's idealistic suggestion that arms and force count for nothing because soldiers will never fight against their consciences, A replies, with a touch of cynicism, that religiously based power is strong enough to foment rebellion; but, "if they have money" (18), kings can always rout such opponents. Money can tip the balance against inspiration, as is well known, because "there are but few whose consciences are so tender as to refuse money when they want it" (18). Yet religion can sometimes override interest, and it is an especially powerful force when the scales of material advantage otherwise rest in delicate equilibrium. (This is true of norms and names as well.) The power of a religiously legitimated actor depends on the overall power situation in which he finds himself: "The great mischief done to kings upon pretence of religion is, when the Pope gives power to one king to invade another" (18). The Pope survived because kings, driven by irrational envy of rivals, "let his power continue, every one hoping to make use of it, when there should be cause, against his neighbour" (21). The power of religion does not cancel but does seriously qualify and interfere with the authority of money and arms.

## Death Is Not the Greatest Evil

What is the secret of religious authority? How did "so many poor scholars" (21) acquire so much power? Hobbes occasionally suggests that the sole source of power is the ability to inflict physical pain; that is, the capacity to deliver a believable threat to crush rivals by force in cases of conflict. For example, "he that is master of the *militia,* is master of the kingdom" (98). This statement raises an obvious question, however. If a government imposes its authority by means of the police and the army, "what shall force the army?" (59); that is, how can a sovereign gain "the power of pressing and ordering soldiers" (79)? How can he attain authority over his own authority-enforcing machine? (This is not merely a philosophical question, but also a practical one which, as is well known, plagued and eventually destroyed the Long Parliament [109].) The sovereign's "right" to control the army "signifies little" if the soldiers entertain "seditious" opinions (27–28). If force were the only source of authority, then state building or militia building could never get off the ground. Luckily, there is another source of social power: fraud.[71] A king can govern his subjects by the psychological manipulation of his soldiers' beliefs. While these beliefs will not appear or disappear on demand, they can be indirectly channeled and shaped.

Mankind's *summum malum,* according to Augustine, is not violent death but eternal damnation.[72] The belief that damnation is worse than death obviously weakens the deterrent power of secular punishments. The crucial biblical passage on this theme is Matthew 10:28: "Fear not them which kill the body and after that have power to do naught; but rather fear Him who after He has killed the body, has power to condemn to hell."[73] Taken literally, this advice would cripple peacekeeping authorities and swell the power of rebellious ecclesiastics: "What can be more pernicious to any state, than that men should, by the apprehension of everlasting torments, be deterred from obeying their princes, that is to say, the laws."[74] Hobbes stresses the same dilemma in *Behemoth:* "As much as eternal torture is more terrible than death, so much [the people] would fear the clergy more than the King" (14–15). A says he would rather obey the King, who can inflict real punishment, than religious authorities, who fulminate about the afterlife. Qualms about excommunication, B responds, hinge on the premise that salvation and damnation are controlled by the Church: "Which supposition, it seems, you believe not; else you would rather have chosen to obey the Pope, that would cast your body and soul into hell, than the King, that can only kill the body" (8).

At times, Hobbes denies that anyone "when his life is in extreme danger . . . will voluntarily present himself to the officers of justice" (50). But he cites with approval a contrary claim by Diodotus Siculus, concerning the extraordinary power priests can wield in civil affairs. In ancient Ethiopia, individuals would voluntarily submit themselves to capital punishment by the order of religious officials (94). This zombie-like self-sacrifice testifies to the entrancing power of theological beliefs. Most amazing of all, as noted earlier, priests issued orders for kings themselves to commit suicide; and the monarchs would sheepishly take their own lives. They complied because they were men of simple judgment and "educated in an old and indelible custom" (94). Thus, Diodorus concludes, "in former times the Kings did obey the priests, not as mastered by force and arms, but as having their reason mastered by superstition" (94). Mind mastery and custom are sources of power sharply distinct from the capacity to employ force.[75]

## The Source and Limits of Power

Power belongs to those who can plausibly threaten to crush rivals by physical force as well as to those who master opinion by rhetoric and fraud. But it also flows, according to Hobbes, toward those who can plausibly threaten to withdraw their cooperation when it is most in need. The theory of power implicit in *Behemoth* is complex. Hobbes's insistence that rulers must be "skilful in the public affairs" (70) certainly implies that no one can rule by monopolizing force alone. Kings need cooperation and cannot afford to ignore the reasonable and unreasonable requests of their most important collaborators. In particular, kings need "money, men, arms, fortified places, shipping, counsel, and military officers" (110) adequate to their political aims. Such resources cannot be wrung from subjects by force. The limited effectiveness of brute force is what Hobbes has in mind when he laments "that unlucky business of imposing upon the Scots, who were all Presbyterians, our book of Common-prayer" (28).[76] Acknowledging the independent causal efficacy of religious ideas, Hobbes stresses the self-defeating character of attempts to change people's minds by brutal means: "Suppression of doctrine does but unite and exasperate, that is, increase both the malice and power of them that have already believed them" (62). This is a stunning admission from a champion of unlimited sovereign power. Indeed, it sounds more like Locke than Hobbes.[77]

Regret about the prayer book episode, indeed, is the closest Hobbes comes to admitting, in a Lockean vein, that royal misgovernment or overreaching, rather than insubordination among miseducated subjects, led to the breakdown of authority. In the abstract, he was committed to the notion that the "private interest" of an absolute monarch automatically coincides with the interest of "the publique."[78] But this claim was historically implausible. The rebellion began not with Parliamentary disobedience but with a series of annoying royal coups. Charles I extorted money in unconventional ways from influential subjects and persecuted religious nonconformists. These arrogant actions alienated important individuals from his dynasty and barred his access to "the purses of the city of London" (2). In other words, unlimited power can be self-weakening and even self-destructive. When the Scots army invaded the country, Charles found himself all alone, literally helpless. As a result of his absolutist ambitions, the nation withdrew its cooperation, went on a tax strike. The King would have been more powerful if, having submitted himself to Parliamentary limitations, he could have counted on Parliamentary cooperation.

Hobbes admired the Romans for their capacity to win power through strategic concessions (33–34).[79] They gained obedience from newly conquered peoples by offering, not merely protection, but also citizenship, status, and the right to influence policy. By restricting their own arbitrary discretion, they gained useful cooperation and support. Limited power, they recognized, was more powerful than unlimited power. A flickering awareness of the self-defeating character of unconstrained authority helps explain an obscure sentence of the preface to *Leviathan* where Hobbes claims to advocate a middle way between "too great Liberty" and "too much Authority."[80] How can there be too much authority for Hobbes? Most commentators are unsure. But the answer may lie here: authority is excessive when it is self-defeating, when it undermines itself by alienating potential cooperators.[81]

This surprisingly liberal train of thought may also explain the surprising passage in *Behemoth* in which Hobbes categorically denies that all the commands of the sovereign can be considered laws. Laws are only those commands that attain a high level of generality, naming no names: "By disobeying Kings, we mean the disobeying of his laws, those his laws that were made before they were applied to any particular person" (51). A bill of attainder, by this standard, would not be a valid law. To his prohibition on retroactive laws,[82] Hobbes adds a clear affirmation of the person-office distinction: the sovereign "commands the people in general never but by a precedent law, and as a politic, not a natural person" (51). The requirement that laws be general and published in advance is an obvious limitation on the discretion of the King. But it is also useful as a means for winning cooperation, not merely compliance, from proud subjects.

## Gatekeeper-Priests

We are now in a position to answer more fully our question about the origins of clerical power. Priests insinuate themselves with the sick and the dying, bilking them of money in order to build religious houses. Before "women and men of weak judgment" (16), clergymen pose as magicians able to transform bread into Christ's flesh, claiming "at the hour of death to save their souls" (15). Similarly: "When they shall have made the people believe that the meanest of them can make the body of Christ; who is there that will not both show them reverence, and be liberal to them or to the Church, especially in the time of their sickness, when they think they make and bring unto them their Saviour?" (41). Ecclesiastics successfully present themselves as gatekeepers to heaven, as intermediaries between man and God. Such mind mastery pivots upon their *threat to withdraw cooperation* from those who would forgo eternal damnation and taste eternal bliss. Imagining what it would be like to confront churchmen holding the key to salvation, B exclaims: "For my part, it would have an effect on me, to make me think them gods, and to stand in awe of them as of God himself, if he were visibly present" (15). More crudely, if you believe you cannot be saved without a priest's help, you will probably do whatever he requests.[83]

Such subservience is based on emotion as well as opinion. The principal passion favoring Church authority is fear. But religious apprehension is distinct from the rational fear that induces obedience to a sovereign's laws. It is more like hysteria or, to use Hobbes's word, *anxiety.* Emotional turmoil afflicts an individual who is "over provident," that is, who "looks *too far* before him" and is irrationally obsessed with possible future calamity. Such a person is "gnawed on" by anxiety.[84] He suffers from a form of shrieking misery and near dementia especially easy for clerical merchants of repose to exploit.

## The Political Utility of Religious Fraud

Christianity is dangerous to the state. But it is "not in man's power to suppress the power of religion" (82).[85] *L'infâme* can never be *écrasé.* As a consequence, a prudent sovereign will attempt to monopolize the pretense of spiritual power along with the reality of physical force. He will attempt to become the Pope, or the head of the Church, in his own lands: *cuius religio, eius regio,* to reverse the common phrase. While subversive in the wrong hands, the ability to threaten damnation and interpret God's law can be tremendously useful if controlled exclusively by the King. For authority is more easily established by hocus-pocus than by a rational exchange of obedience for protection. Remember that the colossus on the frontispiece of *Leviathan,* bestowing his protection on a peaceful city, holds the secular sword in one hand and a bishop's crosier in the other. There is no question here of any separation between Church and State.[86] On the contrary, Hobbes's main intellectual target is "that seditious *distinction* and *division* between the power *spiritual* and *civil.*"[87] In a way, his life's work was a sustained attempt to obliterate this distinction, to erect a commonwealth that would be, as he explained in the subtitle to *Leviathan,* simultaneously ecclesiastical and civil.

Hobbes describes his peacekeeping state as a "mortal God." In this way, he hopes to divert religious piety away from Puritan sects, Presbyterian ministers, Anglican bishops, and, of course, the Pope. Popular reverence should be channeled exclusively toward national and centralized political authority. For the same reason, Hobbes calls the governor of the state "Gods Lieutenant,"[88] and describes the ascent from the state of nature to civil society as a welcome transition from *homo homini lupus* to *homo homini deus.* He rhetorically divinizes the state in order to strengthen its claims against rival authorities, especially religious ones.[89]

By wrapping himself in a religious mantle, in effect, a clever monarch can acquire divine legitimacy, can obtain the "reverence" (13) due to God's agent. If he can manage to make the content of religion "indisputable" (43) within his kingdom, he will have repulsed the main danger posed by religion to civil concord. As the noncelibate Pope or archbishop of England, he can have "the laws of England" read from the pulpits once a week (16). Following the Catholic Pope's example, he can use the universities as *his* Trojan horse, as a vehicle for indoctrinating his subjects into Hobbes's "science of *just* and *unjust*" (39).[90] An appeal to divine authorization, indeed, is essential for stable monarchy. Subjects who think "of this present life only" are almost impossible to control (54).

Hobbes obviously respects the papacy's no-translation policy. He nevertheless concedes that putting the Scriptures into the vernacular can prove useful to secular authority: "The reading of them is so profitable as not to be forbidden without great damage to [the people] and the commonwealth" (53). True, the Bible's disobedience passages can never be wholly eclipsed by its obedience passages. But the greatest source of anarchy is pride; and, as Pascal showed, there is no mythology more effective in attacking pride than the mythology of sin and redemption.[91] Society would certainly be more peaceful if both "glory" and "vengeance" could be reserved to God, as Scripture says they should be. It is no accident that Hobbes lifted his central metaphor, the state as the king of the children of pride, from the Bible. And his insistence that *inoboedientia* stems from *superbia* shows the degree to which he is indebted to an old Christian, even papal, tradition. If military training inculcates a willingness to "dare" (45) and even an eagerness to die with one's boots on, Christian training does the opposite. The notion that the last shall be first, that the meek shall inherit the earth, sedates the soul into "a quiet waiting for the coming again of our blessed Saviour" (58). So valuable is this unmanning or discouragement to the state, that the appalling risks of a book-based religion must be run.

According to Bacon, "It often falls out, that *Somewhat* is produced of *Nothing:* For Lies are sufficient to breed Opinion, and Opinion brings on Substance."[92] Hobbes emphatically concurs. Religion solves the problem of how to create political power in the first place, how a ruler can initially gain control over an armed retinue that will, in turn, enable him to impose his authority by force. Indeed, this is the central example of self-fulfilling prophecy in Hobbes's theory: if people believe you are an (immortal) god, you will be a (mortal) god. Power is based on nothing more substantial than a "reputation" for power (95). Fiction becomes reality. If you can cajole people into believing that you have power, you *will* have power.[93] Authority cannot be stably based on either reason or force. It depends, ultimately, on sleight of hand.[94] A social *creatio ex nihilo* presupposes the gullibility of most people. By a primitive bootstrapping operation, political institutions can be created even though no one possesses, at the outset, visible political resources. Thus priests have challenged the authority of secular rulers. Thus political society originally emerged from the war of all against all.

Hobbes hopes to confiscate the intangible power of religious fraud from dangerous clergymen and bestow it safely on the King. He therefore asserts that legal positivism should *not* be the official doctrine of the Crown. Indeed, the sovereign must pretend "that the civil laws are God's laws" (58). To admit that law is exclusively man-made is to expose its contingent or might-have-been-otherwise character to public view. The King can increase his power only if he conceals it to some degree. For one thing, less (apparent) power will provoke less (real) envy. Thus, the claim that *auctoritas non veritas facit legem,* that authority, not truth, makes the law, gives only a partial picture of Hobbes's approach to lawmaking power. When publicly professed, legal positivism implies precisely the kind of liberal responsibility and accountability for legislation that he hopes to avoid.

## Sexual Guilt

Like the Grand Inquisitor, Hobbes believes that "it is the desire of most men to bear rule" (193). But the inborn need to be told what to do can be powerfully reinforced by clever manipulation of circumstances. By spreading confusion and bitter disagreement, power seekers can create a pent-up need for a higher authority able to settle disputes by fiat. As Richelieu, Hobbes's onetime protector in France, purportedly said, "Le désordre fait partie de l'ordre." Occasional doses of anarchy will help remind subjects of why they should meekly obey their king.

Divisions can also be introduced *within* the person. You can increase an individual's distaste for autonomy and desire to be ruled by bifurcating his mind, making him feel nauseated at himself.[95] The traditional Christian ploy was to teach people that physical attraction to a member of the opposite sex, with no untoward action whatsoever, was a disgrace before God, that "the delight men and women took in the sight of one another's form" was "a sin" (26).[96] Thus, power-hungry ecclesiastics "brought young men into desperation and to think themselves damned, because they could not (which no man can, and is contrary to the constitution of nature) behold a delightful object without delight." By inducing guilt and self-hate, the clergy increased prodigiously the need for a rescuing authority: "By this means they became confessors to such as were thus troubled in conscience, and were obeyed by them as their spiritual doctors in all cases of conscience" (26). The mechanism here is partly this: inner divisions make you feel disoriented, unable to govern your own actions, and therefore in need of authoritative instruction to get you through the day. When you feel faint, you reach dizzily for a crutch. But the psychological dependency created in this way can also be interpreted in a more rationalistic vein, as an extremely subtle version of the obedience-for-protection exchange, assuming rational advantage seeking on everyone's part. The Christian clergy implants a fictive danger in the minds of the people, the danger of burning in hell for experiencing creaturely desire. After inculcating a sense of peril, they sell their protection from this phantom threat for the price of total obedience. That, at least, might be a rational-choice reconstruction of the opium of the people.[97]

## Conclusion

*Behemoth* represents Hobbes's mature understanding of political breakdown and the reconsolidation of authority. This time his theory of "human nature in general" (29) is not filtered through a set of political recommendations. It is expressed in a description, not of the way human beings might behave under imaginary or ideal conditions, but of the way they actually did behave in England between 1640 and 1660. Not surprisingly, an anatomy of disorder is more realistic than a blueprint for order. Particularly noteworthy is *Behemoth*'s fine-grained account of human motivation. True, the psychological assumptions inspiring its historical narrative are ultimately indistinguishable from those expounded almost two decades earlier, in *Leviathan*. But they are illustrated with greater concreteness and color. Thus, the later work still makes an invaluable contribution to our understanding of both Hobbes and his liberal successors. The general impression left by his dialogues on the civil war is that many human beings are, first of all, incapable of calculative reasoning and, second, doltishly indifferent to self-preservation. Human behavior is largely determined by beliefs, and most beliefs are irrational, even absurd. Religion is the most obvious example. Herein lies the second main theoretical achievement of *Behemoth*. The all-importance of religion in Hobbes's theory is displayed more clearly here than in any other work. We see in picturesque detail why religion is both an irrepressible danger and an indispensable resource for the peacekeeping state. Every reader of

*Leviathan,* perplexed by the sheer bulk of parts 3 and 4, has asked, why is religion such an obsession for Hobbes? Readers of *Behemoth* know the answer: because the minds of human beings will never be freed from discombobulating passions and intoxicating doctrines, norms that mesmerize and names that slander or beguile.

# 4

# The Constitution of Sovereignty in Jean Bodin

*On a commencé à se guérir du machiavélisme, et on s'en guérira tous les jours.*

—MONTESQUIEU

Not unlike Hobbes, Jean Bodin is a preliberal and nondemocratic theorist, whose writings repay careful study by students of liberal and democratic politics. Admittedly, a chapter on Bodin seems even more out of place in a book on the theoretical foundations of liberal democracy than a chapter on Hobbes. But the incongruity is intentional. A reading of Bodin can help us upend some of the most well-established conventions of liberal historiography. As Hobbes sheds new light upon liberal thinking about the passions, so Bodin illuminates, in an unexpected way, the liberal theory of constitutional constraint.

Liberal democracy presupposes the existence of the state. The core norms of equality before the law and majority rule cannot be put into practice until territorial borders have been firmly established and the question of who is a member of the community has been clearly answered. In short, philosophers of liberalism must take elementary processes of state building for granted. This is obvious, in a way, for no nation can become liberal unless it is already a nation. The ideal of limited government will never have much popular appeal, moreover, unless political authority has already managed to secure a minimum of social order and protection from mutual violence. For this and other reasons, liberalism cannot be plausibly understood as an ideology deeply opposed to historical processes of centralization and state building. Even the liberals most fearful of tyranny acknowledged the utility of a consolidated state. As Alexis de Tocqueville remarked, "For my part, I cannot conceive that a nation can live, much less prosper, without a high degree of centralization of government."[1] Once we see Tocqueville's point here and recognize that liberal rights themselves are dependent for their enforcement on consolidated statehood and concentrated political capacities, we should be open to the paradoxical thought that preliberal theorists of "absolutism," such as Bodin, might be more relevant to the evolution of liberal democracy than has conventionally been assumed.

Allegedly an unflinching advocate of autocratic power, Bodin turns out to have been a subtle theorist of the art of indirect rule. Most importantly, he understood, well before any liberals had appeared on the scene, that "unlimited" power is often crudely ineffective for achieving desirable objectives, not to mention being personally dangerous to its wielders. Later on, this counterintuitive line of argument became a central tenet of liberal thinkers such as Montesquieu, who were naturally eager to stress the graspable political advantages, not merely the laudable moral superiority, of constitutional regimes.

That a sixteenth-century exponent of absolute monarchy had something essential to teach seventeenth- and eighteenth-century liberals may still seem fairly implausible. But it begins to make more sense when we reflect on the central political problem of Bodin's time: religious civil war. The desire to eliminate or subdue bigoted fundamentalists and cruel fanatics was to remain just as strong among liberals as it had been earlier among the proponents of strong centralized states. Indeed, the idea that the liberal state should establish social peace by enforcing an attitude of "neutrality" toward conflicting moral ideals can be traced back to various étatist theorists, Bodin among them, who struggled to find a solution to the wars of religion that ravaged France between 1562 and 1598. It is not altogether surprising, therefore, that a rationale for religious toleration which eventually became indispensable to liberals was already formulated with brilliant clarity by a sixteenth-century monarchist. But Bodin's central contribution to liberalism was even greater than a focus on tolerance alone would suggest. He framed and popularized a practical argument in favor of constitutional limitations on power. By studying the roots of liberal constitutionalism in his thought, therefore, we can avoid repeating and reinforcing one of the most common blunders of constitutional theory. I have in mind the view that the primary or even sole purpose of a constitution is to secure individual liberty by hamstringing the government and its agents.

What this *negative constitutionalism* neglects is that a constitution also creates institutions, assigns responsibilities, inculcates aims, and makes a country governable. Bodin, of course, is essentially concerned with the construction of a strong monarchy, capable of dealing effectively with the problems of religious civil war. Limited government he accepts as a means to this end. His constitutionalism, such as it is, is explicitly designed to strengthen the state. By tracing out his argument in some detail, we can prepare ourselves to see the constitutionalism of his liberal successors in a similar light. Better than any other theorist, Mill aside, Bodin teaches us the attraction and persuasiveness of *positive constitutionalism*. This is a vital lesson, for the idea that state capacities can be sharply increased by strategic limitations on power turns out to be a fundamental premise of liberal-democratic thought.

## Toleration and *Raison d'état*

Generalizing from the English and American cases, political theorists conventionally assume that liberal ideals initially emerged in a struggle against the politics of absolutism. Rights, they tend to think, are shackles imposed upon a restive sovereign. The relation between power and freedom, however, was never so unequivocally antagonistic as the legendary account makes it appear. In crucial cases, rights (including modern property rights) were created and maintained by the state to promote the goals of the state. The slow and irregular advance of religious freedom, in particular, was inextricably entwined with the consolidation of dynastic rule, especially in France. The subsequent conflict between liberalism and absolutism should not be allowed to obscure their common filiation in this respect. By the 1570s, a disjunction of temporal and spiritual domains was already being advocated as a technique for strengthening the sway of secular rulers over nonreligious matters. Privatization of religious disputes or the withdrawal of public officials from theological controversies was widely acclaimed as sovereignty enhancing. Important theorists urged the government to steer clear of "the religious thicket," to speak anachronistically, in order to augment effectiveness and credibility in other domains. With benefit of hindsight, a cynic might even claim that the cause of religious toleration succeeded chiefly because it proved advantageous to power wielders, humane respect for rights of conscience providing little more than a fig leaf of morality for an otherwise self-interested policy. Be this as it may, advocates of toleration were prudently solicitous of political authorities. As a result, they placed uncommon emphasis on the state-building function of the depoliticization of religion.

Accustomed by historical accident to an alliance between toleration and antiroyalism, American scholars tend to slight the decisive role played by absolutism in establishing, throughout Europe, a taken-for-granted separation of religious and political domains. French political theory provides a useful corrective here because so many of its major representatives presuppose a mutually supportive relation between state power and individual freedom. To mention a very late instance:

Émile Durkheim argued forcefully that the modern state, far from being an implacable enemy of individual rights, actually created and sustained such rights by dissolving the oppressive "communal" bonds of clan, castle, sect, and parochial village.[2] In advancing this argument, which may seem paradoxical to Americans, Durkheim was simply reiterating a central tenet of French political theory: liberty and sovereignty, far from being hostile alternatives, can enliven and reinforce one another.[3] An important variation on this general theme is the hypothesis of a mutually supporting relation between public authority and the privatization of religion. To reconstruct the arguments that were originally adduced to bolster this thesis, we can do no better than to examine Bodin's *Les six livres de la république* (1576), written to support state authority on the one hand and the toleration of sectarian diversity on the other.[4] Before turning directly to the *République*'s discussion of religion, however, we must pause to introduce Bodin's theory of sovereign power.

## The Bodin Problem

Sovereignty is "the most high, absolute, and perpetual power over the citizens and subjects of a commonweal." It is quite simply "the greatest power to command" (I, 8, 84). This superiority, Bodin adds, is not merely relative but absolute: "It behooveth him that is sovereign not to be in any sort subject to the command of another" (I, 8, 91). Terrible concentration of power is justified as the one acceptable alternative to religious civil war. Mutual butchery of citizens was Bodin's *summum malum,* the uttermost evil, to be avoided at all costs. In a pagan phrase, he defines "civil war" as "the only poison to make empires and states mortal, which else would be immortal" (V, 5, 602). An absolute sovereign alone can put an end to the fratricide devastating France since the early 1560s.

His pronouncements about authority have established Bodin's reputation as a self-appointed spokesman for centralizing monarchs who "put to sleep" representative bodies inherited from the Middle Ages, rejected Papal pretentions to a universal monarchy, and eventually drew into their own hands the scattered fragments of medieval political power. Absolute sovereigns, as Bodin described and admired them, were both internally supreme and externally independent. These two characteristics were complementary sides of the same coin, for a king typically had to assert his authority against unruly forces, such as the Catholic League, which were simultaneously localist and internationalist.

When Bodin contends that "the marks of sovereignty are indivisible," he is not making the merely conceptual point that, by definition, sovereignty ceases to be sovereignty once it is divided. Rather, he is advancing a causal generalization about the viability of divided political institutions. For example: "Where the rights of sovereignty are divided betwixt the prince and his subjects: in that condition of the state, there are still endless stirs and quarrels for the superiority, until some one, some few, or all together have got the sovereignty" (II, I, 194). Or again: states in which lawmaking authority is divided "find no rest from civil wars and broils, until they again recover some one of the three forms," that is, until they settle down as either democracies, aristocracies, or monarchies (II, I, 195). Far from being definitionally impossible, divided sovereignty episodically crops up; but whenever it does, it always proves radically unstable.[5]

Bodin carries this argument to its logical conclusion and thus subverts his own assertion that sovereign power can be stably located in either one, a few, or the majority. He ends up alleging, in fact, that a monarch alone can be an effective sovereign: "The chief point of a commonweal, which is the right of sovereignty, cannot be, nor subsist (to speak properly) but in a monarchy: for none can be sovereign in a commonweal but one alone" (VI, 4, 715). His fundamental premise, here and throughout, is that a powerful king is best equipped to prevent the sedition, faction, and civil war that are perpetual threats to every commonwealth and that have become particularly perilous to France during the Catholic-Huguenot struggles. Because of this general line of argument, the *République* is usually, and not unjustly, described as an early statement of the absolutist political program.

Partly accurate, this interpretation is nevertheless incomplete. For one thing, Bodin appears to be a traditionalist as well as an innovator. Alongside his advocacy of radically centralized sovereignty, we find him praising, or seeming to praise, institutions usually associated with the ancient "polity of estates." True, as his reputation would lead us to expect, he repeatedly emphasizes that obedience to the sovereign is not based on consent: "We see the principal point of sovereign majesty, and absolute power, to consist principally in giving laws unto the subjects in general, without their consent" (I, 8, 98).[6] Because it may be whimsically or unpredictably withdrawn by the king's subjects, especially by his nobles, "consent" provides a rickety foundation for political authority. Moreover, if subjects have discordant aims, consent-based authority will be paralyzed or fall into conflict with itself. Hence, every effective sovereign is and must be an independent, uninfluenced, uncommanded commander.

At least Bodin sometimes argues this way. At other times, he forcefully stresses the quid pro quo arrangement whereby, to use Hobbesian language, subjects voluntarily offer obedience in exchange for protection (I, 7, 60). In the relevant passages, he writes unambiguously that the duties of princes are just as binding as the duties of subjects: "As the subject oweth unto his lord all duty, aid, and obedience; so the prince also oweth unto his subjects justice, guard, and protection: so that the subjects are no more bound to obey the prince, than is the prince to administer unto them justice" (IV, 6, 500). The prince too, therefore, has unbreakable obligations; while legally unaccountable, he is nevertheless duty-bound. But what does Bodin mean here? How can an uncommanded commander nevertheless be subject to political obligations? How is this seeming inconsistency to be resolved?

The tension here is pivotal and crucially relevant to Bodin's justification of religious toleration, as we shall see. To cite another case: Bodin avows that the sovereign is at once above the law and subject to the law, that "the prince is acquitted from the power of the laws" and that "all princes of the earth are subject unto the laws of God, of nature, and of nations" (I, 8, 91 and 90). Here Bodin appears to use the word law equivocally, referring to man-made law in one case and natural law in another. But we must not erase the verbal contradiction too hastily. Indeed, the drama of Bodin's position lies precisely here, in his systematic oscillation between two not quite compatible claims.

A sovereign is above the law because he makes the law. Indeed, "the law is nothing else but the commandment of a sovereign, using his sovereign power" (I, 8, 108). A command theory of law is therefore built into the foundations of Bodin's concept of sovereignty: "Under this same sovereignty of power for the giving and abrogating of the law are comprised all the other rights and marks of sovereignty, so that (to speak properly) a man may say, that [legislative power is the] only mark of sovereign power, considering that all the other rights thereof are contained in this, viz., to have power to give laws unto all and every onc of the subjects and to receive none from them" (I, 10, 161–62). Most striking is Bodin's radical claim that a law acquires its validity solely from its source rather than from its content. Even if a law corresponds to reason, it is valid only because it is promulgated by the proper authority: "The laws of a sovereign prince, although they be grounded upon good and lively reasons, depend nevertheless upon nothing but his mere and frank good will" (I, 8, 92). This is pure voluntarism, *voluntas non veritas facit legem,* a doctrine explicitly tailored to the needs of a faction-riven society, where irresolvable controversies rage about what "reason" itself demands. The "justice" of any law is open to dispute, particularly if citizens cultivate inconsistent religious beliefs. On the other hand, even implacably hostile groups (and moral skeptics as well) can be brought to admit that a law has been officially promulgated by a de facto sovereign. Thus, it has sometimes been argued that legal positivism first emerged as a strategy for stabilizing the ship of state in the tumult of religious war.[7] This can certainly be said of Bodin's attempt to locate legitimacy in the easily identifiable source, rather than the infinitely disputable content, of law.

## The Limits on Sovereign Power

Sovereignty is strictly unconditional. Rather than law governing authority, authority establishes law. The king is *absolutus,* utterly absolved from legal accountability. He is unrestricted by custom, the consent of subjects, or even his own laws. These assertions are radical and striking, as Bodin meant them to be. But they are also partial. Throughout the *République,* every such assertion is balanced by a reassuring counterclaim. Sovereignty is conditional, limited, accountable, and surprisingly unfree. Bodin's unbound sovereign is restricted in a number of ways.

First, as already mentioned, the sovereign is limited by divine and natural law. Bodin emphatically denies that "the laws of sovereign princes alter or change the laws of God and nature" (I, 8, 104). Indeed, Bodin upbraids courtiers who accentuate the legally unconditional status of the sovereign: "They that generally say that princes are not subject unto laws nor to their own conventions, if they except not the laws of God and nature, and the just contracts and conventions made with them, they do great wrong both unto God and nature" (I, 8, 104). True, Bodin does not assign to any earthly agency the power to enforce divine and natural law upon a reigning sovereign. But his stress on the total subjection of sovereign princes to a higher law is much too relentless to be treated as marginal or secondary. The laws of God and nature are essential to his theory of political sovereignty. But what are these laws of nature? How do we recognize them? What sort of binding force do they have? And why should a wholly unfettered prince, subject to no one's command, acquiesce in such irksome restraints?

Bodin additionally insists that his unbound sovereign is nevertheless bound fast by the constitutional rules of the kingdom, the wholly secular *leges imperii* or *lois royales.* Like later constitutional theorists, he draws a sharp distinction between "laws concerning ordinary police" and higher laws "such as concern the very state itself." The latter, unlike the former, should be exceptionally "firm and immutable" (IV, 3, 471). Acting within a framework of such presumably unchangeable rules, the sovereign must passively submit, first of all, to the tradition of passing the crown to a male heir: "Touching the laws which concern the state of the realm, and the establishing thereof; for as much as they are annexed and united to the crown, the prince cannot derogate from them, such as is the law Salique" (I, 8, 95). Even absolute power is powerless in some respects. The prince's word may be law; but he dare not freely choose his own successor.

Despite the unboundness of sovereignty, similarly, the prince is explicitly barred from treating the royal domain as conveyable private property: "It is certain by the edict and laws concerning the public domain, that it is not to be alienated" (I, 10, 182). The fundamental principles of French monarchy prohibit the king from whimsically shedding parts of the kingdom. Such "higher laws" are quite unlike the commands of a sovereign. Indeed, they are commands to which the sovereign must submit. The domain lands belong to the commonwealth and cannot be sold—certainly not by an act of royal will and without the consent of the Estates.

Similarly, while the king is allowed to make laws without consent, he is forbidden to levy taxes without consent. "It is not in the power of any prince in the world, at his pleasure to raise taxes upon the people, no more than to take another man's goods from him" (I, 8, 97). This is a remarkably "liberal" assertion, suggesting Bodin's departure from the absolutist party line, articulated more consistently, in this case, by Hobbes. The Estates have the right to decline subsidies. The subversively constitutionalist flavor of this arrangement is emphasized by Bodin's reference to Philippe de Commynes who, earlier in the century, had been imprisoned by the crown for making a similarly seditious suggestion. Bodin is scathing about writers who incite the king to impose taxes without consent. This, he claims, "is as much as if they should say it to be lawful for them to rob and spoil their subjects, oppressed by force of arms; which law, the more mighty use against them that be weaker than themselves, which the Germans must rightly call the law of thieves and robbers" (I, 8, 109). In passages such as these, which seventeenth- and eighteenth-century writers took up and expanded into a liberal theory of the taxing power and its limits, Bodin the royalist echoes the language of antiroyalism.

Furthermore, while "the prince is not subject to his law, nor to the laws of his predecessors," he is nevertheless subject "to his own just and reasonable conventions, and in the observation whereof the subjects in general or particular have interest" (I, 8, 92). The sovereign is especially bound, says Bodin, by covenants issued not of his own free will but rather at the request of his subjects.

It is not wholly correct to say that Bodin empowers no worldly agency to enforce limits such as these upon the king. The legally recognized power of the Estates to refuse subsidies is an obvious counterexample. Note also that the magistrate is not bound "to obey or put into execution the prince's commands in things unjust and dishonest" (III, 4, 312). Moreover, when Bodin asks whether a magistrate may resign rather than enforce a law perceived to be unjust, he answers that such a magistrate *can* resign if a majority of his fellow magistrates agree that the law in question violates natural equity (III, 4, 316). Bodin does not elaborate on this modest mechanism for political protest; but one implication might be that a majority of dissenting magistrates could justly resign as a body. If they did this, however, the king would have no means for enforcing his own laws. So here, too, as in the case of the right of the Estates to refuse subsidies, Bodin may perhaps be granting de facto veto power to men operating independently of royal control.

Here, in short, is a philological and theoretical puzzle: Bodin describes his sovereign as both bound and unbound.[8] This seeming contradiction presents a genuine mystery. And scholars have adopted a variety of attitudes toward it. Some commentators simply declare Bodin to be inconsistent, arguing that he negligently combines the old and the new, medieval constitutionalism with modern absolutism, without making any serious effort at synthesis.[9] Others skirt the problem, suggesting that in the *République*, "the rights of absolute sovereignty must always be tempered by the laws of nature."[10] While true, this analysis does not go very far. Why is sovereignty tempered by higher law? And what is the force of such a limit? Can a sovereign still be sovereign if his power is shackled in this way? Nannerl Keohane does better, advancing the intriguing claim that the "limits" on sovereign power are "most accurately understood as conditions for its exercise."[11] Unfortunately, after introducing this promising suggestion, she leaves it undeveloped. While endorsing the commonplace notion of Bodin's basic "inconsistency," Julian Franklin, too, suggests *en passant* that Bodin embraced limitations on state power as techniques for enhancing state power.[12] John Plamenatz provides the most convincing, though still offhand, assessment along these lines. Bodin, he wrote, "appears more inconsistent than in fact he was. He thought it dangerous to allow that anyone had a legal right to set a limit to royal authority, but he knew that the king could not rule efficiently without devices to retard his actions."[13] In my view, this lucid paradox explains both the underlying unity of the *République* and its vital importance to the political theory of liberal democracy.

## Sovereignty-Reinforcing Restraints

The *République* is a diffuse and slippery work. Its fundamental argument, however, can be restated with some precision. To approach the book as a coherent set of doctrines, we must first notice that Bodin is chronically addicted to paradoxes. He amusingly stresses, for example, both the advantages of deprivation and the disadvantages of overendowment. Echoing classical sources, he notes that "men of a fat and fertile soil, are most commonly effeminate and cowards; whereas contrariwise a barren country makes men temperate by necessity, and by consequence careful, vigilant, and industrious" (V, 1, 565). And this observation about fertility of soil is juxtaposed to another about superior intelligence: "The Florentines in their assemblies spoil all through the subtlety of their wits" (V, 1, 563). In any case, a relish for paradox, most notable in Bodin's illustrations and asides, also inspires his argument about sovereignty. His basic idea, and the key to his importance for us, is that limited power is more powerful than unlimited power. Restraints strengthen. By closing off some options, a ruler can open up others. A king cannot rule effectively without devices to *retard* his action. Formulated somewhat differently, under certain circumstances, legal and institutional rigidities produce political and social flexibilities.

Bodin is far from being a pure decisionist or voluntarist. But neither is he a traditional moralist or pious exponent of natural law. To comprehend the uncommon structure of his argument, we must first set aside our intuitive sense that restrictions inhibit. Limitations may facilitate as well as cripple. Indeed, limits can well be enabling because they are disabling. Consider grammar. Rules governing the use of language cannot be adequately conceived as pure prohibitions on, or obstacles to, speech. By submitting ourselves to constraints, we gain the capacity to do many things we would otherwise never be able to do. Rules of grammar, in fact, are possibility-creating rules and therefore cannot be accurately described as manacles clamped upon a preexistent freedom.[14]

Bodin's massive treatise is much too sprawling and loose-knit to be exhaustively summarized in any compact thesis. Nevertheless, this argument does stand out: laws of nature, laws of succession, nonalienability of domain lands, immemorial customs, a prohibition on taxation without consultation, and the informal prerogatives of parlements and Estates can substantially *increase* the power of a prince. Bodin treats restrictions on power, unconventionally, as a set of authority-reinforcing, will-empowering, and possibility-expanding rules. Meinecke was therefore quite right to describe him as a premier exponent of anti-Machiavellian *raison d'état*.[15]

To deal with the problem of religious civil war, Bodin argues that law is valid solely when promulgated by an authority with the right to make it. As a *raison d'état* theorist, however, Bodin had to confront the question, How can the right to rule be transformed into the capacity to rule? While a "positivist" strategy might stifle disputes about which laws deserve obedience, it raises other difficulties, particularly the problem of getting the laws obeyed in practice. Because he was concerned with this practical dilemma, rather than the scholastic issue of legal right, Bodin turned his attention to strategically designed limitations on supreme power. By allowing his power to be restricted in certain specific ways, a sovereign increases the likelihood of social compliance with his wishes. This bargain explains how he can become a sovereign in fact as well as in law. But how can the wielder of the highest authority be *compelled* to compel himself? A monarch accustomed to thinking of himself as all-powerful will certainly attempt to prevent his subjects from acting unjustly and destroying the peace. But will he permit others to supervise and discipline him in the same way? The challenge Bodin faced, in other words, was to devise a method for persuading the king to accept informally enforceable constraints on royal authority. His solution was to redescribe traditional limits on royal power as conditions for the successful exercise of royal power. Successful does not mean just, or right, or in accord with God's law, but simply capable of preventing civil war and keeping domestic peace. The laws of the realm, for instance, did not destroy, but rather enhanced, the advantages of radically centralized royal power.

Bodin sought to reconceptualize traditional restraints as *instruments* of princely authority. As a result, he was not, as many commentators suggest, an imperfect Hobbes who spoiled his otherwise modern doctrine of sovereignty by a vestigial medievalism. Bodin's doctrine of natural law, for example, is designed to be just as attractive to an unvirtuous as to a virtuous prince. The pessimistic assumption that enlightened statesmen will *not* always be at the helm is historically well grounded because "there have been but few princes for their virtues famous" (IV, 1, 414). Arguing in a way that Madison would later make famous, Bodin adds that "fear" is "the only controller of virtue" (V, 5, 603), more reliable than either moral or religious motives. Accepting this rather pessimistic premise, he focuses almost exclusively on rules that would be self-enforcing, which presuppose no motive nobler than the self-interest of the prince. He also concentrates on de facto diffusion of power: "There is nothing more true, than what was spoken by Brutus the Tribune of the people unto the nobility of Rome, that there was one only assurance for the weak against the mighty, which was that if the mighty would, they could not hurt them: for that ambitious men that have power over another, never want will" (V, 6, 619). The only power wielder who will refrain from abusing his power and brutalizing the vulnerable is the power wielder whose capacity for control is factually limited. Fortunately, institutional arrangements, building upon a series of socially prominent sources of nonprincely power, can make it difficult for the nominally all-powerful sovereign to misuse his position. A prudent sovereign will relinquish some of his power voluntarily when he learns, from Bodin and others, that limitations placed upon his caprice markedly increase his capacity to govern and to achieve his steady aims.

Earlier exponents of natural law had periodically drawn attention to the political advantages of moral self-restraint.[16] But Bodin focuses almost exclusively on the secular side-effects of the prince's virtues. True, the suggestion that he "secularized" natural law to make it appealing even to princes of low moral character confronts an obvious objection. Seemingly sincere references to God's will abound throughout the *République*. This is disturbing counterevidence, but not decisive. For one thing, Bodin also says that "it is better to have an evil commonwealth than none at all" (IV, 3, 469). Furthermore, even "the tyrant," he insists, is in some sense "a sovereign" (I, 8, 87). Tyrants frequently violate justice. But Bodin acknowledges their sovereignty because, stated brutally, oppression is preferable to civil war. Avoidance of civil war is primarily a secular goal, even though it may be incidentally good for religion and pleasing to God. Preventing subjects from slaughtering one another is the immediate worldly purpose of all political authority. The goal of this-worldly civil peace takes precedence over all rival aims, including the most inspiring religious objectives.

Bodin's main argument, once again, is structured to convince unvirtuous rulers that submitting to natural law and other restraints has significant strategic advantages. If a sovereign breaks his word too often and too frivolously, for example, his word will become useless as a tool for mobilizing cooperation. Activity and passivity, influence and adaptation, are not mutually exclusive. Only by adapting to nature can a prince exert power over it (V, 1, 545, 558, 564). To arrive at the port of his choice, a pilot must not imperiously flout natural limits, but must instead "yield unto the tempest" (VI, 4, 720) and learn how to ride out the storm. Similarly, by adapting compliantly to his subjects' habits and beliefs, the prince can increase his ability to influence their behavior. In the preface to the first edition, Bodin attacks Machiavelli for having taught that commonwealths could be stably founded on injustice (A70). To refute this crude Machiavellianism, Bodin points to the political harvest that can be reaped by a prince who respects various limitations on his own power.[17] He even redefines natural law as a set of prudential maxims for avoiding revolution. In general, "a commonweal grounded upon good laws, well united and joined in all the members thereof, easily suffers not alteration: as also to the contrary we see some states and commonweals so evil built and set together, as that they owe their fall and ruin unto the first wind that bloweth or tempest that ariseth" (IV, 1, 434). A tyrant may be a sovereign; but his position is precarious. Cruel princes "hazard their whole states" (III, 7, 373). A tyrant is always terrified: "If he be cruel, he will stand in fear that some one in so great a multitude will take revenge" (VI, 4, 721). Tyrannicide will occur, whether it is legally allowed or disallowed. Constitutional prohibitions on the right of violent resistance are but parchment barriers. By contrast:

> Fear I say of death, of infamy, and of torture: these be the revenging furies which continually vex tyrants, and with eternal terrors torment them both night and day: then envy, suspicion, fear, desire of revenge, with a thousand contrary passions at variance among themselves, do so disquiet their minds, and more cruelly tyrannize over them, than they themselves can over their slaves, with all the torments they can devise. (II, 5, 226)

Tyrants are not punished in the afterlife alone, but also in the here-and-now. The terrible laws of assassination and revolution, which can be rechristened laws of nature, provide a this-worldly seat of judgment. Such dangers are emphasized by Bodin to help rulers focus their minds apprehensively and to provide them with a keen incentive to embrace voluntarily some form of limited rule.

All temporal jurisdiction belongs to the sovereign—all temporal jurisdiction, that is, except for paternal power. At first, Bodin's proposal to delegate some of the prince's authority to the head of the domestic household seems surprising, for "the last and highest degree [of authority] is of such as have the absolute power of life and death; that is to say, power to condemn to death, and again to give life unto him which hath deserved to die; which is the highest mark of sovereignty . . . proper only unto sovereignty" (III, 5, 326–27). But despite

Bodin's avowal that "the marks of sovereignty are indivisible," he makes an exception in this case: "It is needful in a well-ordered commonweal to restore unto parents the power of life and death over their children" (I, 4, 22). But why should the prince divest himself of a crucial mark of sovereignty, the monopoly on punishment by death? Bodin's answer is that, by so doing, the king will be better able, in the long run, to exact obedience from his subjects: "Domestical justice and power of fathers [are] the most sure and firm foundation of laws, honor, virtue, piety, wherewith a commonweal ought to flourish" (I, 4, 23). Here we have a clear case of relinquishing power to gain power: *reculer pour mieux sauter.* If you retreat one step, you can bound two steps forward. Governance is eased by a sharing of burdens. Authority is strengthened when its jurisdiction is narrowed. The public realm becomes easier to govern if some issues are removed from the public agenda. This pattern of argument reappears countless times throughout the *République.* That it forms the centerpiece of Bodin's argument for religious toleration will not, therefore, be altogether surprising.

## The Self-Binding of the Sovereign

Having documented Bodin's concern to place limits on royal authority, we can now return to the prohibition Bodin ostensibly places upon royal self-binding. In his chapter "Of Sovereignty," he writes: "If then the sovereign prince be exempted from the laws of his predecessors, much less should he be bound unto the laws and ordinances he maketh himself; for a man may well receive a law from another man, but impossible it is in nature for [him] to give a law unto himself, no more than it is to command a man's self in a matter depending of his own will" (I, 8, 91–92). This argument is significant, not least of all because of its subsequent history, discussed at length in chapter 5. Thomas Jefferson, among others, took up Bodin's proposition and applied it to the democratic sovereignty of the people.[18] In the course of the *République,* however, initial objections to binding precommitments are severely qualified. Ultimately, Bodin comes closer to Madison, who fiercely defended constitutional precommitment, than to Jefferson, who attacked it. To understand how Bodin accomplishes this reversal, we must discover the purpose he believes served by an injunction against monarchical self-binding.

A prohibition upon self-binding is itself a restriction on the king's freedom of action. This is only logical. To be free in some respects, a king must be unfree in others. For example, the king cannot refuse in advance to hear the complaints of his subjects: "The prince cannot so bind his own hands, or make such a law unto himself [to] prohibit his grieved subjects from coming unto him with their humble supplications and requests" (I, 10, 169). Once he has heard a complaint, the prince can legally do as he wishes; but he *cannot* refuse to listen beforehand because this would be an act of self-destruction, a relinquishing of supreme power to decide what to do.

More profound than the self-binding taboo, and underlying it, therefore, is the self-destruction taboo. Self-binding is illicit when it entails a diminution of royal power. For the same reason, self-binding is permissible and even obligatory when it helps maintain or increase royal power. If the king can retain or extend his authority only by tying his hands, then tie his own hands he must. The sovereign "ought to take away all occasion of discontentment that men might have against him; and better means is there none, than to leave all that may be to the disposition of the laws and customs, no man having just cause to complain of the prince" (IV, 4, 490). Abdication of power is not always an infringement of the prince's will. It can also be a technique for ducking odious responsibilities, insulating oneself against opposition, and asserting one's will.

A concrete example occurs in Bodin's discussion of coinage. One of the main powers of the sovereign, he says, is to "appoint the value, weight, and strength of the coin" (I, 10, 175). But this, too, is a right that the king must never exercise, for his own good: "The prince may not make any false money, no more than he may kill or rob, neither can he alter the weight of his coin to the prejudice of his subjects, and much less of strangers, which treat with him, and traffic with his people, for that he is subject to the law of nations, unless he will lose the name and majesty of a king" (VI, 3, 687). This is a perfect illustration of a self-enforcing restriction on royal whim. To have power, that is, to achieve his objectives, a king must cultivate a reputation for trustworthiness, and this requires him to play by the rules. Public credit is a vital resource for the crown. By committing himself in advance to coins of fixed value, the king can successfully resist pressures to depreciate, cultivate the confidence of creditors, and retain better control of the economy in general.

Self-binding is an effective technique for indirectly increasing one's power. Once we have grasped this paradox, we will have no trouble explaining how Bodin can both advocate absolute sovereignty and argue that a commonwealth "should by laws, and not by the prince's will and pleasure, be governed" (IV, 4, 490). After all, there are only twenty-four hours in a sovereign's day. General laws are much less time-consuming and yield greater return per unit of effort than particular proclamations and decrees. A king is not legally obliged to lay down general rules and obey them, but if he has an iota of political sense, he will do so (IV, 4, 486). An utterly self-interested prince, if he sees clearly, will make numerous prudential concessions to his subjects, whose willing cooperation he needs. The sovereign aristocracy of Venice provides a revealing example. Their willingness to relinquish small bits of privilege and power was neither altruistic, nor pious, nor required by law: "The Venetians, to maintain their Aristocratical estate, impart some small offices unto the people, contract alliances with them, borrow of them to bind them to the maintenance of the state; and disarm them quite: and to make them more mild and pliable, they give them full scope and liberty to all sorts of pleasures: and sometimes they make their rich citizens burgesses" (VI, 4, 711). Voluntary sharing of privilege and power is neither legally nor morally required. But it is a shrewd political bargain negotiated in order to win useful and necessary cooperation.

Constitutions are bargains. Even absolute kings, usually considered the archenemies of constitutionalism, can see the advantage of striking a deal with potential troublemakers. The slyly manipulative strategy of the Venetian oligarchy included disarming the common citizenry and, more subtly, making them creditors to give them a personal stake in the state's stability. The freedoms and minor powers they devolved upon the commoners, in any case, were justified as serving the interests of the sovereign. This, to repeat, is the central paradox of Bodin's theory of sovereignty: less power is more power. He says it explicitly in what I take to be the key sentence in the *République:* "The less the power of the sovereign is (the true marks of majesty thereunto still reserved) the more it is assured" (IV, 6, 517). In other words, by limiting himself, the sovereign is able to preserve and even strengthen himself. By decreasing his power to command his subjects arbitrarily, he increases his capacity to achieve his concrete goals.

The *République* endorses all strategies for maintaining and increasing royal power, for royal power is the sole guarantor of civil peace. The political demand to maintain such centralized control overrides legal taboos against succumbing to limitations on monarchical authority. Traditional prohibitions against alienating the domain lands fit perfectly into this pattern. The force behind these restrictions does not derive from any conventional moral precept, such as: *regnum non est dominium,* or "the goods of the community must not be treated as if they were the prince's private property." Rather, selling the domain is impermissible for the hardheaded reason that it would undermine the king's independence and freedom of action. Stripped of an independent source of revenue, the prince would be forced to irritate and estrange the public by imposing onerous taxes: "To the end that princes should not be forced to overcharge their subjects with imposts, or to seek any unlawful means to forfeit their goods, all monarchs and states have held it for a general and undoubted law, that the public revenues [e.g., from the domain lands] should be holy, sacred, and inalienable, either by contract or prescription" (VI, 2, 651). So kings *do* voluntarily bind themselves. To prevent themselves from acting in a myopic and self-destructive manner, financially pressed monarchs will tie their own hands, withdrawing their principal source of income (the goose that lays the golden eggs) from their own immediate control.

Bodin uniformly, even repetitiously, justifies prohibitions and entitlements by adducing their beneficial consequences for royal power. To tax without consent is, in principle, a violation of the rights of subjects. But it is also, and far more importantly, a danger to the stability of the regime. Writers who encourage the prince to tax without consent are counseling self-destruction:

> Now certainly it is a greater offense to infect princes with this doctrine than it is to rob and steal. They that maintain such opinions, show the lion his claws. Made worse by instruction [the prince proves] to be a tyrant . . . and break[s] all the laws both of God and man: and afterward enflamed with corrupt desires and affections, which altogether weaken the more noble parts of the mind, he quickly breaketh out from covetousness to unjust confiscations, from lust to adultery, from wrath to murder. (I, 8, 109)

Loss of self-control on the prince's part can trigger assassination attempts or, less dramatically, a withdrawal of elite cooperation essential to the effective exercise of power. Contrariwise, by voluntarily accepting stabilizing constraints, a prince can increase his capacity soberly to achieve his ends. Even if the sovereign were not legally obliged to consult the Estates before levying a tax, he could increase his revenues by granting the Estates a role in the taxing process. Flattered by being given an important role in government affairs, parliamentarians will open their purses voluntarily. History shows, according to Bodin, that voluntary compliance is the most efficient method for extracting resources from tight-fisted subjects. (Comparatively heavy English taxes are his primary example here.)

Initially, the command theory of law sounds advantageous for the sovereign. But the power to make law is only valuable to the extent that law is obeyed. Even if there are no formal or legal conditions on his lawmaking authority, therefore, the prince must in fact share power with others and accept limits on his own sweet will, if only to secure obedience. Traditions are valid solely if they are permitted to remain in effect by the king's say-so: "Custom hath no force but by suffrance, and so long as it pleaseth the sovereignty" (I, 10, 161).[19] After salaaming to the all-powerful monarch, however, Bodin proceeds to cast doubt on the superiority of prince-made law over inherited custom. He treats tradition pragmatically, once again, not piously. Interested in obedience, no ruler will casually dissolve age-old customs and promulgate unheard-of laws: "Newness in matter of law is always contemptible, whereas to the contrary, the reverence of antiquity is so great, as that it giveth strength enough unto a law to cause it to be of itself obeyed without the authority of any magistrate at all joined unto it" (IV, 3, 469–70).[20] Lawmaking power is not self-sufficient. To ensure obedience to his laws, the sovereign must rely on prescription, habit, custom.

He must rely also on the voluntary cooperation of the Estates, general and provincial, of the parlements, and of the officers of the realm. Similarly, "There is nothing that giveth greater credit and authority unto the laws and commandments of a prince, a people, or state, or in any manner of commonweal, than to cause them to pass by the advice of a grave and wise Senate or Council" (III, 1, 254).[21] While legally independent, the sovereign lacks a professional civil service and is therefore politically dependent on nonappointed officials who make his laws more acceptable and his deals more durable.

The king is not *formally* obliged to bow to the wishes of magistrates, for instance. While retaining the right of remonstrance, parlements cannot legally refuse to register royal edicts. Nevertheless, the magistrate is the "living and breathing law" (III, 5, 325), and ignoring his wishes may result in the total nullity of the king's most cherished commands. In other words, the informal power of judges is enormous. While the king is officially an uncommanded commander, he must clearly, if he wants to achieve his own goals, expose himself to considerable influence from below: "Neither ought the prince. . . . knowing the magistrates to be of contrary opinion unto his, to constrain them thereunto: for the ignorant and common people is no ways more moved to disloyalty, and contempt of their prince's edicts and laws, than to see the magistrates hardly dealt withall, and the laws by them contrary to their good liking published and enforced" (III, 4, 323). Rather than combining medieval natural law and modern absolutism in an incoherent or eclectic fashion, Bodin focuses single-mindedly on the varieties of informal rights and powers that any calculating monarch must grant his subjects if he is to exert his authority effectively.

In justifying the separation of powers, too, Bodin emphasizes its power-enhancing function. An independent judiciary increases the king's capacity to govern. Malefactors must be punished; but if the king exacts penalties personally, he will inevitably create resentments that may, in turn, weaken his authority. Thus, a clever sovereign will reserve to himself the distribution of pardons and rewards while delegating to truly independent magistrates the job of issuing condemnations and exacting fines: "In which doing, they who receive the benefits shall have good cause to love, respect, and reverence the prince their benefactor; and those who are condemned shall yet have no occasion at all to hate him, but shall still discharge their choler upon the magistrates and judges" (IV, 6, 512). The separation of powers, according to this analysis, allows the ruler to deflect resentment and duck responsibility. An independent judiciary, from this perspective, is not meant to paralyze power but, on the contrary, to increase the government's capacity to do its job.

As Hobbes himself argued in rare moments, absolute power is less powerful than limited power because power wielders need cooperation, not just compliance. This is Bodin's central premise. In both democracy and monarchy, power sharing is prudent: "If the prince or the people shall take upon themselves the authority of the Senate, or the commands, offices, or jurisdictions of the magistrates; it is much to be feared, lest that they, destitute of all help, shall at the length be spoiled of their own sovereign majesty also" (IV, 6, 518). Because he needs voluntary cooperation, a prince (or a sovereign people) cannot safely take personal control of all political functions.

The basic "dialectic" in Bodin's argument can also be illustrated by his praise of mixed regimes. On the one hand, any attempt to subordinate the king to the Estates will lead to chaos: "If the king should be subject unto the assemblies and decrees of the people, he should neither be king nor sovereign" (II, 8, 95). On the other hand, "a combining of a monarchy with a popular government" is "the most assured monarchy that is" (II, 7, 250).[22] In the same vein: "How necessary the assemblies and meeting of the whole people for to consult of matters, are, is hereby perceived, in that the people which may so call together such counsels, with them all things go well: whereas others which may not so do, are oppressed with tributes and servitude" (III, 7, 385). If the king ignores the Estates, civil war will ensue; if he consults the Estates, and sometimes actually defers to its wishes, he can stabilize and enlarge his authority: "So far it is from that such an assembly in any thing diminisheth the power of a sovereign prince, as that thereby his majesty is the more increased and augmented" (II, I, 192). By stressing that consultation is not required legally, Bodin simply emphasizes how indispensable it is politically.

However attractive *les grands coups d'autorité* may seem in the short run, they prove totally contrary to the king's long-term interest. It would be a fatal error to put to sleep the old representative assemblies: "The just monarchy hath not any more assured foundation or stay than the estates of the people, communities, corporations, and colleges. For if need be for the king to levy money, to raise forces, to maintain the state against the enemy, it cannot be better done than by the estate of the people, and of every province, town, and community" (III, 7, 384). The sovereign should retain these traditional bodies not because he is "just," and not because of the sanctity of tradition, but for purely calculating and self-interested motives, because they are the indispensable tools of royal government.[23] The prince's power cannot be measured by his capacity to command a bending of the knee. More significant is his ability to solve whatever problems are at hand. If the problems he faces are exceptionally difficult, he will need a great deal of help. The "rights" of subjects, as a result, may be paradoxically secured by the very needs of power. This is true, for instance, of the right to be represented in a national assembly: "For where can things for the curing of the diseases of the sick commonwealth, or for the amendment of the people, or for the establishing of laws, or for the reforming of the state, be better debated or handled, than before the prince in his Senate before the people?" (III, 7, 384). For subjects aiming to extract political concessions from the king, the threat of violent resistance may be less effective than the threat to withdraw cooperation. Commands backed by threats of force are too crude to mobilize effective teamwork. Self-interest alone shall thus lead a rational prince to establish or retain some kind of representative assembly.

A people free to express itself may sometimes prove difficult to control, but it is also more willing to make voluntary contributions to solving common problems. On this question, Bodin stands squarely on the side of later liberal writers against defenders of censorship and enforced conformity. A wise prince will realize that he can personally benefit from whatever freedom of speech he concedes. A king who repressed the Estates, for example, would deprive himself of a vital source of information. Appearing at the meeting of the Estates, a prince can acquire politically indispensable knowledge which would otherwise be unavailable: "There [the representatives] confer of the affairs concerning the whole body of the commonweal, and of the members thereof; there are heard and understood the just complaints and grievances of the poor subjects, which never otherwise come unto the prince's ears; there are discovered and laid open the robberies and extortions committed in the prince's name; whereof he knoweth nothing" (III, 7, 384). While a king can give orders, he is in a poor position to monitor how his orders are put into effect. A freespoken assembly does this work for him. By granting freedom to his subjects, in other words, a monarch can gain some degree of control over his own inferior agents. In some cases, moreover, criticism can strengthen the monarch. For obvious reasons, no powerful ruler will look benevolently on his critics; but an intelligent king "refuseth not to be freely and discreetly reproved for that he hath done amiss" (II, 4, 212). Before he can correct his own mistakes, a prince has to learn about them, and where can he acquire this knowledge, if not from an outspoken assembly?[24]

## Religion

Bodin's views on religious persecution and state power implicitly allied him with the *politiques*. Unlike the *dévots* or Catholic extremists with whom the *politiques* are usually contrasted, he preferred civil peace to religious uniformity and was thus accused, already in his lifetime, of abandoning "noble" for "base" aims. Toleration was difficult because "the people everywhere [are] most jealous of their religion" and "cannot . . . endure any rites and ceremonies, differing from the religion by themselves generally received." Neither laws nor magistrates can restrain "bands of men" whose "rage will oft times most furiously break out" (III, 7, 381). Ordinary men and women in sixteenth-century France did not understand the need for separating religious and political allegiances. Many preferred civil war to sharing their country with heretics. First-hand experience of self-destructive dispositions on the part of the people surely made Bodin less friendly to majoritarianism than to some form of paternalism.

The unsuccessful Colloquy of Poissy (1561) put an end to most hopes for creedal reconciliation. Calvinists had become too numerous, well-armed, and doctrinally committed to be easily reconverted. Attempts to suppress dissent by force would have imposed unacceptable costs on all Frenchmen. This situation was unprecedented. Faced with what he saw as intractable sectarian divisions, Bodin responded in an appropriately radical way. Along with a handful of others, he took a step that was to have momentous consequences for the future of liberalism. He abandoned the traditional view that social cohesion required all subjects to share religious beliefs. As a deputy at the Estates General of 1576, the very year his great political work first appeared, he vigorously advocated a policy of toleration and conciliation with Huguenots. Compromise, he thought, was the only feasible alternative to civil war.[25]

The *République* issues a plea that "no man be forbidden the private exercise of such his religion" (IV, 7, 539). The king should cease attempting to save souls, punish heretics, or eliminate religious dissonance. Such futile efforts only undermine political order and provoke rebellion. Sovereign authority should lower its sights, resting satisfied with the lesser goal of establishing a modus vivendi between conflicting groups. Bodin praises one ancient emperor for enacting a "law of forgetfulness" and another for issuing an edict of "union and tranquillity or quietness," both aiming "to reconcile the companies of all sorts of religions among themselves" (III, 7, 382). This is essentially the policy he favors for France. Subjects owe obedience to their sovereign on the secular ground that he, in turn, guarantees internal and external peace. Peace is not an end in itself, to be sure, any more than food or shelter are; but it is an essential precondition for every worthwhile goal: "It is impossible for a commonweal to flourish in religion, justice, charity, integrity of life, and in all the liberal sciences and mechanic arts, if the citizens enjoy not a firm and lasting peace" (V, 5, 598).

In his rejoinder to his *dévot* critics, Bodin could well have said: lower goals serve higher ones. Instead of attempting in vain to confer moral perfection or Christian redemption on his subjects, the monarch should attempt to "avoid commotions, troubles, and civil war" (IV, 7, 537). If the king keeps the peace, his subjects can pursue a wide variety of spiritual objectives. The state is a legal framework in which moral antagonists can coexist and cooperate in secular undertakings. Sectarian religions can also flourish, but only so long as they adapt themselves pliantly to the rules of peaceful coexistence.

No sooner was the *République* published than it was vehemently attacked. In *dévot* circles, at least, it was viewed as a foul defense of religious pluralism and, by implication, as blasphemous condemnation of the divinely ordained St. Bartholomew's Day massacre.[26] It is crucial to recall these scandalized reactions of the truly pious when examining Bodin's statements that religion is essential to the state (e.g., Preface, A70; and VI, I, 645). Consider a frequently cited and potentially misleading passage: "There is nothing which doth more uphold and maintain the states and Commonweals than religion" which "is the principal foundation of the power and strength of monarchies and Seignories as also for the execution of justice, for the obedience of the subjects, the reverence of the magistrates, for the fear of doing evil, and for the mutual love and amity of every one towards other" (IV, 7,

536). To understand what Bodin is saying here, we must focus on what he is denying. Remarkable for contemporaries was his refusal to endow the state with an overriding obligation to establish the one true religion. Even a false religion, he says, is better than none. To preempt or outbid his *dévot* opponents, he occasionally declares that the ultimate goal of every commonwealth is religious. But the state's real goal, in his mind as in Hobbes's, is nothing holier than social peace. (This militantly secular teleology, in political matters, makes them proto-liberals as well as preliberals.)

Bodin admits that religion is "a matter very considerable" (VI, 1, 648). The *République* is a fundamentally nonreligious treatise, however: "I here speak not but of temporal sovereignty, which is the subject that I entreat of" (I, 9, 137). As J. W. Allen observed, "You can eliminate from Bodin's *Republic* all his references to God, and to Princes as the lieutenants of God, and the whole structure will stand unaltered."[27] Although it has frequently been disputed, Allen's analysis is basically sound. At several points, for example, Bodin emphasizes the nonidentity of religious and political change.[28] Concerned with maintenance of political communities, he attends not to religion itself but exclusively to religion's secular effects. History shows that vile conspiracies against the commonwealth have often been hatched "under shadow of religion" (III, 7, 380). That religion can be a pretext was memorably demonstrated by the way secular rulers used the Reformation as an excuse to expropriate ecclesiastical property. The Church's enormous wealth "hath ministered occasion of troubles and seditions against the clergy, throughout all Europe, when as in show [the princes] made a color of religion" (V, 2, 575). Bodin was especially concerned with pious pretexts for fear that "conspiracies and rebellions of mutinous subjects against their sovereign princes" might be publicly justified by invoking an "especial commandment of God" (II, 5, 224). If used to undermine obedience, religion can plunge the state into anarchy: "But yet this is especially to be considered, that we pretend not the vain show of religion, or rather of superstition, against our prince's commands, and so upon a conscience evil-grounded open a way unto rebellion" (III, 4, 325). Aware that religion may be adduced as a pretext for rebellion, the sovereign prince will judge every appearance of faith by a severely secular standard.

In the *République,* in short, religion captures Bodin's attention for the same reason it was later to absorb Hobbes's. Bodin is interested in religion almost exclusively because of its influence on the sovereign's capacity to keep the peace. A religion may be false and nevertheless useful because it "doth yet hold men in fear and awe, both of the laws and of the magistrates, as also in mutual duties and offices one of them towards another" (IV, 7, 539).[29] If fear of hellfire lends credibility to the law, then religion is a welcome ally: "Neither is it to be expected that either prince or magistrate shall reduce those subjects under the obedience of the laws that have trodden all religion under foot" (VI, 1, 645). In other words, Bodin advances a social-prop theory of devoutness. The utility of religion hinges in no way upon its truth.

The concept of sovereignty itself, it should be recalled, was implicitly anticlerical. It implied the independence of the crown from papal control. The French king was the model of an absolute sovereign because he cultivated this independence much more assiduously than his fellow European monarchs: "But howsoever the Bishop of Rome pretended to have a sovereignty over all Christian princes, not only in spiritual, but also in temporal affairs. . . . Yet could not our kings even for any most short time endure the servitude of the bishop of Rome, nor be moved with any of their excommunications, which the popes used as fire-brands to the firing of the Christian commonweals" (I, 9, 145). In the same Erastian spirit, Bodin remarks that the Catholic Church owns far too much land, that the king's word should be sufficient without any religious oath being superadded, and that a Christian prince must keep his promises to infidels (I, 8, 92 and V, 6, 628). Religion is even impiously said to vary with climate.[30] Bodin's analysis of sovereignty, in sum, is essentially nonreligious. His idea of supreme authority was designed to fit all states, pagan as well as Christian.

## Toleration and the Power of the Prince

We are now in a position to apply the foregoing analysis of Bodin's theory of sovereignty to his discussion of religion. That the state can increase its authority by restricting its jurisdiction also serves as Bodin's principal argument for toleration. The *République* counsels just such a propitiatory approach. "And albeit a prince had the power by force to repress and reform a mutinous and rebellious people, yet ought he not so to do, if otherwise he may appease them" (IV, 7, 532). Repression is to be avoided, if at all possible, because it is self-defeating. This thesis, so crucial to later liberal writers, brings us quite close to Bodin's central argument for toleration:

> I will not here in so great variety of people so much differing among themselves in religion, take upon me to determine which of them is the best (howbeit that there can be but one such, one truth, and one divine law, by the mouth of God published) but if the prince well assured of the truth of his reli-

> gion, would draw his subjects thereunto, divided into sects and factions, he must not therein (in my opinion) use force. (IV, 7, 537)

Bodin argues against slavery not for moral reasons, because it is sinful, but on the purely practical grounds that it poses a threat to slave-owners (I, 5, 32–46). In advocating toleration, he likewise slights the trampled rights of victims, concentrating instead upon the long-term interests of the persecutors. From the prince's own viewpoint, violence is profoundly counterproductive. It not only fuels civil hatred and weakens authority; but it also prevents the conversion of heretics and even creates hypocrites and atheists. "The more [the minds of men] are forced, the more forward and stubborn they become" (IV, 7, 537).[31] Naturally, kings desire to secure religious homogeneity. But forcing consciences will not do: "Minds resolved, the more they are crossed, the stiffer they are" (III, 7, 382). A king will have a better chance of saving refractory souls if he simply tolerates dissenters and lives a God-fearing life himself according to the teachings of his church. His pious example will win more conversions than force.

Against zealots of all denominations, Bodin—who may or may not have been a believer—argues that tolerance for religious diversity does not necessarily imply personal indifference to religion. Deep devotion does not necessarily require a rabid persecution of nonbelievers.[32] Not only political power, but even the piety of the prince, can survive a reform that leaves religion up to individuals. Even more pertinent to France, perhaps, is the Roman example. The Romans, although they insisted on public worship of Roman gods, "yet for all that did they easily suffer every man privately within the city to use his own manner and fashion, and his own religion" (IV, 7, 538). Private worship leaves the public realm untouched, and perhaps improved.

Bodin's approach to the great question of toleration is consciously eclectic. To forge an alliance among antipersecution parties, he touches almost all bases. He argues (1) that a man's conscience, by natural necessity, cannot be compelled, (2) that persecution leads to hypocrisy, atheism, and disobedience, and (3) that God accepts any form of worship so long as it comes from a pure heart. But his basic concern is to protect neither God nor the individual but rather the state. He never mentions that the violent suppression of dissenters might be morally wrong, while he repeatedly emphasizes the wild imprudence of using violence if the sovereign is at all uncertain of success, for "there can be nothing more dangerous unto a prince, than to make proof of his forces against his subjects, except he be well assured to prevail against them: which otherwise were but to arm a lion, and to show him his claws, wherewith to tear his master" (III, 7, 382). This statement returns us directly to Bodin's fundamental argument. A prince has a perfect right to repress religious dissent; but if he exercises this right, he risks his own destruction. As a self-imposed limit on the king's authority over the lives of his subjects, toleration can reinforce political sovereignty. The very word toleration derives from the Latin for strength: to stand up, support, and sustain. No surprise, therefore, that the doctrine of toleration could be incorporated smoothly into the political program of power-seeking absolutism. Religious liberality strengthens the state, makes possible an armistice among rival sects, and promotes the supremacy of the crown.

Superficially, Bodin agrees that the ideal recipe for social cohesion remains *une foi, une loi, un roi.* Subjects certainly have no inalienable right to freedom of conscience. But religious homogeneity is now impossible and here, as always, the sovereign must adapt to the imperfections of his situation. Reconverting or suppressing dissenters, admittedly, would be the optimal solution,

> but it may be that the consent and agreement of the nobility and people in a new religion or sect, may be so puissant and strong, as that to repress or alter the same, should be a thing impossible, or at leastwise marvelous difficult, without the extreme peril and danger of the whole state. . . . Wherefore that religion or sect is to be suffered, which without the hazard and destruction of the state cannot be taken away: The health and welfare of the Commonweal being the chief thing the law respecteth. (III, 7, 382)

The best is the enemy of the good. Extreme piety can subvert peace. To wield power effectively, the ruler must reconcile himself to denominational pluralism, to irreconcilable sectarian divisions. Religious unity may remain a splendid ideal, but, in the imbroglio of post-Reformation France, religious diversity is the only realistic option.

## Neutrality and Faction

Some great noblemen, it is true, hoped for a *cuius regio, eius religio* solution in France, the king reduced to a figurehead and local princes ruling over semiautonomous religious units. In other words, toleration was *not* the only available alternative to civil war. Partition was also possible. But Bodin emphatically rejects territorial segmentation as a feasible way of handling religious diversity. The dangerous side effects of faction, it seems, are best neutralized in a large kingdom. He asserts repeatedly that "the greater the Monarchy is, the more goodly and flourishing it is, and the subject more happy, and living in an assured peace" (VI, 4, 721). A wide territorial scale promotes peace, he writes in a passage that strikingly resembles Madison's plea for a large republic, because "conversions and changes of commonweals do more often happen in little and small cities or states, than in great kingdoms full of great provinces, and people." A "small commonweal," he goes on to say, "is soon divided into two parts or factions" (IV, 1, 432). Such a polarized situation is extremely dangerous. Since conciliation cannot be imposed, the only peace-promoting and union-preserving alternative is to diffuse tensions by multiplying factions. In the *Heptaplomeres,* the brilliant and mysterious dialogue attributed to Bodin, Toralba cryptically remarks that "many things cannot be opposite by nature to the same thing," meaning that a surfeit of sects renders two-way polarization unlikely. And Octavius adds: "For this reason, I think, the kings of the Turks and Persians admit every kind of religion in the state, and in a remarkable harmony they reconcile all citizens and foreigners who differ in religions among themselves and with the state."[33] For this reason, too, Bodin recommends increasing the size of the population in order to domesticate faction: "There is nothing more dangerous than to have the subjects divided into two factions without a mean, the which doth usually fall out in cities where there are but few citizens" (V, 2, 571). The advantage of large size is its attendant pluralism; peace can be achieved through multiplicity.[34] Two denominations will inevitably be locked in war; while a promiscuous variety of religions will settle comfortably into peace. Although strikingly Madisonian, this argument is also distinctive. Bodin does not, for example, argue that a proliferation of sects will prevent a majority from imposing its wishes on minorities. Rather, "where there be more than two sects or sorts, there must needs be some in the mean betwixt the two contrary extremes, which may set them agreed, which otherwise of themselves would never fall to agreement" (IV, 7, 540). Large states can contain faction because they naturally produce mediators to manage and regulate conflict. A society divided along a single cleavage, by contrast, is unlikely to yield neutral arbiters.

Bodin's discussion of toleration in book IV, chapter 7 deserves to be reconstructed in some detail. He begins by reiterating that, in some circumstances, religion can help quell civil war by striking fear into the hearts of citizens:

> For at such time as the Florentines were fallen out into such a fury among themselves, as the city swam with the blood and

> slaughter of the citizens: and that they could by no means be parted, Francis Soderin the bishop, attired in his bishoplike attire and attended upon with a company of priests, and a cross carried before him, came into the midst of the furious citizens, so bandying it one against another; at the sight and presence of whom, they all for the reverend fear of religion upon the sudden laid down their weapons, and so without more ado, got themselves home every man unto his own house. (IV, 7, 534)

But why, in the 1570s and in France, would Bodin choose to expand on religion's contribution to social peace? He soon adds, again invoking the example of Florence, that "deadly broils" can be resolved only by "mediation" of a neutral bystander. Most important of all, once a cycle of revenge and counterrevenge has become psychologically entrenched, the factions involved cannot bring it to a halt by themselves, even if they ardently wish to, so long as they are attached to an ethic of honor: "Oftentimes it happens that the citizens, divided into factions weary at length of their murders and tumults, seek but to find an occasion for them to fall to agreement; yet being of opinion it to touch them in honor that should first seek for peace, therefore continue their bloody quarrels until they have utterly ruined one another, if some third man interpose not himself betwixt them for the making of them friends" (IV, 7, 535).[35] In popular and aristocratic commonwealths, the mediation of a neutral party is difficult to come by. In a monarchy, nothing could be easier. Indeed, this is the chief advantage of the monarchical form of government. The king, so long as he remains a third man, strategically situated above the battle, can impose peace on warring factions.

In Bodin's France, unlike Soderini's Florence, the Catholic Church could not play the neutral moderator, for Catholicism was one of the partisans. Thus, Bodin's discussion of Soderini cannot plausibly be interpreted as an endorsement of religiously imposed order. Here is a danger that every prudent sovereign must avoid:

> Sometime it happeneth the sovereign prince to make himself a party, instead of holding the place of a sovereign Judge: in which doing for all that he shall be no more but the head of one party, and so undoubtedly put himself in danger of his life, and that especially when such dangerous seditions and factions be not grounded upon matters directly touching his estate, but otherwise, as it has happened in almost all Europe within this fifty years, in the wars made for matters of religion. (IV, 7, 535)

Only by adopting a position of neutrality toward religious conflict, by viewing questions of religion as alien to questions of state, can the prince avoid anarchy and retain power. The Catholic-Calvinist struggle is solely a "matter of religion." When such divisive and essentially nonpolitical issues are at stake, the king must remain sovereignly nonpartisan.

A few pages later, in apparent disregard of his own plea for nonpartisanship, Bodin endorses Solon's famous "law for part-taking," whereby no Athenian citizen was allowed to remain neutral in cases of factious conflict, "which unto many seemed a thing unreasonable, considering that the greatest praise and commendation of a good subject is; to be a quite civil man, desirous and doing the best that he can to live in peace" (IV, 7, 540). This strange law, however, because of the incentives it produced, was not as unreasonable as it initially seems. It inhibited troublemakers who hoped to reap profits from the sidelines after having fomented factional discord. And it also encouraged moderate parties to work more actively to prevent the outbreak of factional war. When conflict had already erupted, the law of part-taking was a reliable mechanism for enlisting the community's otherwise reticent elites, ensuring the presence of some relatively cool heads on each side, thereby helping bring the conflict to a speedy end. By involving everyone, a legal prohibition on neutrality provided a powerful incentive for responsible citizens, who could not stand aside, to steer the community away from civil war.

How is this curious digression related to Bodin's central argument for a policy of religious toleration? It seems, for a moment, that he is now reversing himself and arguing *against* the neutrality of the prince. Engagement, not detachment, is essential. It is always advantageous, in time of war, for weaker parties to join the stronger. During the Peloponnesian War, Theremenes "had kept himself quiet, and stood still looking on, but as an idle beholder, without taking part either with the one or with the other." This was an unwise policy, for he "was himself at the last forsaken of all, and so left unto the mercy of the tyrants, who made him a miserable spectacle unto all men, and in the end most cruelly put him to death" (IV, 7, 541). Does this mean that neutrality is dangerous and partisanship wise? Is Bodin suggesting that the French king should simply side with one party, exactly as the League wished?

Not at all.[36] Any monarch desiring to stay safely aloof cannot remain a passive spectator but must instead, from his position of neutrality, deliberately stage-manage the factional struggle: "He therefore which will stand as neuter, whether it be in civil war, or in wars amongst strangers, ought at the least to do his endeavor to set the rest agreed" (IV, 7, 541). Neutrality is not *fainéantise* but rather a combination of peace enforcment and arbitration. The state must adopt an active role as the midwife and guarantor of a religious truce if a stable polity is to be created. The prince of a religiously divided kingdom cannot simply dispense justice and thereby maintain the pre-existent social balance, for there is no spontaneous social balance. He must be much more dynamic, innovative, creative than traditional kings. He must be a boss as well as a judge. He must be willing relentlessly to pressure and manipulate his subjects without, of course, provoking unnecessary resentments.

Book V, chapter 6, in which Bodin again appraises the politically ambiguous consequences of neutrality, provides another perspective. The topic here is the prince who adopts a stance of nonalignment toward conflicting foreign powers. Bodin's argument mirrors the earlier passage: "It is therefore commendable for the greatest and mightiest princes to remain neuters" (V, 6, 624). This is almost always the best course if the prince has sufficient power to act as a mediator: "It is therefore more safe for him that remains a neuter to mediate a peace, than to nourish war" (V, 6, 624). This is a central tenet of *politique* thought: the state is a neutral power mediating among hostile parties all of whom will thrive best in peace but none of whom can achieve peace without external help. Bodin ably summarizes this precept as follows: "One of the most necessary things for the assurance of treaties of peace and alliance, is to name some great and mightier Prince to be judge and umpire in case of contravention, that they may have recourse unto him to mediate an agreement betwixt them; who being equal, cannot with their honors refuse war, nor demand peace" (IV, 6, 625). Translated into domestic policy this means that the state can serve as an umpire between religious factions only if it refuses to identify itself too closely with the spiritual aspirations of any single sect. By subjecting himself to an extreme Catholic faction, a king who attacked the Huguenots would enfeeble the crown. The peacekeeping regime is necessarily unresponsive; or rather, the king must both represent and not represent his subjects. He must keep their loyalty but he must not reflect their uncompromising and vengeful attitudes when conducting affairs of state.[37]

## The Law of Silence

In book IV of the *Heptaplomeres,* Coronaeus asks: "Is it proper for a good man to discuss religion?" All seven speakers, in fact, agree that discussions of religion can be dangerous. When public debate is forbidden, many other worthwhile activities are made possible for the first time. The withdrawal of intractable problems from the agenda of public discussion makes collective consideration of other issues more congenial, rational, and constructive. Limits strengthen; restrictions are possibility creating. For example: "At Siena the Senate for a long time permitted academies, but the condition was stipulated that there would be no discussions about divine matters and the decrees of the popes. Although one man foolishly violated this edict and suffered capital punishment, there have been no uprisings in that city up to this day." The *Heptaplomeres* itself portrays an extraordinarily freewheeling discussion of religious questions by a multidenominational group including a Catholic, a Calvinist, a Lutheran, a Jew, a Mohammedan, and a skeptic. Lengthy debate, however, leads no one to change his mind. The dialogue concludes: "Afterwards they held no other conversation about religion, although each one defended his religion with the supreme sanctity of his life."[38]

The idea of imposing a law of silence upon religious controversies had already appeared in the *République*. Once a religion is established and coercively enforced by the state, no public disputes about doctrine or even attempts at rational demonstration should be allowed. Some of Bodin's arguments for a legally enforced policy of nondiscussion are overtly religious. Faith, which is ultimately beyond reason, can only be weakened by necessarily unsuccessful attempts to defend it rationally. Once raised, however, doubts will fester, doubts which not only undermine religion but could ultimately destroy the state.

Bodin approves heartily of the truce between Lutherans and Catholics established by the Peace of Augsburg (1555). Strict laws should prohibit public disputations of religion,

> which after long civil war was by the estates and princes of the German empire provided for, and a decree made, that the princes should with mutual consent defend both the Roman and Saxon religion: whereunto that was also joined. That no man should upon pain of death dispute of the religions. Which severe punishments, after that the German magistrates had inflicted upon diverse, all Germany was afterwards at good quiet & rest: no man daring more to dispute of matters of religion. (IV, 7, 536)[39]

To apply his Augsburg sympathies to France, Bodin had to shift ground slightly. Peace can be established, even in a unified kingdom containing a multiplicity of sects, so long as a strict *gag rule* is imposed upon questions of dogma. In a pluralistic realm, especially, public speech should be purged of doctrinal disputes. Here is Bodin's least secular argument for imposing silence on religious controversy:

> Nothing is so firm and stable, nothing so manifest and clear (except it rest upon most plain and undoubtful demonstrations) which may not by disputation and force of argument be obscured or made doubtful: and especially where that which is called into question, or dispute, resteth not so much upon demonstration or reason, as upon the assurance of faith and belief only: which they which seek by demonstrations and publishing of books to perform, they are not only mad with reason, but weaken also the foundations of all sorts of religions. (IV, 7, 535)

The ecumenical appeal implicit in the last phrase is reinforced by the hint that religion cannot yield to rational consideration. Bodin is not saying that the Catholic religion is true and therefore that freedom to dispute it is inherently absurd and immoral. He is saying, rather, that rational proofs of religion are always open to doubt and, to avoid the ravages of doubt, we should simply cease talking about it. The limits of reason dictate removal of rationally irresolvable questions from the public agenda.

## Bodin's Legacy

The paradox that limited power is more powerful than unlimited power, the affiliated notion that religious toleration can enhance sovereign authority, and even the suggestion that irresolvable disputes are best handled by methods of avoidance all play an important role in political theory after the sixteenth century. Liberals, in particular, echoed, reworked, and refined these basic ideas. A few randomly chosen examples will demonstrate that the influence of Bodinian arguments was broad and deep and certainly not limited to France.

According to Spinoza, "an absolute dominion is to the prince very dangerous." Because the sovereign has no right to destroy or even diminish his own power, moreover, he must tolerate religious diversity. For prudential reasons alone, religious controversies should be kept disentangled from political debates. Rulers should realize that "liberty can be conceded to every man without injury to the rights and authority of sovereign power."[40] Spinoza's contemporary, John Milton, argued against censorship in exactly the same way: "This obstructing violence meets for the most part with an event utterly opposite to the end which it drives at: instead of suppressing sects and schisms, it raises them and invests them with a reputation."[41] Religious persecution is an astonishingly bad bargain for public authorities.

Locke not only argues that legal restraints enhance the freedom of the constrained individual.[42] He also claims that, in religious questions, coercion is folly and counterproductive: "There is only one thing which gathers people for sedition, and that is oppression." Similarly: "It is not the diversity of opinions, which cannot be avoided, but the refusal of toleration to people of diverse opinions, which could have been granted, that has produced most of the disputes and wars that have arisen in the Christian world on account of religion."[43] Not liberty but autocracy is the truly anarchical force, not "the Peoples Wantonness" but "the Rulers Insolence." As a result, the people's right to replace the legislature is "*the best fence against Rebellion,* and the probablest means to hinder it."[44]

Montesquieu, along the very same lines, stresses that too much power will expose a sovereign to unnecessary dangers: "In proportion as the power of the monarch becomes boundless and immense, his security diminishes." It turns out, therefore, that "great exertions of authority" are ultimately "impolitic." Similarly, "what would formerly have been called a master-stroke in politics would be now, independent of the horror it might occasion, the greatest imprudence." Indeed, "from experience it is manifest that nothing but the goodness and lenity of a government can make it flourish."[45] From the *Persian Letters,* we learn that harsh rule makes a country ungovernable and, more concretely, that the Revocation of the Edict of Nantes was self-defeating: it undermined the power of the French state by depriving the nation of some of its most useful and productive citizens.[46]

According to Hume, to pick another random example, a free press strengthens the government by making magistrates aware of "murmers or secret discontents" before they become unmanageable.[47] If policies are set publicly and public criticism is encouraged, a government can avoid self-contradictory legislation, nip crises in the bud, and remedy its own blunders. Similarly, a free press can rouse "all the learning, wit, and genius of the nation."[48] Such human resources will presumably improve the performance of government, and not merely intimidate ruling elites back onto the narrow path of legality. According to Kant, too, civil freedoms cannot be infringed without a general decline in state power: "To try to deny the citizen this freedom [i.e., the *freedom of the pen*] means withholding from the ruler all the knowledge of those matters which, if he knew about them, he would himself rectify, so that he is thereby put in a self-stultifying position." Intelligent rulers will see that their own interests are fostered by granting liberties to ordinary subjects. In order to maintain state power, therefore, it is not surprising that "restrictions placed upon personal activities are increasingly relaxed, and general freedom of religion is granted."[49] Finally, Thomas Jefferson, a known reader of Bodin, urged on his fellow Virginians the examples of New York and Pennsylvania, states that were flourishing without any established religion: "Their harmony is unparalleled, and can be ascribed to nothing but their unbounded tolerance, because there is no other circumstance in which they differ from every nation on earth. They have made the happy discovery, that the way to silence religious disputes is to take no notice of them."[50]

The mutually reinforcing relation between individual freedoms and sovereign authority was first elaborated at unforgettable length by Jean Bodin. The opening of a legal path to autocracy was not, therefore, the main intellectual contribution of his great work.[51] With persistence and clarity, Bodin invoked *raison d'état* to justify semiconstitutional restraints on sovereign power. This was his most important legacy to the liberal theorists who read and reiterated him. We might, of course, conclude that he was an immoral realist, cynically reducing the rights of subjects to the utility of princes. Alternatively, we can judge him to be an unrealistic moralist, naively expecting abusive regimes to collapse and authorities voluntarily to limit their own caprice. The vague plausibility of both assessments testifies to the obscure but tantalizing drama of the *République*. Whatever conclusion we draw, however, we cannot deny Bodin's massive importance to later debates. Of special interest are his contributions to positive constitutionalism. Constitutional constraints may be an indirect technique for building effective state institutions and reinforcing governmental power. While often neglected, such a claim lies at the heart of liberal-democratic theory. It is to further considerations of this all-important theme, seen in a much broader intellectual framework, that I now turn.

# 5

# Precommitment and the Paradox of Democracy

*Il est absurde que la volonté se donne des chaines pour l'avenir.*

—ROUSSEAU

A liberal constitution may be minimally defined as a "higher law" that cannot be changed through normal lawmaking procedures in the popularly elected assembly. Exceptional legal entrenchment exempts constitutional rules from the majoritarian controls that govern ordinary legislation. A constitutional text strives to make fast, in this way, the form of government, the limits of government, and the goals for which the government is empowered to act. Is constitutionalism, therefore, fundamentally antidemocratic? Are entrenched rights and an institutionally anchored separation of powers essentially antipopulist? Does a stringent amending formula disenfranchise electoral majorities? Is limited government, therefore, the antonym of self-government? Less abstractly, are restrictions on state power the means by which grasping elites dilute the control wielded by ordinary citizens over their collective existence?

Latent or explicit, the idea of a profound opposition between majoritarian politics and constitutionally anchored restraints remains a commonplace of contemporary political theory. Laurence Tribe, for instance, opens his influential treatise on constitutional law with a concise formulation of the countermajoritarian dilemma: "In its most basic form, the question . . . is why a nation that rests legality on the consent of the governed would choose to constitute its political life in terms of commitments to an original agreement . . . deliberately structured so as to be difficult to change."[1] How can such majority-thwarting arrangements be democratically justified? The same question may be reformulated in a variety of ways. How can the "consent of the governed" be reconciled with the preempting of subsequent consent by a Constitutional Convention? Why should a constitutional framework, ratified two centuries ago, exert such enormous power over our lives today? Why should a minority of our fellow citizens be empowered to prevent amendments to the Constitution? Is judicial review, when based on a superstitious fidelity to the intent of the framers, compatible with popular sovereignty?[2]

## The Tension between Constitutionalism and Democracy

These questions have a long history. In the Flag Salute Case of 1943, Justice Robert Jackson issued the following classical pronouncement: "The very purpose of a Bill of Rights was to withdraw certain subjects from the vicissitudes of political controversy, to place them beyond the reach of majorities and officials and to establish them as legal principles to be applied by the courts. One's right to life, liberty, and property, to free speech, a free press, freedom of worship and assembly, and other fundamental rights may not be submitted to vote: they depend on the outcome of no elections."[3] Constitutionalism, from this perspective, *does* appear essentially antidemocratic. The basic function of a constitution seems to be negative: to *remove* certain decisions from the democratic process, that is, to tie the community's hands.

But how can we justify a "democratic" system that obstructs the will of the majority? On the one hand, we might—in the spirit of Justice Jackson—invoke fundamental rights: if such rights are somehow "inscribed in nature," they may simply override consent. Alternatively, we could focus on the self-defeating character of constitutionally unlimited democracy. This is the line of argument pursued by F. A. Hayek, one of the most prolific exponents of *negative constitutionalism.* A constitution, in his view, is nothing but a device for limiting the power of government.[4] Present-day citizens are myopic; they have little self-control, are sadly undisciplined, and are always prone to sacrifice enduring principles to short-term pleasures and benefits. They may even be tempted to confiscate the wealth of a few, without foreseeing how such an act will affect the living standards of most people. A constitution is the institutionalized cure for this chronic myopia: it disempowers short-sighted majorities in the name of binding norms. A constitution is Peter sober while the electorate is Peter drunk. Citizens need a constitution, just as Ulysses needed to be bound to his mast. If voters were allowed to get what they wanted, they would inevitably shipwreck themselves. By binding themselves to rigid rules, they can better achieve their solid and long-term collective aims.

A different, indeed contrary, perspective is represented by Martin Shapiro. Shapiro's position is subtle and difficult to summarize, but his essay on the meaning of the American Constitution concludes with a rhetorically memorable claim. When we examine a democratically enacted statute, he writes, we should not ask, like text-bound lawyers: Is it constitutional? Rather we should ask, like democratic citizens: Do we want it to be constitutional? We should not be enslaved by "certain dead gentlemen who could not possibly have visualized our current circumstances."[5] We should be guided solely by our collective decision about what sort of community we want to become.

Shapiro and Hayek typify the point and counterpoint of a continuing debate. Their disagreement neatly represents the quarrel—if I can put it this way—between democrats who find constitutions a nuisance and constitutionalists who perceive democracy as a threat. Reform-minded theorists worry that democracy will be paralyzed by constitutional straitjacketing. Conservatives are apprehensive that the constitutional dike will be breached by a democratic flood. Despite their differences, both sides agree that there exists a deep, almost irreconcilable tension between constitutionalism and democracy. Indeed, they come close to suggesting that "constitutional democracy" is a marriage of opposites, an oxymoron.

The existence of an irreconcilable "tension" between constitutionalism and democracy, in fact, is one of the core premises of modern political thought. By calling it into question, I do not intend to deny well-known facts. When a majority of the electorate is fanatically religious, for instance, or where there is no tradition of a separation between church and state, democratic rule will undoubtedly threaten constitutionally entrenched individual rights. In a secularized society with high rates of literacy, on the other hand, limited government and self-government are likely to become mutually supportive rather than mutually subversive. Under modern conditions, in fact, it is "unconstitutional democracy" that sounds like the contradiction in terms. By pursuing the (in some sense obvious) suggestion that constitutionalism and democracy are often mutually supportive, I aim to shed light on some neglected dimensions of democratic and constitutional theory.[6]

John Hart Ely, too, has argued that constitutional restraints, far from being systematically antidemocratic, can be democracy reinforcing.[7] Like all rickety human creations, democratic government requires periodic repair. Its preconditions must be secured or resecured; and this cannot always be achieved by unmixed democratic means. As a consequence, the Supreme Court is constitutionally empowered to be the watchdog of democracy. Elected and accountable representatives, not judges, must determine what "substantive values" are to guide public policy; but in matters of fundamental decision-making procedure, the Court bears major custodial responsibility. It must strike down all legislation, no matter how popular with electoral majorities, that undermines the conditions of a well-functioning democracy: "Unblocking the stoppages in the democratic process is what judicial review ought presumably to be about."[8] This is a democratic, not merely paternalistic, arrangement. The overall power of voters is enhanced when the electorate limits the authority of its own elected officials over basic governmental processes. Ely ably, even brilliantly, develops this thesis in the context of current legal controversies. But he presents his striking claim with little abstract theoretical elaboration and almost no historical background. As a result, he leaves disappointingly untouched the myth of a fundamental tension between constitutionalism and democracy.

For a surprisingly large number of serious thinkers, then, constitutional democracy remains a paradox, if not a contradiction in terms. Yet all working democracies, as nearly everyone admits, operate within boundaries set by stabilizing constraints. Ely's notion that constitutions can reinforce democracy is therefore manifestly superior to the contrary idea that constitutions and democracies are always fundamentally antagonistic. Nevertheless, because constitutions cramp the will of the majority, and are relatively difficult to change, the myth of an underlying tension or paradox or even contradiction lives on.

Discussion of this issue can be advanced by greater theoretical abstraction and a wider casting of the historical net. On the one hand, the relation between constitutionalism and democracy can be significantly clarified by an analysis of the way constraints in general can produce or enhance freedom. On the other hand, the dispute about the relation between constitutionalism and democracy can be traced back to the eighteenth century and even earlier. I will begin with a foray into the history of ideas, expanding on several themes already broached in chapter 4.

## The Prohibition against Binding the Future

In the 1740s, David Hume noted a scandalous self-contradiction at the heart of republican theory. Although seldom discussed, his insight was deep and disturbing. Republicans universally rely upon the fiction of a social contract. But, wrote Hume, "this supposes the consent of the fathers to bind the children, even to the most remote generations (which republican writers will never allow)."[9] Despite their concern to create an enduring framework for self-government, in other words, republican theorists generally insist that a founding generation can never commit its successors to a fixed constitutional scheme. But how is constitutionalism possible, on republican grounds, if our ancestors had no right to contract away our freedom? In the Putney Debates, one speaker remarks: "I presume that all the people, and all nations whatsoever, have a liberty and power to alter and change their constitutions if they find them to be weak and infirm."[10] In the Declaration of Independence, Thomas Jefferson espoused the same principle: "It is the right of the people to alter or abolish" any "form of government" which has become "destructive" to life, liberty and the pursuit of happiness. Alexander Hamilton identified the "fundamental principle of republican government" as "the right of the people to alter or abolish the established Constitution whenever they find it inconsistent with their happiness." And Madison, citing the Declaration, wrote of "the transcendent and precious right of the people to 'abolish or alter their governments as to them shall seem most likely to effect their safety and happiness.'"[11] For republicans, no institution, however important, is unalterable; no law, however fundamental, is irrepealable.

This widely acknowledged republican prohibition against rigid constitutional commitments was itself based upon a more fundamental prohibition, also mentioned by Hume: the principle that no father can rightfully bind his sons. Locke succinctly formulated the underlying rule: "Whatever Engagements or Promises any one has made for himself, he is under the Obligation of them, but *cannot* by any *Compact* whatsoever, bind *his Children* or Posterity."[12] Our ancestors had no right to bargain away our freedom. By the eighteenth century, even those attempting to construct an enduring political order drew the logical conclusion from Locke's radically antitraditionalist and antipatriarchalist premises. In Article 28 of the (unimplemented) Jacobin constitution of 1793, for example, it is written that "one generation cannot subject future generations to its laws."[13] Around this time, the interdiction against precommitting future generations boasted numerous theoretical advocates. To convey the tenor of their arguments, I shall focus on the bold positions defended by Tom Paine and Thomas Jefferson.

## Paine and the Consent of the Living

In 1776, Paine had been the ardent advocate of a "Continental Charter" which he described as a "firm bargain" and "a bond of solemn obligation."[14] But in 1791, without dramatically changing his other views, he mounted a searing attack on the very idea of an inherited constitutional framework. According to Burke, the English Parliament of 1688 had legally bound its posterity to the end of time. Paine countered that no such right or power existed: "Every age and generation must be as free to act for itself, *in all cases,* as the ages and generations which preceded it."[15] It is not only immoral but impossible to preempt the choices of successor generations. The fetters of the past are ropes of sand. Nevertheless, attempts to bind the future, though ultimately futile, can be terribly irritating and destructive. They should therefore be denounced for what they are—open violations of natural justice.

In a way, Paine's blunderbuss assault on constitutional precommitment follows logically from his conception of democracy. For him, democracy is the rule of the living.[16] More belligerently, democracy is a war against the past. The old European world of kings, aristocrats, and hereditary entitlements is thoroughly rotten. The "fraud, effigy and show" of the ancien régime must be relegated to the junk heap of history—for history is a junk heap.[17] Rather than being a storehouse of accumulated wisdom, the result of a thousand tiny adjustments embodying, as Burke admiringly suggested, more experience and knowledge than could ever be possessed by a single individual, tradition is a pestilent sewer of abuses.

The sovereignty of the past is the reign of nobility, which actually means "no-ability." Competence cannot be inherited; so it is not surprising that traditional societies heap power and rewards on imbeciles. Burke had dishonestly implied that traditions, piously received, could relieve the present generation of making arduous choices. But even if such a shirking of responsibility were desirable (which it is not), it would be impossible, because the past is fraught with contradictions.[18] The settlement of 1688, for example, was an innovation forced on Englishmen by the irreconcilable conflict between religious and dynastic traditions. Burke knew this. While belittling the present and aggrandizing the past, he was actually catering to the interests of a small elite—men very much alive.[19]

According to Locke, "an Argument from what has been, to what should of right be, has no great force."[20] Paine took up this classical liberal view and drove it to extremes. Democracy, for him, was the routinization of impiety. There was no reason on earth why people should do things in the future the way they had done them in the past. Democracy was a tirelessly inventive system, oriented toward ceaseless change and reform. The eighteenth-century battle against prescribed sentiments and nonvoluntary obligations yielded no quarter to the earlier choices of individuals. Decisions made by one's past self came to appear imposed and thus illegitimate to one's present self. In Protestant countries, for instance, marriage was no longer a sacrament. A perpetual contract began to appear unnecessary for the purposes of marriage, not to mention inconsistent with the human need to correct unfortunate mistakes.[21] The campaign for a loosening of the divorce laws reflected a general unwillingness to allow the past to enslave the present.[22]

Democracy was the collective counterpart to this personal institutionalization of impermanence:

> There never did, there never will, and there never can exist a parliament, or any description of men, in any country, possessed of the right or the power of binding and controlling posterity to the *"end of time,"* or of commanding for ever how the world shall be governed, or who shall govern it; and therefore, all such clauses, acts or declarations, by which the makers of them attempt to do what they have neither the right nor the power to do, nor the power to execute, are in themselves null and void.

The present generation has an unlimited and illimitable right to new-model the institutions under which it lives. The only consent that legitimates any form of government is "the consent of the living."

Paine's argument here presupposes an irresolvable contradiction between constitutionalism and democracy, between the inheritance of a fixed legal framework and the omnipotence of citizens currently alive. Just as Locke had denied fathers the right to shackle their children, so Paine (at least in these passages) denied the Founding Fathers the right to corset successor generations in an unbending constitutional frame.

## Jefferson and the Self-Sufficiency of Generations

Thomas Jefferson's position was quite similar to Paine's. On the one hand, he explicitly denied the legislature the power to annul the personal liberties enshrined in the Bill of Rights. He endorsed "limited constitutions, to bind down those whom we are obliged to trust with power." And he even wrote, in lawyerly fashion, that "our peculiar security is in the possession of a written Constitution."[23] Again like Paine, on the other hand, Jefferson was a fickle constitutionalist. He, too, launched an uncompromising attack on the very idea of constitutional precommitment. In September 1789 (two years before Paine published *The Rights of Man*), Jefferson wrote to Madison addressing "the question whether one generation of men has a right to bind another."[24] His answer was a resounding No.

Earlier, in his *Notes on the State of Virginia* (1781–82), Jefferson had made a modest effort "to get rid of the magic supposed to be in the word *constitution*." Virginia's ordinance of government was not "perpetual and unalterable" nor, indeed, any more binding than ordinary legislation. He strangely qualified these remarks, however, by arguing that a properly elected constitutional convention could place both basic rights and the form of government itself "beyond the reach of question."[25]

In a polemic published against Jefferson in 1788, Noah Webster poured scorn on these last-minute concessions to unalterable constitutions.[26] Jefferson apparently took Webster's biting sarcasm to heart. In this letter of 1789, he adopted a more consistently majoritarian stance. Like Paine, he argued that "the earth belongs to the living and not to the dead."[27] Years later, he repeated the same argument in an even more callous fashion: "The dead have no rights. They are nothing." Indeed, "the particles of matter which composed their bodies, make part now of the bodies of other animals, vegetables, or minerals."[28] In his letter to Madison, Jefferson went so far as to deny all ordinary assumptions about historical continuity and (thus) national identity: "By the law of nature, one generation is to another, as one independent nation to another."[29] There is no Burkean fatherland, comprising the living, the dead, and the yet unborn. A constituent assembly in Philadelphia, on this logic, can no more legislate for future Americans than for Australians or Chinese.

To Jefferson, the idea of "perpetuity" is morally repugnant, associated as it is with perpetual servitude and self-perpetuating monopolies. The very word *perpetual* should be swept aside with other residua of the old regime: "No society can make a perpetual constitution, or even a perpetual law." People "are masters of their own persons, and consequently may govern them as they please." As a result, "the constitution and the laws of their predecessors [are] extinguished then in their natural course with those who gave them being."[30] The physical death of the constitution makers entails the spiritual extinction of the constitution.[31]

The attack on perpetuities was by no means unique to Jefferson. Lecturing in the 1760s, for instance, Adam Smith had told his students at Glasgow: "A power to dispose of estates for ever is manifestly absurd. The earth and the fullness of it belongs to every generation, and the preceding one can have no right to bind it up from posterity."[32] Writing from Paris in times of financial crisis, Jefferson echoed Smith's revulsion at this traditional way one generation bound the next. Most of his analysis, in fact, revolved around the law of inheritance. He wondered, for example, "whether the nation may change the descent of lands holden in tail."[33] He also inquired if a father had the natural right to bury his children under a mountain of unpaid bills. More politically, he asked if one generation could justify contracting massive debts, while expecting succeeding generations to pay the toll. Jefferson's radical answer, like Smith's, was that successors are "by nature clear of the debts of their predecessors."[34]

On the basis of Buffon's actuarial tables, moreover, Jefferson calculated that "half of those of 21 years and upwards living at any one instant will be dead in 18 years 8 months."[35] An individual can incur a debt only so long as he will repay it in person. Analogously, the political majority should contract no debts it cannot redeem within the course of nineteen years. Jefferson explicitly extended this argument to binding constitutional frameworks. One of his clearest statements on this question occurs quite late, in a letter of 1816: "By the European tables of mortality, of the adults living at any one moment of time, a majority will be dead in about nineteen years. At the end of that period, then, a new majority is come into place; or, in other words, a new generation. Each generation is as independent of the one preceding, as that was of all which had gone before. It has then, like them, a right to choose for itself the form of government it believes most promotive of its own happiness."[36] National plebiscites determining the form of government and enacting fundamental laws should be held every twenty or thirty years. The latent opportunity for constitutional amendment or repeal is inadequate. At set periods, all laws and institutional arrangements must automatically lapse.[37] Only periodic and obligatory constitutional plebiscites can disenthrall the present from the past and assure every generation its proper say.

## Precommitment and the Growth of Knowledge

Paine's impatience with the legacies of the past was fueled by a fierce hatred of aristocracy. Jefferson, too, disliked hereditary monopolies; but just as decisive in his case was a veneration of science and education: "Laws and institutions must go hand in hand with the progress of the human mind. As that becomes more developed, more enlightened, as new discoveries are made, new truths disclosed, and manners and opinions change with the change of circumstances, institutions must advance also, and keep pace with the times."[38] Modern science has made knowledge permanently unstable. The realization that scientific progress will inevitably overturn current beliefs, in turn, makes "precommitment" seem an epistemological absurdity.

This second anticonstitutionalist argument, too, has a long and intricate history. As Hobbes remarked, "no mans error becomes his own Law; nor obliges him to persist in it."[39] Significantly, his more liberal-minded successors rushed to agree. The brief remark already cited from the Putney Debates, for example, implies that the imperatives of public learning override constitutional pieties: if we discover that our constitution is weak and infirm, we should change it. Similarly, Locke argued that the human capacity for learning and self-correction makes void certain kinds of perpetual contract. No promise to remain a lifelong member of a certain religious community, for instance, could possibly be binding. An individual has no right to enter into an irrevocable agreement of this kind: "If afterwards he discovers anything either erroneous in the doctrine or incongruous in the worship, he must always have the same liberty to go out as he had to enter."[40]

Irritation at stupefying obstacles to further learning was also voiced by Immanuel Kant: "One age cannot enter into an alliance on oath to put the next age in a position where it would be impossible to extend and correct its knowledge, particularly on such important matters [i.e., questions of religion], or to make any progress whatsoever in enlightenment. This would be a crime against human nature, whose original destiny lies precisely in such progress. Later generations are thus perfectly entitled to dismiss such agreements as unauthorized and criminal." One pious generation may not fetter the next to a creedal formula. Even more radically, an individual cannot precommit his own future selves: "It is absolutely impermissible to agree, even for a single lifetime, to a permanent religious constitution which no one might publicly question."[41]

To understand what abstract principle is at stake in these assertions, consider a parallel claim advanced by another liberal theorist in a wholly different setting. Sixty-five years after Kant, Mill wrote that "the practical maxim of leaving contracts free, is not applicable without great limitations in case of engagements in perpetuity."[42] This passage concerns not religion but marriage. Present experience, Mill argued, does not provide the individual with sufficient knowledge to make an irrevocable lifetime engagement. A perpetual marriage vow does violence not only to the human capacity to change but also to the human capability to learn and undo previous mistakes. *Precommitment is illegitimate when it stifles and mocks one's own learning capacity or that of subsequent generations.* On this point, Locke, Kant, and Mill concurred. Their common argument against precommitment, however, turns out to have surprising implications. With some conceptual finesse, as we shall see, it can be upended into a powerful argument *for* precommitment.

### Background to the Paine-Jefferson Thesis

As should now be clear, qualms about constitutional limits on democratic majorities date back at least to the eighteenth century. Consciously elaborating on Lockean premises, both Paine and Jefferson argued that one generation has no moral right to bind the next. In other settings, however, both theorists advocated some form of constitutional precommitment; and they did so without doubting the ultimate sovereignty of the majority. The story as I have told it thus far is therefore patently incomplete.

To put the arguments of Paine and Jefferson into perspective, we need to look at earlier arguments about the bindingness of inherited obligations. The first thing we learn when we take a broader view is that Jefferson and Paine were less radical than they initially seem. They located sovereignty in the people, it is true, and not in the government. But otherwise they simply reformulated the classic rejection of precommitment famously enshrined in the British political system itself. As Madison explained, "the British Constitution fixes no limit whatever to the discretion of the legislature" and "the authority of the Parliament is transcendent and uncontrollable as well with regard to the Constitution as the ordinary objects of legislative provision."[43] Although the British government is moderate, therefore, it is not "constitutionalist" in the American sense. In a passage well-known to all the American founders and framers, Blackstone himself had driven this point home: "Acts of parliament derogatory from the power of subsequent parliaments bind not."[44] All power lay with the present generation (of parliamentarians). If constitutionalism requires the legal entrenchment of certain "higher laws" that cannot be changed by ordinary processes of legislation, then British practice, while embodying the liberal ideal of a government limited by public opinion, periodic elections, and judicial independence, was anticonstitutionalist in a technical sense. *Paine and Jefferson were anticonstitutionalists in the very same way.* Despite their populism, even radicalism, they remained essentially wedded to traditional British assumptions. They simply democratized a legally defined anticonstitutionalism they took over wholesale from Blackstone. They fixed no limit whatever to the discretion of the ultimate bearer of legislative authority (in their case, the people rather than Parliament). Their radicalism, therefore, while real, was more conventional than has been commonly acknowledged. This continuity becomes especially intriguing, when we notice that Blackstone, in turn, built his concept of parliamentary sovereignty on very old models. Even Thomas Aquinas wrote that "the sovereign is above the law, in so far as, when it is expedient, he can change the law."[45] This is precisely how Blackstone thought about Parliament. And it is precisely how Paine and Jefferson thought about the sovereign people.

When expressed in such simple terms, the utterly unoriginal conception of sovereignty as legally unconstrained authority *seems* incompatible with any and every form of constitutionalism. If the sovereign can change the law at will, then law cannot possibly bind or restrict the sovereign. But this seemingly logical conclusion cannot be the last word on the subject, for sovereignty and constitutionalism are not actually incompatible. As our analysis of Bodin showed, theorists and advocates of sovereign power managed to integrate important aspects of constitutionalism into their own thinking. To understand how democratic thinkers, in turn, justified constitutional restrictions on the will of the people, it will prove useful to recall once again how some predemocratic theorists justified placing restrictions on the will of the king.

Bodin's contemporary, Richard Hooker, explained the binding power of ancestral decisions in a way strikingly different from Bodin's. Like an individual, he wrote, a kingdom retains its moral identity over time:

> And to be commanded we do consent, when the society whereof we are part hath at any time before consented, without revoking the same after by the like universal agreement. Wherefore as any man's past is good as long as himself continueth; so the act of a public society of men done five hundred years sithence standeth as theirs who presently are of the same societies, because corporations are immortal; we are alive in our predecessors, and they in their successors do live still.[46]

The present generation is bound by the decisions of its forefathers because the dead and the living constitute one people, linked by the same continuities which unite a single individual at the ages, say, of twenty and fifty. Hooker's defense of constitutional precommitment, in other words, is essentially analogical. The dead can distrain the living because living and dead are one flesh. But this reasoning stands and falls with the persuasiveness either of the underlying analogy or of the assumption that a middle-aged man is morally bound by the promise that, as a youth, he made to himself. One might say that, by stressing the radical discontinuity between generations, Paine and Jefferson, as good Lockeans, aimed to discredit the analogy between an individual and a nation that underlay Hooker's acceptance of inherited constraints. But their protest against inherited constraints can also be framed in different terms.

Anticonstitutionalists need not doubt that promises create a prima facie obligation to fulfill them. But what political conclusions can be drawn from this generally accepted premise? According to Grotius, whose reasoning on this point would probably have appealed to progressives such as Jefferson and Paine, "an association as well as an individual has the right to bind itself by its own act, or by the act of a majority of its members."[47] Promises create a duty for the individual or collective promiser, but *only* when they create a right for the promisee. Thus, no legal or moral problems arise in cases of a first-hand and two-party promise of the standard type. Not even Jefferson or Paine thought there was anything controversial about an agreement by which one individual bound himself personally *to another.* Perplexities emerge, instead, in two special cases: (1) where one individual—or generation—tries heteronomously to bind another, and (2) where there are not two parties but only one involved in the contract, that is, where an individual tries autonomously to make a binding promise *to himself.* The dubious legitimacy of the first sort of binding has already been discussed. Let us now consider the second.

## No Man Can Be Obliged to Himself

Medieval "constitutions" such as Magna Carta were contracts between the king and various estates, especially the barons. The obliger and the obliged were distinct parties. Having made a promise to the nobility, the king was not free to release himself. The Whig settlement of 1688 was still styled as a compact between king and people. And even in the nineteenth century, American secessionists inclined to interpret the U.S. Constitution as a pact between pre-existing, sovereign states. In general, however, the modern constitutions which emerged in the United States and France toward the end of the eighteenth century were not conceived as negotiated truces between classes or factions or territorial subunits. As publicly presented, at least, they bear a striking resemblance to proclamations in which absolute monarchs declare their sovereign will. Rather than being conceived as an exchange of promises between separate parties, modern constitutions are typically styled as frameworks which "we the people" give ourselves.[48] This democratic phraseology produces a legal problem, however. In relations between an individual and himself the power to bind entails the power to loose. Legally, what you freely promise yourself, you can freely fail to deliver. The same rule must logically apply to collectivities. What we the people give ourselves, we the people can take away. From this perspective, a constitution which is both binding and democratic seems not merely paradoxical but completely incoherent.

The basic moral principle at issue here can be traced back at least to Seneca. *A binding promise requires two parties and cannot be performed by one party alone.*[49] This principle, if taken seriously, explodes Hooker's influential argument for a binding constitution. Contrary to what Hooker assumed, the old analogy between an individual and a community makes constitutionalism impossible. This important insight was elaborated politically by a host of thinkers from Aquinas to Rousseau. According to St. Thomas, for instance, "the sovereign is said to be exempt as to its coercive power, since, properly speaking, no man is coerced by himself."[50] For Bodin, as we saw, "the sovereign prince" cannot "be bound unto the laws or ordinances he maketh himself; for a man may well receive a law from another man, but it is impossible in nature for him to give a law unto himself."[51] Hobbes collectivized this argument. Because no individual feels bound by a promise he has made to himself, no kingdom can be obliged by its own constitution:

> Neither can any man . . . be obliged to himself; for the same party being both *the obliger* and *the obliged,* and the obliger having the power to release the obliged, it were merely in vain for a man to be obliged to himself; because he can release himself at his own pleasure, and he that can do this is already actually free. Whence it is plain, that the city is not tied to the civil laws; for the civil laws are the laws of the city, by which, if she were engaged, she should be engaged to herself.[52]

Bodin and Hobbes adduced the maxim, "a will cannot be bound to itself" to justify their thesis that the king or sovereign assembly is, at least in principle, *legibus solutus.*[53] Pufendorf was even more explicit in extending this argument to include democracies. The people, in his view, held the same position of untrammeled constituent power occupied by Hobbes's absolute monarch. After stating in conventional fashion that "a man cannot become obligated to himself," Pufendorf went on to claim that "nothing" could prevent a democratic people from abrogating all their fundamental laws at any time.[54]

This powerful argument was given its most famous eighteenth-century reformulation by Rousseau. A careful reader of Bodin and Hobbes, as well as Pufendorf, Rousseau argued that "it is self-contradictory for sovereign authority to shackle itself," that "it runs against the nature of the body politic that the sovereign imposes on itself a law that it cannot transgress," and that "in the state there is no fundamental law that cannot be revoked, not even the social contract."[55] This seemingly radical rejection of constitutional precommitment, or the self-binding of the sovereign, is, once again, unexcitingly traditional or conventional. The novelty of Rousseau's position lies, instead, in his passionate concern for moral and psychological transformation. It is not so much that a sovereign nation has no right or power to bind itself, but rather that firsthand participation in the ritual of laying down fundamental laws lifts man up from animality and transforms him into a moral creature. The making and ratifying of regime-founding constitutions, one might say, changes an individual from "a stupid and limited animal" into "an intelligent being and a man."[56] Periodic revision or reaffirmation of the fundamental law, too, can have a humanly redemptive function. This was much more important to Rousseau than the practical concern for government maneuverability so essential to *raison d'état* thinkers such as Bodin or Hobbes.

Nevertheless, just as Paine and Jefferson followed Blackstone in stressing that one generation cannot legally bind the next, so Rousseau faithfully followed his great predecessors in mocking the very suggestion that a sovereign people might have an obligation to keep a promise made to itself. In doing so, however, he explicitly assumed that nations *can* be adequately conceived of as individuals. This Hookerian assumption is questionable, however. It is not obvious that "the people" can have anything like a coherent "will" prior to and apart from all constitutional procedures. If popular sovereignty can be expressed only on the basis of pre-existing legal rules for aggregating preferences, it becomes manifestly incoherent to locate the source of *all* legal regulation in the will of the people, as we shall see.

## Why One Generation Can Bind the Next

Most early-modern theorists (not Rousseau alone) admired Solon, Lycurgus, Numa, and the other great legislators of antiquity. The most glorious achievements of the ancient world would have been impossible, they realized, had one generation been unwilling or unable to create a difficult-to-change political framework within which subsequent generations could predictably live.[57] From this perspective, the real question was not whether a constitution maker could realistically secure the conditions of good government by establishing more or less unalterable laws. The question was how to *justify* binding obligations to which successor generations had had no chance to consent.

We now know that the anticonstitutionalist arguments advanced by eighteenth-century radicals were more traditional than is commonly recognized. Wittingly or not, Rousseau, Paine, and Jefferson reproduced old patterns of thought. There was nothing new about their two basic claims, the first, revived by Paine and Jefferson, that one generation cannot bind the next, and the second, renewed by Rousseau, that the sovereign cannot make a binding promise to himself. What counterarguments can be advanced against these two seemingly irrepressible claims? What counterarguments were advanced?

Those who *favored* constitutional precommitment did not have to shift for themselves. They, too, were able to draw upon venerable traditions. Numerous earlier writers, for instance, had been concerned to establish that a newly crowned king was obliged to pay the debts of his predecessor. Even cautious monarchs were sometimes obliged to incur debts greater than they could personally repay during their own brief reigns. Thus, there was a pressing practical reason for arguing that successors are, in fact, obliged to pay the debts of predecessors.[58] Later theorists, writing in a liberal-democratic context, modeled their own arguments for inherited constitutional obligations on just such legal precedents.

In principle, one individual's or generation's promise cannot oblige another. But this rule, as Pufendorf remarks, has a crucial exception: "The act of one generation can bind another only when some man [for instance, a creditor] has acquired a right from it."[59] More specifically, if you inherit another's property (for instance, his throne) you also inherit his debts. "By the strict law of nature no one is bound by another's act, except the one who inherits his property; for the principle that property should be transferred with its obligations dates from the establishment of proprietary rights."[60] Against the *legibus solutus* tradition, in short, seventeenth-century natural law theorists argued that kings were obliged by the promises and contracts of their predecessors because they *voluntarily* accepted a throne to which these promises were legally attached.[61]

A skimpily veiled version of the same argument resurfaces at a crucial point in the *Two Treatises of Government*. Paine and Jefferson relied heavily on Locke's claim that a father could not legitimately bind his children. As Hume noted, however, this principle sits uncomfortably with the liberal belief in an original compact, binding on successors. How could Locke have accepted the validity of an original contract and, simultaneously, have rejected the right of ancestors to bind their posterity? The solution to this problem, which we may call Hume's Paradox, is fundamental for the theory of constitutional democracy. Locke circumnavigated the dilemma, it turns out, by invoking the concept of tacit consent. Only the original covenanters consent expressly to the social contract. To explain why latecomers are nevertheless obliged to obey political authorities, Locke followed Grotius. Whenever he accepts a bequest, a nonsigner of the original contract implicitly or tacitly consents to the political constitutions that make enjoyment of this property possible. Since an heir could, in principle, refuse to accept a bequeathed estate (with political obligations annexed), the republican principle of voluntary consent has not been violated. The father has not bound the son. Instead, the son has, of his own sweet will, bound himself to the father's creditor's and to the government that both protects property rights and makes inheritable property possible in the first place. The only consent of any value is the consent of the living. The government's legitimacy rests not on heredity, therefore, but on conscious, present-day agreement to a reasonable exchange.[62]

According to Sheldon Wolin, Locke employed "the institution of property inheritance to undercut the favorite notion of radicalism that each generation was free to reconstitute political society."[63] Alternatively, Locke's argument here could serve as powerful evidence of *his own* radicalism: if bequests alone justify the obedience of successor generations, inheritable property must become widely diffused as quickly as possible. (Thus, the entire legitimacy of government, in Locke's eyes, "necessarily supposes and requires, that the People should *have Property*.")[64] This argument, in any case, powerfully suggests that Lockean premises do not compel Jefferson's and Paine's anticonstitutionalist opposition to inherited obligations. An adamant constitutionalist, such as Madison, could be a Lockean too, as we shall see.

## Why a Will Can Be Bound to Itself

The prohibition against one generation binding the next can be, and was, overcome in this indirect way. But what about the alleged impossibility of an individual (or, by analogy, a nation) making a binding promise *to* himself (or itself)? A striking contribution to resolving this second problem was made in theology. As is well known, many pagan religions stressed the indispensable social role played by a "binding god" who limits and fetters human beings. Christian theologians, too, occasionally toyed with the same idea. Joseph de Maistre himself, a contemporary of Jefferson and Madison and the father of European antiliberalism, invoked the idea of a *Dieu lieur* to demonstrate the utter futility of constitutional democracy. Self-rule is logically impossible, he argued, because no man can have coercive powers over himself. Moreover, "the essence of a fundamental law is that no one has the right to abolish it: but how is it beyond human power if it has been made by someone?" Liberal constitutionalism is absurd because no political community can voluntarily create a legal framework today that it cannot arbitrarily alter tomorrow. A higher law "necessarily and obviously presupposes a superior will enforcing obedience."[65] How can people view with reverence a rule they created by choice? Liberal democracy represents a vain attempt at bootstrapping. Constitution making is the futile endeavor of a purely human will to devise a law that can, preposterously enough, oblige that very same will. But such efforts will be unavailing. Without an external enforcer, people (singly and collectively) cannot be prevented from breaking their promises. As a result, constitutional obligations can be imposed only by a higher will or a "binding God."

This argument is interesting. But it is less orthodoxly Christian than Maistre believes. For one of the distinguishing features of Christianity, in contrast to pagan religions, is the idea of a God who *can* bind himself. This innovative concept, in fact, seems to have been an important intellectual precondition for the emergence of constitutionalism in the West, that is, the improbable modern idea of a self-binding human community.

God's astonishing capacity to bind Himself, so several late-medieval thinkers persistently argued, is an expression of His awesome freedom and power. Summarizing Ockham and others, Francis Oakley writes: "The only force, after all, capable of binding omnipotence without thereby denying it is the omnipotent will itself."[66] Hooker echoes this earlier tradition when he argues that God's commitments to himself are unchangeable: "Nor is the freedom of the will of God any whit abated, let, or hindered, by means of this; because the imposition of this law upon himself is his own free and voluntary act."[67] It is absurd, even blasphemous, to say that God cannot make a binding promise to Himself, for this would be to place a limit on God's freedom and power.[68]

To my knowledge, the first sustained attempt to adopt this classic theological argument, making it applicable to the political organization of human communities, occurs in the *Six livres de la république*. Bodin sometimes asserts that no sovereign can be bound by promises he makes to himself. But his basic position, as we have seen, is much more flexible than this rigid stipulation would suggest. At the heart of his great treatise is a list of restrictions that every sovereign should, and indeed must, impose upon himself. There was nothing unfamiliar about this idea, for Christian theology itself devoted elaborate attention to the concept of a self-binding highest power. Bodin's political theology, in fact, is explicitly based on a loose analogy between God's self-binding and the self-binding of the political sovereign: constitutional restrictions are less *limits on,* than *expressions of,* sovereign freedom and power. Illicit when it involves a diminution of the crown's authority, monarchical self-binding is possible, permissible, and even obligatory when it maintains and increases royal power. If the king can retain and extend his authority only by tying his own hands, then tie his hands he must.[69] In many circumstances, in fact, abdication of power is not at all an infringement of the prince's will but rather an indirect technique by which he can assert his will.[70]

The idea that self-binding can be a strategy of freedom explains why Bodin—the celebrated advocate of absolute monarchy—nevertheless agrees that the commonwealth "should by laws, and not by the prince's will and pleasure, be governed." Whether or not the sovereign is legally obliged to consult the Estates before levying a tax, for example, he can significantly augment his revenues by granting such assemblies a pivotal role in the resource-extraction process. Analogously, to ensure obedience to his own law, the sovereign must limit his own authority over the parlements and other officers of the realm.[71] As we saw, Bodin overcomes his own injunction against self-binding by claiming that constitutional precommitments, institutional constraints that cannot be waived on an ad hoc basis, are vehicles of royal freedom—strategies by which sovereigns may most effectively assert their authority. Applied imaginatively to a democratic sovereign, this important argument eventually became the basis for the modern theory of liberal constitutionalism.

## Madison's Defense of Precommitment

In criticizing Jefferson's anticonstitutionalist attack on precommitment, James Madison was able to resuscitate these and other arguments that pointed in a proconstitutionalist direction. The two prohibitions (the first against one generation binding the next and the second against a will being bound to itself) had been challenged in the past, and with considerable success. While one man's promise could not bind another directly, it could do so indirectly by means of rights and benefits bequeathed along with obligations and burdens. A will, viewed theoretically, cannot be bound to itself; but self-binding can often be, in practice, a marvelously effective and stable instrument of human agency.

In his reply to Jefferson, Madison essentially denied that a constitution is a dead weight or obstruction. The ultimate source of his argument may have been Bodin's writings or even medieval speculations about divine self-limitation. But the proximate source was surely Locke, who argued forcefully that "the end of law is not to abolish or restrain but to preserve and enlarge freedom."[72] Bonds are not necessarily a form of bondage, Madison concurred. Constraints can promote liberty, not so much limiting a free agent as directing him to his "proper interests." The American Constitution is an instrument of government, not an obstacle to government; it is not disabling, but enabling. Unlike contemporary constitutionalists in France, who were reacting against centuries of autocracy, the American framers had been moved to action when they saw their federation suffering from "weak government" and "impending anarchy." The Articles of Confederation presented "the extraordinary spectacle of a government destitute even of the shadow of constitutional power to enforce the execution of its own laws." This was "a striking absurdity."[73] By helping establish a firm and energetic government, the framers thought, a constitution could remedy these failings. It would not merely limit power; it would also create and assign powers, cement and secure the Union, put democracy into effect, and mandate governmental concern for the general welfare.

In England, at this very time, Burke was describing society as "a partnership . . . between those who are living, those who are dead, and those who are to be born."[74] But his argument was curiously medieval, reminiscent of Hooker, appealing to the organic unity of the cosmos. Madison's similar-sounding idea of an intergenerational division of labor was much more secular and pragmatic. If we can take for granted certain procedures and institutions fixed in the past, we can achieve our present goals more effectively than we could if we were constantly being sidetracked by the recurrent need to establish a basic framework for political life. An inherited constitution can institutionalize as well as stabilize democracy. It is not only, and not essentially, a hedge against arbitrary government. For instance, it also designs and erects those institutions that render rulers accountable. Because it is relatively hard to change, a constitution can disencumber the present generation. Thus, it cannot plausibly be characterized as an oppressive force, an autocratic attempt by the past to enthrall the future. Precommitment is justified because it does not enslave but rather enfranchises future generations.[75]

In *Federalist* no. 49, published three years before he formulated his famous rejoinder to Jefferson, Madison had already criticized the swing-door amendment procedure proposed in his friend's 1783 draft of a constitution for Virginia. Madison's objections to Jefferson's scheme were primarily psychological. He agreed that "the people are the only legitimate fountain of power" and that "a constitutional road to the decision of the people ought to be marked out and kept open, for certain great and extraordinary occasions." But the frequent convoking of constitutional conventions would create periodically a legal vacuum in which rational decisions, based on "the true merits of the question," were not likely to emerge. In this legally anomalous and extraconstitutional condition, "the *passions,* not the *reason,* of the public would sit in judgment." Madison warned that the exceptionally positive experiences of his own generation with constitutional conventions were not typical. In immediate postrevolutionary America, patriotic enthusiasm, popular confidence in national leaders, and universal resentment and indignation against Great Britain had created favorable psychological conditions for trust and cooperation outside the framework of a written constitution. Such conditions were unlikely to endure.[76] In more ordinary circumstances, it would not necessarily be democratic to step casually outside the constitutional framework and pretend to ask "the people" to revise the ground rules. Skeptical of republican theatrics and wary of informal coercion—that is, the disproportionate power of self-selected elites—in systems of so-called direct democracy, Madison wanted to discourage plebiscitary appeals. Because they threatened to nullify democracy-stabilizing constitutional precommitments, periodic plebiscites played into the hands of antirepublican forces. Madison opposed Jefferson's excessively relaxed and optimistic amendment scheme for this reason alone.[77]

In his brilliant letter of February 1790, Madison pursued the same line of attack. Jefferson's assertion that "a living generation can bind itself only," that a living generation of debtors can bind itself alone, not its posterity, to its creditors, he wrote, is "not *in all respects,* compatible with the course of human affairs." The call for ventennial plebiscites ignored certain basic features of republican politics. "However applicable in theory the doctrine may be to a Constitution, it seems liable in practice to some weighty objections."[78]

Refusing to meet Jefferson on the plane of high theory, Madison repeatedly drew the dispute down to practical questions. His principal criticism stemmed from a worry, not shared by Jefferson, about the turbulent psychological conditions likely to prevail between the lapsing of one constitution and the ratifying of another.[79] Jefferson's plan for a constituent assembly every twenty years would make the government "too subject to the casualty and consequences of an interregnum." The attendant turmoil would surely decrease the significance of popular consent while markedly increasing the role of chance and skillful demagoguery.[80] Frequent constituent assemblies would not be, as Jefferson imagined, transparent windows on to the wishes of the majority. Indeed, the hopeful or fearful anticipation of such periodic refoundings would exert a warping force on the political scene, creating otherwise nonexistent interests: "A periodic revision [would] engender pernicious factions that might not otherwise come into existence." Similarly, "a frequent reference of constitutional questions to the decision of the whole society" would awaken "the passions most unfriendly to order and concord."[81] If the ground rules were placed beyond easy reach, by contrast, aggrieved parties would be encouraged to husband their resources. Citizens would benefit from having their hands tied in this regard: by avoiding a wasteful struggle over abstract rules, they could achieve more of their concrete aims than if hotly contested amendment campaigns were waged and even won.

According to Jefferson, "some men look at constitutions with sanctimonious reverence, and deem them like the ark of the covenant, too sacred to be touched."[82] Madison was not one of these men. He did not wish to insulate the ground rules from all criticism and reform; he did not advocate an unalterable constitution. "That useful alterations will be suggested by experience," he wrote, "could not but be foreseen." With Article V, in fact, the framers managed "to provide a convenient mode of rectifying their own errors, as future experience may unfold them."[83] They aimed to make the amendment process complicated and time-consuming, admittedly, requiring not a simple majority but rather a sequence of extraordinary majorities within various bodies over an extended period of time. But they sought not an absolute but only a relative permanence. Article V, in Madison's view, balances the needs of flexibility and rigidity, that is, "guards equally against that extreme facility, which would render the Constitution too mutable; and that extreme difficulty, which might perpetuate its discovered faults."[84]

The unwieldiness of the amending power, while permitting useful changes, is meant to discourage frivolous attempts to revise the Constitution every time political deadlock occurs. The unavailability of constitutional amendment as an ordinary political strategy encourages democratic processes of bargaining and mutual learning. Obligatory delays also heighten the quality of successful amendments, because cumbersome procedures give all parties time for thought. Jefferson's scheme was unrealistic, Madison thought, because it ignored the nerve-wracking psychology of interregna and the way periodic opportunities to rescind the entire Constitution would both (mis)shape preferences and squander scarce resources.

Madison also considered the question of the public debt and specifically Jefferson's extreme claim that one generation never has a right to bind its successors to repay debts contracted earlier. Once again, Madison's objection was practical and had, as he cautiously suggested, "some foundation in the nature of things." Following the seventeenth-century natural law theorists, he wrote that financial obligations may descend from one generation to another because some essential national purposes can be achieved only on the basis of an intertemporal division of labor: "Debts may be incurred with a direct view to the interest of the unborn as well as of the living: Such are debts for repelling a Conquest, the evils of which descend through many generations. Debts may even be incurred principally for the benefit of posterity: Such, perhaps, is the [Revolutionary War] debt incurred by the U. States. In these instances the debts might not be dischargeable within the term of 19 years."[85] If benefits are distributed across many generations, burdens should be allotted in the same broad way. Such an arrangement corresponds to equity and provides rewards for all parties in an intergenerational alliance. This is the reasoning, it seems, that underlies Article VI of the Constitution: "All Debts contracted and Engagements entered into, before the Adoption of this Constitution, shall be as valid against the United States under this Constitution, as under the Confederation." Here again the framers deftly adapted the arguments of Grotius and Pufendorf to a republican context. True, future generations are seldom asked if they wish to accept a benefit (say, the defeat of an aggressive enemy) in exchange for assuming a debt. But if all civilized contracts required copresence then each generation would be reduced to a separate nation, that is, would be calamitously deprived of the advantages to be reaped from cooperation across time in which partners cannot, in principle, encounter one another. This explains why the framers rejected "the pretended doctrine that a change in the political form of civil society has the magical effect of dissolving its moral obligations."[86] Practical considerations alone suggest that, in such cases, we should override Jefferson's philosophical principle that no obligations can be incurred without express consent.

Madison next considered property law. The rights of property are not natural but "positive," that is, conventional and revocable. Even in the case of such lesser law, however, periodic assemblies for repeal or reaffirmation would have deleterious effects. On Jefferson's scheme, at twenty-year intervals, "all the rights depending on positive laws . . . become absolutely defunct," to be reenacted or not as the latest constituent assembly sees fit. Once again, such an arrangement would not merely register preference change over time. A constituent assembly is a thermometer that drastically alters the temperature of the room. In the case of property law, the anticipation of such assemblies would provoke "the most violent struggles . . . between the parties interested in reviving and those interested in reforming the antecedent state of property." True, conflicting interests concerning property law exist with or without periodic constituent assemblies. But the inevitability of latent conflict does not imply that a cyclical outburst of violent struggles will necessarily work to the long-term advantage of, say, debtors. A "general uncertainty" would "discourage every useful effort of steady industry pursued under the sanction of existing laws" and, most important of all, would bestow an unearned and undemocratic advantage on those who are clever and unscrupulous enough to exploit social chaos for political and economic gain.

Jefferson was dissatisfied with a formal opportunity to repeal laws and amend the constitutional order because he rejected the idea that tacit consent alone could legitimate rules and decisions. Consent can be inferred, according to traditional doctrine, "from the omission of express revocation," say, from the failure of the public to invoke the right of rebellion. In a modified form, as we have seen, Madison embraced this familiar view. Resigned acquiescence is not a sign of consent; but when citizens do not invoke their rights of amendment and repeal, although they know they could do so easily and without being punished, they are implicitly agreeing to whatever framework is currently in place. No need to schedule magical moments in which express consent must be proclaimed aloud, so long as the uninterrupted chance to protest and lobby for revocation is guaranteed.

Jefferson demurred, but the problems afflicting his own proposal, too, were manifold and obvious. Only the doctrine of tacit consent, according to Madison, could provide "relief from such embarrassments." Madison admitted that, in the past, the doctrine of tacit approval had had "pestilent" consequences. But he believed that its noxious side effects could be neutralized by a deftly designed constitution that would also avoid "the evils" necessarily attendant upon Jefferson's scheme of recurrent constituent assemblies.

Implied or tacit consent, Madison concluded by arguing, is indispensable to "the very foundation of Civil Society." Majoritarianism itself, so essential to Jefferson's scheme, depends on the assumption that individuals born into a society tacitly assent to "the rule by which the majority decides for the whole."[87] To require the express consent of every generation to the constitutional framework (or of every individual to majority rule) would introduce an element of nervous hysteria into the heart of democratic politics, weakening its capacity to resolve conflicts and aggregate diverse interests without violence. To require express and constantly reiterated consent, paradoxically, would *decrease* the influence of the bulk of citizens over the direction of public policy and thus over their own lives.

Jefferson had associated his idea of government by the living, moreover, with an implausible postulate of discrete generations: "Let us suppose a whole generation of men to be born on the same day, to attain mature age on the same day, and to die on the same day, leaving a succeeding generation in the moment of attaining their mature age all together."[88] Unfortunately, this unrealistic fantasy about citizens who are born and die in parade-like generational cohorts conveys a message opposite to the one Jefferson intended. Hume (who was, incidentally, detested by Jefferson)[89] was quite skeptical about the concept of tacit consent. But he drew a distinctly non-Jeffersonian conclusion from his observation that one human generation did not "go on the stage at once, and another succeed, as is the case with silkworms and butterflies."[90] Precisely because generations overlap, because individuals enter into and depart from the world one by one, the living have no right to repeal, at set intervals, the legacy of the past. Closing the doors on our predecessors' commitments is impractical, because the members of every new generation must coexist promiscuously with survivors of the old. Less fearful of innovation than Hume, Madison, too, was eager that methods for registering public consent be compatible with the unsynchronized itineraries of human lives.

## Founders and Citizens

Unlike Rousseau's longing for a morally and psychologically transformative experience, the Paine-Jefferson formula has much to be said in its favor. The present generation alone lives in the world. Who else should be responsible for the workings of a democratic government if not the living? Ancestor worship, a "blind veneration for antiquity," must be kept under control.[91]

As Madison suggested, however, the idea of a government conducted exclusively by the living is not as problem-free as it might at first seem. For one thing, repudiation of the past is a two-edged sword. Present decisions, made with the future in mind, will soon belong to the past. If we can assume that subsequent generations will treat our future-minded choices with haughtily sovereign contempt, why should we give more thought to the future than to the past?[92] We want to act responsibly toward succeeding generations, while we tend to reject the notion that previous generations are responsible for us. But is this really a consistent attitude to adopt? Adding the suggestion that those who are presently alive yearn to control the future, Jon Elster formulates the "paradox of democracy" in the following way: "Each generation wants to be free to bind its successors, while not being bound by its predecessors."[93]

Jefferson and Paine never squarely faced this problem. Imbued with the ideology of unlimited progress, they probably assumed that the future would take care of itself. Convinced that the genuine problems of politics were minimal and decreasing, neither thinker perceived clearly the advantages that might be reaped from an intergenerational division of labor. Viewing the past primarily as dead weight, they failed to appreciate that predecessors might lighten the load on successors. Neither was sufficiently impressed by the utility of organizing in advance future democratic life. Neither recognized each generation's need to unclutter and systematize its own agenda by acceding to certain power-granting, procedure-defining, and jurisdiction-specifying decisions of the past. In sum, neither managed to conceive the constitution in a positive manner, as an indispensable *instrument of government.* Only theorists such as Madison, less intoxicated by the guarantee of progress, became conscious of Elster's paradox and (more importantly) of the paradoxical dependence of the sovereignty of the present on the precommitments of the past. As Bodin, among others, clearly taught, individuals tend to forfeit power and freedom whenever they attempt to solve all their problems alone. By accepting a preestablished institutional framework, a people, like a king, ties its own hands; but it also frees itself from considerable burdens.

Present decisions set in motion irreversible processes which, in turn, necessarily box in future generations. This is true whether we embody our decisions in "irrevocable" charters or not. We must adjust to this fact about historical continuity even if it violates Paine's and Jefferson's curious belief that each generation has an inviolable right to start from scratch, *ex nihilo,* with no inheritances whatsoever from the past.[94] Jefferson himself helped foreclose the options of future generations by agreeing to deprive such states as Virginia of some of their sovereignty. This decision opened some doors by shutting others. Its impact, moreover, was far from negligible: it led, among other things, to a civil war fought explicitly over the legal perpetuity of the Union.

In his remarks on constitutional precommitment, Elster also suggests that there is a radical dissimilarity between the political action of the framers and the political action of subsequent generations. "Only the constituent assembly is a political actor, in the strong sense of *la politique politisante;* all later generations are restricted to *la politique politisée,* or to the day-to-day enactment of the ground rules."[95] Elster does not claim, of course, that his analytical contrast is adequate to the realities of history. A constitutional framer can never be an unbound binder, any more than a sovereign can be an uncommanded commander. Mythmakers aspiring to legitimate a written constitution may invoke an analogy with God's creative act standing in a transcendent relation to acts within the created world.[96] But it would not necessarily be prudent to repackage old myths as new theories. To influence a situation, an actual power wielder must adapt himself to preexistent patterns of force and unevenly distributed possibilities for change. Autonomy in some respects requires heteronomy in others. *Every influencer must be influenced.* This is a central axiom of any realistic theory of power. The capacity to initiate and the need to adapt are never so sharply disjoined, therefore, as Elster's distinction suggests.[97] The framers of the American Constitution, for example, were heavily indebted to the political theories of Harrington, Locke, Trenchard and Gordon, Hume, Montesquieu and Voltaire, to the experiences gained during the seventeenth-century English Commonwealth, and to "the example of the State constitutions."[98] Moreover, they were faced with intractable realities (notably Southern slavery) and only performed *la politique politisante* because they were simultaneously able to practice the art of compromise with unlovable realities, that is to say, because they were engaged in *la politique politisée*.[99]

Individuals who set the side constraints exercise greater influence than those who make particular decisions. Because a constituent assembly allocates authority and establishes decision-making procedures, it can, in some sense, be considered "privileged" with respect to succeeding generations.[100] But, on balance, it is not so clear who exerts more *power* in this relation. Elster expresses grave doubts about the concept of a continuous national "self" (such as Hooker assumed) exercising self-command through a constitutional framework.[101] But the idea that framers exert power over their descendants is no less controversial. The concept of power is difficult to apply in a situation where power wielders, being long defunct, can no longer glean any possible benefit from modifying the behavior of their posterity.

Just as framers are not omnipotent angels intervening from outside the stream of history, subsequent generations, laboring within a framework established by law and custom, should not be likened to Pavlov's dog. While the Constitution has certainly shaped the course of American history, cultural drift and political crisis have returned the favor by reshaping the Constitution in unforeseeable ways. Even though (and, in some cases, precisely because) they are precommitted by the past, descendants possess ample room for maneuver, innovation, and reform. The chance for liberal construction—that is, imaginative interpretation—of the Constitution, even more than Article V, reconciles loyalty to the past with responsiveness to the present. To satisfy rival interests and muster majority support, participants at the Federal Convention incorporated conflicting and ambiguous provisions into the Constitution, thus delegating essential discretionary powers to their descendants.[102] They deliberately strove to avoid sacrificing posterity to their own limited foresight.

The process of framing a constitution, which we might as well call *la politique politisante,* continues long after a constituent assembly has been dissolved. Indeed, it never stops. Many of the basic features of the American Constitution (for example, the strength of the Union, the broad legislative responsibilities of the President, and especially judicial review) were innovations introduced without any formal amendment procedure having been invoked. The Constitution is silent about political parties; but their subsequent development has decisively affected the influence of the Constitution, disappointing the framers' expectations about the Electoral College, for instance. Furthermore, fundamental terms such as "cruel and unusual punishment" tend to alter their meaning from generation to generation. In comparative perspective, the "authorial" powers of later generations are probably greater than those of the original framers.[103] Successors, it could be argued, are not such hapless prisoners of the moment as were the founders. They are no longer victimized by the urgent need to put an end to the turbulence of a sovereignless nation—a need that may have made the framers somewhat timid and conservative about change. Freed from the enormous task of launching and legitimating a new regime in a time of troubles, latecomers can devote themselves to achieving particular political goals.

## Disabling and Enabling Rules

Paine and Jefferson took comfort from the observation that no generation had the ability to bind its successors irreversibly. After witnessing the "suicides" of several democratic regimes, we cannot revive their complacency, their naive trust in the good sense of the present generation, once unleashed from the vexatious commitments of the past.[104] The admittedly real difficulty of binding the future is not always a cause for celebration for the simple reason that our incapacity to commit successors in a semiautocratic manner may lead to the destruction of a fragile system of representative democracy. True, the collapse of the Weimar Republic was due more to the disloyalty of its elites than to Article 48 or defective constitutional design. Still the catastrophe of 1933 suggests, once again, that constitutional precommitment and democratic politics may not be so antagonistic as Jefferson and Paine sometimes believed. There is paradox but no contradiction here. Theorists who recognized the paradox, such as Madison, also embraced it.

A preceding generation cannot use legal entrenchment to prevent a succeeding generation from saying: "No more freedom!" No constitutional arrangement, however well-designed, can protect reliably against a "violent popular paroxysm."[105] But this factual incapacity does not imply that predecessors have no right or reason to design institutions with an eye to inhibiting the future destruction of electorally accountable government. When attempting to bind the future, constitution makers are not simply trying to exercise domination and control. Precommitment is justified because, rather than merely foreclosing options, it holds open possibilities that would otherwise lie beyond reach.

The Paine-Jefferson formula, in truth, is convincing only if we restrict our view to the short run, to relations between two generations. A wider perspective changes the equation. By means of a constitution, generation *a* can help generation *c* protect itself from being sold into slavery by generation *b*. To safeguard the choices available to distant successors, constitution makers restrict the choices available to proximate successors. Ultimately, therefore, Hume was wrong to discern a self-contradiction at the heart of republican theory. Our ancestors *did* have the right to contract away our freedom to contract away the freedom of our descendants. The framers strove to create not merely a popular government but a popular government that (unlike the turbulent Greek republics) might endure. They had a right to bind subsequent generations minimally to prevent them from binding *their* successors maximally. In practice, to be sure, this arrangement will function only if latecomers, currently alive, acknowledge its essential fairness. But this is not an unreasonable expectation. Recognizing the rights of its posterity, a current generation may voluntarily limit its own power over the future; and the easiest way for a large and diverse community to do so may be to submit to the univocal authority of the past. Seen in this light, Madisonian precommitments appear, in principle, both democratic and majoritarian. To grant power to all future majorities, of course, a constitution must limit the power of any given majority. Liberal constitutions, in fact, consist largely of metaconstraints: rules that *compel* each decision-making authority to expose its decisions to criticism and possible revision, rules that *limit* each generation's ability to rob its own successors of significant choices.

Paine and Jefferson shuddered at the idea of binding the future because they could not conceive of "binding" in a positive or emancipatory way. They did not grasp clearly that constraints can enhance freedom, that rigidities can create flexibilities. Their blind spot was due partly to a naive belief in progress. But it also resulted from their overly conservative conception of how constitutions function. The common metaphors of checking, blocking, limiting, and restraining all suggest that constitutions are, in the main, negative devices used to prevent abuses of power. But rules are also creative. They organize new practices and generate new possibilities which would not otherwise exist.

As I explained in the last chapter, constitutions may be usefully compared to the rules of a game and even to the rules of grammar. While *regulative* rules (for instance, "no smoking") govern preexistent activities, *constitutive* rules (for instance, "bishops move diagonally") make a practice possible for the first time. Rules of the latter sort should not be thought of as hindrances or chains. Grammatical principles do not merely restrain a speaker, repressing his unruly impulses while permitting orderly ones to filter through. Far from simply handcuffing people, linguistic rules allow interlocutors to do many things they would not otherwise have been able to do or even have thought of doing. Flexibility should not be contrasted with rigidity, therefore, for the simple reason that rigidities can create flexibilities. A democratic constitution, by analogy, does not merely hobble majorities and officials. The American Constitution helped create the Union. It also assigns powers (gives structure to the government, guarantees electoral accountability, protects the rights of the opposition, and so forth), and regulates the way in which these powers are employed (in accord, for example, with principles such as due process and equal treatment). To say that constitutional rules are enabling, not disabling, is to reject the notion that constitutionalism is exclusively concerned with limitations on power.

We can begin the move from negative to positive constitutionalism simply by rethinking our concept of *limitations*. Limits do not necessarily weaken; they can also strengthen. For one thing, "that ill deserves the Name of Confinement, which hedges us in only from Bogs and Precipices."[106] Constitutions, moreover, can be binding in a way that engenders unprecedented possibilities. By having himself bound to the mast, Ulysses could enjoy an event (song without shipwreck) that he could not otherwise have experienced. His strategy of preventive self-incapacitation, however, is not precisely analogous to the designing and ratification of a constitution. In America, if the framers had not "bound" their successors, there would have been no country. That is why the framers are often assimilated to the Founders. Constitutions do not merely limit power; they can create and organize power as well as give it direction. Most important of all, limited government can subserve self-government by helping create the "self" (or national unity) which does the governing. That constitutionalism can contribute to nation building provides powerful evidence that it has a positive, not merely a negative, function.

## Enabling Functions of the Separation of Powers

For classical liberals, a separation of powers was the centerpiece of modern constitutionalism. Locke, for example, wrote that in every "well-framed Government," the legislative and executive powers must be placed "in distinct hands." When such powers are united, what results is tyranny and atrocious despotism, as in Turkey. If powers are ever fused in England, political freedom will be lost. As Montesquieu remarked, "when the legislative and executive powers are united in the same person, or in the same body of magistrates, there can be no liberty." According to Hume, too, "the government, which, in common appellation, receives the appellation of free, is that which admits of a partition of power among several members." According to Madison, finally, "the accumulation of all powers, legislative, executive, and judiciary, in the same hands, whether of one, a few, or many, and whether hereditary, self-appointed, or elective, may justly be pronounced the very definition of tyranny."[107]

Negative constitutionalists, those who conceive constitutions in primarily prohibitory or inhibiting terms, routinely describe the separation of powers as a machine for preventing encroachments.[108] Authority is assigned to rival offices or individuals to avoid excessive concentrations of power, and thereby to protect a sphere of private freedom. Because of the natural ambitiousness of man, writes Hume, every single branch in any government you establish will attempt to "engross the whole power of the constitution."[109] If nature gets her way, power will be monopolized. Authority can be limited, therefore, only "by placing several parts of it in different hands," to avoid excessive concentrations of power.[110] One branch of government can "check" another, inhibiting despotism and disclosing corruption. When countervailing branches are correctly arranged, then, as Montesquieu stated, "power arrests power."[111]

The most common criticisms of the separation of powers concern its alleged destructive consequences. Divided authority is said to make coherent government impossible. Shared authority is said to blur lines of political responsibility. That there is some truth to these claims, no observer of separation-of-powers regimes can deny. But neither is this the whole story. Here, too, the negative and static connotations of constitutional binding obscure the positive and dynamic purposes of institutional design.

As a corrective to the conventional view, it is useful to conceive the separation of powers as a form of the division of labor, permitting—in some cases—a more efficient distribution and organization of governmental functions. Specialization improves everyone's performance. According to Adam Smith, for example, "the separation of the judicial from the executive power seems originally to have arisen from the increasing business of society, in consequence of its increasing improvement."[112] Initially, kings established quasi-autonomous judicial agencies in response to governmental overload. An independent judiciary was originally established not to limit power but, on the contrary, to increase the capacity of the government to do its job.

Like other constitutional provisions, the separation of powers can enhance governmental authority. It can disentangle overlapping jurisdictions, sort out unclear chains of command, and help overcome a paralyzing confusion of functions. As a political version of the division of labor, it is creative to the extent that specialization enhances sensitivity to a diversity of social problems. The evolution of three distinct (though cooperating) branches of government may be compared with the development of the modern cabinet system. New institutions and offices were gradually developed to cope with a growing volume of highly diverse social problems. Each branch, moreover, recruits personnel in a distinct manner, thus increasing the variety of social interests and perspectives reflected in government decision making.

Early justifications of the separation of powers, long before Smith, emphasized its power-enhancing function. Bodin, remember, argued that an independent judiciary would increase the king's capacity to govern. Malefactors must be punished; but if the king exacts penalties personally, he will arouse resentments that will, in turn, weaken his authority. Thus, a clever sovereign will reserve to himself the distribution of pardons and rewards while delegating to independent magistrates the job of issuing condemnations and exacting fines.[113] Montesquieu took over and refined this argument: a king who relinquishes the power to punish crimes will actually increase his overall power because this arrangement will prevent the parties involved from applying extortionate pressure on the crown.[114]

The separation of powers may not only enhance political power; it can also help sustain democracy. The maxim "divide and rule" was traditionally employed by the masters of mankind to keep their subjects in thrall. Democratic constitution makers usurped this ancient principle and used it in an inverted way, as a strategy by which the governed might enforce their will upon their would-be governors. Rather than weakening government, the separation of powers helps secure the conditions of popular government.

Locke in particular emphasizes the representative function of the separation of powers. Why should legislative and executive powers not be combined in the same hands? If they were so united, the lawmakers would know that the laws they enacted would never be applied to themselves (because *they* would be doing the applying and doing it selectively). If legislators also have executive power, then "they may exempt themselves from Obedience to the Laws they make, and suit the Law, both in its making and execution, to their own private advantage." This opportunity for self-exemption is "too great a temptation to humane frailty apt to grasp at Power." If the executive power rests in other hands, by contrast, legislators will be more likely to make laws with the expectation that these laws will be applied to themselves as well. In other words, the separation of powers heightens the possibility that the perspective of the ordinary citizen, subject to the law, will be represented within the lawmaking process. It increases the likelihood that legislation will serve "the good of the whole" and not just the private advantage of a few lawmakers.[115]

An additional, somewhat more speculative, thought may be worth mentioning. The separation of powers is often described as a balance of powers.[116] Political theorists have tended to conceive this equilibrium as inherently motionless and stable. But a "balance" may be more accurately described as a situation easy to upset: a single straw will tip the scales. If the different branches of government balance one another, then the government as a whole may be much easier to influence from the outside. Hamilton makes this very argument about federalism,[117] while Madison extends it to bicameralism. A constitutionally imposed equilibrium may make the government as a whole resemble a barometer, more sensitive to fluctuations in public opinion than any single-branch regime would be. In this sense, too, checks and balances may contribute directly to popular sovereignty.

### Democracy-Reinforcing Restraints

Tribe asks: if we believe in the sovereignty of the people, why do we accept all these constitutional restrictions on majority rule? The answer proposed by the American framers was simple and bold: these are not restrictions; these *are* the people (or the decisions of the people).[118]

*Popular ratification* justifies the exceptional legal entrenchment of the Constitution, its immunity to change by ordinary legislative means: "The people are the only legitimate fountain of power, and it is from them that the constitutional charter, under which the several branches of government hold their power, is derived."[119] These derived powers have no authority to rewrite the commission under which they function. The British lodge sovereignty in Parliament, rather than in the people, and are therefore clueless about constitutionalism in the American sense. As Madison explains, "the important distinction so well understood in America between a Constitution established by the people and unalterable by the government, and a law established by the government and alterable by the government, seems to have been little understood and less observed in any other country." Although "the rights of the Constitution" are much discussed in Great Britain, Parliament's authority over the form of government remains "transcendent and uncontrollable."[120] Constitutional amendment by a simple parliamentary majority, obviously enough, is incompatible with constitutionalism as Madison and Hamilton understood it. As a popularly ratified document that the government cannot redesign by ordinary means, the constitution is an instrument of self-government, a technique whereby the citizenry rules itself. How else could a large democratic community manage its own affairs? A collectivity cannot formulate coherent purposes apart from all decision-making procedures. "The people" cannot act as an amorphous blob.

Carl Schmitt, an ardent opponent of liberal constitutionalism, loftily spurned such down-to-earth considerations. Like many less cynical theorists, he subscribed to the legendary opposition between constitutional limitations and democratic government.[121] Because *das Volk* is the ultimate constituent power, he claims, it must be conceived as an unstructured "Urgrund" or even as "das 'formlos Formende'" which cannot be precommitted by constitutional procedures.[122] But Schmitt's democratic mysticism, not to mention its practical consequences, suffices to discredit this approach. It is meaningless to speak about popular government apart from some sort of legal framework which enables the electorate to express a coherent will. For this reason, democratic citizens require some organizational support from regime-founding forefathers.[123] Unless they tie their own hands, with the help of their predecessors, "the people" will be unable to deliberate effectively and act consistently.

Decisions are made on the basis of predecisions. Electoral choices are made on the basis of constitutional choices. When they enter the voting-booth, for instance, voters decide who shall be president, but not how many presidents there shall be.[124] Similarly, they do not decide, at that moment, the date when the election is to be held. (As Locke recognized, "this power of chusing must also be exercised by the People, either at certain appointed seasons, or else when they are summoned to it."[125]) Arguing that constitutionalism was an American innovation, alien to Great Britain, Madison noted that British parliamentarians had "actually changed, by legislative acts, some of the most fundamental articles of the government." His principal example of a higher-order law that ought not to depend upon the discretion of elected deputies is electoral law itself. "They have in particular, on several occasions, changed the period of election; and, on the last occasion, not only introduced septennial in place of triennial elections, but by the same act, continued themselves in place four years beyond the term for which they were elected by the people." Under the system developed at Philadelphia, by contrast, the legislature cannot, of its own sweet will, rewrite the rules of the electoral game. For the House of Representatives, for instance, "biennial elections" are "unalterably fixed by such a Constitution."[126]

Fixed-calendar elections, which may well be constitutionally prescribed, deny discretion to both public officials and present-day electoral majorities on a very important question. In practice, liberal democracy is never simply the rule of the people but always the rule of the people within certain predetermined channels, according to certain prearranged procedures, following certain preset criteria of enfranchisement, and on the basis of certain predrawn electoral districts. The last example is revealing, even though districting schemes are not usually entrenched in the constitution. (As a product of federalism, the American Senate is an exception.) While placing supreme authority in an elected legislature,[127] Locke granted the power to reapportion the elected assembly to the unelected executive.[128] Population shifts make it undemocratic to fix electoral districts in an unalterable charter. But the authority periodically to readjust the system to unforeseen demographic changes can be constitutionally assigned. It would be unwise, Locke thought, to ascribe the task of remedying gross malapportionment to the very assembly created by gross malapportionment. Such a negligent allocation of oversight power would make legislators judges in their own cause.[129]

Citizens can enforce their will only through elections held on the basis of a preexistent apportionment plan, a plan which may be unfair or obsolete. As a result, the responsibility for flexible redistricting must be lodged outside the popularly elected legislature (for instance, in the courts). To preserve democracy, in this case, voters must partially *abdi-*

*cate* the power of apportionment, that is, must remove it from the hands of elected and accountable representatives. Here we encounter the paradox of democracy not as a theoretical puzzle but as a functioning institutional arrangement: citizens can increase their power by tying their own hands. Limited dedemocratization subserves continuing democratic rule.

## Securing the Conditions of Public Debate

The best example of a constitutional limit which pries open more doors than it slams shut, that gives subsequent generations more room for maneuver than they would have had in the absence of a constitution, is the First Amendment. The primary function of constitutionalism, it could even be argued, is to protect the hazardous freedom of political discussion, not private property or liberty of contract. An open society can be preserved only if the government is prevented from silencing its critics and if diverse political opinions can be freely aired. Formulating just such a public-debate rationale for the First Amendment, Justice Brandeis wrote that the freedoms of speech, association, and the press, including the right of legally dissenting from government policy, are "indispensable to the discovery and spread of political truth."[130] Liberty of expression is vital to the growth of knowledge and the nonviolent reform of constitutional democracy itself—a theme we will explore further in the next chapter. This argument was not novel with Brandeis, of course, but had long been a staple theme of classical liberal thought.

Milton, who defined "civil liberty" as the capacity of government, on the basis of a free press, to correct its own mistakes, advanced the optimistic notion that truth will always defeat falsehood in open combat: "Let [Truth] and Falsehood grapple; who ever knew Truth put to the worse in a free and open encounter."[131] Locke modestly echoed this claim, writing that "the truth would do well enough if she were once left to shift for herself." He also drew attention to the advantages of making political decisions in an atmosphere of uninhibited public disagreement. When legislators hear "all sides" on a controversial question, they are more likely to make an intelligent decision. We elect our deputies so that they may "freely act and advise, as the necessity of the Commonwealth, and the Publick good should, upon examination, and mature debate, be judged to require. This, those who give their Votes before they hear the Debate, and have weighed the Reasons on all sides, are not capable of doing."[132] Good political advice presupposes the free circulation of information and requires the advisers to hear all sides on every important question.

Cato continued this tradition: "Truth has so many Advantages above Error, that she wants only to be shewn, to gain admiration and Esteem."[133] Jefferson also concurred, somewhat more robustly: "Truth is great and will prevail if left to herself." Despite extreme personal bitterness toward his critics, Jefferson agreed that, of all the instruments useful for discovering the truth, the "most effectual hitherto found, is freedom of the press."[134] Madison and Hamilton were equally concerned to secure "the benefits of free consultation and discussion," concluding that the "jarring" of ideas yields suggestions no one would have dreamed of in isolation.[135] Throughout the Enlightenment, as a matter of fact, the clinching argument for the freedoms of speech, press, peaceable assembly, and petition was that public disagreement sharpens the minds of all parties, producing decisions that are much more intelligent than any proposals presented at the outset.[136] The truth-generating capacity of uncensored debate was the standard rationale for freedom of the press: "If we should be sure of the truth of our opinions, we should make them public. It is by the touchstone of contradiction that we must prove them. The press should therefore be free."[137]

Among nineteenth-century liberal theorists, none focused more persistently on the freedom-enhancing and citizen-involving nature of constitutional rules and institutions than Mill. The burdens and opportunities of a written constitution were foreign to the English experience, as Madison pointed out. But, as we shall see, Mill devoted much of *Considerations on Representative Government* to a discussion of various semiconstitutional devices for organizing popular government. Such devices are stimulants as well as depressants. They mobilize decentralized information and imagination, encourage fact-mindedness, and create incentives for mutual criticism and learning. In advocating an institutional arrangement, Mill typically stressed its creative functions: "It would not be exclusively a check, but also an impelling force."[138] He strove for a constitutional balance between two sorts of mechanism: those that ensured tolerance for poor performance (without being "idiot-proof," of course) and those that encouraged or induced high performance. "Publicity" was a fundamental device in his scheme because it functioned in both ways, as a mobilizer and as a hindrance.

The heart of Mill's constitutionalism, if we can call it that, was a system of incentives encouraging thoughtful public participation.[139] His least attractive proposals, such as the public ballot and supplementary votes granted to those holding university degrees, were designed not merely to prevent the abuse of power but also to enlist intelligent citizen participation: "The general prosperity attains a greater height, and is more widely diffused in proportion to the amount and variety of personal energies enlisted in promoting it."[140]

Democracy is government by rational and free public discussion among legally equal citizens, not simply the enforcement of the will of the majority.[141] Public disagreement itself, conducted with Rawlsian "civility," is an essential instrument of popular government.[142] Not any "will," but only a will formed in vigorous and wide-open debate should be given sovereign authority. The legally guaranteed right of opposition is therefore a fundamental norm of democratic government; it provides an essential precondition for the formation of a democratic public opinion. Without being threatened or deprived of their livelihood, citizens must be able to articulate and publicly defend heterodox political views. Consent is meaningless without institutional guarantees of unpunished dissent.[143] Popular sovereignty is unavailing without legally entrenched rules to organize and protect public debate.[144] Indeed, in the absence of such protections, unanimity on political questions may be a sign of irrationality rather than of rational agreement. As Mill wrote, unless unanimity results from a full and free comparison of opposite opinions, it is not at all desirable.[145]

A well-crafted liberal constitution can protect and nourish political opposition, preventing political elites from innoculating their decisions against future criticism and revision. Powerful individuals naturally resent being contradicted and refuted in public. Rules forbidding the punishment of dissenters and gadflies and stringently limiting the officeholder's resort to secrecy compensate for a lack of better motives. The narrowly legalistic definition of *treason* in Article III, section 3, provides another important protection for potential critics of the party in power. Similarly, by means of a constitutional provision ("Congress shall make no laws . . . abridging the freedom of speech"), a community can defend its rational decision-making capacities against its own inherent tendency to lapse into "group think."[146] Decisions made without canvassing diverse viewpoints are likely to be ill-considered. Uninformed and uncritical deliberation has thus been described as a "mutilation of the thinking process of the community against which the First Amendment to the Constitution is directed."[147]

After a decision is made, the outvoted minority must in practice submit to the will of the majority. But constitutionalized rules of the game allow losers to mount an aggressive campaign of public sarcasm and to focus public attention irritatingly on the unforeseen consequences of the decision reached. In the long run, such a momentarily annoying arrangement makes for better decisions. Some rights, in other words, are designed less for the protection of the minority than for the correction and instruction of the majority. No "popular will" worth taking seriously has a mystical preexistence. In a large nation, at least, public deliberation is always the product of constitutional restraints. Such restraints cannot be plausibly described as antidemocratic so long as they are explicitly designed to evoke "the cool and deliberate sense of the community."[148] Because well-functioning constitutional limits tend to make government more intelligent, the majority of living citizens may even be willing to impose such limits upon itself.

Accepting this basic line of argument, both Mill and Madison rejected the claim that democracy is "based on the right to current intervention in all matters."[149] Democrats who advanced this anticonstitutionalist view were unwitting heirs to a crude version of the ideology of absolute monarchy. If the people is truly *legibus solutus,* if all the ground rules are perpetually on the verge of being rescinded, there will be no possibility of recording or even forming an intelligent public will.

The idea of "possibility-generating restraints" helps explain the contribution of constitutionalism to democracy. It also helps clarify the relation between inherited obligations and express consent. The framers indubitably assumed that future generations would want to live under a government in which most obligations arose from express consent. To make this possible, however, a constitution already had to be in place: a procedural document securing the preconditions for rational consent and dissent, public debate, conflict resolution without violence, and the thoughtful and cumulative revision of the constitutional framework itself. *For such an imposed or inherited constitution, there could be no warrant other than hypothetical or presumed consent.* In a democracy, ideally, everyone affected by a decision has a right to participate in making it. Because the unborn are permanently disenfranchised, however, the framers consciously acted on their behalf. To make subsequent consent meaningful, predecessors had no choice but to act without the leave of their successors. These traces of paternalism cannot be eliminated from the actions of the Founding Fathers. The constitutional "limits" they imposed, of course, remain morally binding and factually in force only so long as citizens currently alive find them appealing and continue to impose them voluntarily upon themselves.

## Constitutional Self-Command

All members of a community can share a common objective. But no individual will be willing to make sacrifices for the sake of this objective unless he can be assured that others, too, will do their part. According to Hobbes, peace is such a goal. Conservation of natural resources and relief of poverty are examples pertinent to developed societies today. Hume adduces the example of draining a meadow: It is "very difficult, and indeed impossible, that a thousand persons shou'd agree in any such action . . . while each seeks a pretext to free himself of the trouble and expense, and wou'd lay the whole burden on others."[150] To achieve such widely valued outcomes, therefore, members of a political society must acquiesce in legal arrangements which bind their wills. If *all* are obliged to pay taxes, then every individual will contribute willingly, and the government will be able, say, to drain a meadow for the benefit of the entire community.

A democratically ratified constitution should be looked at in the same light. A liberal constitutional framework is a classic solution to a collective action problem. People may voluntarily relinquish their ability to choose (in some matters) in order to accomplish their will (in other matters). Collective self-binding can therefore be an instrument of collective self-rule. Rules restricting available options can enable individuals and communities to achieve more of their specific aims than they could if they were all left entirely unconstrained. Such is the democratic function of constitutional restraints.

In *The Strategy of Conflict,* Thomas Schelling examines how one party could exert power over another by means of self-incapacitation, for instance by chaining himself to a railroad track.[151] More recently, he has explored ways in which an individual can exercise power over himself by adopting comparable binding tactics: "We place the alarm clock across the room so we cannot turn it off without getting out of bed. We put things out of sight or out of reach for the moment of temptation. We surrender authority to a trustworthy friend who will police our calories or our cigarettes."[152] An individual can be crafty and strong-willed enough to bind his future selves even if he is too dim-witted and weak-willed to act as he would prefer without precommitments. To achieve his desired ends despite his melting resolve, an individual must restrict his available options. A voter, for example, can support compulsory seat-belt legislation in order to force himself to be free, that is, to do what he really wants to do but would not otherwise be able to do because of laziness, habit, absent-mindedness, or social pressures to appear free and easy.[153] Similarly, laws which prevent employees from voluntarily consenting to work below the minimum wage will increase the capacity of some individuals to get what they want by restricting what they can freely choose. (This is not to deny that minimum wage laws simultaneously restrict employment opportunities for other sectors of the workforce.)

It is tempting to think of constitutionalism in these terms, as a cluster of techniques for collective self-management. By tacitly consenting to judicial review, for example, electoral majorities voluntarily abdicate power. They tie their own hands for what they presumably see as their own good. My entire analysis in this chapter has been premised on the fruitfulness of this perspective. Nevertheless, we should pause before asserting, in a Schellingian manner, that a constitution is basically a community's indirect strategy for self-command.

Nations are not individuals writ large; and constitutions may be misunderstood (not merely trivialized) by being compared with New Year's resolutions and explained in terms originally devised to describe the behavior of pigeons.[154] The Peter sober/Peter drunk analogy is not totally apt, because even a perfectly rational, clear-eyed, and virtuous future generation could benefit from preestablished procedures for resolving conflicts. The framers, moreover, did not have specific aims (to lose weight, stop smoking) which they wished to achieve despite the weakness of will which would foreseeably afflict their posterity. They were neither forging chains to prevent future citizens from tumbling off a ledge nor tying on soft mittens to prevent them from scratching their hives during sleep. In general, Schelling's concept of self-command is much too *negative* to capture the enabling functions of constitutional precommitment. Among other things, the framers wanted to guarantee that, whatever decisions were eventually reached, alternatives were canvassed and counterarguments heard. As mentioned, the Constitution is in part an attempt to program fact-mindedness and self-criticism into American life. It represents not only an endeavor by knowledgeable forefathers to prevent self-destructive behavior, but it is also a set of incentives encouraging future citizens to think for themselves.

"Autopaternalism" is a useful category for highlighting the democratic function of constitutional restraints. But there are, I think, at least three important disanalogies between constitutionalism and self-command as Schelling conceives it:

(1) Self-incapacitation is a bizarre metaphor to apply to nation building. The American Constitution was explicitly designed to cement the Union. Liberal constitutions in general organize processes of deliberation and decision making in order to improve the quality of laws and policies. They contain various inducement mechanisms, devices for focusing attention, sharpening awareness of options, mobilizing knowledge, involving citizens and guaranteeing that future choices will be made under conditions where alternatives are discussed, facts are marshalled, and self-correction is possible. When one of Schelling's

individuals binds himself, he limits his preexistent ability to choose (even if, as a consequence, his subsequent range of choices is enlarged). When a constituent assembly establishes a decision procedure, rather than restricting a preexistent will, it actually creates a framework in which a nation can, for the first time, have a will. Only when procedures for aggregating preferences are already in place can a majority of "the people" exercise control over public policy.

(2) Constitutional devices, such as checks and balances, are not meant simply to compensate for a deplorable but predictable lack of moral fiber; they are actually considered as superior to personal virtue and strength of character. The fat man who wishes to be thin would like to have a strong will. In lieu of inner fortitude, he binds himself. For liberal framers, by contrast, it would be positively undesirable to build political stability on the basis of collective virtue or an unflinching uniform will. This would overburden individual conscience, force a character standardization on citizens, and deprive society of an extrapolitical variety of selves. Discussion would be pointless in such a preharmonized society. Thus, liberal framers do not want citizens transfixed on an overpowering common purpose. They reject virtue-based politics for a looser, less all-engaging, more procedural and discussion-stimulating sort of common framework.

(3) Without accepting Hayek's political views, we can admit the plausibility of his claim that "like most tools, [constitutional] rules are not part of a plan of action, but rather equipment for certain unknown contingencies."[155] While only partly accurate, this characterization of constitutional rules suggests a third disanalogy between constitutionalism and Schelling's strategies of self-incapacitation. The latter are monopurposive, while the former is multipurposive and intentionally designed to serve future aims currently unknown.

## The Prohibition against Self-Enslavement

The principle of voluntariness itself requires paradoxically that certain options be foreclosed. Modern constitutions typically outlaw self-sale into slavery.[156] Slaves cannot enter into binding agreements. Thus, an act of voluntary self-enslavement would be a contract to relinquish, among other things, the right to make subsequent contracts. According to Mill, this would be a practical contradiction, a willing to give up your will. By selling himself for a slave, a person "abdicates his liberty; he foregoes any future use of it beyond that single act. He therefore defeats, in his own case, the very purpose which is the justification of allowing him to dispose of himself. . . . The principle of freedom cannot require that he should be free not to be free. It is not freedom to be allowed to alienate his freedom."[157] Here we are faced with another fundamental norm of liberal constitutionalism. *You cannot voluntarily agree to give up your right voluntarily to agree.*

One paradoxical "solution" to the paradox of constitutional democracy may lie here. To preserve voluntariness, voluntariness itself must be restricted.[158] The prohibition against selling oneself into slavery logically implies the acceptance of some sort of binding precommitment. Openness in one respect presupposes closure in another. Precommitment is morally permissible when it reinforces the prohibition against self-enslavement. Among its other functions, constitutional binding is an attempt to foreclose the possibility that the nation (or any generation) will sell itself (or its posterity) into slavery. In this spirit, Article IV, section 4 of the U.S. Constitution purports to make a "Republican Form of Government" obligatory in the states and unalterable by future majorities. To guarantee republicanism on a national level, in turn, was the purpose of the Constitution as a whole. In general, a democracy choosing to destroy the framework in which nonviolent disagreement and conflict resolution can occur would be acting suicidally. The framers proposed, and subsequent generations have accepted, constitutional precommitment because it is a useful device for forestalling this sort of collective self-destruction.

Additionally relevant here is Bodin's assertion, already cited, that "the prince cannot so bind his own hands, or make such a law unto himself [to] prohibit his grieved subjects from coming unto him with their humble supplications and requests."[159] Self-binding is illicit whenever it impedes the free flow of information and squelches the learning capacity of the sovereign prince. A liberal constitution, by analogy, can prevent the sovereign people from renouncing its capacity to learn from criticism and dissent.

Originally set in opposition to constitutional restrictions, the freedom of the sovereign people actually presupposes certain inflexible rules. Once it is recognized that learning capacity can be enhanced by strategic self-binding, then self-binding becomes not only permissible but obligatory. In a liberal democracy, elected legislators must *make no laws* which interfere with voting rights, the free flow of information, freedom of assembly, and political access for protesting minorities. They cannot obstruct activities "which can ordinarily be expected to bring about *repeal* of undesirable legislation."[160] The majority must limit its own powers in order to guarantee that it will remain a majority that can learn.

Paine and Jefferson believed that democracy was a system oriented toward change, innovation, and improvement. Rationality itself requires future chances for reconsideration and self-correction. Mill, to whom we now turn, accepted this principle but was convinced that beneficial change required a careful structuring of the conditions under which political reforms were evaluated and discussed. An institutional and legal framework must be devised for keeping open the widest gamut of alternatives for new and better decisions. According to liberalism, our humanity is best located in our capacity for choice, our ability not merely to decide but also to undo unsatisfactory past decisions and decide again.[161] A cleverly designed constitution can create a regime which is roughly adequate to the precious human capacity for self-correction. Only a rather inflexible precommitment to certain procedural rules (guaranteeing, for example, the continuing right of unpunished dissent) makes public learning possible. Constitutional democracy is the most humane political system because it thrives on the ability of individuals and communities to recognize their own mistakes. While prohibiting precommitments which obstructed further learning, Locke, Kant, and others endorsed durable—though certainly not unalterable—constitutional rules. They did so, among other reasons, because they recognized that such rules can foster further learning. The dead should not govern the living; but they can make it easier for the living to govern themselves.

# 6

# The Positive Constitutionalism of John Stuart Mill

*Men's natural abilities are too dull to see through everything at once; but by consulting, listening, and debating, they grow more acute, and while they are trying all means, they at last discover those which they want, which all approve, but no one would have thought of in the first place.*

—SPINOZA

The interdependence of constitutionalism and democracy presents a paradox, not a contradiction. Liberal restrictions on the powers of the majority, such as the legally protected right to criticize publicly those who win political power in fair elections, are designed not only to ward off majority tyranny, but also to organize popular decision making and put deliberative democracy into effect. No theorist devoted more attention to this second pattern, to the mutually supportive relation between popular government and limited government, than John Stuart Mill. Focused especially on this issue is his *Considerations on Representative Government,* of 1861, which draws attention to the creative rather than merely protective functions of liberal-democratic institutions. Mill endorses representative government for its creative potentials, not merely as a safeguard against tyranny and corruption. Representative government, he argues, is much more restless and onward-moving than the "government by consent" praised by Locke. A defeated minority may agree to a decision-making procedure even while disapproving of a particular decision. But to the outcome of such a procedure, those who are outvoted, by definition, do not consent. What they *can* do is discuss and, in discussing, they can contribute vitally to a process of collective learning. Public learning is the heart of liberal democracy, or so Mill believed. Constitutionalism, whether it involves a written charter or not, should increase the thoughtfulness of collective deliberation.[1] The institutional reforms Mill advocated, therefore, were aimed not merely at protecting private rights and fostering personal development. They were also, and more centrally, meant to promote the advance of publicly useful knowledge. To analyze and criticize Mill's defense of this important thesis is to deepen our understanding of the practical inseparability of liberalism and democracy.

## Publicity and the Growth of Knowledge

Representative government is itself a cognitive process, fashioned to maximize the production, accumulation, and implementation of politically relevant truths. Because he conceived of representative government in this way, Mill rejected an economic or privatistic interpretation of liberal citizenship. Voting is not a private right but a public trust. The voter should not be exclusively concerned to press his private case, but should also take the community's general good, as he comes to see it, into account. Truth on such matters does not hinge upon given preferences, but on preferences shaped and reshaped by open, strenuous debate. Seen from this angle, liberal democracy is a set of institutionally anchored procedures *both* for aggregating pregiven interests *and* for rationally evaluating and redefining interests in the course of public discussion. Because of this preference-transforming function, representative government, as Mill portrays it, cannot be adequately described in categories used for analyzing consumer satisfaction and economic exchange.

Since he advocated the flourishing of personality and imagination in all their manifold diversity, Mill is often grouped among the self-realization theorists of democracy. And no reader can fail to notice the glaring traces of romanticism in such essays as "Coleridge" and "The Spirit of the Age." But this is certainly not all there is to Mill. For one thing, his deep commitment to an analogy between politics and science (to be criticized below) jars rudely with one-sidedly romantic interpretations of his thought. True, he considered political participation to be personally rewarding—a way to cultivate one's feelings, widen one's horizons, exercise one's higher faculties, and enrich one's character. But his central argument was less focused on the personal than on the social or collective advantages of civic engagement. Free speech is valuable less because of the chance it affords the individual to hone his sensibilities or unbosom his innermost convictions, than because of its beneficial influence on the quality of collective decisions. Indeed, participation in politics has a rewarding effect on individual character itself only when citizens pursue a goal less personal than self-improvement. Their principal end in view should be the intelligent governance of the community. Character development will then be a welcome by-product, not an achieved aim.

Uninhibited public discussion allows truth to prevail over error. So runs the public-debate rationale for freedom of expression. Compared with the position adopted by ostensibly "more democratic" theorists, this Miltonian thesis is quite radical. (Rousseau, for example, denied that disagreement can be politically creative just as adamantly as any exponent of absolute monarchy.) True, publicity is a disinfectant, a way of flushing out corruption and exposing abuses of power. But publicity also exerts a more positive influence: it is a stimulant as well as a depressant. As Mill described it, public discussion is a machine for gathering facts, correcting past errors, generating new policy suggestions, and enlisting the creative energies and decentralized intelligence of citizens in solving common problems. Not only representatives, moreover, but *all* citizens are called upon to take part in public debate: "By the utmost possible publicity and liberty of discussion . . . not merely a few individuals in succession, but the whole public, are made, to a certain extent, participants in the government."[2] Like an economic market, the free market of ideas mobilizes dormant resources (for example, underemployed minds, working at one-half capacity), which can help make government more intelligent, better informed, and more aware of troubling side effects. Both representative institutions and freedom of the press have a crucial *mobilizing function*.[3] They stimulate the thinking of ordinary citizens and bring it to bear on the conduct of public affairs. Autocratic governments, issuing commands from on high and expecting their subjects submissively to obey, deprive themselves of a powerful resource locked within their own citizens. This is Mill's version of the Bodin thesis, discussed at length in chapter 4. Arbitrary regimes are self-impoverishing.[4]

A legally guaranteed right of opposition is an essential component of democratic government. To help make collective decisions as intelligent as possible, critics of governmental officials and policies must not only be protected but even institutionally encouraged. Uncriticizable rulers never learn of their problems until it is too late. If policies are set publicly and public criticism is rewarded, by contrast, a government can promptly correct its own mistakes. Furthermore, as Spinoza had already explained with admirable clarity, the "collision" of ideas sharpens the minds of all parties, yielding suggestions no one would have lit upon in isolation and producing decisions more adequate than any proposal presented at the outset.[5] Public opinion is a progressive force only when it is formed in a free-for-all public debate. Without institutional inducements for public criticism and opposition, in fact, political unanimity is likely to be a sign of irrational conformism.[6] For the sake of collective rationality, "a perpetual and standing Opposition to the will of the majority" must be kept up.[7] Only then will the reason, rather than the passions, of the public stand in judgment. Only then will "the cool and deliberate sense of the community" prevail.[8]

Beneath these political claims lies an epistemological principle that later came to be known as fallibilism. We cannot remove an idea from our minds and compare it with "reality" to determine if the two correspond. So how can we know if our beliefs are true? Mill's trenchant answer was that "the beliefs which we have most warrant for, have no safeguard to rest on, but a standing invitation to the whole world to prove them unfounded."[9] Indeed, intellectual honesty demands that we energetically strive to refute our own convictions. If you have not played the devil's advocate, attempting vigorously to disprove your own opinions, you have no reason to believe what you believe.

This fallibilist epistemology inspired many of Mill's political proposals. Consider, for example, his support of a trustee as opposed to a delegate theory of representation. A delegate is a mere agent, sent to Parliament to express the opinions of his constituents and subject to immediate recall if he deviates an iota from his mandate. A trustee, by contrast, has ampler room for maneuver. He can vote as he thinks best, using his discretion, disregarding occasionally, if only temporarily, the opinions of his electors.

The delegate model is objectionable, according to Mill, because it implicitly rejects the epistemology of fallibilism. It implies that a representative has nothing important to learn from an uninhibited give-and-take with fellow deputies. But this assumption is unrealistic: "If he devotes himself to his duty," a representative "has greater opportunities of correcting an original false judgment, than fall to the lot of most of his constituents."[10] The decisive superiority of deputies over citizens lies not in higher intelligence, virtue, or education, therefore, but in the unusual nature of the legislative situation itself, a situation which, according to Mill, fosters self-correction. Voters are parochial. They are seldom exposed to the clashing viewpoints of fellow citizens who live in remote parts of the country. No one is ever invited to prove them wrong or rewarded for disclosing their follies. Voters should defer to representatives, therefore, although only in the short run, not because members of an elected assembly are likely to be especially virtuous, but rather because representatives enjoy the eye-opening benefits of exposure to stinging criticisms and relentless debate.

In medieval assemblies, a deputy would represent his constituents before the king or a court of nobles. In modern parliaments, by contrast, citizens represent themselves *to each other.* This nonhierarchical mutuality creates an unprecedented situation. A modern legislative assembly is a machine for public learning because it guarantees that rival political proposals will be "tested by adverse controversy."[11] Deputies are encouraged not only to uncover each other's errors but also to change their own minds whenever they become convinced that they have been laboring under an illusion. If recanting is intelligent, then it can be justified publicly, even to the voters back home, at least eventually. Accountability requires that deputies explain their decisions to their constituents. Because explanations of difficult issues take time, however, a system of immediate recall would make a mockery of government by discussion. Far from being antidemocratic, the trustee theory of representation simply recognizes that public learning, or the collective correction of collective mistakes, can never be instantaneous.

## Freedom and Knowledge

Mill's entire theory of personal liberty assumes, without proving it, that we can distinguish clearly between actions that affect the interests of others and actions that directly affect the actor alone. Government should limit itself to regulating the former; and therefore public officials must have cognitive capacities adequate to discerning the line Mill has in mind. Significantly, Mill also justifies his ideal of personal liberty by advancing a striking claim about *the lack of knowledge:* "The strongest of all the arguments against the interference of the public with purely personal conduct, is that when it does interfere, the odds are that it interferes wrongly, and in the wrong place."[12] Governments, which must know when the interests of others are being wrongfully damaged, almost never have sufficient information to save someone from himself.

The Mill of *On Liberty* was less concerned with the tyranny of the magistrate than with the tyranny of social ostracism and gossip. The entire book is a defense of personal eccentricity, nonconformism, and deviance in the face of censorious peer-group pressures. The right to be different must be respected above all else. But what does a handbook for heretics have to do with representative government? Mill's often-cited definition of liberty ("the only freedom which deserves the name, is that of pursuing your own good in your own way") is deafeningly silent about a nation's freedom collectively to govern itself.[13] Thus, the political relevance of *On Liberty* is not immediately clear. It would be emphatically wrong, however, to conclude that Mill did not consider collective self-rule to be a freedom worthy of the name.

Civic shirkers unwittingly jeopardize their private independence because control of political decision making entails control of the police. Thus, even if Mill believed (which he ultimately did not) that the only freedom worthy of the name was that of pursuing your own good in your own way, he would have advocated representative institutions: when government officials are not held accountable, they soon begin to harass private citizens, preventing the latter from pursuing their own good as they conceive it. The reverse is also true: when private independence is destroyed, citizen participation in collective decision making is essentially worthless. Intimidated sheep cannot criticize each other in constructive ways. Liberal democracy cannot function if citizens are routinely brutalized by the police and their pseudoconsent is extorted by credible threats. Thus, private rights make an essential contribution to public debate: in a democratic nation, citizens must be well shielded from reprisals by government agents whenever they choose to criticize wielders of power.

*On Liberty* is concerned not only with personal eccentricity but also with democracy-reinforcing freedom of speech. Mill stressed not the origins but the consequences of this right. In addition to his hopes for the cultivation of character, he advanced several nonromantic arguments for near-absolute freedom of expression. For example, from the double premise that human minds are fallible and that everyone will benefit from knowing the truth, he drew the logical conclusion that censorship is an irrational, self-destructive policy. To censor an individual is to deprive mankind of his potential contributions to the advancement of knowledge, contributions that censors will, at the outset, be too obtuse to discern. Because human minds are frail and mistakes are common, citizens should have the right publicly to defend any opinion, no matter how immoral or offensive it may happen to seem to other people. "All silencing of discussion is an assumption of infallibility."[14] Such an assumption is both unwarranted by experience and damaging to the growth of knowledge.

Mill was not exactly a skeptic. For one thing, he considered censorship to be irrational because it conflicted with *indisputable facts* about human ignorance and knowledge. But while censorship is irrational, it can easily be explained. Man is a self-flattering animal. Most people vastly minimize their own proneness to error. Human beings seldom hesitate before deciding what is right and wrong, especially what is right and wrong for others. They are irrationally wedded to their own parochial perspectives and expect the circumambient world pliantly to conform. Disagreement and disobedience shock the mind. But, however natural, such arrogance is self-defeating in the long run.

Put simply, the epistemological principle underlying Mill's defense of free speech is that *no opinion is so certain that we can justify using force to prevent it from being criticized.* This principle is simultaneously liberal and democratic. To adduce it as evidence for Mill's unhinged moral nihilism is unwise, to say the least.[15] Conservative theorists who shun unfettered discussion, lacking confidence in their own views and expecting that wide open debate will demolish all universally respected truths, have a better claim to the title of skeptic than Mill, who justified freedom as a necessary precondition for discovering the truth. If anything, as we shall see, Mill was overconfident about the production of moral knowledge through uncensored political debate.

## Skepticism, Empiricism, and Reform

Political and moral skepticism are quite distinct. Mill was not a moral but only a political skeptic: he did not trust unaccountable political authorities intelligently to enforce a valid conception of the good life on passive citizens. As every reader of *Utilitarianism* knows, doubts about the perceptiveness and virtue of rulers did not lead Mill to disavow any difference between right and wrong. True, he believed that a widespread lack of inner certitude among powerful people about the one and only good might be politically beneficial. To undermine persecutorial imperiousness, therefore, he strove to make religious bigots aware that their own deepest beliefs were the fruits of happenstance. A religious crusader is a victim of his birthplace: "The same causes which make him a Churchman in London, would have made him a Buddhist or a Confucian in Pekin."[16] Presumably, a *chevalier de la foi* will hesitate to burn "heretics" for entertaining certain beliefs, if he can be convinced that he would have held the very same beliefs if he had himself been raised in similar circumstances. Homilists who ascribe all manner of moral catastrophe to relativism and historicism should reflect upon the contribution that, at least according to Mill, such doctrines make to the triumph of toleration.

In many ways, Mill's reformism rested squarely on claims about knowledge: "The practical reformer has continually to demand that changes be made in things which are supported by powerful and widely spread feelings, or to question the apparent necessity and indefeasibleness of established facts; and it is often an indispensable part of his argument to show, how those powerful feelings had their origin, and how those facts came to seem necessary and indefeasible."[17] Opponents of reform naturally seek to demonstrate that an offending institution "cannot" be changed. In response, a reformer must first of all prove that concrete alternatives are available. To be truly effective, however, he must also explain how the obfuscatory appearance of *false necessity* initially arose. Explanations of fatalistic delusion almost always direct our attention to the environmental origins of such a cognitive bias. As a result, "there is a natural hostility between [the reformer] and a philosophy which discourages the explanation of feelings and moral facts by circumstances and association, and prefers to treat them as ultimate elements of human nature; a philosophy which is addicted to holding up favourite doctrines as intuitive truths, and deems intuition to be the voice of Nature and of God, speaking with an authority higher than that of our reason."[18]

As reflected in this passage, Mill's battle against innate ideas was, in part, politically motivated.[19] His socio-psychological approach to the genesis of (fatalistic) beliefs was designed to advance the cause of reform. He presented fallibilism itself as an attack on illusory certainties. And he turned the psychological theory of associationism, initially introduced to undermine the dogma of original sin, into a powerful technique for shaking the self-assurance of the moral police. In short, the philosophy of experience was an epistemology for reformers.

Besides ensuring that political decisions will be based on inadequate information, censorship also enfeebles the minds of individual citizens. If a government allows people to think for themselves, then, in future unknown situations, they will be more likely to act rationally without needing a public official to hold their hands. Understood as the capacity to give plausible arguments for one's beliefs and plausible justifications for one's actions, rationality develops with use. But such a healthy exercise of reason is suffocated by censorship. As a result, opinions sheltered from criticism, far from being fortified, are impaired. Beliefs defended not by reason but by the censor's blotter "are apt to give way before the slightest semblance of an argument."[20] A government inadvertently confers an unearned persuasiveness on rotten arguments by preventing its citizens from witnessing unsound ideas routinely being trounced by sound ones.

Absolute freedom of expression should be protected, among other reasons, because an opinion the government desires to suppress may turn out to be true. But Mill also argues that errors themselves are worth protecting. False beliefs serve an important intellectual function: "Teachers and learners go to sleep at their post, as soon as there is no enemy in the field."[21] By assailing a correct opinion, dissenters, no matter how misled, force those who know the truth vigorously to defend their beliefs. When we defend a belief, we transform it from a mechanical assertion into a profound conviction capable of influencing action. The vibrancy and vitality of truth can be sustained only in a continuous struggle with error.

We are now in a position to recapitulate Mill's main argument. Liberal democracy is the best form of government, given a certain minimal level of education, because it protects the interests of all citizens, develops their mental alertness and fact-mindedness, enlists their creative capacities in solving common problems, and improves the quality of collective decisions. *Mill justifies liberal-democratic institutions positively, then, not negatively. The justifying aim of such institutions is the growth and application of publicly useful knowledge.* To repeat the argument, accentuating its epistemological side: representative government protects the governed from the ignorance of those who govern, promotes the growth of knowledge among citizens, mobilizes preexistent knowledge for public purposes, and improves legislative proposals by submitting them to uncensored processes of mutual criticism.

### The Use and Abuse of Political Ignorance

The irrepressible human capacity to *withhold knowledge* also has important consequences for legislation and institutional design. At the time Mill wrote *On Liberty,* English law required witnesses in court to swear a religious oath. The intended effect of this law was to exclude atheists from testifying on the assumption that only believers had an incentive to tell the truth. According to Mill, this rule was a howling absurdity, for it allowed mendacious atheists to testify, depriving the courts only of testimony from atheists who tell the truth.[22]

Institutions designed to create public ignorance about private motives, on the other hand, can be politically useful. James Mill, for instance, believed that the secret ballot could do for the many what ownership of land had done for a few: it could protect voters from manipulation and retaliation by the powerful. It performed this function by artificially obstructing the flow of information, that is, by selectively replacing knowledge with ignorance. When people vote secretly, they can have a will of their own: they can vote as they think best, not as they think their superiors or employers think best.

Convinced that fidgety intolerance of dissent and an ape-like urge to conform were deep-seated proclivities of human nature, the younger Mill might well have followed his father's lead and sprung to the defense of the secret ballot. To vote publicly is to expose oneself to the intolerance of others. The desire to "fit in" might impoverish political life in a society where all participation was publicly exposed. But Mill, ignoring such considerations, attacked the secret ballot. What were his reasons? His principal argument was psychological, it seems. Institutions, such as the mode of voting, make an indirect impression on the minds of citizens, leading them to conceive citizenship in a particular way. The secret ballot teaches voters to regard their votes as private possessions. In other words, the secret ballot educates citizens to underestimate the common interest and to act for selfish motives even in public life.

Renowned for his hostility to paternalism, Mill nevertheless argued that citizens must be subjected, against their will, to the moral education provided by public voting. They need to learn that the franchise is a public trust and not a private right; and they must be psychologically coaxed, in the act of voting, to focus on broad public advantages rather than on their own puny selves. Public voting will not lead to slavish conformism, he optimistically promised. It will merely compel citizens to concoct plausible rationales for unpopular causes: "To be under the eyes of others—to have to defend oneself to others—is never more important than to those who act in opposition to the opinion of others, for it obliges them to have sure ground of their own."[23] In other words, Mill supported public voting because of its effect on public knowledge. The glare of publicity, it turns out, is an irresistible spur to moral behavior: "Even the bare fact of having to give an account of their conduct, is a powerful inducement to adhere to conduct of which at least some decent account can be given."[24] This last statement should tantalize students of Mill's life. Bitterly wounded in his private existence by public pressure to conform to conventional standards of decency, Mill nevertheless proposed using a threat of shame to induce thoughtful participation in public affairs.

With the same enthusiasm for openness and publicity, Mill describes the diffusion of useful information as one of the main positive functions of liberal government. At the very least, the government has an affirmative duty to disrupt those cognitive monopolies which form "spontaneously" in the social world. Many illiberal social patterns depend upon asymmetries of information. Knowledge is power; and if a seller can prevent a buyer from learning the low price of a product at a competitor's shop, he can earn an extortionate profit that no genuinely "free" market would tolerate. To correct this sort of problem, according to Mill, the government must become an aggressive purveyor of information.[25] The *Principles of Political Economy* contains an enthusiastic endorsement of "the course so seldom resorted to by governments, and of which such important use might be made, that of giving advice and promulgating information."[26] While no étatist, Mill insisted that the government should achieve "the greatest possible centralization of information, and diffusion of it from the centre."[27] The state must provide essential social preconditions for individual autonomy; and the most important of these is universally accessible knowledge.

### Elitism and Expertise

A liberal-democratic regime will mobilize the critical and creative talents, the imagination, knowledge, and intelligence of its citizens for the solution of common problems. Such admirable traits are not distributed evenly throughout the population, however. A landed aristocracy has little to offer the community; but a scientifically educated elite can make a contribution to political life out of all proportion to its small numbers. Here we encounter what unfriendly critics have derided as Mill's elitism, including his avowed wish that most people be guided "by the counsels and influence of a more highly gifted and instructed One or Few" or by "the acquired knowledge and practiced intelligence of a specially trained and experienced Few."[28]

Bentham's principle of utility was essentially antiauthoritarian: it decentralized the right to define happiness, dispersing it into the hands of individuals.[29] Mill found the egalitarian and republican implication of Bentham's theory quite congenial. Nevertheless, he notoriously departed from Benthamite premises when he claimed that "some *kinds* of pleasure are more desirable and more valuable than others."[30] When exercising our higher faculties, we experience a "higher" form of pleasure. To rank one pleasure above another, obviously enough, is to make a cognitive claim; rankings can be true or false. Just as Aristotle (whom Mill labels, anachronistically, a "judicious utilitarian")[31] had said, human beings are so constituted by nature that they necessarily attain the greatest utility when engaged in superior forms of activity. This is an empirical claim about universal traits of human psychology. The correct ranking of pleasures cannot be established by counting noses. When comparing two activities, the majority should defer to "the judgment of those who are qualified by knowledge of both."[32]

Here we find the moral, and morally questionable, foundations of Mill's praise for intellectual authority in political affairs, an aspect of his thought which is interesting and worth discussing, although it should not be allowed to overshadow his lasting contributions to the theory of positive constitutionalism. Consider, as a supplementary example, his commentary on the claim that local government is a "school" of political capacity. (Only someone who never went to school could deem this metaphor high praise.) In any case, "a school supposes teachers as well as scholars: the utility of the instruction greatly depends on its bringing inferior minds into contact with superior, a contact which in the ordinary course of life is altogether exceptional, and the want of which contributes more than anything else to keep the generality of mankind on one level of contented ignorance."[33] Intelligent politics requires not merely robust and wide open debate but also a "deference to mental superiority" on the part of most citizens.[34] Such passages reveal the limits of Mill's antipaternalism, and his own deviation from the liberal norm.

In his chapter on the suffrage, Mill argues that people with university degrees should be granted three or four votes while uncertified individuals should be allotted only one. Why Mill believed that an academic education would create useful citizens remains unclear.[35] Having never attended school, he probably overlooked the oppressive dimension of institutional education, viewing academic training, unrealistically, as nothing but a means of liberating the young from inherited conventions and prejudices. The extra votes awarded to those who had received higher university degrees, in any case, were primarily symbolic.[36] Plural voting must not allow the "educated class" to impose its minority views on an uneducated majority. That would be exactly the sort of class legislation Mill consistently opposed.

Indeed, a charitable interpreter might argue that Mill advocated plural voting for the same reason that he supported public voting. Both institutions can be seen as clever—if ultimately unpersuasive—attempts at positive constitutionalism. Both are designed to make an impression on the minds of average citizens, teaching that knowledge is preferable to ignorance. "It is not useful but hurtful that the constitution of the country should declare ignorance to be entitled to as much political power as knowledge."[37] To induce future citizens to become knowledgeable participants in public controversies, a prize for knowledgeableness, that is, symbolic prestige for thoughtful and informed citizens, must be built into the constitutional system itself. Seen from this perspective, elitism serves an educative function simply by providing ordinary citizens with visible examples of well-developed talents, tastes, and understanding. For most people, Mill reasons, personal growth will be stimulated by the belief that some preferences are superior to others.

"No progress at all can be made towards obtaining a skilled democracy," Mill adds, unless democratic citizens "are willing that the work which requires skill should be done by those who possess it."[38] And he did not shrink from employing Platonic metaphors to underscore the need for democratic deference to a knowledgeable class: "The people ought to be the masters, but they are masters who must employ servants more skillful than themselves: like a ministry when they employ a military commander, or the military commander when he employs an army surgeon."[39] In passages such as these, the instructed minority consists of technical experts, not glowing moral exemplars. The educated few have skills that make them better qualified for certain specialized tasks than untrained individuals. But the extent to which ordinary citizens, according to Mill, should *defer* to technical specialists on broad questions of public policy remains somewhat obscure.

## Doubts about Expertise

Mill's brilliance as a theorist of positive constitutionalism does not lift his version of democratic liberalism beyond critical appraisal. The most questionable aspect of his thinking, as I have already suggested, concerns the authority he ascribed to intellectual superiors. This problem surfaces, for example, whenever he stresses the cumulative and slights the destructive sides of scientific progress. He emphasized the present generation's contribution to truth, rather than the near certainty that today's beliefs will be ridiculed or ignored in the future. Despite his fallibilism, in other words, Mill hesitated to acknowledge that modern science makes knowledge permanently unstable: "As Mankind improve, the number of doctrines which are no longer disputed or doubted will be constantly on the increase: and the well-being of mankind may almost be measured by the number and gravity of the truths which have reached the point of being uncontested."[40] As a young man, under the influence of the Saint-Simonians and Comte, he declared that the present was "an age of transition" and that, if the instructed few managed to provide a coherent set of beliefs, intellectual authority would be reestablished in the future.[41] Doubt is seasonal; criticism is a waking interlude between dogmatic slumbers, a fleeting storm between the lulls. Even in his mature writings, Mill sometimes suggested that freedom of discussion is only a provisional virtue, appropriate solely for the disoriented present.[42]

Most people, he also implies, will *never* be able to grasp truth with their own unaided intelligence. Fortunately, except during ages of cultural confusion, the majority of mankind will (and should) defer to intellectual superiors. That, according to the early Mill, is nothing more than what the division of labor demands.[43] Among those who think scientifically, a moral and political consensus does not yet exist;

but it will eventually emerge. This is fortunate because social cohesion ultimately hinges upon the integrating power of a coherent set of beliefs. When a new and well-rounded belief system finally takes shape, the unschooled will acquiesce in the intellectual elite's authoritative opinions with appropriately submissive minds.

Mill's exaggerated confidence in intellectual superiority may have been reinforced by his experience as an administrator in the East India Company. Making decisions about a country so different from England required "professional knowledge" and, indeed, "specially Indian knowledge and experience."[44] It could not be left to an ignorant populace and their elected representatives. Indeed, despite his enthusiasm for parliamentary debate, Mill expressed a general contempt for the competence of legislative assemblies: "A numerous assembly is as little fitted for the direct business of legislation as for that of administration." A long-time observer of Parliament, he wrote that "there is hardly any kind of intellectual work which so much needs to be done not only by experienced and exercised minds, but by minds trained to the task through long and laborious study, as the business of making laws."[45] Unfortunately, British lawmakers were not qualified to do this job.

Mill's fondness for expertise and intellectual superiority, in other words, led him to retreat from what at first seems an unreserved commitment to government by public discussion: "*Doing,*" and he includes lawmaking here, "as a result of discussion, is the task not of a miscellaneous body, but of individuals specially trained to do it."[46] Statutes must meet certain minimal standards of rationality, such as internal coherence and consistency with other laws. Elected legislators, lacking intellectual discipline, will inevitably write bills one at a time and in response to a shifting variety of pressures and problems. The mindless incrementalism of parliamentarians will breed a host of practical confusions. Mill's proposal for a solution was the establishment of a standing panel of experts. If a special commission prepared bills, then "legislation would assume its proper place as a work of skilled labor and special study and experience."[47]

To be sure, Mill's fantasies about an authoritative clerisy were less extreme than these passages, wrested from their original context, might suggest. For one thing, he insisted that elected generalists should always control appointed specialists. Lacking narrow expertise, legislators may nevertheless possess superior breadth of mind, an ability to see the connectedness of things, which no technical education could provide. Experts, therefore, should be on tap, not on top. Parliament approves and rejects bills; and it can charge the Commission of

Legislation with preparing bills on designated topics. The panel of experts would "merely" be the intelligence enabling legislators to carry out their will in a coherent and effective manner.[48] Such passages lend a liberal-democratic hue even to Mill's most unpalatably elitist lucubrations.

Ultimately, Mill's miscellaneous views on the political value of intellectual superiority do not seem completely consistent. But for the mainstream liberal tradition, as outlined in chapter 1, his doubts about elitism have greater weight than his speculations about mental superiority. Consider his skepticism about expertise, eloquently expressed in his discussions of pedantocracy. He wrote admiringly of Rome and Venice: their policies were intelligent because public business was consigned to "governors by profession."[49] They were not aristocracies so much as bureaucracies. Such specialists, however, are quite unspecial in one respect: like everyone else, they display a bias toward their own particular interests, and an uncritical fondness for acquired habits. Technical knowledge, unlike Platonic wisdom, makes no one virtuous. Even if an expert understood the interests of nonexperts better than these nonexperts could understand their interests themselves, there would be no reason to suppose he would respect or foster them.

Furthermore, knowledge that was useful at one time inevitably becomes out of date. Truths do not simply accumulate like stones heaped upon a pile; some are destroyed by the advance of knowledge. Under rapidly changing conditions, bureaucrats and specialists can be crippled by what they "already know." Hard-won insights tend to become objects of veneration and irrational loyalty—as we are constantly being reminded by all those generals anachronistically fighting the last war. "The disease which afflicts bureaucratic governments, and which they usually die of, is routine. They perish by the immutability of their maxims; and, still more, by the universal law that whatever becomes a routine loses its vital principle, and having no longer a mind acting within it, goes on revolving mechanically though the work it is intended to do remains undone."[50] Necessary innovations, in fact, are usually introduced despite the drag of bureaucratic inertia. As a result, final control of the government must never rest with professionals. Only a "popular element," happily free from the debilitating effect of obsolete but self-assured expertise, can cure bureaucracy of its predictable fixation on stale truths. Such is Mill's *raison d'état* argument for the democratic accountability of even the most talented public officials.

Another antielitist strand in Mill's argument appears in his principle of the "pinching shoe."[51] The people most likely to initiate needed reforms are those most adversely affected by bad laws. That is a crucial argument for universal suffrage. Knowledge is not distributed evenly throughout society; but neither is it monopolized by a university-trained elite. Indeed, the ignorance of technical experts themselves is almost encyclopedic. Firsthand knowledge of what problems need to be solved is concentrated not in the well-upholstered bureaus but among those who suffer directly from such problems. Victims are grassroots experts, so to speak. Mill's belief in the all-importance of knowledge was not always elitist, therefore, but sometimes had unmistakable democratic implications. Without universal suffrage, the knowledge of disenfranchised citizens will be unavailable to policy makers. One conclusion, which Mill draws, is that the working class must be directly represented in Parliament. The consistency of this liberal-democratic strand in Mill's argument with his convictions about intellectual superiority is not, it must be said, always perfectly clear.

## The Authority of Science

A related cluster of problems concerns the status of science, as Mill understands it. An intriguing, insufficiently examined, and ultimately misleading analogy lurks in the background of his theory of representative government: the analogy between political and scientific discussions.[52] The limits of this analogy must be explored if we mean to embrace Mill's account of the mutual interdependence of limited government and democratic citizenship. Mill's tendency to assimilate political to scientific discussions was already mentioned in passing. To decide if a particular policy or statute is good or bad, whether it promotes the general interest or not, voters must not express their preferences but rather choose the right answer. Like scientists, they must abstract from all personal, sectional, or group interests and devote themselves solely to increasing the GNT, the gross national truth.[53] This argument usefully highlights a fundamental difference between politics and markets. It also shows that Mill did *not*, like a German romantic, view politics principally as an arena for individual self-realization. But despite its virtues, the Millian notion that political discussions produce political "truth" goes too far. It leaves no room for ordinary horse trading among private interests; and no room is not enough, even by the terms of Mill's own account.[54]

In *On Liberty*, along the same lines, Mill conspicuously fails to distinguish between freedom of scientific thought and freedom of moral choice. We must tolerate public disagreement, he explains, because it promotes intellectual progress. To argue in this manner about political and moral questions does not seem completely plausible, however. Notoriously, questions such as "How should I live?" or "What should I do?" have no single correct answer. Certainly, allowing people to do whatever they want will not lead them to an inevitable convergence on *the* true answer to practical questions. But Mill clearly suggests that freedom will generate consensus in morals as well as in science. This may have been due to his conviction that the "worth" of different modes of life is a cognitive question to which a univocal answer is inscribed in human nature.[55] Be this as it may, scientific metaphors pervade his moral writings. For example, he wrote nonchalantly of successful and unsuccessful life experiments. Experience is said to demonstrate which modes of conduct and existence are superior to others. If we want to be rational, we must profit from "the ascertained results of human experience."[56]

At times, it is true, Mill emphasized the "experimental" character of politics in order to dishearten arrogant fanatics who pretend to have all the answers in advance. Referring to communist revolutionaries aiming "to substitute the new rule for the old at a single stroke," he wrote:

> It must be acknowledged that those who would play this [revolutionary] game on the strength of their own private opinion, unconfirmed as yet by any *experimental* verification—who would forcibly deprive all who have now a comfortable physical existence of their only present means of preserving it, and would brave the frightful bloodshed and misery that would ensue if the attempt was resisted—must have a serene confidence in their own wisdom on the one hand and a recklessness of other people's suffering on the other, which Robespierre and St. Just, hitherto the typical instances of those united attributes, scarcely came up to.[57]

In this passage, Mill associates science with a tentative or questioning attitude, opposed to the dogmatism and insolence of revolutionaries. But elsewhere he associates science with sure-footed progress toward incontestable truths. This second suggestion underlies some other dubious and dispensable aspects of Mill's liberalism. We must examine it more closely to determine which aspects of Mill's positive constitutionalism can be detached from his misleading science-politics analogy and preserved in a mature theory of liberal democracy.

## Character and Choice

What is the relation between human character and human choice? At times, Mill writes that character is the *result* of choice: individuals sculpt their own lives, hurling themselves voluntarily into personality-shaping circumstances and thus actively forming their own characters. A person's way of laying out his own existence is best, he tells us, because it is his *own* way. In other passages, however, Mill treats character as a preexistent natural standard which, far from being choosable, itself guides (or should guide) all choice. Individuals must select a life to "suit" their characters, just as shoppers pick shoes which fit their feet.[58] The "worth" of a life is a cognitive question not only because of what human nature *in general* demands. Instead *each individual* has a unique pregiven nature, which a style of life can either violate or match. Mill did not simply delight in diversity. He justified tolerance for moral nonconformity in much the same way as he justified tolerance for scientific disagreement. Both lead to "the truth." By tolerating an abundance of life experiments, society helps individuals discover the distinctive lives which their idiosyncratic natures demand.

We can choose shoes to fit our feet; but we cannot very easily choose our foot size. Despite his commitment to personal liberty and development, Mill sometimes seems so devoted to the pregiven uniqueness of each individual's character that he denies any significant character-shaping role to choice. The value of a life, in any case, comes less from its being chosen (a life of crime may be chosen, after all), than from making the *one right choice.* This last-minute subordination of voluntariness to obligatoriness, free choice to fate, is expressed most clearly in Mill's decision to use the commonplace (but nevertheless weird) metaphor of the man-tree: "Human nature is not a machine to be built after a model, and set to do exactly the work prescribed for it, but a tree, which requires to grow and develop itself on all sides, according to the tendency of the inward forces which make it a living thing."[59] Trees make no choices; they do not have to. Incumbent on an oak is merely the strain of unfolding the unique promise or "tendency" inchoate in the acorn. That, to say the least, is a curious way to conceive the moral life of human beings.

Conformists are miserable creatures: "By dint of not following their own nature, they have no nature to follow."[60] But what does it mean to follow one's own nature? Elsewhere, in a brilliant essay, Mill demolished the fallacious belief that "nature" can serve as a moral standard.[61] In his ethical writings, however, he sometimes ignored his own persuasive strictures on this point. Preferences should be judged not only by their *natural* worth but also by their correspondence with inborn individual character. He insisted that "our desires and impulses should be our own."[62] But what does personal "ownership" contribute to inherent value? And what does it mean to call a desire "our own" anyway? Mill's entire discussion, in fact, hinges upon a latent distinction between autonomous and heteronomous desires, but he never even tries to make this controversial distinction clear or even intelligible.

Mill sometimes lapsed, it seems to me, into the same fallacy which plagues all philosophers who rely on "athletic arguments" when advancing moral claims. An individual has many capacities which are unique to himself or to his species (e.g., the capacity to be absurd). But his "possession" of these capacities is obviously not a moral reason for his exercising them to the hilt. A Darwinist perspective, unfamiliar to Mill himself, helps illuminate the hidden teleological premises behind his wholesale assertion that human beings should realize their inborn potentials and exercise their authentic capacities. Many people have the ability to flash hot with aggression because, at some earlier stage of evolution, such a capacity was useful for the survival of the species. Changed circumstances, however, have made this "inborn capacity" obsolete and even converted it into an albatross needlessly hampering and shortening human life. In other words, to assume that people have a moral obligation to realize their natural potentials is to assume that these potentials were purposely granted by God or nature and were not the result of selective adaptation of bundled traits to ephemeral circumstances.

## Consent and Assent

Indifferent to individual preferences, "truth" is also independent of majority will. To the extent that Mill believed political problems susceptible to correct solutions ("correct" in the scientific sense of dictating the acquiescence of *all* rational minds), he also denied that popular consent could ever legitimate a political choice. This undemocratic conclusion results not from liberalism, however, but from an unwise reliance on the science-politics analogy. A commitment to "truth" in politics makes "consent" redundant—which may explain why Mill so often displays an unwarranted confidence in intellectual superiors. His scientism also surfaces in his disembodied and overintellectualized conception of public debate. His ideal political discussions have been so thoroughly sanitized of love and hatred, of partial interests and partial loyalties, that they do not even resemble university seminars. The politics-science analogy suggests that if members of a community discuss moral and practical questions long enough, they will eventually reach agreement about what to do. But this assumption is unrealistic if fundamental conflicts between rival values cannot be resolved by rational argument.

To preserve the core of Mill's argument, which I believe, remains basically convincing, we must distinguish between *consent* and *assent*. Assent is agreement to empirical or mathematical truths. We assent to the proposition that "it is snowing in Chicago," and our assent is essentially redundant: it will still be snowing whether we say so or not. In fact, it makes little sense to categorize acquiescence in empirical truths as either voluntary or involuntary. The truth that "Paris is in France" depends in no way on our accepting it; nor does accepting it in any way diminish our freedom.

Neither personal nor political choices are of this sort. For such choices, knowledge is necessary, but not decisive. Collective decisions to break a military alliance or build a nuclear reactor are risky ventures. The question of what to do in such circumstances does not have a true or false answer. For this reason, political choice demands consent, not assent. Unlike assent, consent implies an assumption of responsibility in a situation where outcomes are still unknown. Indeed, political decisions require consent precisely because they may prove to have been foolhardy. If things turn out badly, a community will have only itself to blame for a decision based on popular consent.

The distinction between consent and assent strongly suggests that freedom of political debate must be justified in a slightly different manner than freedom of scientific discussion. Debate on important public issues is not desirable because it produces "true answers," but for other reasons. For one thing, wide-open discussion and tolerance for criticism helps encourage government flexibility, awareness of alternatives, self-correction, and the ability to rethink and respond again. Discussion provides a mechanism for introducing political change without resort to violence. If *all* citizens have a chance to protest and discuss public issues freely, moreover, those who are eventually outvoted will probably be more willing than they otherwise would be to abide by the decisions made. Political debate may not guarantee the triumph of truth; but it remains a useful method for challenging false certainties, mobilizing consent, and promoting the trial of new ideas.

The politics-science analogy, for all its shortcomings, does help us see that the "rules of the game" in a liberal democracy are enabling, not merely disabling. Mill's tendency to assimilate political to scientific discussion is telling to the extent that the former, too, helps uncover relevant facts and launch novel ideas. But political debate also keeps public consciousness focused on rival, perhaps irreconcilable, values; and it simultaneously fosters private and sectional bargaining. Discussion is a perfect medium for the simultaneous pursuit of factual knowledge, moral agreement, and pragmatic compromise among clashing values and conflicting interests. This is why there are no authoritative experts in political matters as there are in medicine or physics. Mill was right to note that public debate can set in motion a process of preference transformation. But this process takes time; and time is permanently scarce. Decisions often have to be made in haste and, as a result, the labor of reshaping individual and group interests will sometimes be cut short. Thus, the transformation of preferences will always have to be supplemented by the ad hoc aggregation of preferences.[63] Deliberation must be supplemented by majority rule, by decision making in the absence of true answers, accepted by all. Within all well-organized public discussions, as Mill would probably have recognized, room is made for both processes to go on. That, at least, is the principal aim of positive constitutionalism.

## Private Fallacies and Public Insights

A voter should vote not for his private interests but for the public advantage, as he sees it, "exactly as he would be bound to do if he were the sole voter, and the election depended upon him alone."[64] There is no suggestion here of an invisible hand, squeezing public benefits from private vices: each citizen must be completely public-minded, must act with the common good in mind. In several other passages, however, Mill makes greater concessions to human partiality and thus to the metaphor of a free market of ideas. He argues, for example, that one-sided and even bigoted debaters are naturally led, through a process of almost unwitting "collision," to produce something resembling the whole truth. Invisible to the debaters, such a fortunate outcome can be appreciated only by lucky bystanders. This particular *Harmonielehre* requires no directing intelligence, but only the watchfulness of an observing intelligence. Unfettered debate can be justified because it induces auditors to hear both sides of an issue; but it cannot be justified from the standpoint of the controversialists themselves.

The attempt to see the whole picture is valuable only when *all* participants in a debate rise above party spirit and seek a wider view. Unfortunately, this seldom occurs because "in the human mind, one-sidedness has always been the rule and many-sidedness the exception."[65] When popular truths are one-sided, however, as they often are, they can be effectively opposed only by equally one-sided fanatics. Evenhanded debaters will be completely ineffectual. If one individual is fanatically biased and another strikes a reasonable balance, the outcome of a compromise between the two is likely to be skewed toward the selfish commitments of the former. In other words, what is rational for the individual (to see both sides) may not necessarily be rational for society.

After making an obligatory nod to intellectual superiority, Mill acknowledges the importance of an invisible hand for the successful functioning of the free market of ideas: "Truth, in the great practical concerns of life, is so much a question of the reconciling and combining of opposites, that very few have minds sufficiently capacious and impartial to make the adjustment with an approach to correctness, and it has to be made by the rough process of a struggle between combatants fighting under hostile banners."[66] Useless or even harmful to the debaters themselves, public controversy can be indispensable to an intelligent audience able to appreciate the composite truth that emerges from the clash of two one-sided views.[67] Private errors produce public truths.

At one point in *On Liberty,* Mill recklessly wrote that "no belief which is contrary to truth can be really useful."[68] This assertion is utterly contradicted by his repeated claim that one person's error can fortify another person's truth. Even those who are hopelessly wrong can prevent teachers and learners from dozing off at their posts. This instrumental attitude toward the false beliefs of the deluded is limpidly expressed in the *Autobiography.* Looking back, Mill wrote that he "earnestly hoped that Owenite, St. Simonian, and all other anti-property doctrines might spread widely among the poorer classes; not that I thought those doctrines true, or desired that they should be acted on, but in order that the higher classes might be made to see that they had more to fear from the poor when uneducated, than when educated."[69] Deluded individuals are stepping-stones to a higher consciousness that they themselves may be unable to attain.

This conclusion follows directly from the tendency to assimilate political to scientific truths. It should have been—but apparently was not—disturbing to a liberal such as Mill. Marxists are usually the ones accused of conspiring to make omelets by breaking eggs, experimentally sacrificing the happiness of the present generation, which has but one chance to be happy, to the expected bliss of later generations. Without being so callous toward other people's suffering, Mill came close to making a parallel argument. He did so because he unwisely allowed the scientific rationale for freedom of debate to dominate his understanding of political liberty. In science, all that matters is the *outcome* of uninhibited inquiry and uncensored debate. Using this model, Mill sometimes reduced human discussants to disposable cogs in a truth-maximizing machine. The virtue of some individuals, that is their evenhandedness, must be sacrificed to promote the advancement of the species. Mill does not quite say that one man's disability is justified by its contribution to another man's ability, but he says something similar. But do "the permanent interests of man as a progressive being" really *justify* the mistakes of individuals?[70] Did Mill's enthusiasm for scientific progress require him to embrace an updated form of theodicy? Did his belief in an alliance between liberal politics and scientific inquiry lead him—as other beliefs had led Marx—to espouse a doormat theory of the present generation? Arguments can be given on both sides. What Mill's writings on this question reveal, in any case, is a tension between his epistemology and his ethics, between his commitment to science and his commitment to individualism. From its very inception, after all, modern science pursued the growth of knowledge ruthlessly, with no particular regard for individuals. To adapt Mill's cognitive justification of constitutional democracy to a more consistently liberal outlook, therefore, we must take greater care to distinguish between the scientific and the political functions of discussion, that is, between assent and consent.

## Conclusion

The strength of Mill's thought lies in its stress on positive constitutionalism, on the possibility-creating effects of institutional constraints. Its weakness lies in its bias toward mental superiority, its over-intellectualized conception of politics, and especially in its reliance on an analogy between political and scientific discussions. These criticisms, it should be said, while valid in general, do not take every detail of Mill's complex presentation into account.

By way of conclusion, let me note one way in which Mill questions, and even rejects, the politics-science analogy that otherwise bedevils his thinking. In politics, unlike science, he surprisingly explains, free debate can sometimes be counterproductive. "I acknowledge that the tendency of all opinions to become sectarian is not cured by the freest discussion, but is often heightened and exacerbated thereby."[71] This is a remarkable admission by the nineteenth century's premier advocate of free debate. Public discussion of political questions can undermine both individual and collective rationality. Open debate may lead to a hardening of battle fronts, far beyond what would result from a silent assessment of conflicting interests. Because of the plentiful opportunities it offers for cornering, insulting, embarrassing, losing face, and tripping over one's own feet, uninhibited discussion can cause disputants irrationally to dig in their heels. Controversies also have a certain dynamic of their own. Controversialists may come to appreciate the sweet benefits of facing down bitter opponents. After all, enemies help clarify life. Once a friend-enemy pattern has been established, however, an individual's willingness to acknowledge the valid insights offered by his antagonist markedly shrinks, "the truth which ought to have been seen, but was not, being rejected all the more violently because proclaimed by persons regarded as opponents."[72]

In this case, an institutional guarantee of openness may actually decrease the reasonableness of democratic life. This paradoxical insight not only explodes the deceptive analogy between political and scientific discussion. It also suggests the need, in some circumstances at least, to inhibit freedom of expression for the sake of liberal democracy itself. It is to this controversial relation between self-censorship and self-rule that I now turn.

# 7

# Gag Rules or the Politics of Omission

*Le Roy de Moschovie, voyant son peuple divisé en sectes et seditions, pour les presches et disputes des Ministers, fit defense de prescher, ni disputer de la Religion, sur peine de la vie.*

—BODIN

A conversation is invariably shaped by what its participants decide not to say. To avoid destructive conflicts, we suppress controversial themes. In Cambridge, Massachusetts, old friends still shun the subject of Israel in order to keep old friendships intact. Burying a divisive issue, of course, can be viewed censoriously—as evasiveness rather than diplomacy. But conflict-shyness is not merely craven; it can serve positive goals. By tying our tongues about a sensitive question, we can secure forms of cooperation and fellowship otherwise beyond reach.

Strategic self-censorship occurs in a variety of settings, from international summits to midnight trysts—including perhaps the limiting case of amnesia. In collective life, unmentionables abound. Within every group, speaking about tabooed subjects will provoke general consternation and embarrassment. After all, no one should wash his dirty linen in public. At faculty meetings, even garrulous professors will not prattle interminably about their alcoholism or marital problems. Such universally appreciated uncommunicativeness can be easily explained. For one thing, no group's information-processing capacity is infinite—people cannot talk about everything at once. Life is short; to avoid cognitive overload, different groups focus on different topics at different times.

Other reasons for sealing one's lips are less general and more pertinent to the theory and practice of liberal democracy. Sometimes an issue appears "unspeakable" because open airing would mortally offend prominent individuals or vulnerable subgroups and irreparably injure the cooperative spirit of the organization. Alternatively, a collectivity can often utilize its scarce resources more effectively if it dodges an irksome issue. By refraining from opening a can of worms, discussion leaders can prevent its lively contents from attracting the whole of everyone's attention—at least for the time being. Despite the warnings of popular psychology, in other words, repression can be perfectly healthy.

## Some Preliminary Illustrations

To suggest the range and variety of self-censorship common in liberal-democratic societies, let me begin with a few nonpolitical examples. In law, statutes of limitation preclude prosecutions for temporally remote crimes. Similarly, various nonjusticiability doctrines enable the Supreme Court to silence itself about difficult legal issues. The "political questions" doctrine, as well as "case and controversy," "ripeness," and "standing" are all "devices for deciding not to decide," strategies by which members of the Court limit the range of problems on which they are required to pronounce.[1] Every institution is equipped to resolve certain difficulties better than others. By staying its hand, the Court can improve its overall performance. By refusing either to uphold or overturn a governmental action, it can avoid decisions that might damage its credibility and overtax its limited problem-solving capacities.

Scholarly communities similarly regulate the area of permissible and pertinent speech. Universities, for example, are generally thought to have a limited mission. True, controversy rages about the banning of hate speech on campus and about how audible or muted, say, the university's political voice should be. Conservatives used to assert that divestment from companies doing business in South Africa was not a suitable subject for formal consideration by a university faculty. But liberals, while castigating what they perceived as moral evasiveness, always concurred that the docket of faculty meetings must be confined in *some* ways, for example, that they should not schedule time for an exhaustive analysis of faculty spouses.

Finally, to select a quite different example, John Rawls has argued for the political utility of what he calls "the precept of avoidance." In any group, a cleverly formulated gag rule can profitably shift attention away from areas of discord and toward areas of concord. Certain metaphysical assumptions about the human person are now, and will probably remain, controversial. But we can agree upon the right while differing on the good. To establish a public conception of justice, acceptable to all members of a diverse society, we must abstain from questions which elicit radical disagreement. In a liberal social order, "certain matters are reasonably taken off the political agenda." The basic normative framework of society must be able to command the loyalty of individuals and groups with widely differing self-understandings and conceptions of personal fulfillment. Theorists of justice can achieve such broad consensus on ground rules only if they "bypass religion and philosophy's profoundest controversies," only if they steer clear of irresolvable metaphysical disputes.[2]

Similar side-stepping techniques are familiar in political life as well. Hand-tying in general has been discussed in chapter 5. Tongue-tying, as a narrowly targeted version of this universal technique, may be one of constitutionalism's main gifts to democracy. Some constitutional limits, at least, can be usefully redescribed as expressing a community's decision to silence itself, or its representatives, on selected issues. Legislators are enjoined from officially discussing questions which, if placed under the control of electoral majorities, would (it is thought) induce governmental paralysis, squander everyone's time, or exacerbate factional animosities.

## Self-Denying Ordinances

Conspiracy theorists have taught us to conceive of agenda narrowing as a technique by which sinister elites exert power over their hapless victims: "Power may be, and often is, exercised by confining the scope of decision making to relatively 'safe' issues," or, less circumlocutiously, "He who determines what politics is about runs the country."[3] Indeed, power wielders do not always act surreptitiously when silencing others or constricting the range of issues which can be freely discussed. By limiting campaign contributions or discontinuing legal aid to the poor, public officials may stifle the voice of some particularly annoying citizens without actually commanding them to remain silent. But coercively enforced censorship, at least since the invention of printing, has easily rivaled the withdrawal of resources as an instrument of political control. Today, for example, the United States government no longer forbids medical personnel in federally-funded family planning clinics from offering counseling services about abortion; but the Supreme Court has upheld the constitutionality of such a gag rule, which may therefore be reimposed when the next Republican candidate is elected President.[4] And even now, many important restrictions on, say, commercial speech remain in force, including, for example, statutes preventing tobacco companies from advertising cigarettes.

Freedom of speech, as this principle has evolved in American constitutional thinking, does not outlaw every sort of gag order. Judges seal records, telling lawyers not to inform the jury about a defendant's earlier mistrial for the same offense. More rarely, a judge may issue a gag order, prohibiting lawyers, police detectives, and court employees from discussing a case with reporters while the trial is going on. The common law itself restricted courtroom communications, rejecting written testimony as valid evidence, for example, on the grounds that a lack of opportunity for visual observation and cross examination of witnesses substantially diminished its reliability.[5] Today, various laws regulate disclosure by government employees, where military secrets, for example, are at stake. A court may even, in exceptional circumstances, impose prior restraint to prevent newspapers from publishing a story that might endanger national security. Similarly, and of probably greater significance, libel law is a system of rules specifying what people cannot say. In the common law that British settlers brought to America, libel was a criminal as well as a civil offense, an injury against the public, not merely against the defamed individual. Because insults, even if true, predictably ignited a yearning for violent revenge, libel was originally considered a conspiracy to break the public peace.[6]

One individual or group can obviously gag another, brandishing threats or paying hush money. But it is much more intriguing that individuals and groups can also, under certain conditions, gag themselves. Self-denying ordinances are perfectly possible. Witnesses plead the Fifth Amendment, declining to testify for fear that they may incriminate themselves by what they say. Analogously, nominees to the federal bench, if they wish to be confirmed, evade senatorial queries that try to force them to state how they would decide a future case. Panel members recuse themselves because of conflicts of interest. Legislators abstain from voting when countervailing pressures cannot be reconciled and taking a position one way or the other might cost them essential electoral support.

Such garden-variety examples of strategic self-censorship could be multiplied almost indefinitely. Legislative bodies interdict debate on delicate issues in a somewhat more systematic manner. In the early American Senate and House, a parliamentary technique was employed "for avoiding either undesired discussions or undesired decisions, or both."[7] Like individuals, in other words, organizations and collectivities can deliberately keep selected topics undisclosed for what they consider their own advantage. In order to present a united front, members of a political party may refrain from publicizing internal conflicts. To attract public attention, by contrast, members of rival parties may choose to highlight their differences, remaining strategically mute about the principles and goals they share in common. Sometimes important objectives can be achieved only so long as they are left unspoken. Marriages may founder on attempts to delineate, in a written contract, precisely who is to perform what tasks and when. Affirmative action may be yet another example: if the government talks too freely about what it is trying to do (for instance, create the conditions for self-respect among racial or ethnic minorities), it may needlessly throw obstacles in its own path. In such a case, public officials are probably well-advised to gag themselves. Conservatives may object to what they see as governmental hypocrisy here, but soft-spokenness remains desirable whenever it helps prevent not only unwanted conflict but also counterproductive humiliation. To make their policies successful, in any case, groups and governments often find it prudent to cultivate the arts of omission.

## Positive Uses of Negative Liberty

No issue is more frequently classified as "worthy of avoiding" than religion. Sectarianism is rightly feared as a divisive force, a potential threat to communal cooperation. Religious disputes cannot always be resolved politically, or even rationally. On this premise, some multidenominational communities with liberal aspirations have decided to draw a "line" between the public and the private—to consign controversial religious attachments to the nonpolitical sphere, beyond the jurisdiction of majorities and officials. Paradoxically, a religiously pluralistic country devoted to majority rule can be *united* by a deftly drawn *division* between public and private spheres. Compartmentalization can reinforce social cohesion. Other controversies, in this case, will be easier to resolve because religious schisms are not allowed to crystallize into political factions.

If accepted, such a claim throws interesting light on the doctrine of nonentanglement. The "wall" between church and state may not create tolerant human beings, but it can nevertheless solve certain social problems. Not merely does it shelter the private sphere from unwanted incursions, it also unburdens the public sphere of irresolvable problems. In general, students of "negative liberty" have neglected this second achievement, the disencumbering or agenda-uncluttering function of private rights.[8] Limits on the government's jurisdiction are typically justified by reference to the fragility and intrinsic value of protected domains. But why not invert the picture and examine what benefits accrue to public life if certain issues are precluded from the public agenda? While screening one realm, private rights may simultaneously lighten the charge on another. Negative liberty "privatizes" certain questions, erasing them from the list of problems to be resolved politically. This unloading tactic makes all remaining controversies more amenable to compromise. When viewed from a slightly different angle, what formerly seemed a protective device now appears as a disencumbering strategy. By gagging themselves about religion, to return to that example, public officials seem to gain as much freedom as do private sectaries. The autonomy of politics increases simultaneously with the autonomy of religion.

According to Isaiah Berlin, "there is no necessary connection between individual liberty and democratic rule." This connection, he continues, "is a good deal more tenuous than it seemed to many advocates of both."[9] If my suggestion has any merit, Berlin is at least partially mistaken. Some private rights, at least, contribute vitally to democratic government by expunging irresolvable disputes from the public sphere. By narrowing the political agenda to problems manageable by discussion, certain individual rights may be said to subserve self-government. By helping secularize politics, religious freedoms also help democratize collective life. Legal protections of individual conscience, once again, do not merely shield the private; they also disencumber the public.

Issue suppression sounds tyrannical, for to gag is to choke. But self-denial may be indispensable in self-regulating polities. For one thing, conflict resolution often presupposes conflict avoidance. Democracy becomes possible, according to many democratic theorists, only when certain emotionally charged solidarities and commitments are displaced from the political realm. By keeping religious questions off the legislative agenda, or so I want to suggest, the liberal principle of nonentanglement may help fashion a certain kind of public—a public susceptible to democratic methods of conflict resolution. Self-gagging is thus a form of self-control, not of self-strangulation. By agreeing to privatize religion, a divided citizenry can enable itself to resolve its *other* differences rationally, by means of public debate and compromise.

Democracy is conventionally associated with *glasnost,* freedom of speech, and the overthrow of censorial government. The abolition of the crime of seditious libel, for instance, helped define American democracy.[10] And liberalism in general was born in protest against religious authorities who attached cruel penalties to hazardous and heterodox speech. Thus, it seems perverse to focus on the contribution of gag rules to self-rule. Nevertheless, the shape of democratic politics is undoubtedly determined by obligatory silences, by the strategic removal of certain items from the democratic agenda. Some theorists have even argued that issue suppression is a necessary condition for the emergence and stability of democracies.

According to Joseph Schumpeter, for instance, one of the essential prerequisites for a successful democracy is that "the range of political decision should not be extended too far." Robert Dahl argues that moral conflict need not subvert democracy: disagreement about ultimate goals is compatible with collective self-rule, but only if there remains ample group autonomy within a society, that is, plenty of leeway for groups to follow their own goals unharassed. Because he views religion as a prime source of rationally irresolvable conflict, Samuel Huntington asserts that cultures lacking a sharp separation between religion and politics, between spiritual and secular domains, are not "hospitable to democracy."[11] When ultimate ends color all concrete political acts, compromise or piecemeal reform becomes next to impossible. Democratization is doomed from the start, according to this line of argument, without some sort of socially acknowledged boundary between religion and politics.

## A Typology of Gag Rules

Let me broach my main subject in this chapter by making a few analytical distinctions which will prove useful later on. Gag rules can be either autonomous or heteronomous, that is, self-imposed or imposed by others. Self-imposed gag rules, in turn, can be ratified by unanimity or only by a majority. They can also be either formal or informal. For example, some legislative vows of silence are explicitly incorporated into the constitutional framework, while others are based on a tacit agreement among political elites. I will return to the autonomous/heteronomous, unanimous/majoritarian and formal/informal distinctions in my analysis, below, of two classic attempts at issue avoidance: the efforts, in the United States, to suppress political controversy first about slavery and then about religion. Several other variations among kinds of gag rule should also be mentioned at the outset.

Some gag rules are designed solely to postpone discussion or avoid a precipitate decision; others are meant to bury a topic definitively.[12] Some gag rules debar everyone from raising a ticklish question; others are more narrowly targeted, silencing only a selected class of speakers. (For instance, when a technical question arises, as Mill explained, laymen should defer to specialists.) Modern democracies contain many semiautonomous institutions, each with its own agenda. Thus, we must also distinguish between the universal suppression of a theme and the mere transferal of that theme to a different institutional context. Unspeakable in one room or *devant les enfants,* embarrassing revelations may be thoroughly canvassed in a more secluded part of the same house. Rather than tinkering with an explosive issue, a high official may pass the buck, handing it over to expendable functionaries not too closely associated with the party in power.

Less deviously, some topics are excluded from the national legislative agenda only to be consigned to state legislatures or to the courts. Contrariwise, by decamping from the political thicket, the Supreme Court silences itself, but it simultaneously invites executive and legislative officials to speak out. In such cases, gag rules institute a division of labor which can help clarify responsibilities for all parties. Much more radical is the decision to remove an issue from the jurisdiction of all branches and levels of government.

Finally, some items are excluded from the political agenda without any conscious decision having been made. Agendas are not infinite; it would be preposterous to assume that all issues would naturally appear on the agenda unless they have been consciously removed. Parochial habits of mind, cultural blinders, and lack of wit all help explain why politicians fail to seize upon (what seems to us) an important theme. The United States, unlike West European nations in the second half of the twentieth century, has never debated the legitimacy of private property in formal legislative settings. But the issue was never deliberately suppressed because, for a variety of reasons, it was never raised.

Political agendas are constantly expanding and contracting. Why an issue captures or escapes public attention is an important subject for historical and sociological research. Seriously to analyze processes of agenda narrowing and agenda broadening would require, among other things, careful attention to the conditions for successful and abortive social movements. Understandably, my concerns in this chapter are more narrow. There are at least some issues which would otherwise be at the center of political attention which are consciously deleted from the range of subjects to be discussed.[13] To make the concept of a *gag rule* useful for comparative analysis, I have chosen to restrict it to such overt, fully purposive, and tactically justified acts of omission.

## The Transition to Democracy

The raging debate about decommunization and lustration in the fledgling democracies of Eastern Europe suggests that gag rules may sometimes be beneficial to processes of democratization.[14] An obsessive desire to air in public crimes of collaboration that were committed under the old regime may well make the consolidation of democracy, including an etiquette of civilized disagreement, more difficult than it would otherwise be.[15] A decade ago, a similar dilemma was raised by the controversial decisions of recently established democracies in South America to offer immunity from criminal prosecution to military leaders who wielded power under the old regime.[16] Although guilty of atrocities, some of these officers proved willing to relinquish power peacefully to a civilian government. But they did so in exchange for a legislative and judicial vow of silence about their past wrongdoings. Amnesties, in fact, can be seen as classic examples of gag rules, meant to stabilize democracy. They embody what Nietzsche called "active forgetfulness," but on a national or at least governmental scale.[17] By closing the books on the past, by keeping retribution for former crimes off the political agenda, the organizers of a new democracy can secure the compliance of strategically located elites—cooperation which may be indispensable for a successful transition from dictatorship to self-government. In the absence of an overriding desire for national unity, however, we can assume that opposing groups will be unlikely to silence themselves about the issues that most radically divide them.

Governments presumably strive to ensure that their abilities and resources are adequate to the problems they face and the objectives they intend to pursue. Excising unanswerable questions from the political agenda is thus a natural strategy for any state, especially a recently founded one. New regimes have shallow roots and may be destroyed by the first storm that strikes, as Machiavelli observed. A newborn government is not likely to survive if forced to make controversial decisions about historically intractable problems.

According to Dankwart Rustow, an intense but obviously unwinnable struggle is an essential precondition for the transition to democracy.[18] All parties will soon become weary of interminable hostilities. If they possess the talent and determination, key elites can then negotiate a settlement—a system of power sharing and mutual accommodation in the interest of all major factions. This bargain among subgroups and sections may assume the form of a constitution. Eliminating divisive questions from the jurisdiction of state officials is likely to be an essential element in any such regime-founding compromise.

If the government is to survive, Rustow adds, the original constitutional settlement must be a bootstrap operation. The constitution cannot be imposed autocratically from above or, as Adam Przeworski remarks, "democracy cannot be dictated; it emerges from bargaining."[19] To have the exemplary power essential to any successful act of founding, the initial peace treaty must at least appear to be designed cooperatively by the rival factions.[20] In other words, consensus on fundamentals should not be overrated as a precondition for democratization. Without major divisions, there would be no incentive to devise democratic institutions in the first place. These institutions, it seems, will only succeed in handling latent conflicts if they incorporate mechanisms for side-stepping divisive issues.[21]

Paradoxically, as Clifford Geertz has argued, citizenship and community can be violently at odds.[22] At the very least, communal loyalties present serious obstacles to the integration of recently created national states. Geertz is concerned with the consolidation of any sort of national state, not solely with the creation of democracies. But his insights are nevertheless revealing for our inquiry, especially given the worldwide resurgence of identity politics in the wake of communism's shattering collapse. "Primordial attachments," as he describes them, can be religious, racial, linguistic, tribal, regional, or customary; but they are always tinged with xenophobia and are thus in tension with membership in the state as a whole. Some of the world's most intractable problems arise when primordial ties are politicized by attempts at national integration.[23]

Minority security is a common good—good for the majority as well as the minority. By designing a constitution to allay the fears of defenseless ethnic subgroups, the framers of a regime-founding compromise can secure the national cooperation necessary for economic prosperity and military independence. Any nation split into "primordially defined groups" must discover a "form competent to contain the country's diversity." This "form," once again, is a political constitution in the broad sense. It establishes law-making and law-enforcing bodies, but also organizations, such as political parties, "within which primordial conflicts are being informally and realistically adjusted."[24]

Party organization, the domestication of factional loyalties and the diplomatic skill of elites are essential for social stability in a religiously and ethnically diverse country. *But such factors must be supplemented by a strategic narrowing of the national political agenda.* Primordial loyalties must be shielded from the police and not only directed into "proper" political channels but also (at least to some extent) channeled away from politics altogether.[25] De-politicization, in conjunction with other forces, can increase the chances for rational compromise in a divided society.

One traditional solution to the problem of primordial divisions is secession or partition. Another is ethnocracy: a single religious, linguistic, racial, or regional group can expel, assimilate or subjugate all others. This is "community" in the strong and antiliberal sense. Serbia provides a recent and sickening example. If diversity can be neutralized constitutionally, however, communitarian secessionism and ethnic cleansing may perhaps be avoidable. Luck is indispensable; but shrewd institutional design may help rival ethnic groups live peacefully within the four corners of a single state. Clever framers *can* craft institutions that cushion conflict. By so doing, they are laying the foundations for "a civil politics of primordial compromise."[26]

A compromise-minded politics of this sort has been the focus of Arend Lijphart's studies of consociationalism. In primordially divided societies, self-government requires "cooperation by the leaders of different groups which transcends the segmental or subcultural cleavages at the mass level."[27] Paradoxically, elites must both represent and not represent their constituents. They must hold their followers' loyalty, but not reproduce their uncompromising attitudes in national negotiations. Such cross-sectarian cooperation among elites requires "a strengthening of the political inertness of the nonelite public and their deferential attitudes to the segmental leaders."[28]

The spirit of compromise among elites is a necessary but not sufficient condition for self-rule in a divided society. Equally important is "segmental autonomy"—Lijphart's expression for the removal of divisive issues from the national agenda. Ideally, there will be a "high degree of freedom for the segments in the conduct of their internal social and cultural affairs." In other words, the national government must muzzle itself on certain issues. On matters of regional or sectarian but not national interest, "decisions and their execution can be left to the separate segments."[29] When national decisions cannot be avoided, each group must be granted influence proportionate to its numbers and, crucially, be armed with a veto. The reason for taking such elaborate precautions is simple: "In a political system with clearly separate and potentially hostile population segments, virtually all decisions are perceived as entailing high stakes, and strict majority rule places a strain on the unity and peace of the system."[30] When the stakes are high, the jurisdiction of national majorities must be narrow. To ensure its own authority on other issues, the national majority must gag itself on issues destined to provoke sectarian animosity. Constitutional constraints can foster democracy by helping avoid an uncontrollable outbreak of group passions.

For divided societies, Lijphart advocates coalition governments, a mutual veto, proportionality in the allocation of civil service jobs as well as government subsidies and, as I mentioned, segmental autonomy. He favors three or four parties over two, a parliamentary to a presidential system, proportional representation to majority rule, and federalism over a unitary government. He also prefers a "coalescent" to an adversarial style of decision making. Political choices should be made in secret negotiations among rival elites (on the basis of logrolling, package deals, and so forth) and should be arrived at by virtual unanimity. Consociationalism, in other words, means democracy without an opposition. According to Lijphart, in fact, the societies in question are too deeply divided to withstand open political contestation.

## The Gag Rule of 1836

Before the Civil War, the United States itself was a profoundly divided society. Its leaders, too, shied away from open conflict over the most divisive of all issues. In 1836, for example, the U.S. House of Representatives adopted the first in a series of gag rules: "*Resolved,* That all petitions, memorials, resolutions, propositions, or papers, relating in any way, or to any extent whatsoever, to the subject of slavery, or the abolition of slavery, shall, without being either printed or referred, be laid on the table, and that no further action whatever shall be had thereon."[31] This act of legislative self-censorship and the parallel measure adopted in the Senate were tactical compromises, "coalescent" attempts to split the difference between North and South. Only a self-denying ordinance would permit mutual adjustments and rational discussion of other issues among the sections. Only a gag rule could scale back the responsibilities of the federal government, making them roughly proportionate to its modest problem-solving capacities. Curiously enough, Congress's decision to stay its own hand was attacked not only, as one would expect, by abolitionists; it was also assailed, for reasons to be explained, by proslavery advocates of states' rights (such as John Calhoun), who themselves yearned for absolute congressional silence on the slave question. The unavoidable precariousness of all self-gagging arrangements, in fact, is beautifully illustrated by unbending southern hostility to this bill.

The debate of 1836 about gagging Congress occurred under the shadow of a larger controversy about gagging the abolitionist press. Northern antislavery societies had decided to use the mails to flood the South with emancipationist tracts. Predictably, southerners refused to allow these works to circulate freely. In their view, such pamphlets threatened their very survival, that is, constituted open invitations to slave insurrection. The federal government, unwilling to enforce its own laws on such a sensitive issue, turned a blind eye while southern states proceeded to censor the mails.[32]

Stanching the flow of abolitionist literature across southern borders was not sufficient for the proslavery forces. They were equally anxious to quell unending congressional debates about slavery. President Jackson himself argued, in the words of his biographer, that "all discussion in Congress of the slave issue" was "ultimately undemocratic."[33] But how can discussion be undemocratic? Incessant slavery agitation was crippling the national legislature's capacity to deal with other issues, Jackson apparently thought. Talk of slavery in the federal assembly was simply disruptionist. Mutual recriminations between proslavery and antislavery forces had even led some congressmen to arrive at the House and Senate chambers armed with knives—a sign that parliamentary courtesy was fraying at the edges.

Of particular concern to the South were petitions requesting Congress to abolish slavery, or at least the slave trade, within the District of Columbia. The antislavery position was that all citizens had a right to petition the government for redress of grievances.[34] According to slavery's advocates, by contrast, Congress should refuse even to *receive* these petitions on the grounds that the federal government had no authority to abolish slavery anywhere. Exactly like the abolitionists, Senators and Representatives should be fully gagged on the slave question: "The subject is beyond the jurisdiction of Congress—they have no right to touch it in any shape or form, or to make it the subject of deliberation or discussion."[35] While appealing to formal rights and lines of jurisdiction, Calhoun was actually concerned almost exclusively with political consequences. The abolitionists were fanatics and incendiaries. Their "insulting petitions" vilified the South, inculcated hatred, and threatened to destroy the Union. Attempts publicly to disgrace and humiliate slaveholding states could not be profitably discussed in Congress. Such discussions, however perfunctory, could only further polarize the nation.

As a compromise measure, Henry Pinckney introduced a series of resolutions in the House stipulating that Congress could not, as a matter of constitutional principle, regulate slavery in the South, and should not, as a matter of expedience, regulate slavery in the District. The attached gag rule clause, cited above, declared that petitions concerning slavery would be formally "received" by Congress; but they would then be automatically tabled and never discussed.

As mentioned, Calhoun and fellow nullificationists in the House "considered Pinckney's gag rule a disastrous southern defeat."[36] It struck Congress dumb, but not deaf. In retrospect, it should be said, proslavery objections to the rule seem almost hysterically legalistic. The resolutions, they argued, implicitly granted Congress the right to discuss slavery and to abolish it in the District, even though Congress currently refused to exercise these rights.[37] Abolition petitions, at any rate, should not be received and tabled but simply not received. Not only should Congress's mouth be gagged; but its ears must also be plugged. The initial reception of petitions, Calhoun explained, was "our Thermopylae." We must, he added, "meet the enemy on the frontier."[38] Halfhearted gag rules were too loose to still the emancipationist tongue. Indeed, Calhoun and his compatriots wanted the impossible, for Congress to be so tightly handcuffed on this issue that it could never even aspire to slip its bonds: "Nothing short of the certainty of permanent security can induce us to yield an inch."[39]

The gag rule of 1836, precisely because it was a political compromise, is emblematic of the mainstream approach to the slavery question in American politics from the Founding to the Civil War. Fortunately or unfortunately, the emergence and maintenance of national self-rule seems to have presupposed the strategic avoidance of this divisive theme. At the very outset, a clause opposing the slave trade was dropped from the Declaration of Independence. The Constitution itself discreetly abstained from using the words "slave" or "slavery." The framers acknowledged the institution of slavery, of course.[40] But they resorted to euphemism and indirectness when describing it—as if the disagreeableness of the thing could really be mitigated by fastidiousness about the name. The sectional compromise at the heart of the Constitution, one might say, demanded that the issue remain latent and largely unspoken.[41] Discussing the bargains by which divided nations are united, Geertz comments that "the mere prejudices that must be tolerated in order to effect such reconciliations are often repugnant."[42] The creation of a national republic in the United States seems to be a case in point. As time went by, northerners found their moral opposition to slavery intensifying. Most, however, remained even more averse to dismembering the Union. Nationalism, as is often the case, made them reticent to stir up sectional hostilities.

## The Constitution as a Bargain

Under any system of majority rule, members of an outvoted minority must agree to an outcome they oppose. That is, they must comply with a decision to which they do not consent. Majoritarianism is therefore inherently paradoxical. It escapes inconsistency only because *consent* can be aimed at different targets. Even if they do not consent directly to the decision being made, members of an outvoted minority can consent to the procedures by which that decision was reached, and they can even bind themselves indirectly to abide by whatever outcome the accepted procedures produce. But the implicit difficulty here cannot be easily dismissed. Why *do* minorities accept majority rule? Without a minority's acquiescence in decisions that its members, by definition, dislike, democracy would be radically unstable. But how is an electoral minority's peaceful submission politically guaranteed?

One classic answer is offered by the theory of "multiple membership." If every individual belongs to several groups at once, then most citizens will be aligned with both majority and minority coalitions on different questions. Outvoted on one issue, citizens will have good self-regarding reasons to accept an unwanted decision: in other circumstances they, too, will benefit from majority rule. Contrariwise, members of an obviously temporary majority will be inspired to display self-restraint. Cross-pressured by their rival group allegiances and expecting to be outvoted on other issues, the winners of the moment will be unlikely to run roughshod over the deepest values of the losers.

When majority and minority coalitions become solidified across the most important political issues, no system of mutual restraint and accommodation based on multiple membership can gain a purchase. Such was roughly the situation in the United States before the Civil War. Only a constitution placing strict limitations on majority power could foster minority security and thereby induce a southern minority to accept the decisions of a northern majority. Federalism, paradoxically, was the structural provision most essential for securing national cooperation in the face of "primordial" divisions. Relative decentralization gave all states a stake in the system and guaranteed that their deepest values would not be trampled upon by national majorities.

In every deeply divided society, majoritarianism is possible only on the basis of privatization of the divisive questions or, alternatively, by segmental autonomy. Not surprisingly, therefore, southern unionists conceived American democracy in proto-consociational terms.[43] For democracy to function in a morally disunified country, national majorities must tactfully yield to intense sectional minorities. Simple outvoting on highly charged issues would bring the entire system crashing down. In the American case, the moral status and political future of slave ownership was too hot to handle and touched nerves too deep to be subjected to majoritarian politics on the national level.

Northerners offered southerners the following quid pro quo: if the slave states would submit other issues to majority control, the free states would agree to exclude the slave question from the national majority's jurisdiction. Legislative self-censorship was justified as essential to national cooperation. This strategy of avoidance seems to have been a working principle of American government in the first half of the nineteenth century. Pinckney's gag rule of 1836 simply codified a generally accepted practice and applied it to a particular case. The Union could be preserved only by removing the slave issue from the Congressional agenda. The Missouri Compromise corroborates this interpretation; it, too, was a package deal in the classic consociational manner.

Calhoun came very close to formulating the argument in precisely this way. Slaveholders had a constitutionally guaranteed private right to hold their property. But the prohibition against federal regulation of slavery did not merely protect a private sphere and the attendant values of personal autonomy; it also unburdened the national public sphere and thus preserved the values of democracy. Orderly democratic consideration of *other* problems would become impossible if such a passion-charged and divisive issue were placed at the center of legislative deliberation.

This prodemocratic defense of agenda narrowing follows directly from Calhoun's general theory of constitutionalism. Constitutions, he argued, are bargains. Indeed, the development and acceptance of a constitutional framework can occur only as the contingent result of irresolvable conflict: "The constitutions [of both Rome and Britain] originated in a pressure occasioned by conflicts of interests between hostile classes or orders and were intended to meet the pressing exigencies of the occasion, neither party, it would seem, having any conception of the principles involved or the consequences to follow beyond the immediate objects in contemplation."[44] And, he adds, it seems "impossible" for constitutional governments of this sort to arise in any other manner.[45]

The initial willingness of rival factions to compromise on a constitutional framework is usually motivated by battle fatigue and a yearning for the fruits of peaceful cooperation. But all parties must be assured that "ultimate values"—the things they care about most—will not be dragged through the mud of contestation. When factions negotiate, they put their differences aside and build on common ground. Both northerners and southerners desired peace and detested the thought of being ruled by foreigners. Burying differences, in Calhoun's view, meant removing them from the national political agenda in order to concentrate on problems likely to mobilize greater social consensus.

Despite all gagging efforts, the slave issue would not subside. Eventually, it cracked the frame, that is, became too explosive to be handled within the institutional structures established by the framers and reaffirmed by the Missouri Compromise. Abolitionists, of course, had always been repelled by the bargain-like character of America's quasi-consociational system. William Lloyd Garrison, for example, denounced the Constitution as "a covenant with death, and an agreement with hell."[46] Slavery was sinful and odious; and it was the essence of immorality for legislators to silence themselves about such an abomination. If forcing slavery on to the legislative agenda caused the breakdown of national democracy, so be it. An issue of this magnitude was worth a civil war.

### What Cannot Remain Unspoken

To a surprising degree, the great Lincoln-Douglas debates of 1858 hinged precisely upon the question of what should and should not be said. According to Douglas, any discussion of the moral status of slavery was a grave insult to southerners, tending to put the Union at risk. By unceremoniously branding slavery as "evil" and declaring that slaves had an inalienable right to self-ownership as well as the right to the fruits of their own labor, Lincoln was acting no differently than extreme abolitionists such as Garrison. He, too, was hazarding the Union and inviting sectional war. Basically, according to Douglas, Lincoln was an agitator who refused to let sleeping dogs lie, a *Gesinnungspolitiker,* driven by abstract idealism and unappreciative of the tactical compromises implicit in the Constitution. By announcing that slavery must be placed on the course of ultimate extinction, he was terrorizing a vulnerable southern minority, engaging in a "conspiracy to wage war against one-half of the Union." The slave question was so charged with "passion," moreover, that rational discussion about it was precluded.[47] Douglas would have concurred with those theorists of negotiation and mediation who urge that "when anger and misperception are high, some thoughts are best left unsaid."[48] In his view, Lincoln simply did not understand that preserving the American republic required self-censorship about the most emotional and galling of all issues.

While painting Lincoln as an extremist, Douglas portrayed himself as a moderate and a *politique.* He was willing to compromise about almost anything except union and peace. The peace party of sixteenth-century France had believed that national unity was compatible with religious diversity, that is, that a divided house could stand. Three centuries later, the unionist Douglas asserted that national unity was compatible with a diversity of laws and customs concerning slavery. The nation was not based upon a moral consensus about black slavery: northerners thought it evil, while southerners thought it good. The Constitution was nevertheless able to unify the country by abstracting from this underlying normative dissonance. Instead of demanding that all citizens adopt a common attitude toward slavery, the framers forged a modus vivendi among a morally divided people. The Constitution was a "form designed to contain the country's diversity." By their incessant ranting about the evils of slavery, Lincoln and the abolitionists were wrecking this skillfully wrought bargain from which great benefits had ensued.

As is well known, Lincoln denied Douglas's fundamental premise. The basic division in the land was not between those loyal and those indifferent to the Union. Much more important was the disagreement between those who believed slavery was wrong and those who considered it comely and beneficial. In a valiant attempt to be evenhanded, to ply an intermediate course between secessionists and abolitionists, Douglas struggled to say *nothing at all* about the moral status of slavery. As Lincoln ironically noted: "He has the high distinction, so far as I know, of never having said slavery is either right or wrong."[49] But tongue-tying neutrality on this explosive issue was unacceptable.[50] Especially in the final debates, Lincoln repeatedly maneuvered his opponent into an either/or situation: Douglas must throw off his conciliatory pose, ungag himself, and take sides. To remove the slave issue from the political agenda may appear fair to all sections, but it actually "muzzled" the nation's conscience. On some questions, self-gagging is simply immoral. To suppress this issue, in any case, was *implicitly to take sides.* According to Lincoln, Douglas was "in favor of eradicating, of pressing out of view, the questions of preference in this country for free and slave institutions; and consequently every sentiment he utters discards the idea that there is anything wrong in slavery."[51] No would-be fence sitter could avoid making a moral pronouncement, one way or the other.

While cautious himself, Lincoln nevertheless ridiculed the idea that conflict avoidance should be a politician's paramount concern. Douglas was opposed to discussing the slave issue in moral terms, he mockingly suggested, only because such discussions "will make a fuss."[52] Conflict was not amusing, of course; and Lincoln was willing to grant important concessions to the South to preserve peace and the Union. But there could be no lasting compromise with evil. Ultimately, political horse trading must yield to moral conscience.[53] Not even a majority of voters, local or national, can make a wrong into a right. Here Lincoln appears at his most antipropitiatory and anti-*politique*. The framers were not solely concerned to establish a modus vivendi between morally discordant sections. They agreed to tolerate slavery, but only on the assumption that it would eventually disappear. The Constitution was not merely a bargain; it was also an acknowledgment of fundamental norms. Despite Calhoun, American democracy was never meant to be a consociational system. The "pluralism" of slaveholding and nonslaveholding states could not be accommodated indefinitely: a house divided *cannot* stand. The nation was founded on a unifying moral creed: all men are created equal. The institution of slavery was an affront to that creed and ultimately had to be extinguished if the nation was to endure.

Douglas was an eloquent spokesman for the democracy-reinforcing function of segmental autonomy. His basic thesis was that national harmony would reign if every state left the others alone. The sovereignty of local majorities promoted national concord by preventing one state from using federal powers to pester another. "Each state must do as it pleases" was his maxim.[54] This was a principle, he proudly announced, that traveled well, that is, could be embraced in Illinois as well as South Carolina. Unfortunately for Douglas and for the unity of his party, deference to local majorities was *not* universally admired. By advocating what he thought was an intermediate position, Douglas (like Pinckney) lost southern support. But why was segmental autonomy ultimately unacceptable in the South?

Even the most extreme nullificationists supported the fugitive slave clause in the Constitution. Article IV, sec. 2, par. 3 placed the weight of federal authority on the side of the individual slaveholder against the pretensions of local majorities who might be inclined to pass laws protecting runaway slaves. Despite talk of states' rights, in other words, southerners were never willing fully to embrace segmental autonomy. If safe havens were available, planters might be deprived of their property without due process of law.

The *Dred Scott* decision, although an act of the federal government, was hailed by proslavery forces because it debarred local majorities from interfering with property rights in slaves. As a shrewd polemicist, Lincoln exploited the contradiction between Douglas's absolute deference to the Supreme Court and his absolute deference to local majorities. The compromise position to which Douglas retreated was remarkably illogical: the territories had no right to prevent the entrance of slave property, but they could exclude slavery in practice by enacting unfriendly legislation. Naturally enough, this "solution" (whereby territorial majorities could make slave property worthless) proved unpopular in the South.

To deny the federal government a power often means depositing that power somewhere else. Everything depends on the arena to which forbidden decisions are subsequently transferred. To take a question off the national agenda may be to place it *on* the local agenda and to subject it to the control of local majorities. On the other hand, a decision may be withdrawn from all branches and levels of government and consigned to private individuals. Some conspicuous examples of the second pattern are the questions of how many children to have, what career to pursue, where to live, what religion if any to embrace, and (to introduce a discordant note) where to establish a plantation with one's slaves. That, according to Lincoln, was the individualistic logic of *Dred Scott*. Given planter concern for property rights, it is small wonder that Douglas's enthusiasm for local majorities alienated southern Democrats.

Lincoln stressed another weakness of segmental autonomy. Local communities might be just as divided by the slave question as the national community. Kansas, in fact, was cursed with just such a division. Territorial sovereignty there, which Douglas believed would place a quietus on slavery agitation, had led instead to bloody conflict.[55] Even from a pure *politique* standpoint, Douglas's *cuius regio, eius religio* solution was inadequate. Local control did not cause any abatement of the slavery turmoil. On the contrary, the struggles in Kansas reopened old wounds and increased rather than decreased national tensions.

The modus vivendi between North and South was destroyed by a thirst for expansion. As Lincoln said, "we have generally had comparative peace upon the slavery question, and . . . there was no cause for alarm until it was excited by the effort to spread it into new territory."[56] The open question of whether the new states to be carved out of the western territories would be slave or free perturbed both factions and enfeebled congressional vows of silence. Slavery in the South was the real evil; but what ultimately mobilized northern indignation, that is, provoked mainstream northern politicians into talking openly about the immorality of slavery, was the mere anticipation of slavery in the federal territories. Reticent about repealing an old gag rule, northerners were nevertheless unwilling to accept a new one.[57]

The old Whig and Democratic parties had purchased internal cohesion by intraparty decisions to suppress the slave issue. Thus, both parties had adherents in the North as well as in the South. After slavery had been placed squarely on the national agenda by the acquisition of vast new territories, however, the old nation-straddling parties were doomed to disintegration. Once slavery became the outstanding political issue, a massive realignment was inevitable: sectional parties arose, notably the Republican.[58] And fissiparous tendencies soon began to threaten the Union.

Strategic self-censorship could forestall but not prevent conflict between the proslavery and antislavery forces in the long run. Although it could be successfully squeezed off the legislative agenda for several decades, the slave issue was never off the agenda of public discussion. Congress could gag itself temporarily; but it could never effectively gag the public or the press. The temporary and selective nature of gag rules, however, does not necessarily destroy their usefulness. By 1860, many historians have argued, the North had finally become strong enough to impose abolition on the South by force. Abolitionists might never have achieved military and industrial superiority, in the context of a common nation, without a provisional agreement to silence Congress on the slave issue. By *postponing* the discussion of a difficult issue, in other words, a group or a nation may increase its capacity to solve the underlying problem later, when it can no longer be repressed.

## The Political Divisiveness Doctrine

This thumbnail sketch of efforts to keep the slave issue off the national agenda suggests the usefulness, for historical analysis, of the concept of gag rules. As a second example, offered in the same tentative spirit, consider now the question of self-government in *religiously* divided societies. I will focus here on recent constitutional disputes. While attempts to sidestep the slave issue were morally questionable and ultimately unsuccessful, collective self-censorship about religious disagreements seems to be a happier arrangement all around.

Even when obviously useful for preventing sectarian conflict, legislative gag orders may be annulled if they appear repugnant to the Free Exercise Clause.[59] But the Establishment Clause has led the Supreme Court to issue gag orders of its own. Most notably, school prayers—even silent prayers conducted on a "voluntary" basis—have been declared unconstitutional.[60] Public schools cannot provide and supervise clergymen who offer prayers in official graduation ceremonies.[61] Religious conservatives claim that the Court has prohibited children from praying. But the Court's intention has apparently been only to impede children of a majority sect from harassing, embarrassing, and pressuring children with different beliefs. More importantly, the school prayer rulings seem reconcilable with free exercise values because the gag orders in question are not aimed principally at children at all but rather at public employees. The government must gag itself (that is, its functionaries) on religious questions to avoid conveying a message that the state endorses or approves any sectarian practice. To send such a message would insultingly suggest that nonadherents of the endorsed religion are second-class citizens. By refusing to be party to sectarian controversies, public officials can not only do their jobs more effectively but can also promote an atmosphere of cross-sect cooperation essential for the proper functioning of the political processes outlined in the Constitution.

Consider, as one historical illustration, the New York state school law of 1842. A fiery, brick-heaving conflict was raging around this time between antiforeigner Protestants and recent Irish-Catholic immigrants. Catholics sought public financial support for their own schools, while anti-Irish nativist forces aimed to reserve all state aid for Protestant schools. Moderate politicians agreed that "it was imperative that this disruptive issue be removed from the political arena."[62] The problem would not subside, however, unless Catholics could be appeased without Protestants being outraged. Various segmental solutions were proposed, allowing local majorities to determine the religious content of publicly financed education. But the New York legislature ultimately rejected segmentation among districts and embraced the separation between church and state: no public funding would go to schools where sectarian practices were inculcated.[63] The gag rule imposed by the bill was quite narrowly targeted. Publicly paid teachers could not indoctrinate students on school premises. But religious indoctrinators remained free to practice their arts outside school walls, or in parochial schools if they could afford to establish them.

In twentieth-century America, at least, when the Supreme Court has removed religious questions from the national agenda, it has not transferred them to local majorities: that would have been a consociational solution. Some conservative and religiously inclined scholars, to be sure, claim that such a solution would have been more faithful to the Constitution.[64] But it is difficult to believe, given the account of factionalism in *Federalist* no. 10, that the framers wished to pacify and harmonize the national political scene by fostering political divisions along religious lines *within the states*. Be this as it may, a strategy of regional segmentation remains incompatible with the Court's present attitude toward separation between church and state. When the Court removes religious questions from the control of national majorities, it privatizes them, that is, turns them over not to localities but to individuals. A public/private or state/society distinction, running across the nation, performs almost the same function, it seems, as a consociationalist partition of the country into semiautonomous units. Privatization, like consociationalism, allows a divided house to stand, and makes democracy possible despite irrepressible moral divisions. But privatization is also superior to consociationalism from a liberal-democratic perspective because it grants majoritarianism a central role in decision making at the national level.

If religion can be transformed into a wholly private matter, then sectarian attachments will no longer provide the basis for "politically salient subgroup solidarity." Political divisions will not directly reproduce or mirror religious cleavages. The de-politicizing of religious conflict is accompanied by the secularization of political conflict. When both occur, the benefits of an adversarial style of decision making begin to outweigh its dangers. The apparent ease with which a government-versus-opposition pattern has been sustained in the United States may be due not merely to the "Lockean consensus" stressed by Louis Hartz, but also to the robustness of a public/private boundary which allows religion to flourish in civil society, while inhibiting religious antagonisms from ossifying into *political* oppositions.

Religious authorities are defanged when they are prevented from using state coercion to punish deviants. This is the principal rationale of the "wall" between church and state. But like other protective devices, this partition can also serve as a disencumbering strategy. It can improve the public sphere while protecting the private sphere. On the one hand, it shelters the integrity of individual conscience. On the other hand, its contribution to social cohesion was noted from the start. Unifying a divided nation may not always require a "naked public square," where rival claims to know God's true will are considered out of place. But a political sphere marked by general indifference to sectarian practices may well be a significant precondition for nation building in a country such as the United States. Neutral territory—such as a schoolroom where children of all sects are debarred from stigmatizing others as un-American—seems to have played an essential role in unifying this religiously pluralistic society.

Justice Frankfurter, calling the public school "the symbol of our democracy," advanced precisely this argument for the democracy-reinforcing function of a secular education:

> Designed to serve as perhaps the most powerful agency for promoting cohesion among a heterogeneous democratic people, the public school must be kept scrupulously free from entanglement in the strife of sects. The preservation of the community from divisive conflicts, of Government from irreconcilable pressures by religious groups, of religion from censorship and coercion however subtly exercised, requires strict confinement of the State to instruction other than religious, leaving to the individual's church and home, indoctrination in the faith of his choice.[65]

In a multidenominational society, rival and exclusive religious communities pose a potential threat to inclusive political citizenship. Frankfurter did not contrast affectless legal neutrality with affective moral community. Rather, he argued that *political* community cannot flourish unless the government adopts a modest institutional neutrality toward contending sects. Nonentanglement is an essential precondition for majoritarian politics in any multidenominational state. By gagging indoctrinators on public premises, a nation can promote a sense of shared identity among Catholics, Protestants, and Jews. Relieved from sectarian harassment, local religious minorities will not develop "a feeling of separatism." Frankfurter emphatically denies that the secularization of public life diminishes the social importance of religion, that is, the role of sectarian attachments in civil society. Even the children of Voltaire may favor the vitality of religion in nonpolitical domains, since a strong *private* attachment to a sect whose membership does not coincide with membership in the nation may usefully prevent citizens from irrationally deifying their country. Nevertheless, liberals in multidenominational societies have generally concluded that a nonsectarian *school system* can help children develop the "habits of community" essential for the proper functioning of democratic institutions.[66]

During the 1970s and 1980s, the need to avoid political divisiveness became a central—although controversial—theme of American Establishment Clause jurisprudence.[67] Because it may "strain a political system to the breaking point," Justice Harlan wrote, "political fragmentation on sectarian lines must be guarded against."[68] According to Paul Freund, too, "while political debate and division is normally a wholesome process for reaching viable accommodations, political divisions along religious lines are one of the principal evils that the First Amendment sought to forestall." Clinching his case, Freund added that "President Kennedy, as a candidate, was able to deflect some of the questions addressed to him on church-state relations by pointing to binding Supreme Court decisions."[69] Lucky the politician who can gag reporters by gagging himself!

A well-functioning majoritarian democracy, as political scientists, too, have argued, may require cross-cutting cleavages. Consociationalism, secession, and civil war seem to be the only available options when political divisions map neatly onto religious schisms. All three solutions, however, are plainly unacceptable in the United States. Thus, a coincidence of political and religious cleavages must be avoided at all costs. Artfully crafted gag rules, giving behavioral significance to the theoretical distinction between public and private realms, can be justified whenever they help prevent the consolidation of religiously defined political constituencies.

In *Lemon v. Kurtzman,* the locus classicus of the divisiveness doctrine, Chief Justice Burger explicitly echoed, or perhaps had his clerks transcribe, Freund's argument.[70] The entanglement between church and state produced by public aid to parochial schools was viewed by Burger as dangerous precisely because of its community-splintering potential. The religious provisions of the First Amendment, too, are meant to foster democratic politics: "Ordinarily political debate and division, however vigorous or even partisan, are normal and healthy manifestations of our democratic system of government, but political division along religious lines was one of the principal evils against which the First Amendment was intended to protect. . . . The potential divisiveness of such conflict is a threat to the normal political process."[71] More concretely, "to have States and communities divide on the issues presented by state aid to parochial schools would tend to confuse and obscure other issues of great urgency."[72] If Protestants, Catholics, and Jews began to battle over yearly school appropriations, the community's capacity for collective self-rule would be severely damaged. To preserve a climate of national cooperation and thus secure the majority's authority on other more pressing issues, citizens must agree to let their public officials gag themselves on religious questions.[73]

Worried that the general prohibition against church-state entanglements is somehow demeaning to religion, conservatives have recently raised numerous doubts about the utility of the divisiveness test.[74] Divisiveness cannot be measured; sectarianism in America has become almost unbearably bland; sects are no different from other interest groups; the danger of explosive conflict among denominations is vanishingly remote. At the very least, the potential for divisiveness alone, without other factors, does not suffice to make a statute unconstitutional.[75] Some antiseparationists even suggest that the idea of political divisiveness along religious lines is a twentieth-century coinage unknown to the eighteenth-century Founders.[76] As the epigraph to this chapter shows, however, the idea that censorship may help avert religious conflict had already occurred to peacemakers soon after the Reformation split the Christian world into rival sects.[77] To eighteenth-century *philosophes*, and thus to the framers of the First Amendment, it was a truism.

Another hostile critic asks: "Does a potential for even minor division justify silencing the churches in public debate over fundamental values?"[78] But such a question reveals an elementary misunderstanding: the divisiveness doctrine requires the government to gag not citizens but itself.[79] A rule of silence is imposed not on civil society, but on public officials alone. Religious groups and individuals can freely express their views; the government, however, is debarred from providing aid which, because it benefits one religion at the expense of other sects and nonbelievers, would significantly deepen sectarian animosities.[80]

More theoretically interesting is the objection that the norm of conflict avoidance exposes a society to manipulation by anyone willing to threaten conflict. In the Pawtucket crèche case, for example, the Court noted that the challenged nativity display had caused no sectarian dissension in its forty-year history.[81] It is farcical for litigants to adduce their own complaint as evidence that an offending governmental action is politically divisive. Along the same lines, the goal of eliminating religious divisiveness does not justify judicial attempts to promote "safe thinking" among citizens or even among public officials.[82] Obviously enough, anodyne and useless political discussions would result if the divisiveness test were carried to extremes.

These and similar demurrers raise some doubt about the legal future of the divisiveness doctrine. But the very debate between its advocates and its opponents confirms once again that gag rules have played (and no doubt will continue to play) a central role in the functioning of democratic political institutions.

## A Note on Abortion

No catalogue of recent acrimonious disputes could omit abortion. The recent conservative attempt to gag abortion counselors shows its crucial relevance to our concerns in this chapter. Some twentieth-century Americans feel as passionately about this issue as nineteenth-century Americans felt about abolition. Walter Berns once wrote quite sympathetically of Calhoun's desire to repress emancipationist pamphlets and petitions. More recently, he has argued that the success of the American legislative process depends upon "its ability to exclude issues—the abortion issue comes to mind—on which there can be only one winner and one loser."[83] Legislators should be gagged, he believes, even if federally funded nurses and doctors should not be.

Such a selectively applied gag rule is justifed, as usual, by invoking dangerous but avoidable conflict. Those who disagree passionately about this question do not hesitate to smear each other publicly with hate-provoking names such as "murderer." Many adherents of one side, at least, seem religiously motivated, and hope to impose their religious beliefs on others coercively. There may be no room for compromise here, and little capacity for either side to listen to the other.

If such a burning issue became central to the federal legislative process, would not Congress's capacity to solve other problems be drastically curtailed? Why waste national resources on an issue that will never command widespread consensus, when there are equally pressing problems (such as preventable teenage pregnancies) about which everyone agrees that something should be done?

These considerations are not without weight. But persuasive arguments have also been mounted on the other side—against the wisdom of removing the legitimacy of abortion from the legislative agenda. For one thing, dire predictions that the issue will necessarily overload and destabilize a democratic political system seem exaggerated.[84] Furthermore, restricting the political process to a limited range of issues is never a perfectly neutral procedure. Even when agenda narrowing is not a tool in the hands of sinister elites, *it still favors some parties and disfavors others.* The congressional gag rules of the 1830s and 1840s were moderate but not impartial; on balance, they were much friendlier to slaveholders than to abolitionists. Similarly, withdrawing the legality of abortion[85] from the jurisdiction of Congress and state legislatures means affirming the status quo, that is, resting content with a pro-choice stance. Legislatures may be compelled to adopt a "hands-off" attitude, but winners and losers remain. In the case of abortion, when the Supreme Court constricted the agenda of state legislatures, it was wielding power and doing so for particular ends. Not surprisingly, some pro-life activists view wresting abortion from the Court and putting it back on the legislative agenda as their principal political objective.

Both slaveholders and abolitionists adduced unassailable rights—property rights, on the one hand, and the rights to self-ownership and to the fruits of one's labor, including the right of all men to own property, on the other. These rights were considered indefeasible, regardless of how political majorities happened to vote. Douglas's majoritarianism position fell between the two rights-based views: let the people of each state decide by majority rule. An uncannily similar pattern reappears in the abortion debate. (Although, not surprisingly, both pro-life and pro-choice advocates compare themselves to abolitionists and their opponents to slaveholders.) Each side asserts an indefeasible right—the fetus's right to life and the woman's right to choose. This time, the intermediary or majoritarian position is occupied by, among others, Justice White: "Abortion is a hotly contested moral and political issue. Such issues, in our society, are to be resolved by the will of the people."[86] The Court, in other words, should loosen its grip on the abortion question and consign it to majority rule in the states.

In *Roe v. Wade*, the Supreme Court decided to take the issue of abortion out of legislative hands. On the basis of a fundamental right to privacy, it assigned the right to decide to the individuals directly involved. But *Roe* also reallocated power from state legislatures to the Court. As a result, all sides in the dispute now argue for the moral, legal, and political appropriateness of some sort of gag rule. Differences arise only over which branch of government should be gagged. What I have described as the intermediate position is antijudicial and deferential toward local majorities. From the divisiveness of the issue, Justice White interestingly concludes that abortion must be handled legislatively rather than judicially. The Court should gag itself because, by constitutionalizing such an explosive issue, it not only has thrown the legitimacy of judicial review into question but also has polarized the national community more radically than if it had allowed the problem to be solved on a decentralized basis by ordinary processes of pluralistic bargaining. Far from dampening conflict, *Roe* exacerbated a diffuse and latent antagonism, drawing it onto the national scene. After the decision, tempers flared and battlefronts hardened. Keeping abortion off the legislative agenda, far from consigning it peaceably to the domain of private conscience, he assumes, has given it higher visibility on the agenda of public agitation and discussion. Removing abortion from the Court's docket might conceivably be a more effective political sedative than deleting it from the legislative agenda of the states.

In contrast to White, pro-life and pro-choice advocates cannot, on principle, consistently defer to the opinions of local majorities, or national ones, for that matter. Despite the tactics and rhetoric of antiabortion forces, they do not believe that a fetus's right to life hinges upon the election-day behavior of voters or the decisions of elected representatives. Pro-choice advocates feel the same way about a woman's right to choose. Unlike White, who advocates a majoritarian solution, one side would welcome a judicial decision which declared abortion unconstitutional just as their mortal enemies welcomed *Roe*. Each side in the abortion debate, in other words, would be perfectly content to gag popularly elected state legislatures, curtailing the authority of democratic bodies to authorize or outlaw abortion.

Like the slavery controversy, though on a less tragic scale, the abortion dispute raises questions about the limits of democracy and the wisdom of political self-censorship. It, too, underlines the important lesson that gag rules, although often presented as impartial measures serving the cause of communal peace, can *very easily* be converted into weapons in a partisan struggle.

### Proscribing Creationist Legislation

In *Epperson v. Arkansas,* the Supreme Court overturned a state law prohibiting the teaching of Darwin's evolutionary theory in public schools and universities. The majority justified its decision on the grounds that "fundamentalist sectarian conviction was and is the law's reason for existence."[87] Antievolution statutes, in other words, were declared to breach the wall of separation. Only because they interpret Genesis in a literalist manner have fundamentalists attempted to gag schoolteachers who would otherwise teach Darwinist theories as a matter of routine.[88]

In his separate opinion, Justice Black suggested that a community could justifiably sidestep this problem by deleting all mention of the development of the human species from classes in biology. Banning evolutionary theory on religious grounds violates the Establishment Clause. But state governments have a right to withdraw emotional subjects from the school curriculum altogether; and nothing prohibits a blanket vow of silence designed to reduce disruptive conflict in the classroom. In Black's view, in sum, there is nothing objectionable about a community's self-muzzling decision that "it would be best to remove this controversial subject from its schools."[89]

For a student of self-imposed gag rules, *Epperson* is interesting for another reason as well. What would be the indirect effect upon democratic government if majorities were allowed to rewrite scientific textbooks? The rationalist outlook central to the development of seventeenth-century science had a decisive influence on the shaping of seventeenth-century parliamentary institutions. Could challenging the autonomy of science inadvertently threaten one of the essential preconditions of democratic government?

According to Robert Bork, what majorities are not allowed to do must be left up to individual freedom.[90] To protect democracy against inherent self-destructive tendencies, the Court must defend the right of individuals to engage in political speech. Because most speech is not political, however, most speakers remain constitutionally susceptible to majoritarian censorship and control. Bork's ultimate concern here is to justify gag orders which his more squeamish colleagues are loath to impose: the Constitution is not a suicide pact, and the government has a right forcibly to silence anyone advocating its own forcible overthrow. Generalizing about the need to silence the talkative, Bork adds: "Government cannot function if anyone can say anything anywhere at any time." *En passant,* he also denies that the Court has a right to protect scientific inquiry against majority rule.[91] Constitutionally speaking, he even suggests, scientific conclusions are a matter of taste; and on questions of taste, the Court should remain aloof and allow majorities to have their way. If he retreated from this implausible claim, moreover, Bork would have only one available alternative: the discovery and propagation of scientific truths must be left to "individual freedom."

But how adequate to the creationism controversy is Bork's dichotomy between majority rule and individual freedom? Not very. For one thing, scientific theories are not preferences. Science is not an interest group (even though scientists may sometimes act like members of one); and the outcome of a scientific inquiry is not a free choice. Science has a logic and dynamic of its own; and its results cannot simply be "adjusted" to either personal or political demands. By the Enlightenment standards on which our constitutional settlement was based, a community's attempt to compel scientific outcomes congenial to its nonrational attachments should probably be described as a form of self-injury. Creationists doggedly reinterpret fossil evidence to make it accord with their reading of Genesis. The conclusion they want to reach is fixed beforehand and is, in principle, a conclusion which no counter-evidence could ever lead them to revise.[92] Why not view the Court's prohibition against creationist tampering with textbooks, which finds its constitutional basis in the Establishment Clause and in the government's duty to provide universal education, in this light? Keeping scientific conclusions off the majority's agenda, in any case, may protect "reason" itself, rather than merely individual freedoms. In the liberal tradition, "democracy" is identified with equality before the law and government by discussion, as well as with majority rule. How could the scientific method, in a minimal sense of the examination of surprising facts and the hearing of rival viewpoints, be overridden without undermining an essential element of democratic government itself?

Keeping scientific results off the political agenda (and thus beyond indirect religious control) may allow a nation to shelter the preconditions of rational debate. A gag rule of some sort is obviously required to defend the integrity of science—and its standards of evidence, argument, inference, and disproof—from nonrational attachments. To prohibit creationist legislation may also be to defend democracy from itself. A majority should be empowered to act for the nation, one might say, only if its religious motivations are neutralized constitutionally. By invalidating creationist legislation, arguably, the Court (implicitly, if not explicitly) intended to confer authority on what the framers called the cool and deliberate sense of the community, that is, on the opinions the majority holds when it *discusses* matters in a consecutive, disciplined, fact-minded, and thoughtful way. *Positive constitutionalism,* as outlined in chapter 5, assumes that liberal constitutions are designed not simply to protect the private sphere and maximize individual freedom, but also to reinforce the deliberative aspects of democratic government. From this perspective, the Court is perfectly within its rights when it attempts, by outlawing creationist legislation, to keep democracy deliberative.

When a decision is withdrawn from national majorities, it may be consigned either to local majorities or to individuals: what majorities are not allowed to do must be left to individual freedom. But the creationist case raises a third alternative. Decisions may be withdrawn from all branches and levels of government and from individuals as well. The proper "place" for discussing evolution and determining the contents of biology textbooks is the social system of *science,* a system which operates under imperatives other than maximizing the independence and preference satisfaction of its individual practitioners and which is largely indifferent to majority opinion. The Constitution nowhere mentions the autonomy and authority of science. But if the Court must protect the preconditions of deliberative government, can it be completely oblivious to the attitude toward *truth,* which is not a private preference, inculcated in public schools? In any case, neither Establishment Clause concerns nor the need to protect political speech and individual autonomy are sufficient to explain what seems at first to be a rationally defensible countermajoritarian ban on antievolution statutes.

## Some Problems and a Cautionary Tale

While substantial, especially in divided societies, the benefits of agenda narrowing are almost always accompanied by significant drawbacks. Democracy is not only made possible but also made imperfect by a systematic winnowing of the issues placed under majoritarian control. In a majoritarian democracy within a unified nation, bowdlerizing the legislative agenda may trivialize public life and drain it of human significance. To remove all issues of outstanding moral importance and assign them to individual conscience or even to the courts, some commentators argue, may make democratic politics unbearably bland and useless as an arena for "national self-education." Gag rules, moreover, are seldom neutral: they implicitly support one policy and undermine alternatives. Suppressing a theme may surreptitiously insure the victory of one party over its rivals. Finally, the strategy of avoidance can exacerbate pent-up social tensions, eventually engendering terrorism or a revolutionary explosion by denying legitimate expression to deeply felt beliefs.

At first glance, it seems reasonable to skirt an issue that promises to unleash paralyzing hostilities. But conflict averseness can make a democratic community hostage to anyone willing to threaten conflict. Prickliness and unwillingness to compromise may be feigned. If a community openly declares conflict avoidance to be its highest priority, it invites the power-hungry to misrepresent their preferences strategically. One party can bluff and allege that any attempt to bargain about his vital interests will lead to civil war. Indeed, intractable conflict is not merely an independent variable to which gun-shy groups respond by imposing vows of silence on themselves. Degrees of intractability can be faked, as any seasoned bargainer knows. If a community habitually gags itself on divisive issues, it will give individuals and subgroups a powerful incentive for dissimulation, for exaggerating their unwillingness to compromise. If threats trigger collective silence, threats will be forthcoming. Willingness to yield will never pay; shortness of temper will always be rewarded. By redescribing their annoyance as unremitting horror, individuals and subgroups can prevent issues from being raised which could otherwise, and more justly, be resolved by compromise. Indeed, a policy of self-gagging may eventually produce a culture where the threat of violence or secession is a common political tactic.

The dangers of founding a relationship on a suppressed theme are strikingly illustrated in a tale recounted by Gregory of Tours. Two noblemen could only remain friends and revelling companions so long as they kept silent about the embarrassing fact that, years earlier, Sichar had butchered Chramnesind's family. One evening, the healing silence was broken:

> Sichar drank far more wine than he could carry and began to boast at Chramnesind's expense. He is reported to have said: "Dear brother, you ought to be grateful to me for having killed off your relations. There is plenty of gold and silver in your house now that I have recompensed you for what I did to them. If it weren't for the fact that the fine I've paid has restored your finances, you would still today be poor and destitute." When he heard Sichar's remarks, Chramnesind was sick at heart. "If I don't avenge my relatives," he said to himself, "they will say that I am as weak as a woman, for I no longer

> have the right to be called a man!" Thereupon he blew the lights out and hacked Sichar's skull in two.[93]

Like the peaceful coexistence of slave and free states, the precarious companionship of Sichar and Chramnesind was destined not to last. An individual's thirst for wine, like a nation's thirst for expansion, may irreversibly destroy a long-established etiquette of omission. To win otherwise unattainable cooperation, people voluntarily muzzle themselves about divisive topics. Self-gagging may be a short-lived experiment, however. At any moment, there can be a return of the repressed.

## Conclusion

Communities, like individuals, can silence themselves about selected issues for what they see as their own good. By using such self-restraint, even citizens who differ greatly in outlook on life can work together to solve common problems. Liberal democracies, in particular, often transfer the discussion of rationally irresolvable issues from the legislative arena into civil society or the private sphere. Although seldom studied in a systematic manner, in any case, strategic self-censorship seems to be an almost universally employed technique of self-management and self-rule. While somewhat slippery and difficult to control, the idea of gag rules, as I have been discussing it, does focus attention usefully on the advantages and disadvantages shared by widely varying techniques of issue-suppression. As a result, the concept may well become a serviceable tool for comparative analysis.[94] To show how such a conception might be developed theoretically and applied to a few important cases, where democratic government was at stake, has been my principal aim in this chapter.

Many questions, of course, remain unanswered. Under what cultural and psychological conditions, for example, can gag rules be adhered to successfully? Normative theorists will want to know when gag rules can be morally justified. Can we provide a principled rationale for removing one issue rather than another from the community's or an individual's agenda? While the slave issue could not (and should not!) have been permanently suppressed, religious disagreements probably can (and should) be. I believe this, but can I explain it? On the abortion question, opinions differ about the advisability of gag rules—just as they do on every other aspect of the issue. In general, the foregoing analysis only reconfirms the moral ambiguity of strategic self-censorship. To prevent overload, all individuals and groups must suppress *some* controversial problems. An author, for instance, may have no choice but to relegate an unanswerable question to a chapter's perfunctory conclusion where he can shiftily "postpone" it to a later work. But issue avoidance, however attractive, will always be one-sided and potentially dangerous. We can neither dispense with gag rules nor allay the guilty consciences they inevitably produce.

# 8

# Welfare and the Liberal Conscience

*The care of the poor is incumbent on the whole of society.*
—SPINOZA

Is Milton Friedman the legitimate heir to Adam Smith? Did Locke's antagonism to cruel and arbitrary tyranny imply a repudiation of public provision for the needs of the poor? Does T. H. Marshall's famous sequence of legal rights, political rights, and social rights map the smooth unfolding of an initial promise or a step-by-step disavowal of the past? What is the relation between the old liberalism and the new liberalism, between the *Rechtsstaat* and the *Sozialstaat*, between constitutional rights and welfare rights?

These questions are neither uninteresting nor unanswerable. But the point of asking them is not immediately clear. Even if we could announce that public assistance represented a betrayal or a consummation of classical liberal principles, no political consequences would necessarily follow, one way or the other. The perpetuation of traditional orientations and commitments may be a sign of heroic tenacity, but "fidelity to the sources" may also be a symptom of mental rigidity and moral sclerosis. Some adversaries of the welfare state try to make us feel derelict for having abandoned our noble libertarian heritage. Contrariwise, friends of the welfare state commend us for having thrown off the shameful inheritance of Social Darwinism. Depending on one's perspective, in other words, historical continuity can deserve praise or blame.

I stress this admittedly obvious consideration to avoid a misconstrual of my objectives in this final chapter. While aiming to highlight some neglected similarities and interconnections between eighteenth-century liberal rights and twentieth-century welfare rights, I remain conscious that such an exercise has limited value. Policy debates, for one thing, cannot be sensibly conducted as legacy disputes. The liberal movement, moreover, was complex and diffuse. It evolved over the course of centuries and assumed different forms in different national contexts. Even when studying a single country during one and the same period, we can employ "liberalism" (which, when used to describe pre-nineteenth-century political thought, is something of an anachronism) only as an umbrella term covering a variety of political tendencies and outlooks. As a result, diverse historical perspectives on liberal thought remain possible; different interpreters of the canon will inevitably produce divergent answers to the continuity question. Furthermore, a similarity or correspondence of beliefs, which is all I shall attempt to document, does not constitute proof of historical continuity. Evidence of transmission and reception would be required to support any kind of stronger claim.

Normative continuity, the bequeathing and inheriting of a system of moral values, moreover, even if it could be established, would not constitute a *causal explanation* of the emergence and stabilization of contemporary welfare regimes. General affluence, a dramatic increase in state revenues during wartime, socially accepted obligations toward veterans, the need to secure political stability in the face of boom-and-slump cycles in the economy, the growing bargaining power of previously disenfranchised groups—these and many other factors played a decisive role in the emergence of contemporary economic rights. Public relief programs, moreover, have sometimes been embraced by political elites for purely self-interested reasons: because, for example, "Rebellions of the Belly are the worst," or because indigence provides a breeding ground for contagious diseases that might eventually infect the rich, or because "poverty in the midst of plenty is likely to increase the incidence of crime."[1] Recognition that the castle is not safe unless the cottage is well-fed was no doubt conducive to the enactment of modern redistributionist legislation. If normative continuity outweighed normative discontinuity, as I think it did, it was only one element among the many that contributed to the rise of the welfare state. The erroneous assumption that classical liberals would have been utterly hostile to transfer programs remains such a commonplace, however, that a succinct refutation can still be useful.

## Four Rival Views

A two-by-two table is the most economical way to survey possible responses to the continuity question. We can distinguish, along a *descriptive* dimension, between those who assert a sharp rupture between liberal rights and welfare rights and those who discern an unbroken continuity linking the two. Along an *evaluative* dimension, we can then contrast those who view continuity with approval and discontinuity with disapproval and those who take the opposite approach (see Figure 1).

Figure 1. Possible Responses to the Continuity Question

| | disapproval | approval |
|---|---|---|
| discontinuity | 1 | 2 |
| continuity | 3 | 4 |

1. In the first cell, we can locate what I have been calling *negative constitutionalism,* the standard Hayekian view that liberalism was a basically antistatist philosophy, concerned solely with limiting abusive government—that is, with preventing tyranny and straitjacketing political power. Liberalism, from this austere perspective, is wholly incompatible with positive programs of public provision, all of which require confiscatory taxation, a "taking" from A in order to give to B, and other "stultifying" acts of governmental intervention into a sphere of otherwise spontaneous and voluntary relations. In a free society, according to this view, all individuals must look after their own material welfare as well as their souls. Liberal citizens can be prevented from harming each other but never forced to make one another prosper or even to relieve each other's distress.

2. The second possibility is equally well known. To build the welfare state, it is said, modern citizens had to leave behind the anticommunal, privatistic, beggar-thy-neighbor, and devil-take-the hindmost attitudes purportedly typical of classical liberalism. Social provision depends on forms of solidarity and civic friendship that liberalism purportedly aims to destroy. It fits poorly into a society where all human relations are meant to be voluntary and instrumental, and where contractual freedom cannot be limited by norms of justice and fairness. Before they could endorse the welfare state, therefore, rulers and ruled alike had to be weaned from a morally impoverished *sauve qui peut* liberalism and converted to morally robust, samaritan values and traditions.

3. Third, and quite distinctly, many theorists and publicists have perceived a continuity between liberalism and the welfare state but have gone on to argue that this continuity is morally deplorable—indeed, that it discloses either the original sin of liberalism or the phoniness of welfare rights. This third category is probably the most interesting because it encourages us to ponder the disconcerting bedfellowship of far-left and far-right critics of economic rights. Remember that both Marxists and Reaganites (the former inhabiting cell

3, and the latter cell 1) blame the dole for weakening the moral fiber of recipients, for infantilizing them into dependency—defusing their revolutionary potential in the one case, destroying their frontiersmanlike self-reliance in the other. A different coincidence of opposites is contained within cell 3 itself. Both radicals and ultraconservatives[2] passionately assail the bourgeois individualism and materialistic euphoria of liberal society—as an obstacle to the classless society on the one hand and as an extinction of deference and hierarchy on the other. Neither sees anything in welfare states that fundamentally changes the picture, anything transcending the limits that, in their view, hideously deform the liberal tradition.

However it is judged politically, the position identified by cell 1 is both historically inaccurate and conceptually confused. Above all, it exaggerates the discontinuity between classical and contemporary liberals. Modern liberalism is best understood as a rethinking of the principles of classical liberalism, an adaptation of these principles to a new social context where individual freedom is threatened in new ways. Hence, even those who sympathize with some of the policy implications of the view represented by cell 2 may find it dissatisfying as a historical account. Cell 3 should evoke a contrary response: even those who find it morally and politically unpalatable may concede that it is historically on the right track, since it recognizes the continuum between the classical liberalism of the seventeenth and eighteenth centuries and redistributionist liberalism today.

4. Having signaled the existence of these three alternatives, I turn now directly to the fourth and, I am convinced, superior claim that there is a demonstrable historical continuity, or at least compatibility, between classical liberalism and the values embodied in the welfare state, and that this common ground is, by and large, a moral and political advantage. If we wished to attach a name to this final position, we would probably be justified in citing John Rawls, a defender of welfarist redistribution as well as a self-proclaimed theoretical descendant of Locke and Kant. (While Rawls's own arguments for welfarist redistribution are not strengthened philosophically by citing such a pedigree, the attacks of those critics who accuse him of betraying the spirit of liberalism *can* be definitively refuted thereby.)

In any case, the evidence favoring cell 4, or at least suggesting some kind of historical continuity, is bountiful. Consider, as a randomly chosen example, Montesquieu's unambiguous affirmation of the state's duty to relieve poverty: "The alms given to a naked man in the street do not fulfill the obligations of the state, which owes to every citizen a certain subsistence, a proper nourishment, convenient clothing, and a kind of life not incompatible with health."[3] No series of such quotations, of course, would demonstrate the compatibility of welfare measures with the principles of classical liberalism, much less the logical derivation or historical emergence of the former from the latter. Montesquieu may well have been an inconsistent or incomplete liberal, unable to free himself from vestigial strains of aristocratic paternalism or Christian almsgiving. Perhaps if he had thought through the implications of the "rule of law," he would have written more like A. V. Dicey. I think not, however. To make my position credible, I must now show how redistributionist conclusions are not merely consistent with but, in a changed context, follow directly from liberal principles themselves.

## The Primacy of Justice

In this concluding chapter, I continue to adopt a nominalist approach to the concept of liberalism, taking as my benchmark the cluster of views advanced and defended by, among others, Locke, Montesquieu, Hume, Smith, Madison, Kant, and Mill.[4] This list allows us to register skepticism, at the very outset, about the Hayekian assumption that classical liberals were fiercely hostile to social planning. One of the theorists mentioned actually wrote a constitution; all the others recognized the benefits of shrewd constitutional design; and a constitution, although it does not involve a central allocation of most goods and services, *is* a "plan" with significant allocative implications.[5] The writings of those theorists listed, moreover, provide virtually no evidence that liberalism is deeply incompatible with democratic or majoritarian politics (which may have further redistributive consequences). All of them believed that choices made collectively by communities were a form of *freedom* that rivaled in importance choices made severally by individuals. When Locke wrote that people should freely choose their form of government, for example, he had collective decision making in mind, not the uncoordinated choices of individual consumers in an economic marketplace.[6]

Claimants to the mantle of Adam Smith, such as Milton Friedman, typically paint welfare measures as profoundly illiberal: "The central defect of these measures is that they seek through government to force people to act against their own immediate interests in order to promote a supposedly general interest."[7] But is there anything particularly illiberal about the realization that, in the absence of coercion, self-love will induce individuals to exempt themselves from generally useful rules? Liberal constitutions, it is worth recalling, are designed to do precisely what Friedman apparently deplores: to *force* officeholders, at least, to act against their own immediate interests in order to promote the general interest. And what does Friedman think is the purpose of criminal law?

As our list of representative liberal theorists suggests, liberalism should not be considered principally an antistatist philosophy of limited government.[8] The fact is, liberals were as wary of anarchy as of tyranny. They advocated not merely freedom from government, but also order through government. Security is impossible without a state monopoly on the legitimate use of violence. To the extent that he defined freedom as security, a definition to which I shall return, even Montesquieu conceived sovereign power, organized along liberal lines, as an indispensable instrument of freedom.[9]

The order that liberals admired, moreover, was not just any kind of order, not simply the suppression of random violence and civil war. Instead, it was a certain kind of order, an order qualified in a specific way: *a just order.* The primacy of justice in liberal thought, alas, is often underestimated. According to Friedman, again, "the egalitarian . . . will defend taking from someone to give to others . . . on grounds of 'justice.' At this point equality comes sharply into conflict with freedom; one must choose. One cannot be both an egalitarian, in this sense, and a liberal."[10] But why should a conflict between freedom and equality, even assuming that one exists, require an either/or choice?

There is nothing so melodramatic about normative dissonance, after all. To put Friedman's liberty-equality conflict into perspective, let us consider the conflict, say, between liberty of the press and the right to privacy. This is a *conflict between freedom and freedom.* It requires not an either/or decision but rather a rough balancing of important but rival interests. The conflict between freedom and equality, which Friedman and other libertarians magnify into a final showdown between the forces of good and evil (where one will emerge triumphant while the other is extinguished) is no different. It is just another example of the everyday moral conflict characterizing all liberal societies and requiring pragmatic compromise. By juxtaposing the conflict between freedom and equality—stressed by libertarians—to the many conflicts between freedom and freedom, we de-dramatize the former and put it into perspective. And we show how we can remain simultaneously egalitarians and liberals, perhaps along Rawlsian lines.

Classical liberals, it should be said, never placed *justice* in disdainful quotation marks; they never sacrificed or subordinated justice to freedom, as Friedman's litmus test would require. On the contrary, Hume urges us "to look at the vast apparatus of government, as having ultimately no other object or purpose but the distribution of justice."[11] In a similar spirit, Montesquieu asserted that "we must therefore acknowledge relations of justice [*des rapports d'equité*] antecedent to the positive law by which they are established."[12] According to Adam Smith, too, justice was the "main pillar" of society. He was committed not simply to the natural system of liberty but to "the natural system of perfect liberty *and justice.*" Every man should be free to follow his own interests in his own way, he argued, but only "as long as he does not violate the laws of justice."[13] Interest-governed behavior can enhance social stability and security, by an invisible hand, but only if the interests propelling action are just.[14] Madison agreed: "Justice is the end of government. It is the end of civil society."[15]

Justice, to be sure, is a slippery and polysignificant concept, difficult to define in a univocal way. Perhaps the theorists cited above were thinking about *just retribution* and not *just distribution.* Perhaps they meant to affirm "the limits of justice," confining the term *just* to the giving and receiving of what individuals voluntarily contract to give and receive. According to a preliberal such as Hobbes, for example, "The definition of INJUSTICE, is no other than *the not Performance of Covenant*" and "the nature of Justice, consisteth in keeping of valid Covenants."[16] Even this restrictive definition of justice, however, includes an explicit entitlement to affirmative state action to protect individuals from harm by third parties.

We can say with some confidence, moreover, that liberals did *not* uniformly conceive justice in this narrow "Hobbesian" fashion, as a simple matter of enforcing contracts. For one thing, they universally associated justice with a more substantive idea of impartiality: *all* individuals must be protected *equally* from third-party injury. They explicitly advocated *equal access to the law,* a norm incompatible in principle with many ostensibly "contractual" relations (e.g., those involving indentured servitude). An underlying egalitarian norm explains, for instance, Madison's advocacy of "a government which will protect all parties, the weaker as well as the more powerful."[17] Access to the courts must not be distributed according to merit, contribution, inherited social status, or even prior consent. A jury trial must be made available to *all* similar offenders. A just distribution of the community's legal resources is, in principle, an equal or universal distribution—not conditional, for example, on the quantity of taxes paid. One might even argue that a just distribution of, say, trial by jury was conceived by liberals as a distribution according to need.

## The Redistribution of Security

The semantic trajectory of the word *security* is obviously germane to any study of the transition from classical liberal rights, such as habeas corpus or protection from arbitrary search and seizure, to modern welfare rights, such as legal aid to the poor or public housing and rent subsidies. As the resources of states grew, one might argue, the concept of security was naturally stretched to include more and more basic guarantees. Originally designating protection from private and public violence, "security" eventually came to include compulsory primary schooling and various economic rights—that is, protection from the caprice of family upbringing and from violent fluctuations in the market. But what is the relationship between the "security" protected by liberal constitutions and the homonymous value guaranteed, for example in the U.S. system of "social security"? Is there a conceptual continuity here or merely a verbal one?

Political theorists may have neglected the possibility of a substantive continuity between classical liberalism and the moral foundations of the welfare state because of their commitment to a misleading contrast between *two kinds of rights,* between rights as liberties from government interference and rights as entitlements to government support.[18] This is particularly unfortunate because the original right to protection from unjustified and unpredictable physical violence was itself a right that *entitled* all citizens to affirmative state action.[19] Despite libertarian denials, *every known liberal state regularly extracts taxes from its citizens to provide resources as a basis upon, or a means by which, individuals can exercise their basic rights.* The most obvious example of such state provision is physical and psychological security. But private property itself (an institution, not a material object) exists only as defined by the state and protected by legal coercion. Similarly, every citizen's right to litigate is made possible by legal institutions established and rendered accessible by the state. Public financing of compulsory primary education is only one example among many, therefore, of affirmative state action designed to *help* citizens exercise their basic rights. If theorists had focused more clearly on these uncontroversially liberal forms of state provision, they would have recognized the inadequacy of the superficially alluring contrast between latitudes and entitlements.

In his fanciful and historically inaccurate redescriptions of classical liberal thought, Friedman routinely slights the importance of state power not only for the establishment of security but also for the enforcement of the norms of fairness and impartiality: "The intellectual movement that went under the name of liberalism emphasized freedom as the ultimate goal and the individual as the ultimate entity in the society. It supported laissez faire at home as a means of reducing the role of the state in economic affairs and thereby enlarging the role of the individual."[20] Reading such a passage, one is forced to ask: Who precisely is "the" individual? Is there more than one? Do some ever suffer while, or even because, others prosper? By discussing *the* individual, in fact, Friedman manages to repress any worries about impartiality *among* individuals or about the *illegitimate uses of private power.* Committed to a norm of fairness, classical liberals did not share this happy insouciance.

True, Smith sometimes made statements that seem to rule out a "taking" from the rich to give to the poor: "To hurt in any degree the interest of any one order of citizens, for no other purpose but to promote that of some others, is evidently contrary to that justice and equality of treatment which the sovereign owes to all the different orders of his subjects."[21] But it is unwise to infer any blanket hostility to redistribution from this claim alone. Would Smith, for example, have opposed the use of state power to break up growth-stifling private monopolies? Privileged groups certainly cannot be expected to relinquish their monopolies voluntarily. Interests, as Locke had already made clear, can be legitimate or illegitimate, proper or improper, just or unjust. And despite his disclaimer, cited above, Smith emphatically believed that natural justice *required* the state to hurt the (sinister) interests of one order of citizens for no other purpose than to promote the (acceptable) interests of most others. In plain language, he thought that the interests of the grasping few must be forcibly sacrificed to the interests of the great majority of the people.

Private power poses just as great a threat to security as does public power.[22] The chief aim of a liberal political order, as a consequence, is not to limit the state alone, but rather "to Limit the Power, and Moderate the Dominion of *every* Part and Member of the Society."[23] Individual rights cannot be guaranteed simply by eliminating the state, since rights can be violated just as brutally by highway murder gangs as by public officials. State power is justified primarily, from a liberal perspective, as a remedy against anarchy, and anarchy means not merely chaos, but rather private injustice and oppression. Strict noninterference in social life by the state would produce not wholesome competition but an outcropping of brutal monopolies. Far from being simply antistatist, as a consequence, liberals ascribed important trust-busting functions to sovereign, centralized, and bureaucratic authority. Hume was speaking for all liberals, therefore, when he wrote that "it is impossible for the human race to subsist, at least in any comfortable or secure state, without the protection of government."[24] State intervention was essential for a just distribution of security, for protecting the vulnerable from the mighty.

Writing under the influence of Hume, Smith too laid great stress not only on freedom from government but also on the affirmative duties of the state in restricting private power: "The second duty of the sovereign," after national defense, is "that of protecting, as far as possible, every member of society from the injustice or oppression of every other member of it." And Madison concurred: "It is of great importance in a republic not only to guard the society against the oppression of its rulers, but to guard one part of society against the injustice of the other part."[25] Classical liberals, in other words, were concerned to prevent the violation of private rights by power wielders, whether public or private. Even the nightwatchman state, moreover, concerned exclusively with preventing mutual harm, was profoundly *redistributionist,* charged explicitly with an equitable allocation of security. But what did "security" mean to classical liberals?

The most ardent enemies of an ideological stance are often its keenest analysts. Both Marx and Nietzsche, in attacking liberalism, reserved particular scorn for the norm of security.[26] This was a shrewd strategy because, in many ways, security was the *idée maîtresse* of the liberal tradition. Mill, for example, describes the interest in security as "the most vital of all interests."[27] When considering Friedman's claim that classical liberals preferred liberty to equality, in fact, we should recall that many liberals actually *defined freedom as security;* that is, they identified liberty with a good that cried out for some sort of just or justifiable distribution. "The ultimate aim of government," according to Spinoza, is "to free every man from fear, that he may live in all possible security."[28] Paraphrasing, not to say plagiarizing, Montesquieu, Jaucourt wrote in the *Encyclopédie:* "The political liberty of the citizen is the tranquility of spirit deriving from the sense each has of his own security; for one to have security, the government must be such that no citizen need fear another."[29] Bentham, too, followed Montesquieu on this point: "A clear idea of liberty will lead us to regard it as a branch of security."[30]

The importance of security for all liberal thinkers suggests that liberal justice, far from being limited to the protection of property and contract, had a marked redistributionist dimension. The idea that security might be allocated more justly, it should be noted, was originally popularized by the ideologues of absolutism.[31] Contemplated, one might say, was a rudimentary "transfer plan." Having hitherto engrossed security by means of private armies, so said the crown, the nobility had to be, to some extent, disarmed. The security of the baron had to be diminished, his fortresses torn down, to increase the security of the *roturier.* The modern French monarchy, for instance, was legitimated not solely by its capacity to keep the peace but also by its trust-busting program aimed at protecting the weak from the strong, destroying the old baronial monopoly on security, and enforcing a norm of legal impartiality.

Theorists of absolutism, such as Bodin or Hobbes, did not identify security with "liberty." But they did invoke security to justify a sharp increase in state power. The same value that eventually became the premier rationale for constitutional restrictions on government power had originally served, therefore, as a justification for centralized authority. This historical detail has important theoretical implications. Liberalism may be mistrustful of accumulated state power. But no theory which makes *security* into a central concern can be dogmatically antistatist. Mill, among others, was acutely aware of this paradox. Reflecting on the general insecurity plaguing early modern Europe, he explained why sovereigns had to be granted such inordinate power: "The passions of those who were strong by station or by personal endowment were in a state of habitual rebellion against laws and ordinances, and required to be rigorously chained up to enable the persons within their reach to enjoy any particle of *security.*"[32] Originally, private power had been the most conspicuous threat to individual liberty. To guarantee the security (and therefore freedom) of the weak, restrictions had to be placed on the freedom (and therefore security) of the strong.[33] Security could not be completely *equalized* in this manner; but some redistribution could guarantee a *bottom floor* or minimum of security to all.[34]

For basic security to be universally available, the state had to retain its monopoly on the legitimate use of violence; but public officials also had to be made accountable and subject to punishment. Mill goes on to describe the transition from the absolute to the liberal state in exactly this way: "To prevent the weaker members of the community from being preyed upon by innumerable vultures, it was needful that there should be an animal of prey stronger than all the rest, commissioned to keep them down. But as the king of the vultures would be no less bent upon preying on the flock than any of the minor harpies, it was indispensable to be in a perpetual attitude of defense against his beak and claws."[35] Constitutionalism, therefore, took the original redistribution of security from nobles to commoners a step beyond where absolutism had left it. The security of rulers, too, had to be diminished in order to increase the security of the ruled.

### Justice and Charity

According to Locke, a person's exclusive property rights are valid only "where there is enough, and as good left in common for others." Our duty "to preserve mankind" requires that we abstain from invading our "neighbor's share," reveling in superfluities while others lack necessities.[36] Property, too, is closely associated with security, or at least with dampening a fundamental human insecurity: the uncertainty of where to find tomorrow's meal. To possess property, in an orderly and predictable political environment, means—in Locke's language—to quell a basic human uneasiness or restlessness, that is, to be somewhat more *secure.* Private ownership of agricultural land is justified because it helps generate a hefty grain surplus, thereby lowering the average price of subsistence goods relative to wages. But if this system does not function as hoped, then state provision is required. It is not unreasonable to read Locke's argument for redistribution of property in case of extreme want, therefore, as an argument for a partial transfer of security in case of extreme danger.

Although quite well known, the critical passage is worth citing again at length:

> We know God hath not left one Man so to the Mercy of another, that he may starve him if he please: God the Lord and Father of all, has given no one of his Children such a Property, in his peculiar portion of the things of the world, but that he has given his needy Brother a Right to the Surplusage of his Goods; so that it cannot justly be denied him, when his pressing Wants call for it. And therefore no man could ever have a just Power over the Life of another, by Right of property in Land or Possessions; since 'twould always be a Sin in any Man of Estate, to let his brother perish for want of affording him Relief out of his Plenty. As *Justice* gives every Man a Title to the product of his honest Industry, and the fair Acquisitions of his Ancestors descended to him; so Charity gives every man a Title to so much of another's Plenty, as will keep him from extream want, where he has no means to subsist otherwise.[37]

That this passage enunciates a universal *entitlement to welfare* cannot be denied. Less obvious is the basis for such an entitlement. Some commentators have argued that, in a Lockean world, our obligation to help the needy is divinely ordained.[38] To justify any sort of redistribution, it is claimed, Locke had to appeal to some wholly nonliberal principle, such as God's will. (The underlying assumption here is that liberal norms themselves cannot justify social provision. A further implication, often explicitly drawn, is that welfare measures will be perceived as increasingly illegitimate as secularization erodes the last residues of our religious heritage.) This approach has something to be said in its favor. Ultimately, however, it underestimates the close parallel between Locke's religiously tinctured argument and the claims advanced by more obviously secular theorists including Hobbes, Hume, Smith, Kant, and Mill. They all justified social provision and they did so *without* appealing to divine commands. In my opinion, Locke did the same, since he explicitly argued that "natural Reason" alone, without support from Revelation, "tells us, that Men, being once born, have a right to their Preservation, and consequently to Meat and Drink, and such other things, as Nature affords for their Subsistence."[39]

Consider first Hobbes, the preliberal, who is quite explicit about the need for public assistance to the incapacitated:

> And whereas many men, by accident unevitable, become unable to maintain themselves by their labour; they ought not to be left to the Charity of private persons; but to be provided for, (as far-forth as the necessities of Nature require), by the Lawes of the Common-wealth. For as it is Uncharitablenesse in any man, to neglect the impotent; so it is in the Soveraign of a Common-wealth, to expose them to the hazard of such uncertain Charity.[40]

In this passage, of course, Hobbes explicitly invokes charity, and for the disabled alone. The most "liberal" aspect of his argument is probably the anticommunitarian assumption that a person's value is not contingent on his contributions to the community. Even noncontributors have basic rights, including the right to subsistence.

What is most remarkable about Hobbes's general argument, however, and even more relevant for our purposes, is his claim that *justice requires redistribution*—that is, a taking from the strong and a giving to the weak. The desire felt by grasping men for superfluities needed by others—let us call it "possessive individualism"—must be dealt with severely. By nature, people wish to profit from the self-restraint of others while simultaneously profiting from their own lack of self-restraint. While the Tenth Law of Nature commands an acknowledgment of human equality, arrogant men continue to assert their own superiority: "The Greeks call the violation of this law *pleonexia;* that is, a desire of more than their share." Whenever hoggish individualists make exceptions of themselves, act partially, and engross more than their fair portion, they must be compelled to climb down and accommodate themselves to others. But despite Hobbes's explicit claim that "equal distribution is of the Law of Nature" the redistributionist dimension of his contractarian argument has seldom been fully appreciated.[41]

The Tenth Law of Nature asserts that "no man require to reserve to himself any right, which he is not willing should be reserved to any one of the rest." This is a classic statement of the self-exemption prohibition, a universalistic principle equally dear to the liberal theorists who built upon Hobbesian foundations. The egalitarianism of the claim is striking. Security must be distributed equally to the "poor and obscure" and to the "rich and mighty." The approach Hobbes advocates toward redistribution, including the redistribution of property when subsistence is at stake, is quite ruthless: "A man that by asperity of Nature, will strive to retain those things which to himselfe are superfluous, and to others necessary; and for the stubbornness of his Passions, cannot be corrected, is to be left, or cast out of Society, as combersome thereunto."[42] Not pity or charity but justice demands a harshly punitive attitude toward possessive individualists. Justice requires that all citizens receive a fair allotment of basic resources. In conditions of surplus, a fair share means enough for survival at least.

For further evidence that redistribution can be justified on purely secular and contractarian grounds, without invoking Revelation or divine commands, consider an argument advanced more than a century later by Immanuel Kant. "Indirectly, inasmuch as he takes over the duty of the people, the supreme commander possesses the right to levy taxes on them for their own conservation, in particular, for the relief of the poor." Kant grounded the obligation to furnish relief to those who cannot provide for themselves on the nature of the original contract, omitting all reference to God's will, adducing the will of the people alone. The social contract, based on an exchange of obedience for protection, creates a duty in the state to preserve the life of contracting citizens. More specifically, it implies a *precommitment* of every member's surplus goods so that, if an emergency arises, subsistence rights can be guaranteed for all:

> The general Will of the people has united itself into a society in order to maintain itself continually, and for this purpose it has subjected itself to the internal authority of the state in order to support those members of the society who are not able to support themselves. Therefore, it follows from the nature of the state that the government is authorized to require the wealthy to provide the means of sustenance to those who are unable to provide the most necessary needs of nature for themselves. Because their existence depends on the act of subjecting themselves to the commonwealth for the protection

> and care required in order to stay alive, they have bound themselves to contribute to the support of their fellow citizens, and this is the ground for the state's right to require them to do so.[43]

My duty to help the impoverished is neither inborn nor God-commanded but, rather, a result of a voluntary social pact. Individuals renounced their primitive right to use violence and possess all things in order to acquire legal and economic security. For the social contract to be a just bargain, *all* signers must actually receive some degree of legal and economic security within civil society. Those who give obedience must receive protection in turn. Because property-holders have gained unprecedented security through the social contract, they are morally obliged to exchange equivalents for equivalents, to ensure that *all* parties to the bargain, including the propertyless, get what they bargained for. Put crudely, they should compensate the poor man for forgoing his original right to grab. In other words—and this is an aspect of contractarianism omitted from Robert Nozick's version—redistribution to relieve distress is a form of *just exchange*. Such an argument, which is wholly unreligious, is explicit in Kant. It may also be implicit in Locke.

That Locke's conventional distinction between justice and charity, derived from classical sources, may be less significant than it first seems is also suggested by a parallel passage in Hume where a title to the product of one's industry is subtly fused with a title to relief of want through redistribution: "Every person, if possible, ought to enjoy the fruits of his labour, in a full possession of all the necessaries, and many of the conveniencies of life. No one can doubt, but such an equality is most suitable to human nature, and diminishes much less from the *happiness* of the rich than it adds to that of the poor."[44] Hume is obviously recommending redistribution in this passage. (Indeed, he even seems to go further than Locke, justifying redistribution of happiness, not merely of those resources necessary for survival.) To guarantee citizens all the necessities and some of the "conveniencies" of life, we must *diminish* the happiness of the rich to some extent. Hume did not view his commitment to subsistence rights, significantly, as incompatible with his belief in a strong system of private property. When individuals are in danger of starvation, he elsewhere writes, then property rights themselves may be justly ignored: "Suppose a society to fall into such want of all common necessities, that the utmost frugality and industry cannot preserve the greater number from perishing, and the whole from extreme misery; it will readily, I believe, be admitted, that the strict laws of justice [protecting private property] are suspended in such a pressing emergence, and give place to the stronger motives of necessity and self-preservation." In case of extreme need, he proceeds to say, there is nothing "criminal or injurious" about disregarding ordinary rules of ownership.[45]

Unsympathetic to the idea of natural rights, Hume regularly appeals to the welfare of the majority. The self-exception taboo required that, in policy decisions, the happiness of one person count no more or less than the happiness of another. This egalitarian principle also governs the discussion of justice in the *Wealth of Nations*. Smith advocates free trade because he believes it will increase the welfare of "the lowest ranks of the people" and will work "for the benefit of the poor and the indigent."[46] Istvan Hont and Michael Ignatieff have usefully demonstrated that, for Smith, "the moral legitimacy of distribution in commercial society lay in the fact that those who were 'left out in the partition' of property, i.e. the wage-earning poor, received adequate subsistence." Writing under the powerful influence of natural law theorists such as Pufendorf, Smith rejects attempts to impose an egalitarian distribution of property and instead embraces a system which, although radically inegalitarian, is immensely productive and can therefore guarantee "equal . . . access to the means to satisfy basic needs."[47]

A utilitarian concern for the greatest happiness of the greatest number, in Smith's view, makes it obligatory to improve the circumstances of the lower ranks of people: "Servants, labourers and workmen of different kinds, make up the far greater part of every great political society. But what improves the circumstances of the greater part can never be regarded as an inconveniency to the whole. No society can be flourishing and happy, of which the far greater part of the members are poor and miserable." In these sentences, Smith refers only to the *utility* of majority happiness. But he then turns a corner and includes justice: "It is but equity, besides, that they who feed, clothe and lodge the whole body of the people, should have such a share of the produce of their own labour as to be themselves tolerably well fed, clothed and lodged."[48] What we have here is a fruits-of-one's-labor argument combined with some kind of Rawlsian assumption that society is a cooperative venture from which all participants deserve to derive some benefit. If we distinguished roughly between contribution-based and needs-based justifications for redistribution, we would certainly place Smith's argument here into the first category.[49] To those who feed and clothe us, we owe, as a quid pro quo or *just exchange*, tolerable food and clothing.

Far from retaining a scrupulous impartiality between workers and employers, Smith wrote shockingly that when a regulation is "in the favour of the workmen, it is always just and equitable."[50] As such passages imply, moreover, he displayed less wholesale hostility to redistributive policies than some of his commentators suggest.[51] For example, he opposed taxes on necessities and favored taxes on luxuries because, in this manner, "the indolence and vanity of the rich is made to contribute in a very easy manner to the relief of the poor."[52] *Redistribution* by progressive taxation is justified not by a theory that the rich got rich at the *expense* of the poor, but on the basis of a more general belief that the rich got rich with the implicit or explicit *cooperation* of the poor.

Such arguments do not exhaust the liberal repertoire, of course. A more consistently needs-based, rather than contribution-based, justification for welfare transfers was advanced later by Mill:

> Apart from any metaphysical considerations respecting the foundation of morals or of the social union, it will be admitted to be right that human beings should help one another; and the more so, in proportion to the urgency of the need: and none needs help so urgently as one who is starving. The claim to help, therefore, created by destitution, is one of the strongest which can exist; and there is *prima facie* the amplest reason for making the relief of so extreme an exigency as certain to those who require it, as by any arrangements of society it can be made.[53]

Mill explicitly refused to qualify this needs-based argument for redistribution with any reference to merit: "The state must act by general rules. It cannot undertake to discriminate between the deserving and the undeserving indigent. It owes no more than subsistence to the first, and can give no less to the last." Equality of needs overrides inequality of virtue, making it politically irrelevant to blame poverty on the improvidence or delinquency of the poor. His commitment to impartiality and fairness, moreover, prompted Mill to reject any suggestion that the task of relieving poverty should be left to "voluntary charity." The state must use tax-derived revenues to provide public assistance because "charity almost always does too much or too little: it lavishes its bounty in one place, and leaves people to starve in another."[54]

Mill supplemented these universalistic needs-based arguments, which may indeed have religious origins, with a more down-to-earth claim about compensatory justice. He too, like his predecessors, asserted that "a legal provision for the destitute" represents a *just exchange* of protection for obedience. For one thing, "since the state must necessarily provide subsistence for the criminal poor while undergoing punishment, not to do the same for the poor who have not offended is to give a premium on crime."[55] In effect, welfare support is a payment to the indigent for refraining from crimes (against the rich, among others). If criminals who are apprehended are given food and shelter, then how, for safety's sake, can the noncriminal poor be guaranteed any less?

## Is Poverty an Incentive to Labor?

In the course of his argument, Mill explicitly challenged the conventional wisdom that poverty is a spur to effort, correcting the one-sided theory that public assistance creates a crippling disincentive to work. "Energy and self-dependence," he wrote, are "liable to be impaired by the absence of help as well as by its excess." Like other liberals, he valued security of ownership not solely for negative but also for positive reasons, not only as a means of repressing fear but also as a stimulant to creativity and innovation. Poverty means insecurity, and insecurity is psychologically debilitating or paralyzing. Not penury, but economic growth and a promiscuous diffusion of private property is the most effective spur to effort: "The greater security of property is one of the main conditions and causes of greater production, which is Progress in its most familiar and vulgarest aspect."[56] Economic security provided by state provision functions in the same way.

Smith had been even more direct in asserting that public provision can foster private initiative. His bold argument in favor of high wages was also based on a denial of the poverty-as-a-spur-to-effort thesis: "That men in general should work better when they are ill fed than when they are well fed, when they are disheartened than when they are in good spirits, when they are frequently sick than when they are generally in good health, seems not very probable." Smith justified high wages by invoking the well-being of the majority. But he chose the *majority's* welfare as the criterion to guide public policy because of a prior commitment to distributive justice. His underlying concern for fairness is made explicit in the following often-cited passage: "Our merchants and master-manufacturers complain much of the bad effects of high wages in raising the price, and thereby lessening the sale of their goods both at home and abroad. They say nothing concerning the bad effects of high profits. They are silent with regard to the pernicious effects of their own gains. They complain only of those of other people."[57] The merchants under attack here had violated the norm of impartiality and fair shares: the self-exemption taboo. They subjected others to a principle to which they had refused to subject themselves.

Impartiality demanded the abandonment of the mercantile system, which was nothing other than an expression of the unjust and unjustifiable partiality of merchants.

## The Inviolability of Private Property

Commentators on the left or the right who discern an unbridgeable gap separating legal rights and welfare rights commonly focus on liberalism's commitment to the "sanctity" of private property. But the liberals I have been discussing were well aware that concentrations of property spelled potentially dangerous concentrations of power. In Hume's words, "where the riches are in few hands, these must enjoy all the power."[58] Because inherited concentrations of property, even in a free enterprise system, can produce inherited concentrations of power, private property must be a source of distress as well as of solace to the heirs of the liberal tradition. An irreproachably liberal sentiment, distrust of concentrated power, surely justifies some degree of state regulation of private property.

If the government did not wield its coercive powers to enforce contract and trespass laws, of course, private property would be worthless. What would be the distribution of income in a stateless society? How civilized would "civil society" be in the absence of a monitored but nevertheless effective and reliable police force? Could a "spontaneous" distribution of social wealth possibly serve as an ideal standard of freedom and justice? For liberals the answer was obvious. Liberal society is a product of concentrated (and limited) state power. The wealthy benefit from state protection of private property, while the impoverished benefit from state protection of even more elementary freedoms. According to Mill, "the rich would be far better able to protect themselves, in the absence of government, than the poor, and indeed, would probably be successful in converting the poor into their slaves."[59] Some might dispute Mill's thesis here and argue that a rich man could never enforce slavery in the absence of coercive government. But stateless societies, such as feudal Europe, were anything but egalitarian.

In stateless societies, the mafia or equivalent wielders of private power, tend, among other things, to engross all available wealth. The dual purpose of the social contract, therefore, is to overcome *anarchy* and to correct the unbearable *maldistributions of private power* typical of the state of nature. That ownership itself will be affected was already made clear by Locke. Private property can be enjoyed in security only because it is a monopoly granted and guaranteed by the government for the sake of the public interest. Later liberals such as Hume and

Montesquieu were even more explicit on this point. Put differently, the pattern of "ownership"—if we can call it that—characterizing sovereignless societies is an unrelieved nightmare. Wherever property is secure, it is defined, protected, and regulated by political authority. The state of nature, where property is unregulated and therefore completely unstable, could provide neither a benchmark of freedom nor a justification for limiting the power of the state.

In the seventeenth and eighteenth centuries, to affirm private property was to attack the politics of confiscation. In those passages where Locke seemed to ascribe a presocial origin to private property, he was simply trying to outbid the presocial credentials of confiscation-prone divine right rulers. One you-can't-touch-me ideology deserved and provoked another. (To this extent, Locke's initial appropriation argument was essentially wedded to the theological premises of seventeenth-century political debate. It is thus anachronistic and obfuscatory to speak, with Robert Nozick, of a sacred or inviolable or natural right to property in a society where government no longer claims divine sanction.) To advocate the rights of property owners, in any case, was to question the state's authority to billet soldiers in one's home—a practice threatening to the integrity of the family and not merely to the profits of acquisitive individualists.

The political meaning of property rights was also underlined by the slogan "No taxation without representation." That is to say, the campaign to protect private property was difficult to disentangle from the campaign to establish effective representative institutions.[60] This connection between private property and self-government is also corroborated by *Federalist* no. 10. There, Madison put forward a wholly democratic—that is, neither an individualistic nor an economic—defense of private property. Unless property-owners are protected from fellow citizens as well as from government employees, they will be too frightened to cooperate in a fragile system of collective self-rule.[61] In this period, moreover, to oppose monopolies and advocate the circulation of legally unencumbered private property was to attack primogeniture and entail—that is, to assault the foundation stone of Europe's landed aristocracy. Indeed, liberals valued the market itself as the most efficient vehicle for redistributing social wealth and, thus, for redistributing security. Despite Hayek's jibes about "teleocracy," liberals were never reticent to engage in *purposive* behavior. Their end-in-view was the collapse of inherited privilege and a general diffusion of private wealth.

Even when condemning destructive confiscatory redistribution, however, Locke suggested strongly that some forms of redistribution were legitimate: "These worldly things cannot therefore be taken away from this man and given to that at the magistrate's pleasure, nor can the private possession of them among fellow citizens be changed, not even by a law, *for a reason which in no way concerns the civil community,* I mean for religion."[62] The obvious implication of this passage is that the magistrate *can* confiscate and redistribute property for certain secular and narrowly political reasons. That Locke, at least, endorses the political regulation of private property is beyond all doubt: "Man, when he, at first, incorporates himself into any Commonwealth, he, by his uniting himself there unto, annexed also, and submits to the Community those Possessions, which he has, or shall acquire." It would be absurd, Locke continues, to deny political jurisdiction over private ownership: "For it would be a direct Contradiction, for any one, to enter into society with others for the securing and regulating of Property: And yet to suppose his Land, whose Property is to be regulated by the Laws of the Society, should be exempt from the Jurisdiction of that Government, to which he himself the Proprietor of the Land, is a subject."[63] Locke is deeply concerned to dissociate the inheritance of property from the inheritance of authority. No surprise, therefore, that he identifies *the regulation of property* as one of the paramount functions of government: "In Governments the Laws regulate the right of property, and the possession of land is determined by positive constitutions."[64] Property does not belong to some sacred private sphere, untouchable by the government or the community.

The liberal concept of property also contained a strong universalist element. It offered hope to at least some commoners and less-advantaged groups. Questions of distribution, of course, were never separated from questions of production in liberal thought. The unequal allocation of property characteristic of commercial society was thought to be a necessary by-product of agricultural productivity, guaranteeing subsistence to all. Equal opportunity to satisfy basic needs could be achieved indirectly, and only by accepting unequal wealth and income as well as unequal rights to control the means of production. With a minimum of violence and pain, growing affluence would, for the first time, provide economic security for the vast majority.

Finally, the institutionalization of modern property rights did not "loose acquisitive instincts onto the world," as followers of Leo Strauss and R. H. Tawney love to regret. For one thing, medieval peasants and barons were no strangers to greed. For another, property law, including its modern variants, required short-term self-restraint. Do not covet thy neighbor's goods! More important, as I have been stressing, the liberal embrace of private property initiated a partial *transfer* of security from the old monopolists of land to other, less well-established, groups. What was "loosed" onto the world, in fact, was not acquisitiveness but disrespect for inherited status.

The questions now arise: What shape does liberalism take when translated into a new context? How does the ideology of freedom change when new threats to freedom move into the foreground and old ones recede? How did liberals react, in particular, when private property and the free market began to generate unprecedented forms of *insecurity* and to allocate security in a blatantly unfair way? As is well known, the simple enforcement of contracts was unable, in the wake of massive industrial development, to provide security for workers or to guarantee any facsimile of justly allocated security. When industrial change overwhelmed modern Western societies, certain doctrinaire heirs of the liberal tradition dogmatically opposed curtailments of property rights despite the insecurities and maldistributions that these rights, because unqualified, tended to generate in new circumstances.[65] Others, more true (I believe) to the experimental spirit of liberalism, agreed to infringe some property rights, by establishing a progressive income tax system, for instance, for the sake of greater and more justly distributed security.[66] This welfarist turn was explicitly conceived as an *alternative* to socialism and collective ownership of the means of production. It was also, it seems to me, fully consonant with the original intention behind the liberal celebration of private property. Well-designed redistributionist measures, based on the expectation and hope that capitalism would remain strong, were meant to provide a "bottom floor" of decent subsistence for all.

## Shifting Sources of Insecurity

With a little effort, we can discern an interesting parallel between, the nineteenth- and twentieth-century shift in attitudes toward private property and the seventeenth-century shift in attitudes toward state power. In both cases, initial reverence changed into partial doubt. Absolute monarchy gained legitimacy by campaigning to eliminate civil wars, to bring physical safety to the highways, and so forth. State power was relatively immune from devastating criticism *so long as* the insecurity it was trying to conquer was socially pervasive and universally feared. After they succeeded in destroying these sources of insecurity, however, the state's peacekeeping agencies began to look somewhat like a solution without a problem. Once centralized authority had overcome the anarchical conditions in response to which it had arisen, its enormous powers were themselves suddenly thrown into question. As one source of insecurity (say, baronial or sectarian squabbling) faded from consciousness, another (the state itself) became more conspicuous and annoying.[67] A similar story can be told about the fate of the ideology of private property.

Proponents of both absolutism and liberalism shared a common commitment to security. The pursuit of security led to different policies in different situations. Where they parted company was in the identification of *the most urgent threats* to secure living and social cooperation—the former worrying most about private armies and the second about the agents of the state. Many historical reasons might be adduced to explain this change in "threat perception." Moreover, a similar transformation seems to have occurred in the shift from classical to welfare-state liberalism. Unchanging principles generated unprecedented policies under new conditions. For historical reasons, classical liberals focused on state-induced insecurity, whereas proponents of the welfare state emphasized market-induced insecurity. The *source* of insecurity changed in both cases. But the *value* of security itself remained the same.

Why did James Madison cling to the rights of private property with what now seems like monomaniacal zeal? For one thing, private property was a symbol of security against the whims of political authority and the violence of rowdy neighbors, not to mention more impersonal forces. It was one of the few supports an individual could cling to in a sea of turbulence. As other sources of security, such as a more reliable legal system, became established, private property had to bear less of this burden and thus absorbed fewer of life's uncertainties. Hence, it lost its former aura, its immunity to criticism. It even became visible as a source of insecurity itself.

As documented above, classical liberals, from Locke to Mill, routinely assumed that, when the need arose, the state could and should infringe the property rights of the rich to satisfy the subsistence needs of the poor. According to Montesquieu, moreover, the security of individuals can be threatened not only by tyrannical rulers and by religious and baronial civil wars, but also by unpredictable fluctuations in the market. Security dictates government intervention to help workers whenever an industry suddenly fails. All citizens profit from a flourishing economy. As a just recompense, the state must compensate those workers who, for the common benefit, expose themselves to the periodic incompetence of the market. Indeed, unemployment compensation makes it more attractive for people to enter socially useful but individually risky occupations. In Montesquieu's words:

> The riches of the state suppose great industry. Amidst the numerous branches of trade it is impossible but that some must suffer, and consequently the mechanics [i.e., workers] must be in a momentary necessity. . . . When this happens, the state is obliged to lend them a ready assistance, whether it be to prevent the suffering of the people, or to avoid a rebellion. In this case hospitals, or some equivalent regulations, are necessary to prevent this misery.[68]

Just as legal rights protect citizens from the tyranny of magistrates, so economic rights protect them from the vagaries of the market. (This passage is additionally interesting for the casualness with which Montesquieu juxtaposes several distinct justifications for redistributive relief measures. To the compensatory justice of helping those who contribute to the common advantage, he adds the wisdom of avoiding a potential revolt as well as a more general humanitarian concern to prevent unnecessary suffering.)[69]

A few subsidiary points also deserve mention here. First of all, competition serves consumers. But it does not serve *all* consumers. For-profit hospitals may well tend to concentrate on profitable illnesses, leaving difficult and costly cases to public institutions, just as private schools tend to exclude children with disciplinary and learning problems. This is a liberal reason for refusing to allocate health care and education by pure market mechanisms. Markets promote freedom by allowing individuals, without the intervention of authority, to purchase what they want. But what happens to individuals with no money? How does a market system enhance their freedom? That even libertarians sometimes feel compelled to propose voucher schemes (for schooling, and so forth) suggests a latent guilt about the partiality of the market toward those who have money to spend. Vouchers reflect a normative commitment not to equality but to a bottom floor of resources provided equally to all out of revenues collected on a progressive basis from the population as a whole.

Liberal hostility to inherited authority hardly needs be mentioned. But property is, or can be, power. So by what right can liberals defend hereditary wealth? Liberals argue against confiscatory inheritance taxes, when they do, on practical grounds, not because of any hidden doubts about individualism or the meritocratic ethic. To undermine a family's capacity to educate and shape its children would do incalculable damage to individual liberty. Nevertheless, liberals remain justly worried about individuals who are left without any resources at birth, who (by a natural lottery) are deprived of a realistic opportunity to participate in the market system. For this reason, too, welfare systems can be conceived as expressions of liberal guilt about the anti-individualistic implications of the inheritance of wealth. Despite the claims of its enemies, welfare-state liberalism is meritocratic. It is based on the indubitable premise that the children of the poor have done nothing to *merit* their disadvantages in life.

## Mutual Obligation without a Common Purpose

Romantically inclined theorists typically argue that no welfare program can be justified without appeal to *solidarity* or *community* or *civic friendship*. (They add, incorrectly, that liberalism is antiwelfarist because it scorns solidarity and undermines traditional forms of communal life.) I will be willing to pay taxes for support of the poor, they also argue, only if I identify, morally and emotionally, with the collectivity to which we all, taxpayers and welfare recipients alike, belong. Identification with a larger unit leads me to a selfless concern for my fellow citizens, and so forth. Man is a social animal; *ergo,* the welfare state!

While simple enough to be committed to memory, this ready-mix analysis is not completely convincing. Indeed, the contrary argument seems much more plausible. To erode primordial loyalties of caste, clan, sect, race, ethnic, or regional group, and so on, it is necessary to convince people to conceive of themselves primarily as individuals. Only after traditional groupings have been disaggregated is it possible to reintegrate individuals into a larger national community. Only when you think of yourself as an individual, rather than as a Capulet or a Montague, can you also think of yourself as a citizen.

Individualism, therefore, far from being normatively at odds with policies of economic redistribution, is indispensable to the justification of welfare measures in a multiethnic and multidenominational state. If inhabitants of Scarsdale were primarily seized by loyalty to their ethnic community, why would they be willing to pay taxes destined for Harlem?[70] Though they acknowledge a socially acquired or perhaps inborn grouping instinct, liberals assume that this propensity sometimes has barbaric consequences. Consider again Hume's view of factions, quintessential expressions of human sociality: "Factions subvert government, render laws impotent, and beget the fiercest animosities among men of the same nation, who ought to give *mutual assistance* and protection to each other."[71] Though entirely selfless or communitarian, factional devotion may destroy all possibility of community-wide mutual support.[72] The willingness of individuals to sacrifice themselves to their subgroup—the "generous" side of xenophobia—must be overcome to achieve the rarer selflessness exhibited in national systems of poor relief.

Critics might concede, of course, that primordial affiliations must be dissolved before individuals can conceive of themselves as members of a national community. But they could counter that a new emotional attachment to the *national* community must emerge to replace old loyalties before people will willingly help their neediest fellows. But is this true? Perhaps. Nationalism, a moral-emotional attachment to one's fellow citizens and a corresponding coolness toward foreigners, probably does help modern states extract taxes for redistributive purposes. And nationalism is indeed particularistic and therefore illiberal. But need it play a role in the *moral justification* of the welfare state? Tending to be universalistic or cosmopolitan rather than nationalistic in outlook, liberals support a territorial rather than ethnic definition of nationhood (that is, co-nationals are those who happen to live together in the same territory, not those who share a common ancestry). They are also more willing to support wars, such as World War II, in which cosmopolitan values are at stake than wars for national aggrandizement or national interest. In the same spirit, liberals would be inclined to support an international transfer plan whereby wealthy individuals helped support the poor wherever they lived.

In reality, liberals support national transfer plans. This fact does not imply any betrayal of cosmopolitan values or covert communitarian ideology, however. Instead, it can easily be interpreted as another concession to the practical. Without sovereign power, notoriously absent in the international arena, mutual assistance on a large scale is impossible to implement effectively. Payments across borders will inevitably line the pockets of the rich and crafty, and may well exacerbate urbanization, making poor countries increasingly dependent for food supply on rich countries. Practical problems and stumbling blocks, in other words, not "bonds" of blood or culture, explain the liberal commitment to *national* transfer programs.

War, it is true, cements citizens into tightly knit communities ready to make individual sacrifices for a common purpose (such as avoiding defeat). That warfare contributes to welfare by accustoming citizens to higher tax burdens seems beyond dispute. That massive welfare programs were inaugurated in France and Great Britain after World War II is no coincidence. Welfare, however, is not quite like military victory, not exactly a common goal. Sparta was not a welfare state. Social provision is less like a goal than a condition for the pursuit of a variety of goals. In any case, it seems possible to justify redistributionist policies by appealing solely to equality or impartiality. This, in essence, is Ronald Dworkin's argument, which I find persuasive.[73] Being unwilling to admit that poor citizens are less worthy of respect than rich ones, or that their ideals deserve less chance of realization, liberals are committed to providing the poor with at least some resources for working out and trying to fulfill their own goals. Redistribution can be justified even in the absence of fraternal sentiments. Welfare rights express liberal neutrality, not blood-based community. Or again: welfare is a precondition for diverse and rival purposes, not itself an homogenizing or collective aim.

## The Facilitative Functions of State Power

A stylized distinction between the state and civil society, between the grim domain of bureaucratic compulsion and the jaunty realm of economic voluntariness, is at the center of many right-wing attacks on welfare rights. Freedom is at an end when, ominously and imperialistically, "government interferes in society." The autonomy of civil society, the "prepolitical" nature of extrapolitical life, the utter absence of power relations within the market sphere—these remain potent myths. There is no denying that they were initially promulgated by some classical liberals—think only of Tom Paine. Originally, however, these exaggerated claims were intended as political programs, not as empirical generalizations. They were exasperated attacks on the temporarily most annoying source of social insecurity, the state, not sociological claims about the capacity of nonpolitical sectors of society to function effectively without any governmental regulation or support.

The writers I have been discussing were all aware that the state created national markets by knocking down traditional barriers to trade. They also knew that government continued to enforce contract law and trespass law and to disrupt spontaneous social monopolies. Without betraying their principles, some liberal states, at least, built railroads, highways, lighthouses, dams, sewers, and canals—providing facilities essential to the community that individuals would not always have been able to fund privately.[74] As Mill says, there are "a variety of cases, in which important public services are to be performed, while yet there is no individual specially interested in performing them, nor would any adequate remuneration naturally or spontaneously attend their performance."[75] In any case, none of our representative liberals dreamed about a politics-free realm or the pristine autonomy of civil society. Indeed, they all conceived "civil society" as society "civilized" by state action. Despite some rhetorical exaggeration, they did not believe that we could realistically choose an inactive rather than an active government. The only open question was: in what sort of activities should the state engage?

What precisely can a liberal state do to "promote the general welfare"? Smith, for one, proposes a publicly financed and compulsory system of education, aimed to lift up the poor. The market alone, he believes, cannot be trusted to deliver this precious good. Indeed, Smith justified state intervention in the educational arena as a necessary response to the incompetence of the market and, more specifically, as a remedy for the humanly disfiguring and crippling consequences of factory work. Specialization transformed workers into miserable citizens, incapable of making informed judgments about political questions.[76] Mill followed Smith in this line of reasoning. Self-government becomes possible only when the majority has reached a certain level of education. Universal education facilitates democratic decision making. The right to an education can therefore be inferred directly from the right to participate in collective self-rule: "I hold it therefore the duty of the government to supply the defect [of schools established on a voluntary basis] by giving pecuniary support to elementary schools, such as to render them accessible to all the children of the poor, either freely, or for a payment too inconsiderable to be sensibly felt." State-supported education is a serious annoyance for the doctrinaire libertarian because, in this case, government intervention obviously enhances individual autonomy. Publicly supported schooling (which does not necessarily imply public ownership and operation of schools), as Mill says, is "help toward doing without help."[77]

But the crucial argument advanced by both Smith and Mill is that educational rights are democracy reinforcing. Frank Michelman has taken a further step and argued that subsistence, shelter, and health care are all "indispensable means of effective participation" in the political processes outlined by the U.S. Constitution.[78] Welfare benefits foster the *inclusion* of all citizens into the system of private and public rights guaranteed by the Constitution. Admittedly, the idea that implicit (educational and economic) rights are necessary preconditions for the proper utilization of explicit (political and legal) rights is vulnerable to some serious criticisms.[79] The basic idea is not, however, a recent invention but, rather, a notion well known to the eighteenth-century liberals who most influenced the American framers.

## Collective Self-Reliance

Opponents of the facilitative state repeatedly denounce its paternalism in the name of citizen self-reliance. But this may well be a false alternative. In the first place, self-reliance must be organized. When individuals walk into court and sue on the basis of a democratically approved statute, they are no less self-reliant than when they establish a labor union. In a complex society, all self-reliance requires social dependency and cooperation, indirect techniques, and institutional strategies. (To "do it yourself," as is well known, you must go to a do-it-yourself store and buy a do-it-yourself kit.) As a result, we cannot use the idea of self-reliance to justify a blanket rejection of redistributionist legislation.

Self-reliance does not occur in a legal and political vacuum; it depends upon preconditions and resources (such as well-defined property rights) that, in some cases, must be provided by the state. Because independence in one respect always implies dependence in another, antipaternalism is an impossible position to espouse consistently. Hobbes, moreover, already provided a partial answer to the accusation of paternalism hurled later at all welfare programs. Peace, as he saw it, is a goal that most citizens share but that no individual is willing to pursue unless he or she can be assured that others will cooperate in achieving it as best they can. Government intervention is justified not merely to protect unwilling victims but also, and primarily, to help citizens do jointly what they all want to do but cannot do severally. In other words, although Hobbes would never have used such language, state help can be freedom enhancing as well as freedom restricting.

Answering the libertarians of his day, Mill explained the autonomy-reinforcing function of state intervention:

> The principle that each is the best judge of his own interest, understood as these objectors understand it, would prove that governments ought not to fulfill any of their acknowledged duties—ought not, in fact, to exist at all. It is greatly the interest of the community, collectively and individually, not to rob or defraud one another; but there is not the less necessity for laws to punish robbery and fraud; because, though it is the interest of each that nobody should rob or cheat, it is not anyone's interest to refrain from robbing and cheating others when all others are permitted to rob and cheat him. Penal laws exist at all, chiefly for this reason, because even a unanimous opinion that a certain line of conduct is for the general interest, does not always make it people's individual interest to adhere to that line of conduct.[80]

Coercive government intervention can be essential for individuals to overcome collective-action problems and achieve their own goals: "It is in the interest of each to do what is good for all, but only if others will do likewise."[81] John Rawls makes the same point: "Even if all citizens were willing to pay their share, they would presumably do so only when they are assured that others will pay theirs as well."[82] By enforcing the norm of fairness (the self-exemption prohibition), the state can enable citizens to do what they genuinely want; that is, it can increase individual self-direction. Thus, justice and freedom, state regulation and liberty, are not nearly so antithetical as right-wing enemies of the welfare state would have us believe.

To recapitulate: even if most Americans wished to help the poor, they might do so only if they believed with some certainty that most of their fellow citizens would pitch in. Alleviation of poverty is a public good that cannot be provided by the market. Transfer programs may be justified on these grounds alone, as even their opponents admit. Interestingly, Friedman himself concurs with Mill and Rawls on this point: "We might all of us be willing to contribute to the relief of poverty, *provided* everyone else did."[83] If some charitable individuals make an effort to alleviate poverty, freeriders will lack an incentive to make efforts of their own. (This economic argument is a powerful one; but how it can get off the ground without an initial acceptance of the right of the poor man to demand support, remains strangely unclear in Friedman's presentation.) In any case, I bring up the free-rider problem solely to make a negative point. All the liberal theorists discussed in this chapter recognize that governmental coercion can help individuals achieve their own goals. As a result, liberalism should not be mechanically associated with a hysterical fear of state paternalism or dependence on government. Liberals have always accepted some degree of paternalism, in education for example, so long as it is autonomy enabling, somehow a reinforcement of individual freedom as well as an expression of collective self-rule.

## Conclusion

Most discussions of the normative foundations of the welfare state suppose a fundamental breach with the classical liberal tradition. Welfare-state liberalism is described as radically "revisionist," for good or ill. Classical liberalism was antistatist, it is assumed, hostile to social planning, fond of liberty above equality, unwilling to engage in redistribution, committed to the inviolability of private property, assured of the spontaneous harmony of interests, trustful of the market, rigidly antipaternalistic, hopeful that the public sector would shrink and that the private sector would expand, and so forth. On all accounts, as I have tried to show, this widely accepted picture of classical liberalism is flawed. As a result, the fundamental continuity between liberal rights and welfare rights is stronger than has ordinarily been realized. It is perfectly plausible to interpret social provision as a faithful application of traditional liberal principles to a new situation. Such considerations do not provide a moral or political justification of the redistributionist state, as I said. They alone cannot compel us to support any specific public policy, without consideration of costs and alternatives. All that the historian of ideas can plausibly demonstrate, in fact, is that redistributive policies *should not be rejected* on the grounds that they are inherently illiberal or represent a betrayal of the great liberal legacy. Without justifying the welfare state, we can nevertheless revoke the bragging license of its enemies.

# CONCLUSION

As described in the foregoing pages, the theory of liberal democracy has a simple psychological premise and a complex institutional strategy. Its psychological premise is the fragility of reason. Its institutional strategy involves the integration of market economics and deliberative politics within a single legal framework, administratively enforced. Premise and strategy are linked in important ways. The various normative aspirations of liberal democracy—including individual liberty, equal dignity of citizens, and tolerance for diversity—are best discussed in relation to such psychological and institutional factors. The same can be said about liberal democracy's undoubted failure to realize these aspirations fully in practice.

## Irrational Desire

Classical liberals cannot plausibly be accused of naive rationalism. Neither Locke nor Montesquieu, Kant nor Mill conceived of human beings as rational egoists or calculating maximizers of personal advantage, much less as selfish materialists. Ordinary human motivation, they assumed, is shot through with habit and passion, custom and impulse. The rational assessment of costs and benefits has a real but modest and episodic role in shaping human behavior. Reason's importance varies enormously from context to context and is seldom the only decisive factor. People frequently act in ways they do not themselves understand and cannot explain when asked. They may be overcome by emotions that derail consecutive thought, preventing them from clearly anticipating the consequences of their actions, focusing simultaneously on conflicting aims and values, and coolly pursuing their palpable interests.

Liberal theorists incorporated these psychological tenets into their political theories. From classical and scholastic thought, as I have argued, they inherited the concept of *irrational desire.* Their well-corroborated belief that human striving is often unreasoning has important practical consequences. They feared tyranny, for example, because of the terrifying latitude it gives to unconstrained passions.

Above all, classical liberalism does not identify freedom with the unrestrained capacity to satisfy immediate or given desires.

Among mankind's most headstrong passions is factionalism, the subrational tendency to identify emotionally with an exclusive group that may be locked in real or imaginary struggle with another. The decisive importance of factionalism, religious persecution, and (eventually) racist bigotry for the evolution of liberal thought belies the suggestion that liberals were chronically unaware of the power exerted by groups over individuals. The starting point for liberalism is not the atomistic individual, but the conflicts that ensue when differently socialized individuals, immersed in contrasting creeds, customs, and affective attachments, clumsily rub shoulders and attempt to coexist. Far from being blind to loyalty, liberals simply assume that loyalty is sometimes good and sometimes bad, depending largely on the way conflicting affiliations and affinities are handled politically.

While liberals see no reason to be anticommunitarian in a militant sense, they reasonably refuse to interpret loyalty as the highest human good, suggesting that a distinction be made between group identifications to be encouraged and those to be discouraged. To draw a line between creative and destructive loyalties, liberals usually invoke another set of values, necessarily distinct from loyalty itself—justice, peace, rational discussion, and the mutually enriching and enlivening power of human diversity.

As Hume argued, emotional identification with a clan or sect can produce behavior at odds not only with the public good but also with the rational self-interest of the individual involved. Some people, at least, are mortally offended when their subgroup is publicly humiliated and seem willing to pay steep personal costs to exact retribution. Moreover, people may feel vexed and out of their element when confronting outsiders whose manners have not been homogenized by local culture. This psychological irritation can occur even when there is no question of competition over scarce resources. Sometimes people shun contact with strangers or even lash out aggressively in their presence, not because it is in their rational self-interest to react in a parochial and unwelcoming way, but simply from dread or disorientation in the face of those who appear unintelligibly different.

By institutionalizing a commitment to religious toleration, the political system of liberal democracy attempts in a modest fashion to take account of intense group loyalties and the threat they sometimes pose to social comity. The majority of human beings will never shed their particularistic allegiances and local identities, of course. How to handle group rivalry and mutual distrust, therefore, will always be a problem in any liberal-democratic state. One relatively successful attempt to solve this problem is the "wall" between church and state, meant to depoliticize sectarian animosities, not to obliterate group life or rinse particular attachments from the repertoire of human interaction. (Endeavors to employ a similar sequestering technique to problems of racial diversity have not been successful.) In any case, liberals strive, wherever possible, to desacralize or relativize group identity just enough to increase the chances for peaceful coexistence and mutually beneficial cooperation, across denominations and ethnic communities.

This ambivalent attitude of classical liberals toward group loyalty is inseparable from their well-known commitment to individualism. Liberal individualism is misunderstood as a celebration of egoism or the callous lack of social conscience. On the contrary, the essence of liberal individualism is best expressed in the double imperative to take moral *responsibility* for oneself and to treat *others* as individuals, rather than as members of a group. Far from being antisocial, liberal individualism was, from its inception, an ideology targeted against the subgroup loyalties most likely to generate factional bloodshed and civil war. An intensely loyal member of an insular subgroup will be more willing to risk his skin in an attempt to mutilate or kill members of an offending tribe if he is consoled in advance by the thought that his faction will survive his own demise. Individualism attempts to deal with this perennial problem by denying that group glory compensates for personal death. We might call this the Hobbesian Moment in liberal thought. The ideology of secular individualism represents a conscious attempt to put the sting back into mortality, counteracting the reassurances of membership and blocking the understandable tendency of individuals to project their identities onto something less ephemeral than their own bodily selves.

## State Power as a Solution and a Problem

When Madison wrote that "the passions ought to be controlled and regulated by the government," he meant that deliberative politics presupposes the cooling off or damping down of violent and irrational affect.[1] While commercialism can contribute to this end, by habituating ordinary citizens to methodical lifestyles and cross-denominational cooperation, it is far from sufficient. In general, markets do not provide everything people need. Among the most vital public goods that must be provided by a bureaucratically organized state, because they cannot be provided by a free market, are law and order and stable political frontiers. (The latter includes an answer to the question of who is a member of the community.) Most important, the violence that persists even in highly commercial societies must be dealt with by police. In the absence of such public goods as safe homes and streets, individuals live in a stressful state of anxiety that interferes with their ability to organize their lives productively. As is well known, weak-state pluralism is a recipe not for liberalism, but for a proliferation of rival and coercive mafias, clans, gangs, and cults.

One anti-individualist consequence of statelessness, or the state's failure to assert effectively its monopoly on the legitimate use of coercion, is the ability of private groups to enforce loyalty on their restless members by punishing defection with torture and death. Members may describe their unswerving adherence to group norms and directives as a product of ethnic pride or selfless fidelity, but the contribution of physiological panic to "dutiful" behavior is not decreased simply because it is publicly denied. From this perspective, the problem of anarchy suggests that the liberal state must monopolize the means of physical coercion in order to make individualism possible, outlawing the violent enforcement of loyalty on the part of exclusive private groups.

More generally, statelessness means rightlessness. Rights, including property rights, must be enforced by the administrative and judicial machinery of the state. This is a two-way street, because the impartial enforcement of rights can enhance the legitimacy and hence effectiveness of the state. Liberal democracy has no need for a heavily militarized, land-grabbing police state. But it does presuppose an effective and reliable public administration, for no organization except the state is ever likely to represent the interests of the majority of citizens against the behavior of strategically located and well-organized social predators. This is not to deny that state power can be, and often is, used for the benefit of the few against the many. The state monopoly on the legitimate means of coercion, in fact, while it solves the problem of anarchy, simultaneously raises the problem of tyranny. Any agency that wields enough power to protect me against the depredations of my neighbor, wields enough power to destroy or enslave me. This paradox lies at the root of modern state-of-nature theory. How can we exit from anarchy without falling into tyranny? How can we assign the rulers enough power to control the ruled, while also preventing this accumulated power from being abused?

The liberal-democratic solution to this problem is constitutionalism. Today, there are still a handful of liberal-democratic regimes that operate without a written and legally entrenched basic law. But they, too, organize government in a broadly constitutional way, subordinating citizens to the authority of government while simultaneously subordinating government to the authority of citizens. Liberal government is a remarkable innovation for this reason, because it is meant to solve the problem of anarchy *and* the problem of tyranny within a single and coherent system of rules.

While the police power gives government the capacity to control citizens, the countervailing power of the people over public officials is most clearly visible in the famous right to "throw the rascals out." While dependency on the people, in periodic elections, is the most effective hedge against tyranny, checks and balances can provide an important set of auxiliary precautions. This divide-and-rule strategy may prove democratically useful because the public at large is likely to be preoccupied with nonpolitical affairs and is, in any case, a highly diffuse body, difficult to keep mobilized and focused for any length of time. To compensate for its own inability to subject public officials to ongoing scrutiny, the democratic electorate creates divided government. The theory behind divided government, as it developed in the United States at the end of the eighteenth century, is not the libertarian dogma that government action is inevitably counterproductive. The underlying idea, rather, is that public officials will act more consistently in the interest of the public if they believe they are being scrutinized by rival politicians who, in turn, have clear incentives to alert otherwise distracted voters to gross public malfeasance and ineptitude. Checks and balances have been persuasively criticized on a number of grounds. But the separation of powers is potentially democratic in this simple sense. It can create a governmental power that, while strong enough to repress anarchy, will not fall into the opposite extreme of tyranny. Under favorable conditions, constitutionalism may help avoid tyranny by creating a system in which institutionally autonomous representatives of the people monitor each other and publicly report their findings, thus increasing the chances that rulers will be held accountable by the ruled.

## Passions, Constraint, and Deliberative Democracy

It is easy to understand why a democratic people would want to subject its rulers to the constraints of a relatively inflexible basic law. And when liberal constitutions function well, they help ensure that public officials, to some extent, govern under conditions laid down by the public at large. But why would a secular people, freed from the vise-grip of tradition, subject *itself* to binding constraints? Why would a modern democratic citizenry agree to a relatively strict amending formula, thereby limiting *its own* capacity to act however it happens to wish?

Citizens are willing to bind themselves, for the same reason that they are eager to bind their rulers: distrust. In liberal-democratic societies, ordinary people distrust themselves when acting collectively just as they mistrust themselves individually, because they know they have a tendency to make unwise decisions which they might live to regret. They are willing to accept limits on their own discretion if they perceive that these limits will improve the quality of the decisions that they eventually make.

A democratic constitution is an instrument of government. It is a way not only of protecting private rights but also of organizing the process of deliberation and decision making; it is a means of implementing the ideal of collective self-rule. An eighteenth-century liberal, such as Madison, used a simplified faculty psychology to dissolve the paradox of democracy: a democratic citizenry will submit itself voluntarily to enforceable restrictions on its own whim in order to ensure that its reason will outweigh its passion in the public realm. Autonomy cannot flourish in the absence of constraining rules because, freed from all restraints, a democratic public, like a royal sovereign, will fall victim to its own irrational impulses, incurring large long-term costs for the sake of small short-term benefits. Freedom, as Spinoza argued, means emancipation from the turbulent and myopic passions. To achieve a desirable clarity of mind, individuals and communities will willingly part with some degree of arbitrary discretion. More generally, binding rules can be accepted, consciously and voluntarily, because they *create valuable possibilities* that would otherwise not exist.

Early enemies of liberal democracy, such as Joseph de Maistre, asserted dogmatically that constitutionalism is impossible since the power to bind entails the power to loose, and therefore no community can voluntarily bind itself to enforceable restraints. Only religious subjects who believe that God authoritatively delivered their basic law, or tradition-bound peoples who never question inherited customs, can live acceptingly within the bounds of a stable constitutional framework. Because modern and secular citizens know perfectly well that they have *made* their constitution, they will have no inhibitions about casting it off when the first crisis strikes.

While intriguing, this argument fails to grasp the enabling or possibility-creating function of constitutional restraints. Relatively rigid constitutions can be, and have been, accepted democratically because of their *consequences,* not because of their *source.* A democratic people will submit itself voluntarily to enforceable limits on its own discretion because it wants not merely to have its way or express its untrammeled will but also to improve its thinking. A liberal constitution can improve the thinking of democratic citizens by the way it organizes the process of deliberating and deciding. One of the strongest passions that an individual is subject to, for instance, is the aversion to being criticized, contradicted, and exposed as a fool before an onlooking crowd. This abhorrence of public reproach presents a serious obstacle to learning, including the timely perception of oncoming dangers. Constitutionalism, in part, is meant to overcome this obstacle, to free people from the effects of a debilitating passion.

Communication rights, including most importantly the right to criticize democratically elected wielders of power, are productive, not merely protective. They are designed to help generate more intelligent solutions to collective problems. A majority will allow its own agents to be criticized in this way not only because it distrusts public officials, but also because it distrusts itself, or realizes that, up till now, it may have identified its own interests incorrectly and that it may need to change its mind in the light of new arguments and information. Desire can be irrational because, among other things, attention is always selective. A democratic people will acquiesce in a free-speech regime, however psychologically stressful, because it recognizes that the *pour et contre* of public debate can help overcome the natural blindsidedness of human thought. Freedom of speech, in political matters, helps shake a community free from ossified routines and liberate the public and its representatives from the excesses of fixated thought. Deliberative democracy, by preventing us from silencing our annoying critics, *compensates* for the disabling inflexibilities and obsessions of spontaneous thinking. The way a privatization of religion, the legal severance of church and state, may contribute to this same goal has been discussed in chapter 7.

Even "consumerist unbelievers," casually irreligious and lax about custom, will willingly submit to restrictive rules, if they believe that such rules, while sometimes emotionally trying, will shake them out of their ordinary torpor and bring to bear on collective problems talents that are strewn throughout the population and would otherwise lie unused. Citizens, who can reasonably wonder if they have been identifying their interests in an intelligent way, presumably prefer to make intelligent decisions (the term is relative) rather than foolhardy ones. They also want to prevent, or inhibit somewhat, the capture of public resources by clever private groups who know how to camouflage their partial interests as the common good. A well-designed constitution cannot solve such problems, but it can improve democracy's ability to deal with them, and ordinary citizens know it. Democratic citizens want to make good decisions today because, among other reasons, they realize that they will personally pay the costs of bad decisions tomorrow. Not ancestor worship, then, but an understandable concern for their future selves leads citizens in a liberal democracy to favor a system in which at least some of their mistakes can be corrected some of the time.

They embrace constitutionalism not only because it increases the probability of intelligent decision making, then, but also because it maximizes the opportunity for intelligent self-correction later on. The present electoral majority will submit to irritating criticism of its decisions by the opposition because it knows that it may want to change its mind in the future and that it needs to hear and consider, on an ongoing basis, possible reasons for doing so. Constitutional democracy, in short, is fallibilist democracy. It is neither voluntarist majoritarianism, designed to implement a preexistent will, nor the pious submission of the people to eternal verities handed down by God or elaborated slowly by a reverenced tradition. Constitutionalism is a technique. It assumes that the passions of men will not conform to the dictates of reason and justice without constraint. It is the way a democratic nation strives to make itself into a community that can continue to learn and thus adapt itself intelligently to unfamiliar circumstances as they arise.

# NOTES

## Introduction

1. John Stuart Mill, "De Tocqueville on Democracy in America," II, in John Stuart Mill, *Collected Works,* ed. J. M. Robson, vol. 18, *Essays on Politics and Society* (Toronto: University of Toronto Press, 1977), pp. 176–77.

2. *The Federalist Papers* (New York: Mentor, 1961), no. 15 (Alexander Hamilton), p. 106.

3. As the last item shows, constitutionalism will always be as much an ideal standard or unattainable goal as a political reality.

## Chapter 1

1. On non-Marxist writers who nevertheless use "liberalism" as a term of obloquy, see Stephen Holmes, *The Anatomy of Antiliberalism* (Cambridge: Harvard University Press, 1993).

2. Adam Smith, *An Inquiry into the Nature and Causes of the Wealth of Nations* (New York: Modern Library, 1937), pp. 11, 609.

3. John Locke, *Two Treatises of Government,* ed. Peter Laslett (Cambridge: Cambridge University Press, 1988), II, § 22.

4. Giovanni Sartori, *The Theory of Democracy Revisited* (Chatham, N.J.: Chatham House, 1987), p. 380.

5. This is not to deny that illiberal states may sometimes prove superior to liberal ones in certain domains—making the trains run on time, for instance.

6. Alexander Solzhenitsyn, *Warning to the West* (New York: Farrar, Straus & Giroux, 1976) and *A World Split Apart* (New York: Harper & Row, 1978).

7. Locke, *Two Treatises of Government,* II, § 42.

8. Émile Durkheim, *Leçons de sociologie* (Paris: Presses Universitaires de France, 1969), p. 96.

9. For instance, J. G. Merquior, *Liberalism: Old and New* (Boston: Twayne, 1991), p. 2.

10. Absolutism was the only practicable remedy to clerical oppression because only an all-powerful monarch could "keep the tribe of ecclesiastics in their place," enforcing a sharp dissociation of this-worldly and other-worldly authority. Far from being a despotic abuse of undivided power, Bayle believed, the Revocation of the Edict of Nantes symbolized Louis XIV's inability to enforce his sovereign will upon religious authorities. While further enfeebling the state, a policy of intolerance and persecution was already a sign of crippled sovereignty (Elisabeth Labrousse, *Bayle* [Oxford: Oxford University Press, 1983], pp. 75–86).

11. David Hume, "Of Commerce," in *Essays Moral, Political, and Literary* (Indianapolis: Liberty Classics, 1985), p. 262.

12. Immanuel Kant, "Idea for a Universal History," *Kant's Political Writings,*

trans. Thomas Nugent, ed. Hans Reiss (Cambridge: Cambridge University Press, 1970), p. 50.

13. Jean Bodin, *The Six Bookes of a Commonweal [Les six livres de la république],* trans. Robert Knolles, ed. K. D. McRae (Cambridge: Harvard University Press, 1962), bk. 3, chap. 7, p. 384.

14. *The Federalist Papers* (New York: Mentor, 1961), no. 1 (Alexander Hamilton), p. 35; no. 49 (James Madison), p. 317.

15. *Federalist Papers,* no. 30 (Hamilton), pp. 188–89; no. 21, p. 139.

16. William Blackstone, *Commentaries on the Laws of England* (Chicago: University of Chicago Press, 1977), bk. 2, chap. 1.

17. Mill, *Principles of Political Economy,* in John Stuart Mill, *Collected Works,* ed. J. M. Robson, vol. 3 (Toronto: University of Toronto Press, 1965), p. 949.

18. Max Weber, *Wirtschaft und Gesellschaft* (Tübingen: Mohr, 1972), p. 725.

19. John Rawls, *A Theory of Justice* (Cambridge: Harvard University Press, 1971), pp. 271–74; *Political Liberalism* (New York: Columbia University Press, 1993), p. 364.

20. "Pour les libéraux, l'homme—en générale et en moyenne—est un être égoiste et rationnel" (Maurice Flamant, *Le libéralisme* [Paris: PUF, 1979], p. 62).

21. Locke, *A Letter on Toleration,* ed. R. Klibauski and J. G. Gould (Oxford: Clarendon Press, 1968), p. 141.

22. Isaiah Berlin, *Four Essays on Liberty* (Oxford: Oxford University Press, 1969), pp. 118–72.

23. Wilhelm von Humboldt, *The Limits of State Action* (Cambridge: Cambridge University Press, 1965).

24. Quentin Skinner, "The Idea of Negative Liberty: Philosophical and Historical Perspectives," in Richard Rorty, J. B. Scheewind, and Quentin Skinner, eds., *Philosophy in History* (Cambridge: Cambridge University Press, 1984), pp. 193–221.

25. *Federalist Papers,* no. 51 (Madison), p. 325.

26. Judith Shklar, "The Liberalism of Fear," *Liberalism and the Moral Life,* ed. Nancy Rosenblum (Cambridge: Harvard University Press, 1989), pp. 21–38.

27. Locke, *Two Treatises of Government,* II, § 131.

28. *Federalist Papers,* no. 10 (Madison), p. 77.

29. For a critical analysis of the conservative saw that new reforms inevitably put old reforms in jeopardy, see Albert Hirschman, *The Rhetoric of Reaction* (Cambridge: Harvard University Press, 1992), pp. 81–132.

30. Locke, *Two Treatises of Government,* II, § 98.

31. Montesquieu, *The Spirit of the Laws,* trans. Thomas Nugent (New York: Hafner, 1949), vol. 1, p. 155; Blackstone, *Commentaries on the Laws of England,* vol. 1, p. 165.

32. Montesquieu, *Spirit of the Laws,* vol. 1, p. 154.

33. Locke, *Two Treatises of Government,* II, § 149.

34. John Dunn, *Locke* (Oxford: Oxford University Press, 1984), pp. 22–59.

35. *Federalist Papers,* no. 51 (Madison), p. 322.

36. Mill, "Considerations on Representative Government," in John Stuart Mill, *Collected Works,* ed. J. M. Robson, vol. 19, *Essays on Politics and Society* (Toronto: University of Toronto Press, 1977), p. 403.

37. Milton, *Areopagitica,* in *Complete Prose Works of John Milton* (New Haven: Yale University Press, 1959), vol. 2, p. 564.

38. Milton, *Areopagitica,* p. 490.

39. *Federalist Papers,* no. 63, p. 387; cf. ibid., no. 10, p. 80; no. 37, p. 227; no.

40, p. 253; no. 41, p. 260; no. 46, p. 294; no. 49, p. 313; no. 51, p. 321; no. 57, p. 351.

40. Spinoza, "The Ethics," in *The Chief Works of Benedict de Spinoza,* trans. R. H. M. Elwes (New York: Dover, 1955), vol. 2, part 4, appendix, sec. xvii, p. 239.

41. This last condition, it should be noted, excludes most forms of job security.

42. The reasons why economic inequality is treated differently than political and legal inequality have already been discussed. Recall, however, that liberal tolerance for economic inequality, justified by reference to the common benefits produced by a decentralized economy, tends to wane when vast accumulations of wealth begin to produce inequalities in political and legal realms.

43. *Federalist Papers,* no. 17 (Hamilton), p. 119.

## Chapter 2

1. Spinoza, *The Ethics* in *The Chief Works of Benedict de Spinoza,* vol. 2, ed. R. H. M. Elwes (New York: Dover, 1955), part 4, Prop. LIV, p. 223.

2. For the contrary and, I believe, implausible claim that the rationality hypothesis needs no modification to take account of such mind-boggling passions, simply because a perfectly irrational person will, all things being equal, buy less of a product if the price goes up, see Gary Becker, "Irrational Behavior and Economic Theory," *Journal of Political Economy* 70, 1 (February 1962): 1–13.

3. George Stigler, "Smith's Travels on the Ship of State," in A. Skinner and T. Wilson, eds., *Essays on Adam Smith* (Oxford: Clarendon Press, 1975), pp. 237, 244, 245, 246.

4. Ibid., p. 239.

5. Thus, Jacob Viner, too, is mistaken when he argues that, in the *Wealth of Nations,*"every possible impulse and motive to action is included under self-interest except a deliberate intention to promote the welfare of others than one's self." Viner, "Adam Smith and Laissez Faire," *The Long View and the Short: Studies in Economic Theory and Policy* (Glencoe, Ill.: Free Press, 1958), p. 227.

6. Adam Smith, *An Inquiry into the Nature and Causes of the Wealth of Nations* (New York: Modern Library, 1937), pp. 582, my emphasis, 362, my emphasis, 365, 553, 751.

7. Ibid., pp. 279, 389.

8. J. A. W. Gunn, "'Interest Will Not Lie': A Seventeenth-Century Political Maxim," *Journal of the History of Ideas* 29 (1968): p. 558; although Smith relied extensively on the calculation-impulsiveness polarity, he also wrote lucidly about subrational emotional *dispositions*—toward envy, for example, or xenophobia or indecisiveness or sycophancy—which endure over time and cannot be considered impromptu or impulsive.

9. Thomas Macaulay, "Mill's Essay on Government: Utilitarian Logic and Politics," in J. Lively and J. Rees, eds., *Utilitarian Logic and Politics* (Oxford: Clarendon Press, 1978), p. 125.

10. David Hume, *Enquiries concerning the Human Understanding and concerning the Principles of Morals,* ed. L. A. Selby-Bigge (Oxford: Clarendon Press, 1966), p. 298; cf. Third Earl of Shaftesbury (Anthony Ashley Cooper), *Characteristicks* (London: J. Purser, 1737–38), vol. 1, p. 115; Francis Hutcheson, *An Essay on the Nature and Conduct of the Passions and Affections,* 3d ed. (1742; rpt., Gainesville, Fla.: Scholars' Facsimiles and Reprints, 1969), p. ix.

11. Hume, *Enquiries,* p. 296.

12. David Hume, "Of the Dignity or Meanness of Human Nature," in *Essays: Moral, Political, and Literary* (Indianapolis: Liberty Classics, 1985), p. 85; cf. Shaftesbury, *Characteristicks,* vol. 1, p. 120.

13. The distinction between calculating and noncalculating behavior does not correspond neatly to the distinction between interested and disinterested behavior. As economists (see note 2) love to point out, altruists, too, weigh costs and benefits and try to allocate scarce resources in an efficient manner. Similarly, the desire to taste the inferiority of others is not self-interested in a narrow sense, but it can nevertheless set in motion the most elaborate of Machiavellian calculations. Conversely, the "pleasure principle" seems to refer to a form of self-interested motivation that is almost wholly free of rational forethought or the comparison of alternatives. Disinterested motives can be calculating and interested motives can be something close to "second nature." In what follows, I restrict myself largely to the starkest contrast, that between the calculating pursuit of private advantage and noncalculating behavior that is damaging to one's self.

14. Hume, *Enquiries,* p. 301.

15. Ibid., pp. 216, 234n.

16. We may take pleasure in expressing an emotion or conforming to a norm, according to Hume, but this pleasure is secondary and derivative, not primary or causally decisive. "We get the pleasure because we do the action; we do not do the action because we get the pleasure" (ibid., p. 85).

17. Ibid., p. 226.

18. Ibid., p. 218; in the same vein, Hutcheson mentions "disinterested hatred" (*Nature and Conduct of the Passions,* p. 105).

19. Politically, Samuel Johnson was no liberal and certainly not a Humean skeptic; but he nevertheless displayed an enormous, we might even say liberal, range of human sympathies. Exactly like Hume and Smith, moreover, he claimed that "the great law of mutual benevolence is oftener violated by envy than by interest." Johnson, *Rambler,* no. 183 (17 December 1751), in *Rasselas, Poems and Selected Prose,* ed. Bertrand H. Bronson (New York: Holt, Rinehart, & Winston, 1958), p. 125. Crazily enough, an envious man will pay steep costs to ruin another's accumulated assets even without expecting any subsequent benefits for himself.

20. Hume, *Enquiries,* pp. 251n., 302; "Of the Delicacy of Taste and Passion," in *Essays,* p. 4.

21. Adam Smith, *The Theory of Moral Sentiments,* ed. D. D. Raphael and A. L. Macfie (Oxford: Clarendon Press, 1976), pp. 34–43.

22. Ibid., p. 40; Smith's "unsocial passions" are modeled on Shaftesbury's "unnatural affections" that "lead neither to a publick nor a private Good" (*Characteristicks,* vol. 2, p. 163).

23. Hume, *Enquiries,* p. 301, my emphasis; ibid., p. 281; ibid., p. 302.

24. Montesquieu, *The Spirit of the Laws,* trans. Thomas Nugent (New York: Hafner, 1949), vol. 1, bk. 12, chap. 4, p. 186.

25. John Locke, *Two Treatises of Government,* ed. Peter Laslett (Cambridge: Cambridge University Press, 1988), II, § 230; see, in addition, Robert Burton, *The Anatomy of Melancholy* (New York: Farrar & Reinholt, 1927), pp. 231–33.

26. Hume, "Of Parties in General," in *Essays,* pp. 54–63; in what follows, I have also drawn upon "Of the Parties of Great Britain," in *Essays,* pp. 64–72.

27. Hume, "Of Parties in General," pp. 56, 58; "Where difference of interest is removed, whimsical and unaccountable factions often arise from personal favour or enmity" (Hume, "Idea of a Perfect Commonwealth," in *Essays,* p. 529); Madison

makes the very same observation about "the propensity of mankind to fall into mutual animosities" (*The Federalist Papers,* [New York: Mentor, 1961], no. 10, p. 79).

28. Hume, *Enquiries,* p. 275.

29. Hume, "Of Parties in General," p. 55.

30. Hume, *Enquiries,* p. 224.

31. Hume, "Of Parties in General," p. 57.

32. Ibid., p. 301.

33. Ibid., p. 59.

34. The *relative* harmlessness of self-interest was an important thesis of all liberal theorists; people are rarely so innocently engaged as when they are making money, it seems obvious, for at least they are not then brutalizing, torturing, and murdering their imagined enemies or detractors.

35. Hume, "Of the Parties of Great Britain," p. 614; this is a nice reversal of the contemptuous view, expressed by prebourgeois elites, that "the great mob of mankind" has only interests, while noble pride, moral insight, and so forth are reserved for the refined upper classes.

36. Ibid., p. 65; note that a reductionist approach to motivation, stipulating that all behavior is ultimately rational and arises from self-interest, would block this sort of causal analysis of the relation between different sorts of motive.

37. Hume, "Of Parties in General," p. 58.

38. Ibid., p. 63; cf. *Federalist Papers,* no. 10 (Madison), p. 79.

39. Hume, "Whether the British Government Inclines Most to Absolute Monarchy or to a Republic," in *Essays,* p. 51; the domination of opinion over interest is another liberal commonplace; cf. "One person with a belief, is a social power equal to ninety-nine who have only interests" (Mill, "Considerations on Representative Government," in John Stuart Mill, *Collected Works,* ed. J. M. Robson, vol. 19, *Essays on Politics and Society* [Toronto: University of Toronto Press, 1977], p. 381).

40. Hume, "Of Parties in General," p. 59.

41. Ibid., p. 63.

42. Hume, "Of the Parties of Great Britain," p. 610.

43. "Born originals, how come it to pass that we die copies?" in Edward Young, "Conjectures of Original Composition" (1759), in *The Complete Works* (London: W. Tegg & Co., 1854), vol. 2, p. 561.

44. David Hume, *A Treatise of Human Nature* (Oxford: Clarendon Press, 1978), bk. II, part 1, sec. xi, p. 316.

45. Hume, "Of the Parties of Great Britain," p. 610.

46. Ibid., p. 68.

47. Albert O. Hirschman, *The Passions and the Interests: Political Arguments for Capitalism before Its Triumph* (Princeton: Princeton University Press, 1977); for Hume's own contrast between calm and violent passions, see the *Treatise,* II, i, p. 276.

48. Admittedly, Hirschman may exaggerate somewhat the novelty of this idea. There does not seem to be anything specifically modern or protocapitalist about the attempt to repress violent passions by appealing to material interests. Archaic legal codes—hinted at, for example, by the arbitration-like procedure described in Homer's shield scene (*Iliad* 18, 497–508)—were typically concerned not with the punishment of the guilty but rather with establishing monetary equivalents for broken teeth, gouged eyes, and amputated fingers. Individuals were encouraged not to retaliate for injury but to come to the king's court where the culprit might be made to pay an indemnity. The long history of *wergild* compensation sug-

gests that, well before the seventeenth century, Europeans were hoping to replace the blood feud by the cash nexus. While premodern Europeans did not have the language (although some people might be impressed by the coincidence that the word *interest* originally meant compensation for damages), they did have the idea of overcoming the passions with the interests. Hirschman might plausibly respond, of course, that a recognition of the advantages of compensation over retribution cannot ultimately be equated with the modern celebration of the salutary side effects of materialism and acquisitiveness.

49. Shaftesbury, *Characteristicks,* vol. 1, p. 116.

50. According to Marchamont Needham, "if you can apprehend wherein a man's interest to any particular game on foot doth consist, you may surely know, if the man be prudent, whereabout to have him, that is, how to judge of his design." *Interest Will Not Lie, or a View of England's True Interest* (1659), cited in J. A. W. Gunn, *Politics and the Public Interest in the Seventeenth Century* (London: Routledge & Kegan Paul, 1969), p. 44.

51. "He that falls by the attacks of interest is torn by hungry tigers; he may discover and resist his enemies. He that perishes in the ambushes of envy, is destroyed by unknown and invisible assailants, and dies like a man suffocated by a poisonous vapour, without knowledge of his danger, or possibility of contest." Johnson, *Rambler,* no. 183 (17 December 1751), in *Rasselas, Poems and Selected Prose,* p. 126; for an argument that the wholly nonenvious man, who has probably never existed, is the best maximizer of his own utility, see Jon Elster, "Envy in Social Life," *Strategy and Choice,* ed. Richard J. Zeckhauser (Cambridge: MIT Press, 1991), pp. 49–82.

52. R. H. Tawney, *Religion and the Rise of Capitalism* (New York: Harcourt, Brace, & World, 1926).

53. Some of Hirschman's other writings have proved particularly useful in this regard, notably his analysis of "the tunnel effect," whereby people will tolerate disparities in well-being when they believe that their turn is coming up next, in "The Changing Tolerance for Income Inequality in the Course of Economic Development," in *Essays in Trespassing: Economics to Politics and Beyond* (Cambridge: Cambridge University Press, 1981), pp. 39–58.

54. Compare the shorter and sweeter list given in Joseph Butler, *The Analogy of Religion* (Oxford: Clarendon Press, 1896), p. 121n.

55. In the *Wealth of Nations,* Smith also explains how three historically powerful moral codes have successfully repressed the taste for conduct conducive to material gain. He discusses (1) the aristocratic belief that economic effort is defiling, (2) military traditions of unquestioning obedience, and (3) religious commitment to otherworldliness and self-abnegation. Moreover, the third book of the *Wealth of Nations* revolves around the distinction between two types of character, between the maximizer and the nonmaximizer, between the calculating and the noncalculating spirit. By temperament, inclination, and training, the nobles of Europe are unsuited to improve the land. Heedlessness of profit is built into their character or "turn of mind." They do not scrutinize their preferences and resources and, on this basis, rationally choose a noncalculating life. They simply have no taste for calculation (*Wealth of Nations,* pp. 364, 279, 384–85, 379, 389, 578–79).

56. Indeed, the entire argument of the *Wealth of Nations* depends on an underlying contrast between interest and envy. Smith denounced the "invidious and malignant project" whereby Britain excluded other nations from the colony trade; for by beggaring its neighbors, a country actually impoverishes itself (p. 561). Mer-

chants supported trade barriers because of "private interest," but governments and people were drawn to mercantilism by motives which, while no more admirable, were *much less* rational. Politicians, for instance, tended to be mercantilists not by interest but by "national prejudice and animosity" (p. 441). Smith's polemical intent here was not merely to turn attention from short-run to long-run interests. More profoundly, he hoped to draw the political classes of Great Britain away from envy and unreasoning animosity and toward interest—away from the ideal of relative and toward that of absolute wealth.

57. Smith, *Theory of Moral Sentiments,* pp. 52–53; cf. Hume, *Enquiries,* p. 247.

58. Francis Bacon, "Of Death," in *The Essayes or Counsels, Civill and Morall,* ed. Michael Kiernan (Cambridge: Harvard University Press, 1985), pp. 9–10; Bacon describes vengefulness, in particular, as a bewitching, noncalculating, and self-destructive passion: "a Man that studieth *Revenge,* keepes his owne Wounds greene, which otherwise would heale, and doe well" ("Of Revenge," ibid., p. 17); similarly: "Anger is like Ruine, which breakes it Selfe, upon that it falls" ("Of Anger," ibid., p. 170); envy, "the vilest Affection, and the most depraved," arises only when we compare ourselves to others ("Of Envy," ibid., pp. 31, 29); we poison our own existence by focusing obsessively—as we do not have to do—on a person whose success has no causal relation to our lack of success; what offends most, in any case, is not inequality but leapfrogging, seeing others advance while we stand still (p. 28); it is palpably absurd, but nevertheless people do "thinke other Mens harmes, a Redemption of their owne Sufferings" (p. 28). Finally, Bacon also discusses the irrational tendency to believe that an achievement which has cost us a great deal of effort must therefore be extremely valuable. *The New Organon,* ed. Fulton H. Anderson (Indianapolis: Bobbs-Merrill, 1960), p. 54 (LIV).

59. While Aristotle, for example, believed that human beings were often calculating and selfish (Aristotle, *Politics,* 1261b, 34–35), he also distinguished between morally praiseworthy and morally despicable forms of self-love or *philautia* (*Nicomachean Ethics,* 1168a, 28–1169b, 1), and devoted careful attention to the unreasoning and self-forgetful passions (*Rhetoric,* bk. 2, 1377b–90b); particularly noteworthy is his claim that a person exclusively concerned with his private advantage could never successfully insult another, because social slights must be seen to be gratuitous, not instrumental (1378b–79a); see, also, the classic treatise on the passions in Thomas Aquinas, *Summa Theologica* (Westminster, Md.: Christian Classics, 1948), vol. 2, pp. 691–790 (pt. 1–2, questions 22–48).

60. D. D. Raphael and A. L. Macfie, "Introduction," in Smith, *Theory of Moral Sentiments,* p. 5.

61. Diogenes Laertius, "Zeno," in *Lives of Eminent Philosophers,* trans. R. D. Hicks (Cambridge: Harvard University Press, 1971), vol. 2, pp. 214–23 (vii, 110–17).

62. Cicero, *Tusculan Disputations,* trans. J. E. King (Cambridge: Harvard University Press, 1971), p. 345 (IV.7).

63. Martha Nussbaum, "The Stoics on the Extirpation of the Passions," *Apeiron,* 20, no. 2 (Fall 1987): 129–77.

64. Cicero, *Tusculan Disputations,* p. 349 (IV.9).

65. Seneca, "On Anger," in *Moral Essays,* trans. John Basore (Cambridge: Harvard University Press, 1970), vol. 1, p. 107 (I.1).

66. The irrational craving for approval and the irrational dread of insults, too, lead individuals to neglect their own well-being (Seneca, "On Firmness," in *Moral Essays,* 103 [xix]). People like to have their interests satisfied, of course, but

they prefer to have their vanity caressed. They are much more concerned that you remember their names than that you give them material assistance; Quintus Cicero (attribution doubtful), "Handbook of Electioneering," in Cicero, *Letters to Quintus, Brutus, and Others,* trans. Mary Henderson (Cambridge: Harvard University Press, 1979), p. 779 (41–42); also: "people are charmed more by looks and words than by the substantial benefit received" (p. 783 [46]). Smith was simply echoing this old tradition when he commented on the all-conquering intensity of mankind's desire "to be observed, to be attended to, to be taken notice of with sympathy, complacency, and approbation" (*Theory of Moral Sentiments,* p. 50), a desire that both explains and occasionally overrides the longing to better one's material condition.

67. Stoic "apathy" is not complete impassivity or insensibility but merely the absence of uncontrollable and irrational impulses. J. M. Rist, *Stoic Philosophy* (Cambridge: Cambridge University Press, 1969), p. 35.

68. Nussbaum, "The Stoics on the Extirpation of the Passions," p. 161.

69. This pair of motivations is discussed by economists today as aversion to, or preference for, risk.

70. Thomas Schelling, *The Strategy of Conflict* (Cambridge: Harvard University Press, 1960), p. 143.

71. Jon Elster, "Sadder but Wiser? Rationality and the Emotions," *Social Science Information* 24, no. 2 (1985): 381.

72. Hume notes that the "amours" of Henry IV of France "frequently hurt his interest" (*Enquiries,* p. 258); in the Western code of love, there seems to be a powerful taboo against the appearance of economic exchange between lovers; thus, according to Michel de Pure, "l'intérêt ne sert jamais de rien à l'amour" and "l'intérêt est impuissant pour l'amour; il est sterile et ne produit rien dans un coeur" (*La prétieuse ou le mystère des ruelles* [1657; Paris: Droz, 1939], vol. 3, p. 78).

73. Some individuals become so upset when cheated that they will incur a significant financial loss to eradicate the unpleasant sensation of having been fleeced. This psychological attachment to the norm of "justice," if an individual publicizes it well enough, may deter some prospective con artists. But it may nevertheless be pathological, and should therefore not be adduced as decisive evidence of the nobility of the human spirit.

74. John Trenchard and Thomas Gordon, *Cato's Letters* (New York: Da Capo Press, 1971), vol. 2, p. 52 (5 August 1721).

75. Leo Strauss, *The Political Philosophy of Hobbes* (Chicago: University of Chicago Press, 1973).

76. Galatians 5:26.

77. Hume, "Of Superstition and Enthusiasm," in *Essays,* p. 77.

78. Romans 8:6–7.

79. 2 Timothy 3:2.

80. Augustine, *The City of God,* trans. Philip Levine (Cambridge: Harvard University Press, 1966), 4:404 (XIV, p. 28).

81. Hume, "Of Superstitions and Enthusiasm," in *Essays,* p. 75.

82. Voltaire, *Letters on England* (Harmondsworth: Penguin, 1980), pp. 120–45.

83. Curiosity was sometimes regarded as a Christian sin. We should therefore note that the word *interesting,* too, became fashionable around 1700. Hume and Smith repeatedly state that we can be legitimately "interested" in other people even when our "interests" are not at stake. News in general, for example, is "ex-

tremely interesting even to those whose welfare is not immediately engaged" (*Enquiries,* p. 223).

84. Karl Marx, "On the Jewish Question," *The Marx-Engels Reader,* ed. Robert Tucker (New York: Norton, 1978), p. 52; it seems that the notion of "long-term interest" was originally introduced by theologians to refer to the "pursuit of happiness" in the afterlife as opposed to concern for short-run interests here below.

85. Thomas à Kempis, *Imitation of Christ* (Harmondsworth: Penguin, 1984), p. 137; "Whosoever will come after me," said Jesus, "let him deny himself" (Mark 8:34).

86. Thomas à Kempis, *Imitation of Christ,* p. 33.

87. Walter Hilton, *The Stairway of Perfection* (New York: Doubleday, 1979), pp. 116–18. Despite the Christian injunction to "love thy neighbor," people were generally asked to love others not for themselves, but only as "carriers"—we should love not so much others as God in them.

88. Hume, *Enquiries,* p. 270.

89. Writing of Thomas à Kempis, Tocqueville remarked: "It is not *healthy* to detach oneself from the earth, from its interests, from its concerns, even from its pleasures, when they are honest, to the extent the author teaches; and those who live according to what they read in such a book [*Imitation of Christ*] cannot fail to lose everything that constitutes public virtues in acquiring certain private virtues" (letter to Louis de Kergolay, 4 August 1857, in Alexis de Tocqueville, *Selected Letters on Politics and Society* [Berkeley: University of California Press, 1985], p. 357).

90. Mill, "Considerations on Representative Government," p. 407.

91. Interest in others may be stimulated, for example, by a realistic reminder of the ephemeralness of one's own self: "all selfish interests must be terminated by death" ("Utilitarianism," in John Stuart Mill, *Collected Works,* ed. J. M. Robson, vol. 10, *Essays on Ethics, Religion and Society* [Toronto: University of Toronto Press, 1969], p. 215). A similarly detached and objective view may explain Rawls's striking claim that "rational agents approach being psychopathic when their interests are solely in benefits to themselves" (John Rawls, *Political Liberalism* [New York: Columbia University Press, 1993], p. 51).

92. Mill, "Considerations on Representative Government," p. 410; Mill also emphasizes the therapeutic value of efforts to better one's condition: "those who, while desiring what others possess, put no energy into striving for it, are either incessantly grumbling that fortune does not do for them what they do not attempt to do for themselves, or overflowing with envy and ill-will towards those who possess what they would like to have" (ibid., p. 408).

93. "It is love of self that encourages love of others" (Voltaire, *Letters on England,* p. 128).

94. "Intérêt," in *Encyclopédie, ou Dictionnaire raisonné des sciences, des arts et des métiers* (Neufchastel: Faulche, 1765), vol. 8, pp. 818–19; for polemical reasons, the author accepts a purely negative definition of the word "interest" (as gross selfishness based on a neglect of others and indifference to the rules of justice), reserving wholly positive connotations, however, for "self-love."

95. Hirschman, *Passions and Interests,* p. 16; Dale Van Kley, "Pierre Nicole, Jansenism, and the Morality of Enlightened Self-Interest," in Alan Kors and Paul Korshin, eds., *Anticipations of the Enlightenment in England, France, and Germany* (Philadelphia: University of Pennsylvania Press, 1987), pp. 69–85.

96. Spinoza, *The Ethics,* part 4, prop. XXII, pp. 203–4.

97. This idea can be traced back at least to Erasmus, and possibly to Cicero.

98. Cf. "the Affection toward Self-Good, may be a good Affection, or an ill-one" (Shaftesbury, *Characteristicks,* vol. 2, p. 24). Consider also in this regard Rousseau's famous contrast between, on the one hand, a sickly and culturally induced *amour-propre* and, on the other, a wholesome and biologically original *amour de soi* in "Discours sur l'origine de l'inégalité," in *Oeuvres complètes,* vol. 3, ed. Bernard Gagnebin and Marcel Raymond (Paris: Pléiade, 1964), pp. 219–20.

99. I am thinking, of course, of the butcher, the brewer, and the baker. But are their hearts really emptied of all motives except self-interest? Perhaps. The merchant who does not ask what the traffic will bear will soon be out of business; he will not be able to pay a rent equivalent to the value of his location, or competitive wages. On examination, however, Smith's language proves ambivalent. He may be making no claim about actual motives, after all, but only about knowable and predictable motives: "*We address ourselves,* not to their humanity but to their self-love" (*Wealth of Nations,* p. 14, my emphasis). In a commercial society based on an extensive division of labor, we are all involved in long chains of interdependence with people whose characters we will never have an opportunity to judge. Smith's attitude toward self-interest, in other words, may well have been misinterpreted in the same manner as Machiavelli's remarks about the essential wickedness of man. Machiavelli did not advance an empirical generalization but rather a prudential maxim. It was prudent for the Prince to expect the worst. This reading of Smith as a worst-case theorist is also suggested by Hume's claim that the precept "every man must be supposed a knave" is "true in politics" but "false in fact" ("Of the Independency of Parliament," in *Essays,* p. 43). Our belief that the butcher, the brewer, and the baker are motivated solely by self-interest may be similarly true in the market, while false in fact.

100. Albert O. Hirschman, "The Concept of Interest: From Euphemism to Tautology," in *Rival Views of Market Society* (New York: Viking, 1986), pp. 35–55.

101. Trenchard and Gordon, *Cato's Letters,* vol. 4, p. 96 (23 February 1722).

102. Mill, "Considerations on Representative Government," p. 406; in other words, the concept of interest prepared the way for the radical egalitarian claim that "the interests of the members of the community matter, and matter equally" (Ronald Dworkin, "In Defense of Equality," *Social Philosophy and Policy,* 1 [1983]: 24).

103. R. Hooker, *Of the Laws of Ecclesiastical Polity* (London: Everyman, 1954), vol. 1, p. 192 (I, X, 6); as mentioned in note 35, it was generally believed that the upper classes alone could feel and act on exalted and dangerous passions such as pride (cf. Hirschman, *Passions and Interests,* pp. 108–12; also, "Concept of Interest: From Euphemism to Tautology," pp. 40–41).

104. James Harrington, "The Commonwealth of Oceana," in *The Political Works of James Harrington,* ed. John Pocock (Cambridge: Cambridge University Press, 1977), p. 173.

105. Locke, *Two Treatises of Government,* II, § 165.

106. J. A. W. Gunn, *Politics and the Public Interest in the Seventeenth Century* (London: Routledge & Kegan Paul, 1969).

107. Mill, "Considerations on Representative Government," p. 377.

108. Alexis de Tocqueville, *Democracy in America,* trans. George Lawrence (New York: Doubleday, 1969), p. 247.

109. Trenchard and Gordon, *Cato's Letters,* vol. 2, p. 22 (8 July 1721). The earlier Hobbesian claim that monarchy was the best system for making the interests of the ruler coincide with the interests of the ruled (Thomas Hobbes, *Leviathan*

[Oxford: Clarendon Press, 1965], p. 144 [chap. 19]) was an open invitation to such a democratic response.

110. About merchants seeking to sell dear, Smith noted that "their interest is, in this respect, directly opposite to most of the great body of the people" (*Wealth of Nations,* p. 461); about employers and employees, he wrote: "their interests are by no means the same" (p. 66); for other nonharmonizable conflicts of interest, see ibid., pp. 361–62, 460, 568, 578–79, 582, 603, 605, 625, 765.

111. Trenchard and Gordon, *Cato's Letters,* vol. 2, p. 53.

112. Locke, *Two Treatises of Government,* II, § 98.

113. *Federalist Papers,* no. 51, p. 323; no. 10, pp. 79–80; no. 37, p. 230 (Madison); *Federalist Papers,* no. 36, p. 217 (Hamilton).

114. Trenchard and Gordon, *Cato's Letters,* vol. 2, p. 232 (6 January 1721); according to Madison, "the people can never wilfully betray their own interests; but they may possibly be betrayed by the representatives of the people" (*Federalist Papers,* no. 63, p. 386).

115. Locke, *Two Treatises of Government,* II, § 111; cf. *Federalist Papers,* no. 4 (Jay), p. 46.

116. *Federalist Papers,* no. 52 (Madison), p. 327; see also Locke, *Two Treatises of Government,* II, § 216.

117. Trenchard and Gordon, *Cato's Letters,* vol. 3, p. 15 (17 March 1721).

118. James Mill, *An Essay on Government* (Indianapolis: Bobbs-Merrill, 1955), p. 82.

119. Mill, "Bentham," in John Stuart Mill, *Collected Works,* ed. J. M. Robson, vol. 10, *Essays on Ethics, Religion and Society* (Toronto: University of Toronto Press, 1969), p. 109.

120. Mill, "De Tocqueville on Democracy in America" I, in John Stuart Mill, *Collected Works,* ed. J. M. Robson, vol. 13, *Essays on Politics and Society* (Toronto: University of Toronto Press, 1977), p. 71.

121. Mill, "Bentham," p. 109.

122. Mill, "Considerations on Representative Government," p. 402.

123. Smith, *Wealth of Nations,* p. 651.

124. Mill, "Thoughts on Parliamentary Reform," in John Stuart Mill, *Collected Works,* ed. J. M. Robson, vol. 19, *Essays on Politics and Society* (Toronto: University of Toronto Press, 1977), p. 330.

125. Locke, *Two Treatises of Government,* II, § 57, my emphasis. Hume says that the justice system will force men "to consult their own real and permanent interests" ("Of the Origin of Government," *Essays,* p. 38). As John Rawls reformulates Locke's point, "interests requiring the violation of justice have no value" (*A Theory of Justice* [Cambridge: Harvard University Press, 1971], p. 31). I interpret these passages as telling evidence against Isaiah Berlin's thesis that political liberals steadfastly refuse to distinguish between "higher" and "lower" selves (Isaiah Berlin, *Four Essays on Liberty* [Oxford University Press, 1969], pp. 131–34).

126. Hume, "Of the Origin of Government," *Essays,* p. 38; *Federalist Papers,* no. 10 (Madison), p. 78.

127. That Locke does not build his political theory on the natural or given wants of mankind is also made clear in the following passage: "principles of Actions indeed there are lodged in Men's Appetites, but these are so far from being innate Moral Principles, that if they were left to their full swing, they would carry Men to the over-turning of all Morality" (John Locke, *An Essay Concerning Human Understanding,* ed. Peter Nidditch [Oxford: Clarendon Press, 1975], p. 75).

128. Mill even writes of the "inherent tendency of man" to disguise his self-interest as a duty and a virtue. What concerns him is not imposture, incidentally, but the way individuals deceive themselves—"the artifices by which we persuade ourselves that we are not yielding to our selfish inclinations when we are" ("Bentham," pp. 109–10).

129. Locke, *Two Treatises of Government,* II, § 12.

## Chapter 3

1. For instance, Leo Strauss, *Natural Right and History* (Chicago: University of Chicago Press, 1953), pp. 166–202; C. B. MacPherson, *The Political Theory of Possessive Individualism* (Oxford: Oxford University Press, 1962), pp. 9–106.

2. *The English Works of Thomas Hobbes,* ed. William Molesworth (London: John Bohn, 1839–45, reprint 1966), vol. 4, p. 411.

3. An interesting parallel could be drawn between Charles II's wary attitude toward *Behemoth* in 1668 and Louis XIV's refusal to lift an ecclesiastic ban on another powerful expression of seventeenth-century anticlericalism, Molière's *Tartuffe,* between 1664 and 1669.

4. All parenthetical citations refer to Thomas Hobbes, *Behemoth or the Long Parliament* (Chicago: University of Chicago Press, 1991).

5. The claim that, in *Behemoth,* Hobbes "treated the war as an attempt to destroy the old constitution and replace it with one more favorable to the new market interests" (MacPherson, *Political Theory of Possessive Individualism,* p. 65) is baseless.

6. As permanent features of human nature, of course, irrational passions cannot, all alone, provide an explanation of why a civil war broke out in England only in the 1640s and not earlier or later. Attention must also be paid, as we shall see, to the unique circumstances of the time.

7. Summarizing recent scholarship, Norman Habel reports that "Behemoth" is now identified as (a) "the red Hippopotamus," i.e., "a symbol of the wicked to be hunted and conquered"; (b) "a symbol of the mighty historical enemies of Israel"; (c) a symbol, together with Leviathan, of "the forces of chaos which are overcome by Baal in Canaanite tradition"; and (d) a mortal creature like Job (*The Book of Job: A Commentary* [Philadelphia: Westminster Press, 1985], pp. 557–58). In rabbinical literature, too, "the monster Behemoth, a spirit of the desert, is associated with Leviathan. The Hebrew demons could cause illness, death, pollution, and sins both moral and ritual" (Jeffrey Burton Russell, *The Devil: Perceptions of Evil from Antiquity to Primitive Christianity* [Ithaca, N.Y.: Cornell University Press, 1977], p. 216). It is not altogether clear that Hobbes himself gave the title "Behemoth" to his book on the civil war. For a discussion of the inconclusive evidence on this question, see the excellent essay by Royce MacGillivray, "Thomas Hobbes's History of the English Civil War: A Study of *Behemoth,*" *Journal for the History of Ideas* 31, no. 2 (April 1970): pp. 184–85.

8. "In the language of Hobbes, Leviathan is the only possible corrective of Behemoth" (C. E. Vaughan, *Studies in the History of Political Philosophy before and after Rousseau* [New York: Russell & Russell, 1960], vol. 1, p. 53).

9. Hobbes, *English Works,* vol. 5, p. 27.

10. This is the title of part 4 of *Leviathan,* which is concerned with ecclesiastical imposture.

11. According to MacGillivray, "'Behemoth' is, etymologically, plural" ("Thomas Hobbes's History of the English Civil War," p. 185).

12. Hobbes, "Philosophical Rudiments concerning Government and Society," *English Works,* vol. 2, p. 38.

13. Hobbes, *Leviathan* (Harmondsworth: Penguin, 1986), part 2, chap. 29, p. 371.

14. Ibid., Introduction, p. 83.

15. According to Hobbes, the Augustinian invocation of free will, meant to solve the dilemma of theodicy, was also designed to increase ecclesiastical power: "Because there must be some ground for the justice of the eternal torment of the damned; perhaps it is this, that men's wills and propensions are not (they think) in the hands of God, but of themselves; and in this also I see somewhat conducing to the authority of the Church" (42). The sly clerical attempt to attain power by inducing irrational guilt is discussed below.

16. Here are some nonreligious examples of Hobbes's cynical perspective on human nature: London merchants supported the rebellion because they thought a change in government would increase their profits (4). Indeed, many participants "longed for a war" for the sake of riches and land, as if warfare were a private business deal, as well as a distracting escapade (4, 115). The Scots did not invade England in response to political grievances (e.g., Laud's imposition of the Anglican prayer book), but solely "with a promise of reward and hope of plunder" (31). Similarly: "There were in the army a great number (if not the greatest part) that aimed only at rapine and sharing the lands and goods of their enemies" (136). Taking precautions against free riders, in a literal sense, "the plundering foot" at one siege "kept the gates shut, lest the horse should enter and have a share of the booty" (171).

17. Along the same lines, the Parliamentarians "were resolved to take from [the King] the sovereign power to themselves" (83).

18. Hobbes exaggerates the relative importance of self-interest for an important moral reason, of course. As already mentioned, political theorists traditionally divided humanity into two groups: a vast majority, motivated by lowly self-interest, and elites, propelled by higher ideals such as glory or the common good. (See chap. 2, note 103.) When Hobbes writes of universal self-interest, he means the stress to fall on *universal.* He is universalizing, so to speak, the morality of the common man. His disproportionate emphasis on self-preservation is profoundly egalitarian or majoritarian, therefore. The goals of traditional elites—to rule, or to taste superiority, etc.—are stiffly rebuffed. Hobbes believed that most people were pitiable chumps, but he nevertheless wrote sincerely on their behalf. He allied himself unswervingly with the "anti-violence interest group" (Arthur Bentley, *The Process of Government* [Bloomington, Ind.: Principia, 1935], p. 361) comprising the vast majority of the population.

19. *Leviathan,* part 1, chap. 5, pp. 116, 115.

20. Ibid., part 1, chap. 6, p. 129.

21. Cf. *Leviathan,* part 1, chap. 11, p. 166.

22. Ibid., part 2, chap. 25, p. 309.

23. On the characteristic human folly of destruction without construction, see also pp. 78–79, 109, 192.

24. This usefully simple list can be supplemented by religious or political *doctrines* and psychological *identification* with leaders or groups.

25. Interestingly, Hobbes expressed moral revulsion at Pym for his "knavery

and ignoble shifts" (38); that is, for being a Machiavellian calculator rather than a man of unbending principle.

26. Parliament hoped to dishonor the King by forcing him publicly to betray his friends (81).

27. "They were Presbyterians," he explains, "id est, cruel" (133); the Gunpowder Plot was "the most horrid act that ever had been heard of before" (20); Cromwell's executions in Ireland were "horrid" (163); and "condign punishment" (86–88) is but "cruelty" well liked.

28. Even though he elsewhere defines tyranny as but monarchy misliked, Hobbes here expresses indignation about both the "Pope's tyranny" (172) and "Presbyterian tyranny" (169). Nothing could be worse, it seems, than "a tyranny over a king" (81). Once Parliament has sovereignty it will tyrannize over England, he says, implying that tyrannical sovereignty, in a pejorative sense, is a perfectly cogent idea (88).

29. Despite appearances, it should be said, Hobbes was not ultimately a value-subjectivist. If he were, how could he have based all his political works on the assumption that human beings are almost always mistaken about their own good? When he said that "peace is good," moreover, he certainly did not think he was expressing a mere personal preference. Consider, in this regard, the First Law of Nature discussed in *Leviathan*. This law takes the unusual form of a *conditional imperative,* distinct from both the categorical and hypothetical imperatives discussed by Kant, namely: *if* all others put down their weapons, *then* you must put yours down as well. More precisely: you must put down your weapons if *almost* everyone else does so too—and the state should then forcibly disarm the diehards. (At what percentage of compliance, short of universal cooperation, the First Law of Nature becomes morally obligatory remains perhaps intentionally obscure in Hobbes's presentation of the argument.) In any case, Hobbes's self-exemption prohibition is a moral imperative, although a conditional one. It can be understood neither as a convention, established on the say-so of the sovereign, nor as a subjective preference, nor as a mere maxim of prudence, i.e., as a mere instrument of personal advantage. It is a norm of fairness. The minority of diehards who pursue goals incompatible with peace, and who refuse the Hobbesian program of reeducation, must be exiled from the state or killed (*Leviathan,* part 1, chap. 15, p. 209; part 2, chap. 18, p. 232). To them, obviously enough, the First Law of Nature cannot possibly be a maxim of prudence. Formulated somewhat differently, state-enforced cooperation will make not everyone, but rather *almost* everyone, better off than they would have been under conditions of noncooperation. As a result, Hobbes's theory, although based on a norm of fairness, is not universalist, but merely supermajoritarian (see note 18).

30. The "only glory" of merchants is "to grow excessively rich by the wisdom of buying and selling" (126). Their aim is less material than spiritual: accumulated treasure is but a mirror in which they can contemplate their superior talent. They become wealthy, moreover, "by making poor people sell their labour to them at their own prices" (ibid.). These asides, of course, do not prove that Hobbes was either an ascetic or a devotee of martial glory, much less that he lost sleep over poverty.

31. But note the touch of cynicism in this passage: "For what other cause can there bee assigned, why in Christian Common-wealths all men either beleeve, or at least professe the Scripture to bee the Word of God, and in other Commonwealths scarce any; but that in Christian Common-wealths they are taught it from

their infancy; and in other places they are taught otherwise?" (*Leviathan,* part 3, chap. 42, p. 614).

32. Today, we might call this rage against apostasy the Salman Rushdie effect.

33. Why are inherited inequalities perceived as less injurious than recent inequalities, according to Hobbes? Because habits naturally crystallize into norms: "The reason why we conceive greater *indignation* against new than ancient riches, is that the former seem to possess that which is none of theirs, but the ancient seem to have but their own: for with common people, to have been so long, is to be so by right" ("The Art of Rhetoric," *English Works,* vol. 6, p. 643).

34. Cf. *Leviathan,* part 2, chap. 18, p. 231.

35. For an attempt to address this issue, disfigured to some extent by a far-fetched analogy between England in the 1640s and West Germany in the 1970s, see Bernard Willms, "Staatsräson und das Problem der politischen Definition: Bemerkungen zum Nominalismus in Hobbes' Behemoth," in *Staatsräson: Studien zur Geschichte eines politischen Begriffs,* ed. Roman Schnur (Berlin: Duncker & Humblot, 1975), pp. 275–300; and the same author's "Systemüberwindung und Bürgerkrieg: Zur politischen Bedeutung von Hobbes' Behemoth," in *Freiheit und Sachzwang: Beiträge zu Ehren Helmut Schelskys,* ed. Horst Baier (Opladen: Westdeutscher Verlag, 1977), pp. 277–93.

36. *Leviathan,* part 3, chap. 42, p. 527.

37. The concept of "liberty" employed in *Behemoth* is not altogether clear. Hobbes defines it in at least three different ways: first, scoffingly, as "a liberty of everyone to govern himself" (38), fulfilling people's desire "to do what they list" (157); second, approvingly, as an arrangement giving people "their voice in the making of laws" (34), such as the Union which made the Scots "free," because it "gave them equal privilege with the English" (172); and third (with dictatorial insistence that this is the one true meaning), as freedom from private power (38)—men enjoy "liberty" when they enjoy "an exemption from the constraint and insolence of their neighbors" (59).

38. After first denouncing the common people as one of the "seducers" of the commonwealth (2, 4), Hobbes shifts to accusing them of being one of the commonwealth's "distempers" (20). This is a switch from active to passive, from craft to disease, from player to played-with. Thus, while Hobbes tends to view the few as more inclined to strategic reasoning than the many, he also describes *all* people as episodically calculating but habitually noncalculating.

39. For slightly different catalogues of seditious opinions see Martin Goldsmith, *Hobbes's Science of Politics* (New York: Columbia University Press, 1966), pp. 237–38; and Deborah Baumgold, "Hobbes's Political Sensibility," in *Hobbes and Political Theory,* ed. Mary G. Dietz (Lawrence, Kans.: University of Kansas Press, 1990), p. 83.

40. Ancient political works taught "a great many gentlemen" to love "popular government" (23), even though such an arrangement would obviously damage their material interests. But why did Hobbes refer to Aristotle as a radical democrat who viewed all kings as ravenous beasts (158)? The answer seems to be, first, that he cared less about what Aristotle actually wrote than about the ways in which he was currently being read. Second, Aristotle viewed good monarchy as a utopian dream; he spoke favorably of participation and advocated a mixed constitution; and despite some tough criticisms, he also considered democracy to be the *best* of the bad forms of government. Third, Aristotle's "natural" morality (as opposed to a "conventional" morality, based on the say-so of the sovereign) was a weapon any

would-be revolutionary could seize. Equally dangerous was his irresponsible use of that perilous smear word, *tyranny*.

41. People will fight for what they think England *is*. If they falsely, although sincerely, believe it to be a *mixed monarchy*, they will fight on the wrong side, less for personal profit than from an irrational addiction to the perceived status quo—a motive Hobbes is willing to exploit, of course, when it redounds to the King's advantage.

42. *Leviathan*, part 2, chap. 18, p. 233.

43. See *Leviathan*, part 3, chap. 42, p. 527.

44. Blaise Pascal, *Pensées*, in *Oeuvres complètes*, ed. Jacques Chevalier (Paris: Pléiade, 1954), p. 1129.

45. He also concluded that to govern human beings you must govern their opinions; and if you cannot do this by force or threat of force, you must find other means, such as fraud.

46. Francis Bacon, "Of Death," in *The Essayes or Counsels, Civill and Morall*, ed. Michael Kiernan (Cambridge: Harvard University Press, 1985), pp. 9–10.

47. Bacon, *The New Organon*, ed. Fulton Anderson (Indianapolis: Bobbs-Merrill, 1960), p. 52.

48. Bacon, "Of Death," p. 10.

49. The contrast between self-preservation and other motives appears with great clarity in Hobbes's account of Ergamenes's anticlerical coup: he killed the priests "for the safety of his person" while they had killed his predecessors "out of ambition, or love of change" (94); on the restless yearning for "change," see also *Leviathan*, p. 380.

50. For the intriguing but exaggerated claim that Hobbes reduces all human behavior to the pursuit of intellectual vainglory, see Robert P. Kraynak, "Hobbes's Behemoth and the Argument for Absolutism," *American Political Science Review* 76 (1982): 837–47.

51. "The Art of Rhetoric," in *English Works*, vol. 6, p. 464.

52. The bishops, Hobbes repeats elsewhere, faced "the envy of the Presbyterians" (89).

53. Hobbes expresses bewilderment at ethnic identification and cultural animosity: "I think were mistaken, both English and Scots, in calling one another foreigners" (35). Yet the identification of an individual with a group that may survive his death obviously helps solve the problem of mobilizing subjects to protect their protector (*Leviathan*, Review and Conclusion, pp. 718–19). As is well known, Hobbes opts for the implausible idea that dying in war is the wage subjects pay their sovereign for preserving their lives (ibid., part 2, chap. 30, p. 386). Although he consistently counsels the "vertical" loyalty of subjects to their sovereign, his entire approach prohibits any appeal to "horizontal" loyalties among members of the community or group. His aim, one might even say, was to put the sting back into mortality by blocking the projection of individual identity onto the group. His individualism may have been partly formulated in opposition to an ethics of revenge that drove avengers to risk their lives for a larger and more enduring social unit.

54. Hobbes even claims, reductionistically, that quarrels about opinions are actually quarrels "about who has the most learning" (90)—a piquant assertion, given his own outrageous vanity.

55. Public recollection of civil war presents a double problem. People tend to forget the horrors of civil war too quickly and are therefore prone to relapse into insubordination (39). But they also tend to harbor personal grudges too long,

which is why Hobbes, despite his petulance against groups, carefully refrains from naming individual names (117), sanitizing memories of the conflict in order to avoid rekindling quiescent hatreds. The state of nature may be an attempt to solve both problems at once, making quasi-permanent a *depersonalized memory* of civil war.

56. "The Art of Rhetoric," in *English Works,* vol. 6, p. 475; Jean de La Bruyère combined this insight with speculation on the contrary proclivity: the irrational tendency to love those whom we have helped, simply because we have helped them: "Just as we become increasingly attached to those to whom we do good, so we violently hate those whom we have deeply injured" (La Bruyère, *Characters* [Harmondsworth: Penguin, 1970], p. 77).

57. Similarly, Parliament's soldiers were driven partly by a desire for booty; but equally important was the irrational spite they felt toward flatterers, papists, and fortune-seekers (110).

58. *Leviathan,* part 2, chap. 13, p. 185.

59. Hobbes expresses this point more euphemistically: "The unfortunateness of his marriages had so discountenanced his conversation with ladies, that the court could not be his proper element" (112).

60. One of the peculiar characteristics of Hobbes's theory (in contrast, say, to Augustine's) is that the sovereign's own *libido dominandi* is kept out of the picture. Needless to say, this strategic omission raises acute questions given Hobbes's general views about what people—including, presumably, rulers—are willing to do to one another when released from supervision by a superior power.

61. B says, with some despair: "For aught I see, all the states of Christendom will be subject to these fits of rebellion, as long as the world lasteth" (71). Christianity did not make Europeans more *moral* than the inhabitants of pagan antiquity, simply more prone to shed blood for religion (63).

62. Augustine, *The City of God,* trans. William Chase Greene (Cambridge: Harvard University Press, 1960), vol. 5, bk. 16, chap. 4, p. 29.

63. Likewise, "our rebels were publicly taught rebellion in the pulpits" (144).

64. In the same spirit: "I confess also, that considering what harm may proceed from a liberty that men have, upon every Sunday and oftener, to harangue all the people of a nation at one time, whilst the state is ignorant of what they will say; and that there is no such thing permitted in all the world out of Christendom, nor therefore any civil wars about religion; I have thought much preaching an inconvenience" (63–64).

65. Because the Presbyterians were the one dissenting group to survive as an active force into the 1660s, Hobbes may have somewhat magnfied their role in the civil war in order to discredit them politically.

66. "The most frequent praetext of Sedition, and Civil Warre, in Christian Common-wealths hath a long time proceeded from a difficulty, not yet sufficiently resolved, of obeying at once, both God and Man, then when their Commandments are one contrary to the other" (*Leviathan,* part 3, chap. 43, p. 609). Ultimately, the Bible is an anarchy-provoking work because no one can tell with certainty what it means.

67. Under the Commonwealth, Hobbes had written suggestively that "the Independency of the Primitive Christians . . . is perhaps the best" (*Leviathan,* part 4, chap. 47, p. 711). Yet in *Behemoth* he takes a radically antidisestablishmentarian line (46). True, he still makes positive reference to the Independents. The Rump "plucked out the sting of Presbytery" (169) by voting liberty of conscience, and this incapacitation of the Presbyterians was welcome. But, in general, Hobbes fears

religious anarchy so much that he praises the Pope's no-translation policy (21), states that the King should monopolize communication with God, and denounces the priesthood of all believers. He dislikes a situation in which "every man became a judge of religion, and an interpreter of the Scriptures to himself" for the simple reason that private interpretation is "the cause of so many several sects" (22). He wants an Erastian "subordination of the Church to the Civil state in the things of Christ" (172) to guarantee that the commands of God never conflict with the commands of the sovereign. Toleration spells chaos, a religious state of nature wherein individuals are "assured of their salvation by the testimony of their own private spirit, meaning the Holy Ghost dwelling within them" (25). The wholesale illiberalism of this approach can be made clear by a comparison with Locke, *Two Treatises of Government,* II, ed. Peter Laslett (Cambridge: Cambridge University Press, 1988), § 168.

68. *The Letters of Ambrose* (Oxford: James Parker & Co., 1881), p. 329.

69. The Pope succeeded in the pernicious erosion of imperial authority only because the Emperor had haughtily refused to "descend into the obscure and narrow mines" (13) of Catholic theology, ignoring the indispensability of religion for the stability of political power. A clever Hobbesian sovereign would not repeat this mistake.

70. Hobbes's specific charge is that the distinction between passive and active disobedience, set forth in *The Whole Duty of Man,* is a distinction without a difference, meant to distract from the quite seditious implications of Anglican theology, which outrageously justifies rebellion (47–50).

71. The two cardinal virtues in war, including the war of all against all, are force and fraud (*Leviathan,* part 1, chap. 13, p. 188).

72. The "ultimate good is eternal life, and . . . the ultimate evil is eternal death" (Augustine, *City of God,* vol. 6, bk. 19, chap. 4, p. 122).

73. Cited in *Leviathan,* part 3, chap. 43, p. 610.

74. *De Cive,* chap. 12, sect. 5, in Hobbes, *Man and Citizen* (Gloucester, Mass.: Peter Smith, 1978), p. 248; similarly: "nor is he less, but rather more a master, whom we believe we are to obey for fear of damnation, than he whom we obey for fear of temporal death" (ibid., chap. 6, sect. 11, p. 179). Elsewhere, while sarcastically rejecting any martyrdom that might serve "the ambition, or profit of the clergy," Hobbes counsels the individual to risk death for the simple principle "Jesus is the Christ," on the assumption that such an ecumenical maxim might justify a war with the Turks, but certainly could not inspire civil struggles within a Christian nation (*Leviathan,* p. 530).

75. Physical violence can be used effectively *against* priests, of course. Having praised Henry VIII for his "nature quick and severe in the punishing of such as should be the first to oppose his designs" (19), Hobbes offers uncharacteristically Machiavellian advice to Charles II, encouraging him, although only by implication, to "fall upon" and "destroy" (58) religious subversives, to cut them off as did Hercules the heads of Hydra (73). A prince worth imitating is Ergamenes: the Ethiopian king, educated in philosophy, who daringly murdered all the priests in his land. This was a cruel act, but one less cruel than letting them live (94–95). Hobbes concludes, on the same Machiavellian note, that it would have been best for the English monarchs to have butchered the one thousand or so Presbyterian ministers "before they had preached" (95).

76. The Pope's stupid decision to vex Henry VIII in his marriage designs (19) is another example of the self-destructiveness of "absolute" power, to which,

admittedly, other theorists of sovereignty paid more attention than did Hobbes. In his famous "Of Empire" from the essays of 1625, for instance, Francis Bacon wrote: "For their nobles: to keep them at a distance, it is not amiss; but to depress them may make a king more absolute, but less safe and less able to perform any thing he desires. I have noted it in my History of King Henry the Seventh of England, who depressed his nobility; whereupon it came to pass that his times were full of difficulties and troubles; for the nobility, though they continued loyal unto him, yet did they not cooperate with him in his business. So that he was fain [forced, obliged] to do all things himself" (Francis Bacon, *A Selection of His Works,* ed. Sidney Warhaft [Indianapolis: Bobbs-Merrill, 1965], p. 96). For a more extensive treatment of this theme, see chap. 4.

77. John Locke, *A Letter on Toleration,* ed. R. Klibanski and J. G. Gough (Oxford: Clarendon Press, 1968), p. 145; *Two Treatises of Government,* II, § 230.

78. *Leviathan,* part 2, chap. 19, p. 241.

79. This Machiavellian point, largely undeveloped by Hobbes, became the centerpiece of Harrington's concept of benevolent imperialism (*The Political Works of James Harrington,* ed. J. G. A. Pocock [Cambridge: Cambridge University Press, 1977], pp. 326–28).

80. *Leviathan,* dedication, p. 75.

81. In the *Elements,* Hobbes admitted that subjects rebel because of excessive taxation: "Great exactions, though the right thereof be acknowledged, have caused great seditions" (*Elements of Laws,* ed. Ferdinand Tönnies [London: Frank Cass, 1969], bk. 2, par. 8, p. 169). Yet he did not fully integrate this insight into his theory. While he fully understood the factors that provoked Parliamentary restlessness, he still defended the King's absolute right to levy as much money as he liked (*Leviathan,* part 2, chap. 30, p. 377). In *Behemoth,* he remains flippantly dismissive about legitimate grievances caused by the Crown's irritating tax policy (37).

82. *Leviathan,* part 2, chap. 27, p. 339.

83. The set of requests that he may decently make, presumably, are limited by the norm of consistency as discussed above.

84. *Leviathan,* part 1, chap. 12, p. 169, my emphasis.

85. The seeds of religion, Hobbes says, "can never be so abolished out of humane nature, but that new Religions may againe be made to spring out of them" by ambitious cultivators (*Leviathan,* part 1, chap. 12, p. 179).

86. See *De Cive,* chap. 17, sect. 21, p. 353; and Norberto Bobbio, *Thomas Hobbes and the Natural Law Tradition* (Chicago: University of Chicago Press, 1993), pp. 80–81.

87. *English Works,* vol. 4, p. 432, emphasis in original.

88. *Leviathan,* part 3, chap. 37, p. 478; similarly, when Hobbes defined the sovereign as the "Soule" of the commonwealth (ibid., part 2, chap. 29, p. 375), he may have had *Policraticus* in mind. While John of Salisbury identified the prince as the head of the commonwealth, he considered the priesthood to be its soul (*Policraticus,* ed. and trans. Cary J. Nederman [Cambridge: Cambridge University Press, 1990], bk. 5, chap. 2, pp. 66–67).

89. This is one of the main themes of Carl Schmitt, *Der Leviathan in der Staatslehre des Thomas Hobbes* (Köln-Lovenich: Hohenheim, 1982), a work, originally published in 1938, which is simultaneously spellbinding and repulsive.

90. Hobbes suspends his usual hardheadedness when he optimistically suggests that the problem of social disorder can be solved "by mending the Universities" (71). It seems that the entire course of human history can be permanently

changed if the universities begin to teach "infallible rules . . . for the common people to take notice of" (70). In politics, science is more important than native intelligence (70, 159). Luckily, Hobbesian science is idiot-proof, and truth can never serve sinister ambitions (96); that is, a good theory cannot be misused. These are extraordinary claims for a student of rhetorical manipulation to make.

91. For a similar argument, see Spinoza, *The Ethics,* in *The Chief Work of Benedict de Spinoza,* ed. R. H. M. Elwes (New York: Dover, 1955), part 4, prop. LIV, pp. 223–24.

92. Bacon, "Of Vaine-Glory," in *Essayes,* p. 161.

93. In one well-known passage, he says that "the Religion of the Gentiles was a part of their Policy" (*Leviathan,* part 1, chap. 12, p. 178). That is, "the peace of the Commonwealth" is enhanced by religious myths: "The first Founders, and Legislators of Common-wealths amongst the Gentiles, whose ends were only to keep the people in obedience, and peace, have in all places taken care; First, to imprint in their minds a beliefe, that those precepts which they gave concerning Religion, might not be thought to proceed from their own device, but from the dictates of some God, or other Spirit; or else that they themselves were of a higher nature than mere mortalls, that their Laws might the more easily be received. . . . Secondly, they have had a care, to make it believed, that the same things were displeasing to the Gods, which were forbidden by the Lawes" (ibid., p. 177).

94. The beginnings of commonwealths can never be morally justified (*Leviathan,* Review and Conclusion, p. 722). What is true for foundation by conquest is equally true for foundation by religious deception.

95. Similarly: Aristotle's writings "puzzle and entangle men with words, and . . . breed disputation, which must at least be ended in the determination of the Church of Rome" (42). This guileful divide-and-rule strategy is based on the assumption that dispute and discord are psychologically intolerable.

96. Hobbes sometimes objects to this sort of guilt-inducement on humanistic grounds: "The Desires, and other Passions of man, are in themselves no Sin" (*Leviathan,* part 1, chap. 13, p. 187).

97. Hobbes approves of government by guilt, so long as this tactic is monopolized by the sovereign. People are "lesse apt to mutiny against their Governors" (*Leviathan,* part 1, chap. 12, p. 178) if they blame their misery on themselves. Fear of having neglected the gods, apparently, cripples subjects, making them feel recreant and unwilling to rebel.

## Chapter 4

1. Alexis de Tocqueville, *Democracy in America,* trans. George Lawrence (New York: Doubleday Anchor, 1969), p. 88.

2. Émile Durkheim, "Rapport de l'état et de l'individu," in *Leçons de sociologie* (Paris: Presses Universitaires de France, 1950), pp. 91–99.

3. Another notable proponent of this counterintuitive thesis was Pierre Bayle. Universally acknowledged as a central figure in the history of toleration, Bayle fully supported the politics of absolutism because he believed that the state's independence from intolerant religious authorities could be achieved only if the king attained full civil supremacy. See chapter 1, note 10.

4. Jean Bodin, *Les six livres de la république,* translated as *The Six Bookes of a Commonweal,* ed. K. D. McRae (Cambridge: Harvard University Press, 1962), I, 8, 84. All references are to book, chapter, and page of this English translation of 1606,

which was based on both the French and Latin versions of the original. Spelling and punctuation have been modernized.

5. Admittedly, a tautological approach, whereby "divided sovereignty" is declared a logical contradiction, is sometimes suggested, as in Bodin's remark that a mixed state "was never found" (II, I, 194).

6. Cf. I, 10, 159–60.

7. Being a traditionalist by training and temperament, Bodin also employs argument by analogy in making his case for the king's monopoly on supreme power. The universe as a whole is organized hierarchically as a great chain of being; everywhere we look, we discern "royal" authority. Nature provides the archetype which society must replicate. First of all, a family, "which is the true image of a commonweal," has but a single father. Moreover, "all the laws of nature guide us unto a monarchy, whether that we behold [the human body] which hath . . . but one head for all the members, whereupon depends the will, moving and feeling: or if we look to this great world which hath but one sovereign God: or if we erect our eyes to heaven, we shall see but one sun: and even in sociable creatures, we see they cannot admit many kings, nor many lords, how good soever" (VI, 4, 718). To some extent, then, Bodin's political theory derives from his metaphysical views about cosmic hierarchy and stability. C. R. Baxter, "Jean Bodin's Daemon and his Conversion to Judaism," in *Verhandlungen der internationalen Bodin Tagung in München,* ed. Horst Denzer (Munich: Beck, 1973), pp. 1–21. On the other hand, the immediate occasion for his endorsement of the absolutist cause was not his pious appreciation of God's handiwork, but rather the chaos of France's religious civil wars. He was more concerned to avoid violent disorder than to achieve divinely anointed perfection. Bodin's hostility toward private armies and private justice was sharpened by personal experience: he was at Paris during the St. Bartholomew's Day massacre. A "miserable anarchy," he says, "is the plague of all states" (VI, 4, 717). True, civil war was also aesthetically displeasing, that is, discordant with the beauties of the *Stufenkosmos.* But Bodin's proposals for avoiding it were more worldly, pragmatic, crafty and responsive to daily events than a disproportionate stress on his outmoded metaphysics would suggest. One might say, of course, that Bodin combines the classical argument that politics should mirror natural order with a quite distinct claim that politics must quell natural disorder. Nature includes sin, that is to say, man's inborn unruliness (I, 5, 35). Human nature, in all its wretchedness, is clearly revealed in primitive societies: "The first sort of men were most given to rapine, murder, and theft, delighting in nothing more, nor accounting any honor greater than to rob and kill, and to oppress the weaker sort as slaves" (III, 7, 362). At all stages of social development, however, human beings must be bridled by external controls. Their spontaneous wishes—for example, their desire to inflict pain on the weak—are unworthy of respect. The bestial and disorderly side of human nature finds better opportunity to express itself in some situations than in others. Denominational conflict seems particularly well suited for releasing such primordial cruelty. To counter this contemporary version of a perennial threat, a strong ruler must take control and gain a firm monopoly on all legitimate use of violence within the realm. Ultimately, however, Bodin justified authority in a wholly secular manner, not as a punishment for sin but rather as the creation of order out of disorder. To prevent France from destroying itself in factious warfare, sovereignty must be located in a monarch whose power is formally—though not actually—unlimited.

8. That this paradox has wider implications, not limited to the *République,* is

stressed by Roland Mousnier: "le concept d'absolutisme est difficile pour nous car l'absolutisme, au sens littéral, est sans limite, et l'absolutisme monarchique au contraire est limité" ("Les concepts d'ordres d'états, de fidelité et de monarchie absolue en France de la fin du XV siècle à la fin du XVIII," *Revue historique* 217 [1972]: 304).

9. J. W. Allen, *A History of Political Thought in the Sixteenth Century* (London: Methuen, 1928), p. 410; Georges Weill, *Les theories sur le pouvoir royal en France pendant les guerres de religion* (Paris: Hachette, 1891), p. 168.

10. Quentin Skinner, *The Foundations of Modern Political Thought,* vol. 2 (Cambridge: Cambridge University Press, 1978), p. 297.

11. Nannerl O. Keohane, *Philosophy and the State in France* (Princeton: Princeton University Press, 1980), p. 74.

12. Julian Franklin, *Jean Bodin and the Rise of Absolutist Theory* (Cambridge: Cambridge University Press, 1973), pp. 69, 87, 70, 92. Franklin gestures toward a distinction between "constitutional restraints" which Bodin disallows and "institutional restraints" which he accepts (ibid., p. 98); but a perhaps exaggerated concern with legal formalities as well as commitment to a stylized "battle" between absolutism and constitutionalism prevent Franklin from exploring this distinction in depth.

13. John Plamenatz, *Man and Society,* vol. 1 (London: Longman, 1963), p. 111.

14. At one point, Bodin suggests that laws are nothing but prohibitions with penalties attached (III, 5, 325). But he subverts this claim, for instance, by his lucid discussion of office-creating laws. (I will return to the subject of enabling restraints in chapters 5 and 6.)

15. Friedrich Meinecke, *Machiavellism: The Doctrine of Raison d'État and Its Place in Modern History* (New Haven: Yale University Press, 1957), p. 56.

16. Cf. Aquinas "On Kingship," in *The Political Ideas of Thomas Aquinas,* ed. Dino Bigongiari (New York: Hafner, 1953), chap. 10, pp. 192–95.

17. Many of these arguments, it should be said, including the presentation of moderate rule as a strategy for avoiding assassination, are drawn from Machiavelli's own writings; and see, most intriguingly, Machiavelli's statement that "the kingdom of France is better regulated [*moderato*] by laws than is any other of which at present we have knowledge" (*The Discourses* [Harmondsworth: Penguin, 1970], p. 253).

18. Bodin himself claimed that his ideas about unlimited sovereignty were especially appropriate to democracies for there "the people make but one body, and cannot bind itself to itself" (I, 8, 99). Jefferson's thinking was perfectly analogous to Bodin's: constitutional precommitments violate the full sovereignty of present and future generations. The only solution Jefferson saw was to hold constitutional conventions every twenty years to reaffirm or rewrite the foundational compact (Thomas Jefferson, Letter of 6 September 1789, in *Writings,* ed. Merrill Peterson [New York: Library of America, 1984], pp. 598–64). See also J. P. Mayer, "Jefferson as Reader of Bodin," in *Fundamental Studies on Jean Bodin,* ed. J. P. Mayer (New York: Arno Press, 1979).

19. As further evidence of Bodin's less than pious attitude toward tradition, consider: "The power of the law is much greater than the power of custom; for customs are by laws abolished, but not laws by custom" (I, 10, 160–61).

20. The same passage continues, "There is nothing more difficult to handle, nor more doubtful in event, nor more dangerous to manage, than to bring in new decrees or laws" (IV, 3, 470).

21. Cf. "Publication or approbation of laws in the assembly of the Estates or parlement, is with us of great power and importance for the keeping of the laws" (I, 8, 103); "As for the names of Lords and Senators, which we oftentimes see joined unto laws, they are not thereunto set as of necessity to give thereunto force or strength, but to give unto them testimony and weight, as made by the wisdom and discretion of the chief men, so to give them the better grace, and to make them to be the better received, and not for any necessity at all" (I, 10, 159–60).

22. Note that Bodin draws a sharp distinction between the sovereign and the government (II, 2, 199), a distinction later made famous by Rousseau.

23. "We see that they themselves [e.g., the king and his court] who would have these estates and communities and societies of the people suppressed and abolished, have in time of their necessity no other refuge or stay to fly unto, but even to these estates and communities of the people: which being united together, strengthen themselves for the defense and protection, not of their prince only, but even of themselves also, and of the whole state and subjects in general" (III, 7, 384).

24. Max Weber makes the same point in his hard-headed defense of parliamentarianism: "If there is no powerful parliament, the monarch is today dependent on the reports of officials for the supervision of the work of other officials" (Max Weber, *Economy and Society,* eds. Guenther Roth and Claus Wittich [Berkeley: University of California Press, 1978], p. 1406).

25. Owen Ulph, "Jean Bodin and the Estates-General of 1576," *Journal of Modern History* 19 (December 1947): 289–96.

26. *Rémonstrance au roi par le sieur de la Serre, sur les pernicieux discours contenus au livre de la République de Bodin,* Paris, 1597, cited and summarized in Weill, *Les Théories sur le pouvoir royal en France,* p. 170.

27. Allen, *History of Political Thought,* pp. 415–16.

28. "For we have seen the kingdom of Sweden, of Scotland, of Denmark, of England, and Cantons of the Swiss, yea and the German empire also, to have changed their religion, the estate of every of these monarchies and commonweals yet standing entire and whole." Whenever the prince unwisely abandoned his position of sovereign aloofness and participated as a party in the denominational struggle, on the other hand, religious transformations have only been accomplished "with great violence, and bloodshed" (IV, 7, 535).

29. In the *Heptaplomeres,* Coronaeus says: "I believe that all are convinced that it is much better to have a false religion than no religion. Thus there is no superstition so great that it cannot keep wicked men in their duty through fear of divine power and somehow preserve the law of nature, since rewards for the good and punishment for the wicked are considered part of divine judgement" (Bodin, *Colloquium of the Seven about the Secrets of the Sublime,* trans. Marion Kuntz, [Princeton: Princeton University Press, 1975], p. 162).

30. "It is no marvel that the people of the south be better governed by religion than by force or reason" (V, 1, 560).

31. Notice the psychological premise underlying this advice: "Such is the nature of man, as they esteem nothing more sweet and goodly than that which is strictly forbidden them" (VI, 2, 670).

32. "The great emperor of the Turks doth with as great devotion as any prince in the world honor and observe the religion by him received from his ancestors, and yet detesteth he not the strange religions of other; but to the contrary permitteth every man to live according to his conscience" (IV, 7, 537).

33. Bodin, *Colloquium of the Seven,* p. 151.

34. This argument could have wound its way down to Madison (*Federalist,* no. 10) through, among others, Voltaire: "If there were only one religion in England there would be danger of despotism, if there were two they would cut each other's throat, but there are thirty, and they live in peace and happiness" (*Letters on England* [Harmondsworth: Penguin, 1980], letter 6, p. 41).

35. Bodin is not thinking of a classical "prisoner's dilemma" here. As he sees it, the crucial problem stems not from a conflict between individual and collective rationality, but rather from an inherited code of honor which makes individuals singly, not just collectively, behave in irrational ways.

36. Bodin's later adherence to the League (1589) was probably motivated by concerns for personal safety and, in any case, has no bearing on the argument of the *République,* which was obviously written in opposition to the extreme Catholics.

37. This argument is very similar to the one advanced by Arend Lijphart when discussing the crucial role played by semidetached elites in governing primordially divided societies. Arend Lijphart, *Democracy in Plural Societies: A Comparative Exploration* (New Haven: Yale University Press, 1977), p. 53.

38. Bodin, *Colloquium of the Seven,* pp. 163, 167, 471.

39. Augsburg, in short, taught the same lesson as Siena: "The princes of the Germans at a great assembly at Augsburg, after destructive and lengthy wars, proclaimed that there would be no more discussion about religion among Catholics and priests of the Augsburg confession. When one man rashly violated this edict, he was put to death, and the uprisings in that city were quelled up to the present" (*Colloquium of the Seven,* p. 167).

40. Benedict de Spinoza, *A Theologico-Political Treatise* (New York: Dover, 1951), chap. 20, 264–65, 334.

41. John Milton, *Areopagitica,* in *Complete Prose Works of John Milton* (New Haven: Yale University Press, 1959), vol. 2, p. 542.

42. John Locke, *Two Treatises of Government,* ed. Peter Laslett (Cambridge: Cambridge University Press, 1988), II, § 57.

43. John Locke, *A Letter on Toleration,* ed. R. Klibanski and J. G. Gough (Oxford: Clarendon Press, 1968), pp. 141, 145; along the same lines, one can say that a tough and effective opposition in Parliament obviates the popularly felt need for a more dangerous form of extraparliamentary opposition.

44. Locke, *Two Treatises of Government,* II, §§ 226, 230.

45. Montesquieu, *The Spirit of the Laws,* trans. Thomas Nugent (New York: Hafner, 1949), vol. 1, p. 114 (VII, 7); p. 366 (XXI, 20).

46. Montesquieu, *Persian Letters* (Harmondsworth: Penguin, 1977), letters 80 and 85, pp. 158–59 and 164–66. Notice that elsewhere Montesquieu had emphasized how religious disputes are peculiarly resistant to rational resolution (*The Greatness of the Romans and their Decline* [Ithaca: Cornell University Press, 1968], chap. 22, p. 208).

47. David Hume, "Of the Liberty of the Press," *Essays: Moral, Political, and Literary* (Indianapolis: Liberty Classics, 1985), p. 11.

48. Hume also stressed the contribution of press freedom to public education: "It is to be hoped that men, being everyday more accustomed to the free discussion of public affairs, will improve in the judgment of them" (Hume, "Of the Liberty of the Press," p. 11).

49. Kant, "On the Common Saying: 'This May Be True in Theory, but It Does Not Apply in Practice,'" in *Kant's Political Writings,* ed. Hans Reiss (Cambridge: Cambridge University Press, 1970), p. 85; "Idea for Universal History," ibid., pp.

50–51; Mill, too, argues that bad government deadens the intelligence and energy of the governed, qualities that would have been highly useful to the governors themselves ("Considerations on Representative Government," in John Stuart Mill, *Collected Works,* ed. J. M. Robson, vol. 19, *Essays on Politics and Society* [Toronto: University of Toronto Press, 1977], p. 393).

50. Thomas Jefferson, "Notes on the State of Virginia," *Writings,* ed. Merrill D. Peterson (New York: Library of America, 1984), p. 287; for further *raison d'état* arguments for liberal political institutions, see Stephen Holmes, "Tocqueville and Democracy," in *The Idea of Democracy,* ed. David Copp, Jean Hampton, and John E. Roemer (Cambridge: Cambridge University Press, 1993), pp. 23–63.

51. Franklin, *Jean Bodin and the Rise of Absolutist Theory,* p. 103.

## Chapter 5

1. Laurence Tribe, *American Constitutional Law* (2d ed.; Mineola: Foundation Press, 1988), p. 10.

2. The Supreme Court, it should be noted, may run afoul of electoral majorities both when it worships and when it disdains the intent of the framers. Thus, the countermajoritarian difficulty is broader than the conflict between strict interpretivism and judicial policy making. Why should nine appointed judges—whether they follow or ignore the letter of the Constitution—have a right to nullify the decisions of democratically elected officials today?

3. *West Virginia Board of Education v. Barnette,* 319 U.S. 624, at 638.

4. Friedrich Hayek, *The Constitution of Liberty* (Chicago: University of Chicago Press, 1960), pp. 176–92.

5. Martin Shapiro (ed.), Introduction, in *The Constitution of the United States and Related Documents* (New York: Appleton-Century-Crofts, 1968), pp. xxi–xxii.

6. On the reciprocally beneficial relations between secularization and democratization, see also chapter 7.

7. John Hart Ely, *Democracy and Distrust: A Theory of Judicial Review* (Cambridge: Harvard University Press, 1980).

8. Ibid., p. 117. Ely's argument is persuasive in many respects; but, as others have noted, he falls needlessly into a reductionist or single-purpose theory of judicial review. The Constitution is not merely a procedural document, silent about all substantive issues. And the Warren Court was concerned about a variety of values, such as fairness, independently of its commitment to democracy. Some rights arise from the needs of representative government; but others do not. The central weakness of his argument, however, seems to lie elsewhere. Ely is right to object to justices who, wrapping themselves in the veil of Reason, Natural Law, or the American Way, actually base their decisions on subjective standards concealed safely beneath obfuscatory language. But he is wrong to suggest that he has solved this perennial problem. His idea of "democracy" is far from being a perfectly noncontroversial standard which can liberate judges from the smudge of subjectivity.

9. David Hume, "Of the Original Contract," in *Essays: Moral, Political, and Literary* (Indianapolis: Liberty Classics, 1985), p. 471.

10. "The Putney Debates" (28 October 1647), *The Commonwealth of England,* ed. Charles Blitzer (New York: Putnam's Sons, 1963), pp. 72–73.

11. *The Federalist Papers* (New York: Mentor, 1961), no. 78 (Hamilton), p. 469; and ibid., no. 40 (Madison), p. 253.

12. John Locke, *Two Treatises of Government,* ed. Peter Laslett (Cambridge: Cambridge University Press, 1988), II, § 116.

13. *Les Constitutions de la France depuis 1789,* ed. Jacques Godechot (Paris: Garnier-Flammarion, 1970), p. 82.

14. Tom Paine, "Common Sense," in *The Life and Major Writings of Thomas Paine,* ed. Philip Foner (New York: Citadel, 1961), pp. 29 and 37.

15. Tom Paine, "The Rights of Man," in *Major Writings,* p. 251.

16. "It is the living, and not the dead, that are to be accommodated," and "as government is for the living, and not for the dead, it is the living only that has any right to it" (ibid., pp. 251, 254); it seems safe to attribute a similar conception of democracy to Martin Shapiro (see note 5).

17. Ibid., p. 366.

18. Ibid., p. 273.

19. In all fairness, Burke argued quite forcefully that constant reform was a necessity of government. His basic position, in fact, was unconscionably caricatured in Paine's account. Burke had written that it is difficult to be rational in politics, since one must be thoroughly acquainted with numerous details in order to judge a situation correctly: "Abstractedly speaking, government, as well as liberty, is good; yet could I, in common sense, ten years ago, have felicitated France on her enjoyment of a government, (for she then had a government,) without inquiry what the nature of that government was, or how it was administered?" ("Reflections on the Revolution in France," in *The Works of Edmund Burke,* vol. 3 [Boston: Little, Brown, 1869], pp. 240–41). Paine "quotes" this passage, irresponsibly or furtively, rewriting it to suggest that for Burke rationality is both impossible and undesirable in politics: "Mr. Burke appears to have no idea of principles, when he is contemplating governments. 'Ten years ago' (says he) 'I could have felicitated France on her having a government, without inquiring what the nature of that government was, or how it was administered.' Is this the language of a rational man?" ("The Rights of Man," p. 258).

20. Locke, *Two Treatises of Government,* II, § 103.

21. See Milton's divorce tracts, in *Complete Prose Works of John Milton,* vol. 2, pp. 217–356 (New Haven: Yale University Press, 1959); Locke, *Two Treatises of Government,* II, §§ 80–83; and Montesquieu, *Persian Letters* (Harmondsworth: Penguin, 1977), letter 116, pp. 209–11.

22. See Roderick Phillips, *Putting Asunder: A History of Divorce in Western Society* (Cambridge: Cambridge University Press, 1988), pp. 116–19.

23. Thomas Jefferson, "Draft of the Kentucky Resolutions" (1798) and letter of 7 September 1803, in *Writings,* ed. Merrill Peterson (New York: Library of America, 1984), pp. 454 and 1140.

24. Letter of 6 September 1789, ibid., p. 959; Jefferson's simultaneous and inconsistent beliefs that the majority both must and must not be limited are expressed concisely in his First Inaugural: "Though the will of the majority is in all cases to prevail, that will to be rightful must be reasonable" (ibid., pp. 492–93); this statement implies that an unreasonable majority should *not* prevail; but it does not specify who should enforce what criterion of rationality upon a democratic majority presumably galloping astray.

25. Ibid., p. 251.

26. "The contest for *perpetual bills of rights* against a future tyranny, resembles Don Quixote's fighting windmills; and I can never reflect on the declaration about an *unalterable constitution* to guard certain rights, without wishing to add another

article, as necessary as those mentioned, viz. 'that no future convention or legislature shall cut their own throats, or those of their constituents'" (Noah Webster, "Government, Mr. Jefferson's arguments in favor of an unalterable constitution, considered," *American Magazine,* no. 1 [1788], reprinted as "On government" in *A Collection of Essays and Fugitive Writings on Moral, Historical, Political and Literary Subjects* [Boston: Thomas & Andrews, 1790], p. 67).

27. Jefferson, *Writings,* p. 963.

28. Letters of 12 July 1816 and 5 June 1824, in *Writings,* pp. 1402 and 1493.

29. Jefferson, *Writings,* p. 962; cf. letter of 24 June 1813, pp. 1,280–81. For Noah Webster's earlier use of this argument, see Gordon Wood, *The Creation of the American Republic* (New York: Norton, 1972), p. 379.

30. Jefferson, *Writings,* p. 963.

31. In the same spirit, Jefferson expressed considerable disquiet about the antimajoritarian character of judicial review (e.g., letter of 23 December 1820, in *Writings,* p. 1,446).

32. Adam Smith, *Lectures on Jurisprudence,* ed. R. L. Meek, D. D. Raphael, and P. G. Stein (Oxford: Clarendon Press, 1978), p. 468 (see also pp. 69–70); cf. *The Wealth of Nations* (New York: Modern Library, 1937), p. 363.

33. Jefferson, *Writings,* p. 963.

34. Jefferson, *Writings,* p. 961; this principle follows, in Jefferson's eyes, from the Lockean denial of inherited guilt (Locke, *Two Treatises of Government,* II, § 182).

35. Jefferson, *Writings,* p. 961.

36. Jefferson, *Writings,* p. 1,402.

37. Paradoxically, this rule, too, represents an attempt to bind posterity. When Jefferson wrote "let us provide in our constitution for its revision at stated periods" (ibid.), he was inconsistently endorsing an attempt to impose unalterable arrangements on successor generations.

38. Jefferson, letter of 12 July 1816, in *Writings,* p. 1401.

39. Hobbes, *Leviathan* (Harmondsworth: Penguin, 1968), part 2, chap. 26, p. 323; from this premise, Hobbes concludes, in an assault on legal precedent, that "the sentence of a Judge, does not bind him, or another Judge to give like Sentence in like Cases ever after" (ibid.).

40. Locke, *A Letter on Toleration,* trans. J. W. Gough (Oxford: Clarendon Press, 1968), p. 73. In early nineteenth-century America, institutional precommitment and majority rule collided on precisely this sort of religious issue. In several states, a legal battle raged over ecclesiastical trusts. Church founders had often granted land to a congregation on the condition that future parishioners would continue to embrace specific doctrinal beliefs. The legal question was: should a court enforce the will of defunct Trinitarians against the wishes of a majority of living Unitarians? This question is interestingly discussed in Mark DeWolfe Howe, *The Garden and the Wilderness* (Chicago: University of Chicago Press, 1965), pp. 32–60.

41. Immanuel Kant, "What Is Enlightenment?," in *Kant's Political Writings,* ed. Hans Reiss (Cambridge: Cambridge University Press, 1970), pp. 57, 58.

42. Mill, *Principles of Political Economy,* in John Stuart Mill, *Collected Works,* ed. J. M. Robson vol. 3 (Toronto: University of Toronto Press, 1965), p. 954.

43. *Federalist Papers,* no. 53, p. 331; no. 41, p. 259 (Madison).

44. William Blackstone, *Commentaries on the Laws of England* (Chicago: University of Chicago Press, 1977), vol. 1, p. 90; for Blackstone's version of the related principle that no man may make a binding covenant with himself, see ibid., p. 430.

45. Thomas Aquinas, *Summa Theologica* (Westminster, Maryland: Christian Classics, 1948), vol. 2, I–II, Q. 96, Reply Obj. 3, p. 1,021.

46. Richard Hooker, *Of the Laws of Ecclesiastical Polity* (1593) (London: Everyman, 1969), bk. 1, chap. 10, sec. 8, pp. 194–95.

47. Hugo Grotius, *De juri belli ac pacis,* trans. Francis Kelsey (Oxford: Clarendon Press, 1925), bk. 2, chap. 14, sec. 10, p. 386.

48. The Weimar Constitution, for example, begins: "The German people . . . has given itself this constitution" (*Die Verfassung des deutschen Reichs von 11 August 1919,* ed. Gerhard Anschütz [Berlin: Georg Stilte, 1933], p. xii).

49. "The word 'owe' has no place unless two persons are involved; how, then, will it apply to one person, who, in the act of incurring a debt, frees himself from it?" (Seneca, "On Benefits" v. 7, in *Moral Essays,* vol. 3, trans. John Basore [Cambridge: Harvard University Press, 1935], p. 313). At v. 9 (ibid., p. 317), Seneca explicitly rejects the notion that a single individual, in any legally decipherable sense, contains multiple selves.

50. Aquinas, *Summa Theologica,* vol. 2, I-II, Q. 96, Reply Obj. 3, p. 1021.

51. Jean Bodin, *The Six Bookes of a Commonweale* (Cambridge: Harvard University Press, 1962), bk. 1, chap. 8, pp. 91–92. Citations from Bodin hereafter will be in the form of book, chapter, page numbers.

52. Thomas Hobbes, *Man and Citizen,* ed. Bernard Gert (Gloucester, Mass.: Peter Smith, 1978), chap. 6, sec. 14, p. 183; the same argument surfaces in *Leviathan:* "The Soveraign of a Common-wealth, be it an Assembly, or one Man, is not Subject to the Civill Lawes. For having power to make, and repeale Lawes, he may when he pleaseth, free himselfe from that subjection, by repealing those Lawes that trouble him, and making of new; and consequently he was free before. For he is free, that can be free when he will: Nor is it possible for any person to be bound to himself: because he that can bind, can release; and therefore he that is bound to himselfe onely, is not bound" (*Leviathan,* part 2, chap. 26, p. 313).

53. For Hobbes, the sovereign's freedom from legal restraints was a matter of political reality, not just of law. Ordinary subjects can be expected to keep their promises because the sovereign compels them to do so. But the sovereign's own promises, even his promises to others (to his subjects or to foreign princes) cannot be similarly binding because no superordinate enforcer is on hand.

54. "A man cannot become obligated to himself, or enter into an agreement with himself, or promise himself something which concerns only himself. For whoever obtains a right by an obligation is at liberty to relinquish it, provided no injury is thereby done to a third party. In this instance the person obligating and the person obligated, that is, the one obtaining a right and the one giving it, are the same, and so, no matter how much a man may strive to obligate himself, it will be all in vain, since he can free himself at his own pleasure, without having carried out any obligation whatever, and the one that can do this is actually free" (Samuel Pufendorf, *De jure naturae et gentium,* trans. C. H. Oldfather and W. A. Oldfather [Oxford: Clarendon Press, 1934], bk. 1, chap. 6, sec. 7, p. 94; and bk. 7, chap. 6, sec. 8, p. 1064.)

55. Rousseau, "Sur le gouvernement de Pologne" and "Du contrat social" (I, 7 and III, 18), in *Oeuvres complètes,* ed. Bernard Gagnebin and Marcel Raymond (Paris: Pléiade, 1964), vol. 3, pp. 981, 362, and 436 (and see the epigraph to this chapter, ibid, pp. 368–69). While claiming that absolutely nothing can bind the will of the assembled citizens, Rousseau also stipulated that the popular will can be expressed *only* through absolutely general laws. As has been noted, this is a limit, whatever Rousseau chooses to call it.

56. Rousseau, "Du contrat social," p. 363; in his more conservative moods, it should be noted, Rousseau admits that "it is above all the great antiquity of laws that renders them sacred and inviolable" and that "the people soon despises those laws that it sees change every day" ("Sur l'origine de l'inégalité," ibid., p. 114).

57. For example, "It is doubtful whether any provision was made for revision of the law in Periclean democracy; certainly fundamental laws could not be altered without a revolution" (C. Hignett, *A History of the Athenian Constitution* [Oxford: Clarendon Press, 1952], p. 300). A spectacular ancient example of constitutional precommitment was the "higher law" Charondas established among the Thurians: "He commanded, namely, that the man who proposed to revise any [ordinary] law should put his neck in a noose at the time he made his proposal . . . but if the proposal of revision did not carry, the noose was to be drawn and the man die on the spot" (Diodorus Siculus, *The Library of History,* trans. C. H. Oldfather [Cambridge: Harvard University Press, 1946], bk. 12, chap. 17, p. 407).

58. Pufendorf, *De jure naturae et gentium,* bk. 8, chap. 10, sec. 8, p. 1,346.

59. Ibid., bk. 4, chap. 2, sec. 17, p. 518.

60. Grotius, *De jure belli ac pacis,* bk. 3, chap. 2, sec. 1, p. 623.

61. Ibid., bk. 2, chap. 14, sec. 10, p. 385.

62. Locke, *Two Treatises of Government,* II, §§ 57, 73, 116–17 (see also § 191); the inheritor or purchaser of land, according to Locke, has given his tacit consent to the government that protects his property; but this tacit consent does not make him a *perfect* member of the commonwealth, since he may sell his land and emigrate to found a new society or join another. To become a perfect member of the commonwealth, the individual must give his *express* consent; and if he does so he is "perpetually and indispensably obliged to be and remain unalterably a Subject to it" (ibid., II, § 121). The perpetual obligation that Locke affirms in this passage would be broken if the government dissolved. But does he really mean to exclude voluntary emigration in all other circumstances?

63. Sheldon Wolin, *Politics and Vision* (Boston: Little, Brown, 1960), p. 311.

64. Locke, *Two Treatises of Government,* II, § 138.

65. Joseph de Maistre, "Essay on the Generative Principle of Political Constitutions," in *The Works of Joseph de Maistre,* trans. Jack Lively (New York: Macmillan, 1965), pp. 147–48.

66. Francis Oakley, *Omnipotence, Covenant, and Order* (Ithaca: Cornell University Press, 1984), p. 62. See also Berndt Hamm, *Promissio, pactum, ordinatio: Freiheit und Selbstbindung Gottes in der scholastischen Gnadenlehre* (Tübingen: J. C. B. Mohr, 1977).

67. Richard Hooker, *Of the Laws of Eccleciastical Polity,* bk. 1, chap. 2, sec. 6, p. 154.

68. The enduring influence of this tradition is confirmed in the *Second Treatise,* where Locke argues that princes are subject to natural law because even the Almighty, who cannot be conceived as bargaining with His subjects or owing them anything, is firmly bound by His own promises (Locke, *Two Treatises of Government,* II, § 195).

69. Bodin, *Six Bookes,* I, 10, 162, and IV, 4, 490; see also IV, 3, 469–70.

70. As argued in chapter 4, Bodin's theological analogy is imperfect, since God's self-binding, while part of his arsenal of omnipotence, does not actually increase his powers.

71. Bodin, *Six Bookes,* IV, 4, 490; VI, 3, 687; I, 8, 109 (see also II, 1, 192; III, 7, 384–85; IV, 6, 518); I, 8, 103; I, 10, 159–60; III, 1, 254; III, 4, 323.

72. Locke, *Two Treatises of Government,* II, § 57.

73. *Federalist Papers,* no. 21, p. 139; no. 18, p. 124; no. 15, p. 106.

74. Burke, "Reflections on the Revolution in France," *Works,* vol. 3, p. 359.

75. Conversely, legally entrenched constitutional provisions will typically lose their appeal when, like "the right of the people to keep and bear arms," they help well-organized minorities frustrate majoritarian attempts to pass socially useful legislation. Gun-control laws would certainly not violate the Constitution. But the seeming inability of the American political system to adopt gun-control laws shows that, in some circumstances, the Constitution can serve as a rallying-point for special interests opposed to the will of the majority. The Second Amendment contains the fine print that reminds us that "we the people" did *not,* in every case, sign the Constitution currently in force.

76. *Federalist Papers,* no. 49, pp. 314, 317, 316.

77. Madison described as his *least important* objection to Jefferson's amendment scheme that "frequent appeals would, in great measure, deprive the government of that veneration which time bestows on everything, and without which perhaps the wisest and freest governments would not possess the requisite stability." The psychology of legalism has roots deeper than rational argument. For one thing, compliance with the law is contagious: "The strength of opinion in each individual, and its practical influence on his conduct, depend much on the number which he supposes to have entertained the same opinion." Most people are not philosophers, and the habits of legality upon which social cooperation depends are an improbable and fragile achievement. Thus, "the most rational government will not find it superfluous to have the prejudices of the community on its side" (*Federalist Papers,* no. 49, pp. 314–15). Nevertheless, constitutional rules are justified, according to Madison, not because they are inherited but because they work well for purposes we cherish today. In this sense, he too was a Jeffersonian.

78. James Madison, letter of 4 February 1790, in *The Papers of James Madison,* vol. 13, ed. Charles Hobson and Robert Rutland (Charlottesville: University Press of Virginia, 1981), p. 22.

79. Here, as elsewhere, Madison revealed his indebtedness to Hume: "Were one to choose a period of time, when the people's consent was the least regarded in public transactions, it would be precisely on the establishment of a new government. In a settled constitution, their inclinations are often consulted; but during the fury of revolutions, conquests, and public convulsions, military force or political craft usually decides the controversy" (Hume, "Of the Original Contract," in *Essays,* p. 461).

80. While acknowledging this aspect of Madison's argument, Bruce Ackerman also writes about "*The Federalist*'s recurring assumption that the People best express themselves through episodic and anomalous 'conventions,' and not through regular sessions of ordinary legislatures" (Bruce Ackerman, "The Storrs Lectures: Discovering the Constitution," *Yale Law Journal* 93 [1984]: 1022; and now *We the People,* I, *Foundations* [Cambridge: Harvard University Press, 1991]); but the passages Ackerman cites do not support this imaginative claim. Madison clearly believes that the people are even more likely to express themselves badly in extraordinary bodies convened in exceptional circumstances than in ordinary legislative assemblies. Far from idealizing moments of "higher lawmaking," Madison sees the success of Philadelphia as a stroke of luck unlikely to be repeated once the spirit of party erupts in the United States as it inevitably will. He concludes, therefore, that such "experiments are of too ticklish a nature to be unnecessarily multiplied" (*Federalist Papers,* no. 49, p. 315).

81. *Federalist Papers,* no. 49, p. 315; Madison, *Papers,* vol. 13, p. 22.

82. Jefferson, Letter of 12 July 1816, in *Writings,* p. 1,401.

83. *Federalist Papers,* no. 43 (Madison), p. 278; no. 37, p. 226.

84. *Federalist Papers,* no. 43 (Madison), p. 278.

85. Madison, *Papers,* vol. 13, p. 23.

86. *Federalist Papers,* no. 43 (Madison), p. 278.

87. Madison, *Papers,* vol. 13, p. 24.

88. Jefferson, *Writings,* p. 960. Here again, an unexamined legacy of absolutism may be at work: while the sovereign people will obviously die in an unsynchronized and staggered manner, a sovereign monarch will die a single datable death, and his sovereignty will pass to his successor all at once.

89. Jefferson, letter of 5 June 1824, in *Writings,* p. 1,481.

90. Hume, "Of the Original Contract," in *Essays,* p. 476.

91. *Federalist Papers,* no. 14 (Madison), p. 104.

92. Analogous points were made by Burke: "People will not look forward to posterity, who never look backward to their ancestors" ("Reflections on the Revolution in France," in *Works,* p. 274), and by Tocqueville: "The surest way of training people to violate the rights of the living is to set at nought the wishes of the dead" (*The Old Régime and the French Revolution* [New York: Doubleday, 1955], p. 190).

93. Jon Elster, *Ulysses and the Sirens* (Cambridge: Cambridge University Press, 1979), p. 94.

94. The French Revolutionary slogan *il faut tout recommencer à zéro* and the associated attempt to restart the calendar at Year I, extreme versions of the Paine-Jefferson attitude, appear absurdly naive in retrospect, as all liberal commentators voluminously explain.

95. Elster, *Ulysses and the Sirens,* p. 94. Ackerman, too, argues for a radical dualism between constitutionalism and politics; even though many of his detailed comments suggest a smooth continuum and not an abrupt dichotomy (e.g., "The Storrs Lectures: Discovering the Constitution," p. 1029).

96. According to Hobbes himself, "the *Pacts* and *Covenants,* by which the parts of this Body Politique were at first made, set together, and united, resemble that *Fiat,* or *Let us make man,* pronounced by God in the Creation" (*Leviathan,* p. 8).

97. Freedom cannot be plausibly conceived as the capacity to inaugurate action in a behavioral, cultural, and institutional vacuum; human "activity" is unimaginable without some "passive" adaptations and reactions to circumstances.

98. *Federalist Papers,* no. 39 (Madison), p. 242.

99. Commenting on the less than omnipotent character of the Federal Convention of 1787, Max Farrand labeled the Constitution a "bundle of compromises" (*The Framing of the Constitution of the United States* [New Haven: Yale University Press, 1913], p. 201).

100. Elster, *Ulysses and the Sirens,* p. 95.

101. Ibid., p. 94.

102. Carl J. Friedrich, *Constitutional Government and Democracy* (Waltham, Mass.: Blaisdell, 1968), p. 140.

103. The accumulated innovations introduced by later generations certainly rival the innovations of the Constitution in relation to the Articles of Confederation (see *Federalist Papers,* no. 40, p. 251).

104. I am thinking, for instance, of the Second French Republic and, especially, of the Weimar Republic.

105. *Federalist Papers,* no. 16 (Hamilton), p. 118.

106. Locke, *Two Treatises of Government,* II, § 57.

107. Locke, *Two Treatises of Government,* II, § 159; Montesquieu, *The Spirit of the Laws,* trans. Thomas Nugent (New York: Hafner, 1975), (XI, 6), vol. 1, p. 151; Hume, "Of the Origin of Government," *Essays,* pp. 40–41; *Federalist Papers,* no. 47 (Madison), p. 301.

108. E.g., *Myers v. United States,* 272 U.S. 52, 293 (1926), Justice Brandeis, dissenting.

109. Hume, "Of the Independency of Parliament," in *Essays,* p. 43.

110. Locke, *Two Treatises of Government,* II, § 107.

111. Montesquieu, *The Spirit of the Laws,* trans. Thomas Nugent (New York: Hafner, 1949), (XI, 4), vol. 1, bk. 11, chap. 4, p. 150.

112. Smith, *Wealth of Nations,* p. 680.

113. Bodin, *Six Bookes,* 4, 6, 512.

114. Montesquieu, *Spirit of the Laws,* vol. 1, bk. 6, chap 5, p. 78.

115. Locke, *Two Treatises of Government,* II, § 143; in "well order'd Commonwealths," he explains, "the *Legislative* Power is put into the hands of divers Persons who duly Assembled, have by themselves, or jointly with others, a Power to make Laws, which when they have done, being separated again, they are themselves subject to the Laws, they have made" (ibid.). In other words, the separation of powers gives the legislators some of the same interests as ordinary people. It does this, as Madison, too, was to observe, by ensuring that "they can make no law which will not have its full operation on themselves and their friends, as well as on the great mass of society" (*Federalist Papers,* no. 57 [Madison], p. 352).

116. Locke, *Two Treatises of Government,* II, § 107.

117. As Hamilton wrote, "Power being almost always the rival of power, the general government will at all times stand ready to check the usurpations of the state governments, and these will have the same disposition towards the general government. The people, by throwing themselves into either scale, will infallibly make it preponderate" (*Federalist Papers,* no. 28, p. 181; see also *Federalist,* no. 16, p. 117): notice that a constitutional balance between governmental bodies requires "the people" to play the role of an external balancer. *Federalist Papers,* no. 63, pp. 389–90.

118. *Federalist Papers,* no. 78 (Hamilton), pp. 467–68.

119. *Federalist Papers,* no. 49 (Madison), pp. 313–14.

120. *Federalist Papers,* no. 53 (Madison), p. 331.

121. Carl Schmitt, *Verfassungslehre* (Berlin: Duncker & Humblot, 1928), p. 41.

122. We might translate "das formlos Formende" as "the shaping power that itself has no shape." Seizing the chance to dismay his legalistically minded colleagues, Schmitt wrote, quite unrealistically: "Ein geregeltes Verfahren, durch welches die Betätigung der Verfassungsgebenden Gewalt gebunden wäre, kann es nicht geben." [There can be no regulated procedure through which the activity of the constituent power would be bound] (ibid., pp. 81–82).

123. *Federalist Papers,* no. 40 (Madison), p. 253.

124. Again, the election itself is carried out on the basis of a preselection of the candidates—which itself can be made more or less democratically.

125. Locke, *Two Treatises of Government,* II, § 154.

126. *Federalist Papers,* no. 53 (Madison), p. 331, 332.

127. Strictly speaking, Locke's "legislative" was King-in-Parliament, and therefore only partially elective.

128. Locke, *Two Treatises of Government,* II, §§ 157–58.

129. Locke's argument, interestingly enough, was echoed by Chief Justice Warren in his majority opinion in *Reynolds v. Sims,* 377 U.S. 533 (1964), whereby the Court compelled Alabama to revise an obsolete districting scheme that had granted some citizens forty times greater influence on the choice of representatives than others.

130. *Whitney v. California,* 274 U.S. 357, 375 (1927).

131. John Milton, "Areopagitica," in *Complete Prose Works* (New Haven: Yale University Press, 1959), vol. 2, pp. 487, 561.

132. Locke, *A Letter on Toleration,* p. 45; *Two Treatises of Government,* II, § 222.

133. Trenchard and Gordon, "Discourse Upon Libels," in *Cato's Letters,* (New York: Da Capo Press, 1971), vol. 3, pp. 298–99.

134. Jefferson, "A Bill for Establishing Religious Freedom" [1777], in *Writings,* p. 347; Jefferson, letter of 28 June 1804, ibid., p. 1,147.

135. *Federalist Papers,* no. 55 (Madison), p. 342; Federalist Papers, no. 70 (Hamilton), p. 427.

136. See especially Benedict de Spinoza, *A Theologico-Political Treatise and A Political Treatise,* trans. R. H. M. Elwes (New York: Dover, 1951), p. 376.

137. Helvétius, *A Treatise on Man* (New York: Burt Franklin, 1969), vol. 2 (sec. 9, chap. 12), p. 328.

138. "Considerations on Representative Government," in John Stuart Mill, *Collected Works,* ed. J. M. Robson, vol. 19, *Essays on Politics and Society* (Toronto: University of Toronto Press, 1977), p. 516.

139. See, for example, ibid., pp. 403–4.

140. Ibid., p. 404; recent treatments of Mill often focus on his vaguely romantic and narcissistic notion that participation beautifies the participant. More serious, however, is his idea that public debate is the most effective way to mobilize decentralized knowledge and utilize the diverse talents of the citizenry in solving common problems.

141. A. D. Lindsay, *The Essentials of Democracy,* 2d ed. (London: Oxford University Press, 1951); also excellent on this point, Samuel H. Beer, "The Strengths of Liberal Democracy," *A Prospect for Liberal Democracy,* ed. William Lingston (Austin: University of Texas Press, 1979), pp. 215–29.

142. John Rawls, "The Idea of Public Reason," in *Political Liberalism* (New York: Columbia University Press, 1993), pp. 212–54.

143. Locke, *Two Treatises of Government,* II, § 176.

144. If a community decides by majority vote to disenfranchise a minority, we would not wish to call their action democratic; but why not? If we define democracy simply by reference to the will of the people, such civic expulsions seem democratic enough. But if we define democracy as popular government through public discussion, then the disenfranchisement of a defeated minority would be a violation of a fundamental *democratic* norm. It would be a foreshortening of rational discussion, a smothering of voices. In other words, the procedural rule that minorities must be permitted (so long as they obey the law) to continue protesting puts substantive limits on what the majority can decide.

145. "On Liberty," in John Stuart Mill, *Collected Works,* ed. J. M. Robson, vol. 13, *Essays on Politics and Society* (Toronto: University of Toronto Press, 1977), p. 260.

146. See Jon Elster, *Sour Grapes: Studies in the Subversion of Rationality* (Cambridge: Cambridge University Press, 1983), pp. 39–40.

147. Alexander Meiklejohn, *Political Freedom* (New York: Harper & Bros., 1960), p. 27.

148. *Federalist Papers,* no. 63 (Madison), p. 384.

149. The phrase is Elster's, in *Ulysses and the Sirens,* p. 93.

150. David Hume, *A Treatise of Human Nature* (Oxford: Clarendon Press, 1978), p. 538.

151. Thomas Schelling, *The Strategy of Conflict* (Cambridge: Harvard University Press, 1960), p. 139.

152. Thomas Schelling, "The Intimate Contest for Self-Command," in *Choice and Consequence* (Cambridge: Harvard University Press, 1984), p. 58. See also "Ethics, Law, and the Exercise of Self-Command" (ibid., pp. 83–112).

153. Libertarians who protest that such legislation interferes with freedom of choice might be reminded that voting, too, is a form of choice.

154. As in Tribe, *American Constitutional Law,* pp. 10–11.

155. Friedrich Hayek, *Law, Legislation and Liberty,* vol. 2 (London: Routledge & Kegan Paul, 1976), p. 23.

156. For instance, Article 15 of the French Constitution of the Year III (1795), *Les Constitutions de la France depuis 1789,* p. 102; see also Locke, *Two Treatises of Government,* II, § 23; and Montesquieu, *Spirit of the Laws,* vol. 1, bk. 15, chap. 2, p. 236.

157. Mill, "On Liberty," pp. 299–300; cf. Immanuel Kant, "Perpetual Peace," *Kant's Political Writings,* ed. Hans Reiss (Cambridge: Cambridge University Press, 1970), p. 75.

158. As Elster remarks, summarizing Thomas Nagel, "too much spontaneity now may reduce the possibilities for spontaneous behavior later on" (Elster, *Ulysses and the Sirens,* p. 41).

159. Bodin, *Six Bookes,* book I, 10, 169.

160. So reads Justice Stone's famous footnote in *United States v. Carolene Products* (1938) 304 U.S. 144, 152, n. 4; my italics.

161. "An individual is capable of rectifying his mistakes, by discussion and experience. Not by experience alone. There must be discussion, to show how experience is to be interpreted. Wrong opinions and practices gradually yield to fact and argument; but facts and arguments, to produce an effect on the mind, must be brought before it" (Mill, "On Liberty," p. 231).

## Chapter 6

1. Cass Sunstein, *Free Speech and the Problem of Democracy* (New York: Free Press, 1993), pp. 241–52.

2. Mill, "Considerations on Representative Government," in John Stuart Mill, *Collected Works,* ed. J. M. Robson, vol. 19, *Essays on Politics and Society* (Toronto: University of Toronto Press, 1977), p. 346.

3. Cf. "The general prosperity attains a greater height, and is more widely diffused, in proportion to the amount and variety of the personal energies enlisted in promoting it" (ibid., p. 404).

4. Conversely, public discussion is a practical strength, not merely a moral norm. This thesis is advanced in Samuel Beer, *To Make a Nation: The Rediscovery of American Federalism* (Cambridge: Harvard University Press, 1993), pp. 264–75. I am much indebted to Beer for ten years of inspiring conversation on this theme.

5. "On Liberty," in John Stuart Mill, *Collected Works,* ed. J. M. Robson, vol. 13, *Essays on Politics and Society* (Toronto: University of Toronto Press, 1977), p. 229; cf. Benedict de Spinoza, *A Theological-Political Treatise and A Political Treatise* (New York: Dover, 1951), p. 376.

6. As a result, "unity of opinion, unless resulting from the fullest and freest comparison of opposite opinions, is not desirable" ("On Liberty," p. 260).

7. "Bentham," in John Stuart Mill, *Collected Works,* ed. J. M. Robson, vol. 10, *Essays on Ethics, Religion and Society* (Toronto: University of Toronto Press, 1969), p. 108.

8. To use Madison's phrase, *Federalist Papers,* no. 63, p. 384.

9. "On Liberty," p. 232.

10. "Considerations on Representative Government," p. 509.

11. Ibid., p. 432.

12. "On Liberty," p. 283.

13. Ibid., p. 226.

14. Ibid., p. 229.

15. That is nevertheless the gist of Gertrude Himmelfarb's imaginative and spiteful diagnosis in *On Liberty and Liberalism: The Case of John Stuart Mill* (New York: Knopf, 1974).

16. "On Liberty," p. 230.

17. John Stuart Mill, "Autobiography," in *Autobiography and Literary Essays,* ed. John M. Robson and Jack Stillinger (Toronto: University of Toronto Press, 1981), p. 269.

18. "Autobiography," pp. 269–70.

19. "The notion that truths external to the mind may be known by intuition or consciousness, independently of observation and experience, is, I am persuaded, in these times, the great intellectual support of false doctrines and bad institutions" ("Autobiography," p. 233).

20. "On Liberty," p. 244.

21. Ibid., p. 250.

22. If atheists do tell the truth, and openly divulge their atheism to legal authorities, as the rule assumes they will, then the rule itself is senseless (ibid., pp. 239–40).

23. "Considerations on Representative Government," p. 493.

24. Ibid., p. 493.

25. See, for instance, "Coleridge," in John Stuart Mill, *Collected Works,* ed. J. M. Robson, vol. 18, *Essays on Ethics, Religion and Society* (Toronto: University of Toronto, 1977), p. 156.

26. *Principles of Political Economy,* in John Stuart Mill, *Collected Works,* ed. J. M. Robson, vol. 3 (Toronto: University of Toronto Press, 1965), p. 937.

27. "On Liberty," p. 309.

28. Ibid., p. 269; "Considerations on Representative Government," p. 434.

29. The state must promote the greatest happiness of the greatest number, and happiness should be defined by unsupervised individuals in a variety of eccentric ways. Political officials cannot prescribe obligatory goals or overrule diverse ideas of happiness on the ground that wise statesmen must be their brothers' keepers. From a *political* point of view—and the restriction is crucial—pushpin is as good as Pushkin. If political authorities could legitimately define happiness, resistance to governmental authority would be extremely difficult to justify. On all these points, see Shirley Letwin, *The Pursuit of Certainty* (Cambridge: Cambridge University Press, 1965), pp. 127–88.

30. "Utilitarianism," in John Stuart Mill, *Collected Works,* ed. J. M. Robson, vol. 5, *Essays on Ethics, Religion and Society* (Toronto: University of Toronto Press, 1965), p. 211.

31. "On Liberty," p. 235.
32. "Utilitarianism," p. 213.
33. "Considerations on Representative Government," p. 539.
34. Ibid., p. 508.
35. Other sorts of education may well serve civic purposes; e.g., Rousseau believed that individuals should be taught habits of identification with their fellow citizens. But academic education does not seem well suited for such a task.
36. "Considerations on Representative Government," p. 476. The private value of a few extra votes was certainly worth much less in purely economic terms than the private costs of additional years of education. But Mill reasons that the symbolic gains of status enhancement will suffice to induce people to pay these costs, showing that his analysis presupposes a psychological theory similar to those examined in chapter 2.
37. "Considerations on Representative Government," p. 478.
38. Ibid., p. 440.
39. "De Tocqueville on Democracy in America," in John Stuart Mill, *Collected Works,* ed. J. M. Robson, vol. 18, *Essays on Politics and Society* (Toronto: University of Toronto Press, 1977), p. 72.
40. "On Liberty," p. 250.
41. John Stuart Mill, "Spirit of the Age," in *Essays on Politics and Culture,* ed. Gertrude Himmelfarb (Gloucester, Mass.: Peter Smith, 1973), p. 3.
42. "On Liberty," p. 252.
43. "Those persons whom the circumstances of society, and their own position in it, permit to dedicate themselves to the investigation and study of physical, moral, and social truths, as their peculiar calling, can alone be expected to make the evidence of such truths a subject of profound meditation, and to make themselves thorough masters of the philosophical grounds of those opinions of which it is desirable that all should be firmly *persuaded,* but which they alone can entirely and philosophically *know.* The remainder of mankind must, and except in periods of transition like the present, always do, take the far greater part of their opinions on all extensive subjects upon the authority of those who have studied them" ("Spirit of the Age," pp. 12–13).
44. "Considerations on Representative Government," pp. 574–75.
45. Ibid., p. 428.
46. Ibid., p. 433.
47. Ibid., p. 432.
48. Ibid., p. 430.
49. Ibid., p. 438.
50. Ibid.
51. Clearly expounded in Dennis Thompson, *John Stuart Mill and Representative Government* (Princeton: Princeton University Press, 1976), pp. 20ff.
52. Mill also employed an equally interesting and (I believe) equally unsatisfying analogy between citizens choosing among various political alternatives and jury members delivering a verdict.
53. A playful phrase of Samuel Beer's.
54. For example, Mill explicitly praises representative government as the regime best able to protect the *interests* of the poor.
55. "On Liberty," p. 261.
56. Ibid., p. 262.

57. John Stuart Mill, "Chapters on Socialism," in *On Politics and Society*, ed. Geraint Williams (Glasgow: Collins, 1976), p. 336.

58. "On Liberty," p. 226.

59. Ibid., p. 263.

60. Ibid., p. 265.

61. "Nature," in *Collected Works*, ed. J. M. Robson, vol. 10, *Essays on Ethics, Religion and Society* (Toronto: University of Toronto Press, 1969), pp. 373–402.

62. "On Liberty," p. 263.

63. Jon Elster, *Sour Grapes: Studies in the Subversion of Rationality* (Cambridge: Cambridge University Press, 1983), p. 38.

64. "Considerations on Representative Government," p. 490.

65. "On Liberty," p. 252.

66. Ibid., p. 254.

67. Mill never explained why the adversary system would necessarily bring *all* sides of every issue to the consideration of observant bystanders. Adversaries might despise each other and yet conspiratorially decide to repress relevant facts and viewpoints because, despite their differences, they have some interests in common. Mill simply assumed that this would seldom be the case.

68. "On Liberty," p. 234.

69. "Autobiography," p. 179; Mill does not mention the dangers presented by the *half-educated*, a group that has provided many eager recruits to antiliberal movements in the twentieth century.

70. "On Liberty," p. 224.

71. Ibid., p. 257.

72. Ibid., p. 257.

## Chapter 7

1. Alexander Bickel, *The Least Dangerous Branch: The Supreme Court at the Bar of Politics* (New Haven: Yale University Press, 1962), p. 133; and, in general, pp. 111–98.

2. John Rawls, *Political Liberalism* (New York: Columbia University Press, 1993), pp. 29, 151–52.

3. Peter Bachrach and Morton S. Baratz, "Two Faces of Power," *American Political Science Review* 56 (1962): 948; E. E. Schattschneider, *The Semisovereign People: A Realist's View of Democracy in America* (Hinsdale, Ill.: Dryden Press, 1975), p. 66.

4. Cass Sunstein, *Democracy and the Problem of Free Speech* (New York: Free Press, 1993), pp. 116–17.

5. William Blackstone, *Commentaries on the Laws of England* (Chicago: University of Chicago Press, 1979), vol. 3, pp. 373–74.

6. Blackstone, *Commentaries on the Laws of England*, vol. 4, p. 150.

7. Joseph Cooper, *The Previous Question: Its Standing as a Precedent for Cloture in the United States Senate* (87th Congress, 2d Session, Document No. 104) (Washington, D.C.: U.S. Government Printing Office, 1962), p. 2.

8. For present purposes, I shall define *positive liberty* as collective self-government (not as "the realization of the real self" or "the exercise of authentic capacities," to which self-government is often narcissistically assimilated); *negative liberty*, by contrast, can be preliminarily defined as the absence of coercive interfer-

ence, in voluntary social interactions, by the government or other wielders of power. It is profoundly confusing to identify positive liberty with both democracy and individual self-realization, I believe, because (1) the absence of coercion is typically prized as a necessary precondition for the development of human faculties, and (2) obligatory and full-time political participation may condemn many humanly important capacities to wither on the vine.

9. Isaiah Berlin, *Four Essays on Liberty* (Oxford: Oxford University Press, 1969), pp. 130–31.

10. Since criminal penalties for defamation of public officials allowed such officials, by alleging sedition, to use the courts to punish their critics, a few eighteenth-century predecessors of the American Founders expressed grave doubts about the common law of libels: "What are usually called Libels, undoubtedly keep Great Men in Awe, and are some Check upon their Behavior, by showing them the Deformity of their Actions, as well as warning other People to be on their Guard against Oppression" (Trenchard and Gordon, "Discourse upon Libels" [1722], in *Cato's Letters,* vol. 3 [New York: Da Capo Press, 1971], p. 292); accountable government is impossible if authorities can terrorize the press into meekness by threatening indictment for seditious libel. That, as is well known, was Madison's response to the Sedition Act of 1798 (James Madison, "Report on the Virginia Resolutions," in *Mind of the Founder,* ed. Marvin Meyers [Indianapolis: Bobbs-Merrill, 1973], pp. 328–42).

11. Joseph Schumpeter, *Capitalism, Socialism and Democracy* (New York: Harper & Row, 1962), p. 291 (see also p. 297); Robert Dahl, *Preface to Democratic Theory* (Chicago: University of Chicago Press, 1956), p. 80; Samuel P. Huntington, "Will More Countries Become Democratic?" *Political Science Quarterly* 99, no. 2 (Summer 1984): 208.

12. The opposite of postponing a discussion is cloture: the decision to prohibit discussion *after* a certain point.

13. Freudian repression must suppress not only the event to be forgotten but also the act of repressing itself (J.-P. Sartre, *L'être et le néant* [Paris: Gallimard, 1943], pp. 88–93). To be effective, by contrast, most gag rules require strategically important parties to know that—and remember why—they are avoiding a touchy question.

14. Vojtech Cepl, "Ritual Sacrifices," *East European Constitutional Review,* 1, no. 1 (spring 1992): 24–26; Stephen Schulhofer, Michel Rosenfeld, Ruti Teitel, and Roger Errera, "Dilemmas of Justice," *East European Constitutional Review,* 1, no. 2 (summer 1992): 17–22; Andrzej Rzeplinski, "A Lesser Evil," *East European Constitutional Review,* 1, no. 3 (fall 1992): 33–35.

15. For this argument, see Bruce Ackerman, *The Future of Liberal Revolution* (New Haven: Yale University Press, 1992).

16. Juan J. Linz, "The transition from authoritarian regimes to democratic political systems and the problems of consolidation of political democracy," unpublished manuscript, presented at the IPSA Tokyo Roundtable, March 29–April 1, 1982.

17. Friedrich Nietzsche, "Zur Genealogie der Moral," in *Werke,* ed. Karl Schlecta (Darmstadt: Wissenschaftliche Buchgesellschaft, 1966), vol. 2, p. 799.

18. Dankwart Rustow, "Transitions to Democracy: Toward a Dynamic Model," *Comparative Politics* 2 (April 1970): 337–63.

19. Adam Przeworski, *Democracy and the Market* (Cambridge: Cambridge University Press, 1991), p. 80.

20. "The first grand compromise that establishes democracy, if it proves at all viable, is in itself proof of the efficacy of the principle of conciliation and accommodation. The first success, therefore, may encourage contending forces and their leaders to submit other major questions to resolution by democratic procedures" (Rustow, "Transitions to Democracy," p. 358).

21. This analysis implies that no "transition to democracy" can begin in post-communist societies before there occurs a consolidation of rival social interests capable of being plausibly represented at national "roundtables."

22. Clifford Geertz, "The Integrative Revolution: Primordial Sentiments and Civil Politics in the New States," in *The Interpretation of Cultures* (New York: Basic Books, 1973). Geertz writes of "the looming headlong clash of primordial and civil loyalties" (ibid., p. 309).

23. Ibid., pp. 263, 272.

24. Ibid., pp. 282–83. What leaders must strive to establish is "an effective civil framework within which very intense primordial issues can be adjusted and contained rather than allowed to run free in parapolitical confusion" (ibid., p. 285).

25. This must be what Geertz means by the importance of "divesting [primordial loyalties] of their legitimizing force with respect to governmental authority" (ibid., p. 277).

26. Ibid., p. 310.

27. Arend Lijphart, *Democracy in Plural Societies: A Comparative Exploration* (New Haven: Yale University Press, 1977).

28. Ibid., pp. 53, 169.

29. Ibid., pp..151, 41.

30. Ibid., p. 28. "When such decisions affect the vital interests of a minority segment, such a defeat will be regarded as unacceptable and will endanger intersegmental elite cooperation" (ibid., p. 36).

31. *Register of Debates,* vol. 12, 24th Congress, 1st session (18 May 1836), p. 3,757. The last of the congressional gag rules was rescinded in 1845, largely through the efforts of Adams: see Samuel Flagg Bemis's chapter entitled "Slavery and the Gag Rule," in *John Quincy Adams and the Union* (New York: Knopf, 1956).

32. William W. Freehling, *Prelude to Civil War: The Nullification Controversy in South Carolina 1816–1836* (New York: Harper & Row, 1965), pp. 346–48. I am indebted to Freehling's entire discussion of the gag rule debate.

33. Robert V. Remini, *Andrew Jackson and the Course of American Democracy, 1833–1845,* vol. 3 (New York: Harper & Row, 1984), p. 406.

34. Politicians are always more eager to gag others, needless to say, than to gag themselves. For instance, a significant majority from *both* sections voted to gag the slaves themselves, i.e., to deny them a right to petition Congress (*Register of Debates,* vol. 13, 24th Congress, 2d session [11 February 1837], p. 1733).

35. *The Papers of John C. Calhoun,* vol. 13 (1835–1837), ed. Clyde Wilson (Columbia: University of South Carolina Press, 1980), p. 393.

36. Freehling, *Prelude to Civil War,* p. 355.

37. For similar reasons, Calhoun rejected President Jackson's offer to debar incendiary publications from being circulated in the South: to accept federal help on this matter would be dangerously to extend federal authority into the internal affairs of the states.

38. *Papers of John C. Calhoun,* vol. 13, p. 105.

39. Ibid., p. 106.

40. They acknowledged it, notoriously, by agreeing to tolerate the slave trade

until 1808 (Art. I, sec. 9, par. 1), and by accepting the three-fifths rule (Art. I, sec. 2, par. 3), which helped balance northern and southern power in the House.

41. The classical "prodemocratic" argument for suppressing a divisive issue was made by Senator Benton in 1848: "This Federal Government was made for something else than to have this pestiferous question constantly thrust upon us to the interruption of the most important business. . . . What I protest against is, to have the real business of the country, the pressing, urgent, crying business of the country stopped, prostrated, defeated, by thrusting this question upon us. We read in Holy Writ, that a certain people were cursed by the plague of frogs, and that the plague was everywhere. You could not look upon the table but there were frogs, you could not sit down at the banquet but there were frogs, you could not go to the bridal couch and lift the sheets but there were frogs! . . . Here it is, this black question, forever on the table, on the nuptial couch, everywhere! . . . I remember the time when no one would have thought of asking a public man what his opinions were on the extension of slavery any more than what was the length of his foot" (*Congressional Globe,* 30th Congress, 1st session, appendix, p. 686; cited in Andrew McLaughlin, *A Constitutional History of the United States* [New York: Appleton-Century-Crofts, 1935], p. 509).

42. Geertz, "Integrative Revolution," p. 310.

43. Lijphart, in fact, expressly modeled his own theory on Calhoun's doctrine of "concurrent majorities"; for his references to Calhoun, see *Democracy in Plural Societies,* pp. 37, 125, 149.

44. John C. Calhoun, *A Disquisition on Government* (Indianapolis: Bobbs-Merrill, 1953), pp. 78–79.

45. Like Rustow and Przeworski, Calhoun believes that it is inconceivable for a constitution to be created within a faction-free society: "It is difficult to conceive that any people among whom [constitutions] did not exist would or could voluntarily institute them in order to establish such governments, while it is not at all wonderful that they should grow out of conflicts between different orders or classes when aided by a favorable combination of circumstances" (ibid., p. 79).

46. Cited in C. Vann Woodward, "The Northern Crusade against Slavery," in *American Counterpoint: Slavery and Racism in the North/South Dialogue* (New York: Oxford University Press, 1983), p. 142.

47. *The Lincoln-Douglas Debates,* ed. Robert Johannsen (New York and Oxford: Oxford University Press, 1965), pp. 121, 265.

48. Roger Fisher and William Ury, *Getting to Yes: Negotiating Agreement without Giving In* (Harmondsworth: Penguin, 1983), p. 37.

49. *The Lincoln-Douglas Debates,* p. 256.

50. Lincoln's reasoning here was surely on Rawls's mind when he wrote: "Certain truths . . . concern things so important that differences about them have to be fought out, even should this mean civil war" (Rawls, *Political Liberalism,* p. 151).

51. Ibid., pp. 233, 225.

52. Ibid., p. 256.

53. For my understanding of Lincoln's mature position on this matter, I am indebted to J. David Greenstone, "Political Culture and American Political Development: Liberty, Union, and the Liberal Bi-Polarity," in *Studies in American Political Development* 1 (1987): 1–49.

54. *Lincoln-Douglas Debates,* p. 216.

55. *Lincoln-Douglas Debates,* pp. 199, 236. As one commentator puts it: "To

publicize Kansas as an arcadia for homesteaders and planters alike, and then to legislate that the people in the territory would decide the burning issue of slavery on the basis of squatter sovereignty, was to thrust two gamecocks into a barrel" (James MacGregor Burns, *The Vineyard of Liberty* [New York: Knopf, 1982], p. 550).

56. *Lincoln-Douglas Debates,* p. 136.

57. Arthur Bestor, "The American Civil War as a Constitutional Crisis," *American Law and the Constitutional Order: Historical Perspectives,* ed. Lawrence Friedman and Harry Scheiber (Cambridge: Harvard University Press, 1978), pp. 219–34.

58. According to Douglas, "the great revolution" was that the new parties "seem to be divided by a geographical line" (*Lincoln-Douglas Debates,* p. 116).

59. Classically, *Cantwell v. Connecticut,* 310 U.S. 296 (1940), where a law construed as barring Jehovah's Witnesses from playing anti-Catholic records in a Catholic neighborhood was declared unconstitutional.

60. *Engel v. Vitale,* 370 U.S. 421 (1962); *Wallace v. Jaffree,* 472 U.S. 38 (1985), striking down, as an unconstitutional endorsement of religion, three Alabama statutes that authorized a one-minute period of silent meditation; *Wallace,* in other words, represented a paradoxical, though not necessarily unreasonable, decision to gag silence.

61. *Lee v. Weisman,* 112 S. Ct. 2,649 (1992).

62. J. W. Pratt, *Religion, Politics, and Diversity: The Church-State Theme in New York History* (Ithaca: Cornell University Press, 1967), p. 185.

63. The bill of 1842 actually contained a mixed strategy: the attempt to separate politics from religion was complemented by a concession to the religious loyalties of local majorities. Bible-reading survived the general ban on sectarian practices in the schools; but the King James version was used in Protestant areas and the Douay edition in Catholic districts (ibid., p. 189).

64. The Establishment Clause is commonly said to have denied the right to establish a church to the national government in order to protect established churches in the states. For a counterargument, see Leonard Levy, "The Original Meaning of the Establishment Clause," in *Constitutional Opinions* (New York: Oxford University Press, 1986), pp. 135–61; in any case, "incorporation" via the Fourteenth Amendment eventually extended the Establishment provision explicitly to the states (see *Abington School District v. Schempp,* 374 U.S. 203 [1963], Justice Brennan concurring, at p. 256).

65. *McCollum v. Board of Education,* 333 U.S. 203, 231, 216–17 (1947). Reviewing the history of the state-church issue as it affected public education, Frankfurter also noted that "in Massachusetts, largely through the efforts of Horace Mann, all sectarian teachings were barred from the common school to save it from being rent by denominational conflict" (ibid., at p. 215).

66. 333 U.S. 203, 227; Scalia's claim that school prayer will, on the contrary, *unify* a denominationally divided society remains rather eccentric and unrepresentative of most Establishment Clause jurisprudence (*Lee v. Weisman,* 112 S. Ct. 2649, at p. 2685).

67. Already in *Everson v. Board of Education,* Justice Black associated church-state entanglement with "civil strife" (330 U.S. 1, 8 [1947]). Consider also *Committee for Public Education and Religious Liberty v. Nyquist,* 413 U.S. 756, 794–98 (1973), Powell's plurality opinion; *Meek v. Pittenger,* 421 U.S. 349, 372 (1975), Stewart's plurality opinion; *Wolman v. Walter,* 433 U.S. 229, 258 (1977), Marshall, concurring in part and dissenting in part; *Marsh v. Chambers,* 463 U.S. 783, 799–806 (1983); *Aguilar v. Felton,* 473 U.S. 402 (1985). For a clear summary by the champion of the divisive-

ness test, see *Meek v. Pittenger,* 421 U.S. 349, 374–85, Justice Brennan, concurring in part and dissenting in part.

68. *Walz v. Tax Commission,* 397 U.S. 664, 694–95 (1970).

69. Paul Freund, "Public Aid to Parochial Schools," *Harvard Law Review* 82 (May 1969): 1692.

70. 403 U.S. 602 (1971).

71. Ibid.

72. Ibid. See also *Aguilar v. Felton,* 473 U.S. 402 (1985), Justice Powell concurring.

73. Recall, once again, that an overriding desire for national unity is probably an essential precondition for the willingness of rival groups to set aside their differences. Only a shared concern for military security, arguably, has induced secular and fundamentalist Israelis to postpone any clear-cut decision about the status of religion in their country (Nadav Safran, *Israel: The Embattled Ally* [Cambridge: Harvard University Press, 1981], pp. 200–19).

74. Justice Rehnquist, for example, refers slightingly to the "rather elusive" inquiry into divisive political potential (*Mueller v. Allen,* 463 U.S. 388, 403, n. 11 [1983]); consider also: "The Court's reliance on the potential for political divisiveness as evidence of undue entanglement is also unpersuasive" (*Aguilar v. Felton,* 473 U.S. 402, 429 [1985], Justice O'Connor, dissenting); and "In my view, political divisions along religious lines should not be an independent test of constitutionality" (*Lynch v. Donnelly,* 465 U.S. 668, 689 [1984]).

75. Justice Brennan concurs but stresses that political divisiveness remains a useful signal of impermissible entanglement (*Lynch v. Donnelly,* 465 U.S. 668, 701 [1984]).

76. Leonard F. Manning, *The Law of Church-State Relations* (St. Paul, Minn.: West Publishing Co., 1981), p. 235.

77. According to Bodin, remember, free discussion exacerbates the tendency of religious opinions to become dangerously sectarian. By force of tradition, most sixteenth- and seventeenth-century political theorists believed that no nation could endure part Catholic and part Protestant. But moderates and *politiques* eventually realized that, if salvation were conceived as a wholly private matter, a divided house could stand. The no-more-discussion rule, glossed by Bodin, was a first and somewhat crude attempt to maintain civil order by excluding religious controversy from the public square.

78. A. James Reichley, *Religion in American Public Life* (Washington, D.C.: Brookings, 1985), p. 167.

79. According to the leading advocate of the divisiveness doctrine: "The State's goal of preventing sectarian bickering and strife may not be accomplished by regulating religious speech and political association" (*McDaniel v. Paty,* 435 U.S. 618, 641 [1978], Justice Brennan, concurring).

80. Technically, the government is also barred from aiding all sects equally; but in practice there is no social pressure for such an arrangement and therefore no real danger that realistically needs to be guarded against.

81. *Lynch v. Donnelly,* 465 U.S. 668 (1984), ruling that a publicly subsidized nativity scene did not convey government approval of Christians or disapproval of non-Christians.

82. *McDaniel v. Paty,* 435 U.S. 618, 641 (1978).

83. Walter Berns, *The First Amendment and the Future of American Democracy* (New York: Basic Books, 1976), pp. 119–28; Walter Berns, "Taking Rights Frivolously,"

in *Liberalism Reconsidered,* ed. Douglas MacLean and Claudia Mills (Totowa, N.J.: Rowman & Allanheld, 1983), p. 62.

84. This is more or less the conclusion of *The Abortion Dispute and the American System,* ed. Gilbert Y. Steiner (Washington, D.C.: Brookings, 1983).

85. But not the question of whether federal funds should be used to pay for abortions.

86. *Thornburgh v. American College of Obstetricians,* 476 U.S. 747, 796 (1986), Justice White dissenting.

87. 393 U.S. 97 (1968), 108.

88. Ibid., 97, 103. Concern with the constitutional protection of the conditions of government by discussion is even more apparent in the U.S. District Court finding in *McLean v. Arkansas,* 529 F. Supp. 1255 (E.D. Ark. 1982), holding unconstitutional a statute requiring balanced treatment of evolutionary theory and creation science; all the relevant documents are available in *Creationism, Science, and the Law,* ed. Marcel La Folette (Cambridge: MIT Press, 1983).

89. 393 U.S. 97, 112–13.

90. Robert H. Bork, "Neutral Principles and some First Amendment Problems," *Indiana Law Journal* 47 (fall 1971): 1, 3.

91. Ibid., pp. 21, 20, 28.

92. As is well known, some philosophers dispute the rationality of the process of scientific inquiry. But even Paul Feyerabend would be able to tell the difference between a criminal justice system in which the verdicts were set in advance by the Party *apparat* and one where prejudgments were at least conceivably revisable in the light of evidence.

93. Gregory of Tours, *The History of the Franks,* bk. 9, chap. 19 (Harmondsworth: Penguin, 1977), pp. 501–2.

94. For an interesting example, see Beryl L. Bellman, *The Language of Secrecy* (New Brunswick, N.J.: Rutgers University Press, 1984).

## Chapter 8

1. Francis Bacon, "Of Seditions and Troubles," in *The Essayes or Counsels Civill and Morall,* ed. M. Kiernan (Cambridge: Harvard University Press, 1985), pp. 45–46; Richard Posner, *Economic Analysis of Law,* 4th ed. (Boston: Little, Brown, 1992), pp. 463–64.

2. *Unlike* Reaganites, the latter repudiate the market for traditionalist reasons, as a violation of inherited customs and attachments.

3. Montesquieu, *The Spirit of the Laws,* trans. Thomas Nugent (New York: Hafner, 1949), vol. 2, p. 25.

4. I shall again be discussing Hobbes as well—the preliberal whose thinking, as I argued in chapter 3, left the most lasting traces on the liberal tradition.

5. *The Federalist Papers* (New York: Mentor, 1961), no. 37 (Madison), p. 225; no. 38, p. 233.

6. John Locke, *Two Treatises of Government* (Cambridge: Cambridge University Press, 1988), II, § 102.

7. Milton Friedman, *Capitalism and Freedom* (Chicago: University of Chicago Press, 1962), p. 200.

8. This view is advanced by, among others, Friedrich Hayek, *The Constitution of Liberty* (Chicago: University of Chicago Press, 1960), pp. 176–92.

9. Montesquieu, *Spirit of the Laws,* vol. 1, p. 183; for a contrary view, see the

one-sided argument of Franz Neumann, *The Democratic and Authoritarian State* (New York: Free Press, 1957), pp. 96–148.

10. Friedman, *Capitalism and Freedom,* p. 195.

11. David Hume, "Of the Origin of Government," in *Essays: Moral, Political and Literary* (Indianapolis: Liberty Classics, 1985), p. 37.

12. Montesquieu, *Spirit of the Laws,* vol. 1, p. 2.

13. Adam Smith, *The Theory of Moral Sentiments,* ed. D. D. Raphael and A. L. Macfie (Oxford: Oxford University Press, 1976), p. 86; Smith, *An Inquiry into the Nature and Causes of the Wealth of Nations* (New York: Modern Library, 1937), p. 572, my emphasis; Ibid., p. 651.

14. A concern for the welfare of others, in other words, was built into the liberal definition of legitimate private action. Locke, in a passage cited above, distinguished *proper interests* from improper ones on the grounds that the former were those compatible with the public good (see *Two Treatises of Government,* II, § 57). Self-interest is subordinate to the just, the right, and the proper, and that means: to the general good. Improper or sinister interests, those violating the norm of justice, must be legally repressed. An ascriptive, hierarchical, demeaning, and oppressive social system, where a few reaped all the benefits and the majority bore all the burdens, might be "peaceful" enough, but it would not qualify as a liberal social order for the simple reason that it would not be just. However orderly, slavery remains a vile and miserable, and therefore unacceptable, estate of man.

15. *Federalist Papers,* no. 51 (Madison), p. 324.

16. Thomas Hobbes, *Leviathan* (Harmondsworth: Penguin, 1968), pp. 202–3.

17. *Federalist Papers,* no. 51 (Madison), p. 325.

18. The analytically unsatisfactory distinction between *droits-libertés* and *droits-créances* is accepted uncritically by, among others, Luc Ferry and Alain Renaut (*Philosophie politique 3: Des droits de l'homme à l'idée républicaine* [Paris: Presses Universitaires de France, 1985], pp. 84–86).

19. The very idea of an "entitlement," writes one conservative opponent of welfare programs for the poor, "challenges the distinction, essential to liberal constitutionalism, between the rights the government exists to protect and the exercise of those rights by private individuals, or between state and society. For an entitlement is a right whose exercise is guaranteed to a certain degree by the government—a right that is therefore exercised to that degree by the government. An equal right to seek a job, for example, becomes an entitlement to a job or rather to the proceeds of a job, which the government performs as it were instead of the worker" (Harvey C. Mansfield, Jr., "The American Election: Entitlements versus Opportunity," *Government and Opposition* 20 [winter 1985]: 13). But liberals have always viewed *security* as a right that the government protects by itself performing basic police functions instead of allowing citizens to do so.

20. Friedman, *Capitalism and Freedom,* p. 5.

21. Smith, *Wealth of Nations,* p. 618.

22. The fundamental superiority of the liberal over the Marxist tradition may lie here: despite their intense concern with political tyranny, liberals never lost sight of the possibility of nonpolitical or nonstate forms of oppression. Marxists, by contrast, because of their one-sided focus on the owners of the means of production, tended to neglect the equal and autonomous threat to freedom posed by the wielders of the means of destruction. Because threatening concentrations of power were always emerging spontaneously even within the freest society, liberals saw state power as an indispensable counterweight—as an instrument of, rather than simply

a threat to, freedom. In my view, their fundamentally double conception of the (political and extrapolitical) obstacles to liberty led the most clear-sighted heirs of the liberal tradition, quite consistently, to embrace the welfare state.

23. Locke, *Two Treatises of Government,* II, § 222, my emphasis.

24. David Hume, "Of the Original Contract," in *Essays: Moral, Political, and Literary* (Indianapolis: Liberty Classics, 1985), p. 466.

25. Smith, *Wealth of Nations,* p. 669; *Federalist Papers,* no. 51 (Madison), p. 323.

26. Karl Marx and Friedrich Engels, *Werke* (Berlin: Dietz, 1972), vol. 1, pp. 365–66; Friedrich Nietzsche's "Verachtung gegen Sicherheit" can be found, among other places, in *Werke,* ed. Karl Schlecta (Darmstadt: Wissenschaftlichebuchgesellschaft, 1973), p. 786.

27. "On Liberty" in John Stuart Mill, *Collected Works,* ed. J. M. Robson, vol. 18, *Essays on Ethics, Religion and Society* (Toronto: University of Toronto Press, 1977), p. 251; and he adds: "security no human being can possibly do without" (ibid.); see also Locke, *A Letter on Toleration,* ed. R. Klibanski and J. G. Gough (Oxford: Clarendon Press, 1968), pp. 85, 119–21, 123, 127; and David Hume, *Treatise of Human Nature* (Oxford: Clarendon Press, 1967), pp. 485, 550.

28. Benedict de Spinoza, *A Theologico-Political Treatise and A Political Treatise,* trans. R. H. M. Elwes (New York: Dover, 1951), p. 259.

29. *Encyclopédie, ou Dictionnaire raisonné des sciences, des arts, et des métiers* (Neuchâtel: Fauche, 1765), vol. 9, p. 472; cf. Montesquieu, *Spirit of the Laws,* trans. Thomas Nugent, vol. 1, p. 183.

30. Jeremy Bentham, "Principles of the Civil Code," *Theory of Legislation* (Bombay: Tripathi, 1979), p. 59; see also pp. 64–68; the liberal definition of liberty as a form of security that may be enhanced by well-designed restraints (Locke, *Two Treatises of Government,* 1, II, § 57) contrasts sharply with Hobbes's preliberal definition of liberty as "the absence of Opposition (by Opposition, I mean externall Impediments of motion)" (Hobbes, *Leviathan,* p. 261).

31. Giving advice to Louis XIII, for example, Cardinal Richelieu wrote: "It is also necessary to see that [the nobles] do not exploit those beneath them." And he continued: "It is a common enough fault of those born to this order [the nobility] to use violence in dealing with the common people whom God seems to have endowed with arms designed more for gaining a livelihood than for providing self-defense. It is most essential to stop any disorders of such a nature with inflexible severity so that even the weakest of your subjects, although unarmed, find as much security [*autant de seureté*] in the protection of your laws as those who are fully armed" (Richelieu, *Political Testament,* trans. Henry Hill [Madison: University of Wisconsin Press, 1961], pp. 20–21)

32. Mill, "On Liberty," p. 264, my emphasis.

33. Defending laissez-faire against what he considered a misguided and antiliberal trend toward collectivism, Dicey wrote, in an often-quoted passage: "Few are those who realise the undeniable truth that State help kills self-help. Hence the majority of mankind must almost of necessity look with undue favor upon governmental intervention" (A. V. Dicey, *Lectures on the Relation between Law and Public Opinion in England during the Nineteenth Century* [London: Macmillan, 1914], p. 258). Dicey's choice of words here is striking. "Self-help" originally referred to the private right to avenge perceived injuries without recourse to the judicial apparatus of the state. This was a form of autonomy or self-reliance that seventeenth- and eighteenth-century liberals, too, hoped would disappear. Self-help was indeed killed by state-help, as Dicey suggests, but not accidentally, as a result of some

quaint prejudice or optical illusion, and not illiberally, in a fit of drunken statism. Self-help (in the avenging of perceived wrongs) was undermined with open eyes for the security of the overwhelming majority.

34. Similarly, according to Brian Abel-Smith, "the architects of our welfare states . . . did not intend to create a more equal society but to establish a floor of protection at the bottom" ("The Major Problems of the Welfare State: Defining the Issues," in *The Welfare State and Its Aftermath,* ed. S. N. Eisenstadt and Ora Ahimeir [Totawa, N.J.: Barnes & Noble, 1985], p. 32); notice that the governing norm here is not Rawls's demanding maximin principle, whereby inequalities are justified only if they help the least advantaged, but rather the more modest rule that inequalities are justified only if a bottom floor of decent existence (culturally defined) is secured.

35. Mill, "On Liberty," p. 217.

36. Locke, *Two Treatises of Government,* II, §§ 27, 6, 37.

37. Locke, *Two Treatises of Government,* I, § 42.

38. James Tully, *A Discourse on Property: John Locke and His Adversaries* (Cambridge: Cambridge University Press, 1980), pp. 131–32.

39. Locke, *Two Treatises of Government,* II, § 25; notice also that the welfare state assumes a genuinely egalitarian ethic, presaged more clearly in Locke's secular or antibiblical state of nature than in the Calvinist elitism of "many are called, but few are chosen."

40. Hobbes, *Leviathan,* p. 387; the more or less contemporaneous assertion by Spinoza, cited in the epigraph, occurs in *The Ethics,* trans. R. H. M. Elwes (New York: Dover, 1955), p. 239.

41. Hobbes, *Leviathan,* pp. 212, 213.

42. Hobbes, *Leviathan,* pp. 211, 209.

43. Immanuel Kant, *The Metaphysical Elements of Justice* (Indianapolis: Bobbs-Merrill, 1965) pp. 92–93.

44. Hume, "Of Commerce," in *Essays: Moral, Political and Literary* (Indianapolis: Liberty Classics, 1985), p. 265.

45. David Hume, *Enquiries Concerning the Human Understanding* (Oxford: Clarendon, 1962), pp. 186–87; Hume's unflustered acceptance of the conflict between property rights and subsistence rights seems to have been commonplace in the eighteenth century; Blackstone, for example, defended "absolute" property rights and nevertheless, took the right to subsistence for granted: "The law not only regards life and member, and protects every man in the enjoyment of them, but also furnishes him with every thing necessary for their support. For there is no man so indigent or wretched, but he may demand a supply sufficient for all the necessities of life, from the more opulent part of the community" (*Commentaries on the Laws of England* [Chicago: University of Chicago Press, 1977], vol. 1, p. 127).

46. Smith, *Wealth of Nations,* pp. 11, 609.

47. Hont and Ignatieff, "Needs and Justice in the 'Wealth of Nations,'" in *Wealth and Virtue: The Shaping of Political Economy in the Scottish Enlightenment,* ed. I. Hont and M. Ignatieff (Cambridge: Cambridge University Press, 1983), pp. 13, 44.

48. Smith, *Wealth of Nations,* pp. 78–79.

49. In other words, this argument would not justify the kind of redistribution to the handicapped advocated by Hobbes in the passage previously cited. A similar contribution-based conception of distributive justice was advanced somewhat earlier by Voltaire: "It took centuries to bring justice to mankind, to make people realize that it was horrible that the many should sow and the few reap" (Voltaire, *Letters on England* [Harmondsworth: Penguin, 1980], p. 48).

50. Smith, *Wealth of Nations,* p. 142.

51. Hont and Ignatieff, "Needs and Justice in the 'Wealth of Nations,'" pp. 24–25.

52. Smith, *Wealth of Nations,* p. 683.

53. *Principles of Political Economy,* in John Stuart Mill, *Collected Works,* ed. J. M. Robson, vol. 3 (Toronto: University of Toronto Press: 1965), p. 962; writing in defense of the Poor Law of 1834, Mill claims that it solved the most important dilemma of all welfare programs: "how to give the greatest amount of needful help, with the smallest encouragement to undue reliance on it" (ibid).

54. Mill, *Principles of Political Economy,* p. 962; his concern for impartiality, of course, does not lead Mill to denounce voluntary charity so long as it serves only as a supplement to public provision. Well-being is not solely a matter of comparative advantage. What the poor need, primarily, is help, not equality. Distributive justice remains an overriding norm, however, so long as some citizens have more than they need while others are starving.

55. Mill, *Principles of Political Economy,* p. 962.

56. Mill, *Principles of Political Economy,* p. 961; "Considerations on Representative Government," in John Stuart Mill, *Collected Works,* ed. J. M. Robson, vol. 19, *Essays on Politics and Society* (Toronto: University of Toronto Press: 1965), p. 386.

57. Smith, *Wealth of Nations,* pp. 98, 82–83.

58. Hume, "Of Commerce," in *Essays: Moral, Political and Literary,* p. 265.

59. "Utilitarianism," in John Stuart Mill, *Collected Works,* ed. J. M. Robson, vol. 5, *Essays on Ethics, Religion and Society* (Toronto: University of Toronto Press, 1977), p. 255.

60. In his study of "the public interest," J. A. W. Gunn demonstrated that property rights and self-interest were *republican* principles in the seventeenth century. Who benefited from the ethics of self-sacrifice? Monarchs intent on dynastic aggrandizement, above all others, learned to appreciate the utility of schooling soldiers to forget themselves. To die selflessly, to die for the state, was actually to die for the king's status, his personal prestige. Republicans aimed at wresting power from a belligerent monarch who capriciously ignored the concerns of his subjects. Thus, they were understandably anxious to rehabilitate the inviolability of private property and the affiliated principle of self-interest. To affirm property rights and the legitimacy of universal self-interest was to deprive dynastic monarchs of self-oblivious cannon fodder. It also required rulers to justify excessive taxation by explaining the good it would bring to those who were taxed (J. A. W. Gunn, *Politics and the Public Interest in the Seventeenth Century* [London: Routledge & Kegan Paul, 1969]).

61. *Federalist Papers,* no. 10, pp. 83–84.

62. Locke, *Letter on Toleration,* p. 127; my emphasis.

63. Locke, *Two Treatises of Government,* II, § 120.

64. Locke, *Two Treatises of Government,* II, § 50; cf. "Political Power then I take to be a Right of making Laws with Penalties of Death, and consequently all less Penalties, for the *Regulating* and Preserving of Property" (ibid., II, § 2; my emphasis).

65. The classic illustration, in the American case, is the Supreme Court's decision in *Lochner v. New York,* 198 U.S. 45 (1905).

66. T. H. Green, "Liberal Legislation and Freedom of Contract," in John R. Rodman, ed., *The Political Theory of T. H. Green* (New York: Appleton-Century-Crofts, 1964), pp. 43–73.

67. The liberal doctrine of rights was fully developed, it is sometimes argued,

only after modern societies successfully centralized formerly diffuse social threats or sources of insecurity in one easily identifiable location ("the state"), thus making it possible to defend against them with systematic efficiency.

68. Montesquieu, *Spirit of the Laws,* vol. 2, p. 26.

69. Insecurity produced by private property and the market, be it noted, did not utterly eclipse other forms. Varieties of insecurity do not simply replace one another in the course of modernization but are cumulative. In other words, welfare-state liberals can still be concerned with the danger of political oppression and even with a residual threat posed by the mafia or the Red Brigades.

70. I borrow this example from Charles Larmore, *Patterns of Moral Complexity* (Cambridge: Cambridge University Press, 1987), p. 128.

71. Hume, "Of Parties in General," in *Essays: Moral, Political and Literary* (Indianapolis: Liberty Classics, 1985), p. 55; my emphasis.

72. The impossibility of mapping the selfless/selfish scheme onto the good/bad scheme appears to have been a fundamental insight shared by all liberals. See chapter 2.

73. Ronald Dworkin, "Liberalism," in *A Matter of Principle* (Cambridge: Harvard University Press, 1985), pp. 181–204.

74. Hume, *Treatise of Human Nature,* pp. 538–39.

75. Mill, *Principles of Political Economy,* p. 968; the same argument, in almost the same words, can be found in Smith, *Wealth of Nations,* p. 681.

76. Smith, *Wealth of Nations,* pp. 716–40.

77. Mill, "Considerations on Representative Government," pp. 413–21; Mill, *Principles of Political Economy,* p. 949.

78. Frank Michelman, "Welfare Rights in a Constitutional Democracy," *Washington University Law Quarterly* 3 (1979): 677; Rawls makes a similar claim (*Political Liberalism,* p. 7).

79. See, for instance, Robert Bork, "The Impossibility of Finding Welfare Rights in the Constitution," *Washington University Law Quarterly* 3 (1979): 695–701.

80. Mill, *Principles of Political Economy,* pp. 959–60.

81. Ibid.

82. John Rawls, *A Theory of Justice* (Cambridge: Harvard University Press, 1971), p. 267.

83. Friedman, *Capitalism and Freedom,* p. 191; see also Posner, *Economic Analysis of Law,* pp. 464–66.

## Conclusion

1. *The Federalist Papers* (New York: Mentor, 1961), no. 49, p. 317.

# INDEX